# HUMAN RIGHTS IN A CHANGING WORLD

# HUMAN RIGHTS IN A CHANGING WORLD

*Edited by*
**P. Sukumaran Nair**

KALPAZ

Human Rights in a Changing World



ISBN: 978-81-7835-901-4



Published in 2011 in India by
Kalpaz Publications
C-30 Satyawati Nagar, Delhi-110052
E-mail: kalpaz@hotmail.com
Phone : 9212729499

*Leser Type Setting by:* Square Vision, Delhi

*Printed at* : Chawla Offset Press, Delhi

*Dedicated to the innumerable for whom*
*'Human Right' is just another word*

# CONTENTS

## Part III
## Environment and Human Rights



## Part IV
## Protection of Human Rights

# FOREWORD

Human Rights and freedom have always been universal concepts but it was not until the nineteenth century that they got any international recognition. Experience of the Second World War resulted in the widespread conviction that international protection of human rights was one of the essential conditions of international peace and progress. "We cannot have peace unless we accept Human Rights. Human Rights can evolve only in an atmosphere of Peace" said Dag Hammarskjeold, former United Nations Secretary General.

Human Rights are those conditions of life that allow us to fully develop and use our human qualities of intelligence and conscience. They are based on mankind's increasing demand for a life in which the inherent dignity of each human being will receive respect and protection. In fact, they are fundamental to our nature: without them we cannot live as human beings. To deny human beings their rights is to set the stage for political and social unrest, wars, hostility between nations and between groups within a nation. Human rights far from an abstract concept for philosophers and lawyers affect the daily lives of everyone.

The beginnings of Human Rights as understood in the modern sense could be traced back to the Magna Carta (1215), Bill of Rights (1689) the Virginia Bill of Rights (1776) and the American Declaration of Independence which asserts these rights. "We hold these truth to be self-evident that all men are created equal, that they are endowed by their creator with certain inalienable Rights, that among these are life, liberty and the pursuit of happiness. That whenever any form of Government becomes destructive of these ends, it is the right of the people to alter or abolish it".

The Universal Declaration of 1948 proclaimed by the General Assembly of the United Nations was a bugle call to all the States to respect those rights. It is a manifesto of man's inalienable rights and fundamental freedoms. It enumerates the political, civil, economic, social and cultural rights of man. It recognizes that the inherent dignity and of the equal and inalienable rights of all members of the human family is the foundation of freedom, Justice and peace in the world. "This message is of undeniable importance in to-day's world as grave human rights violations destroy the lives of millions of People.... I believe that violations of human rights could be avoided, at least in part if the Universal Declaration would be better known and internalized by both rulers and citizens" observed Mrs. Mary Robinson, U.N. High Commissioner for Human Rights on the 50th Anniversary of the Universal Declaration.

The Universal Declaration defines the various human rights in 30 articles. Article 1 states that all human beings are born free and equal in dignity and rights while Article 2 states that Everyone is entitled to all the rights and freedoms set forth in this Declaration, without distinction of any kind. Article 3 states that everyone has the right to life, liberty and security of person while Article 5 states that no one shall be subjected to torture or to cruel inhuman or degrading treatment or punishment. Article 7 states that all are equal before the law and are entitled without any discrimination to equal protection of the law while Article 9 states that no one shall be subjected to arbitrary arrest, detention or exile.

The rights so declared would be mere platitudes unless the constituent states declared them in their respective constitutions and unless national and international machinery was provided to enforce them.

Besides the Universal Declarations of Human Rights, the U.N.General Assembly adopted two international Covenants on 16th December 1966. The first one was a Covenant on Civil and Political Rights while the second one was on Economic, Social and Cultural Rights. The former defined the classical rights and the latter the social and economic rights. The Universal Declaration and the two Covenants present a vision which is characterized by individual freedom, liberal polity and human and just economic development. The Universal Declaration has been more often than not violated in almost all countries. Amnesty International, a London based institution in its annual reports brings out the details of human rights violations in almost all the countries of the World.

In India, human rights are protected not only by the constitution but also by laws. The preamble to the constitution assures the dignity of the individual which is the basic principle underlying the Universal Declaration and in order to implement this assurance certain rights have been preserved by Parts III and IV of the constitution as Fundamental Rights and Directive Principles of State policy. The rights conferred by part III are fundamental in the sense that they are enforceable by courts, while the principles laid down in Part IV are not so enforceable, but they are nevertheless fundamental in the Governance of the country. The traditional civil and political rights enumerated in articles 2 to 21 of the Universal Declaration were enshrined as fundamental rights in the constitution, while the economic and social rights referred to in articles 22 to 28 of the Declaration were set forth as directive principles.

Inspite of the constitutional provisions for protecting human rights in India, instances of human rights violations have occurred frequently in India.

The right to life is central to and is the foremost of all human rights. The most disturbing aspect of the Indian scenario is that instances of persons picked up by the police on 'suspicion' on for interrogation meeting with their death are becoming more and more frequent. That the higher judiciary has had quite a few occasions to come down heavily on the police for flagrant violations of human rights as a damning enough testimony to its record in this critical area. Arbitrary arrests, political killings and extra judicial executions are widely prevalent in India.

The National Human Rights commission (NHRC) has recorded 1305 reports of custodial deaths during April 2001 to March 2002. Of these, 1140 were in Judicial custody and 165 in police custody. Amnesty International in its Annual Report for 1992-93 has stated that in India hundreds of political workers are detained without a trail by the courts. In tension areas the Phenomenon of disappearance is on the increase. The NHRC statistics, reveal that 2,25,817 of 3,04,893 or 74.06% of the total prison population in India are those awaiting trial (undertrails). It also found that 10,414 women were in Jail in India. Of these, 1369 women prisoners had their children living with them. NHRC received till July 2001 for the years 2000-2001 of human rights violations by armed forces and another 212 complaints against paramilitary forces.

In the area of human rights in 2010 the Supreme Court of India declared "illegal" the use of narco-analysis, brain-mapping and polygraph tests on suspects and held that these tests could not be conducted on any person whether he or she is an accused or suspect, without his or her consent.

The pervasive tendency of the political executive to misuse the law enforcement machinery for partisan ends is an important cause for custodial torture and death. Insulating the crime investigation process from political and other external influence will go a long way in reducing the incidence of custodial deaths. But this depends on whether the political class can muster the will to mend its ways. The omissions of the Government to punish officials guilty of custodial deaths lead to repetition of such crimes. The failure of the criminal justice system to bring to account persons guilty of crimes gives rise to extralegal methods leading to violations of human rights.

Another aspect of violation of human rights in India is the endless atrocities against women and children. In the name of dowry a large number of women are brutally murdered. At a meeting of the United Nations General Assembly's Social Committee in December 1991, the Canadian envoy Yves Fortier participating in a debate on human rights voiced concern over the status of women in India in General and over the high rate of dowry deaths in particular. He pleaded for appropriate steps by the Indian Government to tackle this. Social discrimination in the choice of the child resulting in female infanticide, accounting for nearly three million deaths annually in India and the denial of political rights to women are also an insult on the sanctity of human rights. Twenty million children are subjected to forced labour and exploitation in India.

Atrocities against the Dalits constitute another gross violation of human rights. In fact, there is no limit to these atrocities. According to estimates, every day 3 Dalit women are subject to rape and killed. Houses of Dalits are being burnt indiscriminately.

The social and economic exploitation of the poor by the well-to do results in violations of human rights. So also when the state neglects its legitimate duty of rendering succour in times of natural calamities such as flood, earthquake and cyclone, it is attended with violations of human rights. The flushing of industrial waste into nearby rivers or canals, inadequate industrial safety measures by MNCS, adulteration of food, drinks and medicines are also violations of human rights.

As the space for human rights gets narrowed down in the state system, the civil society also gets into a crisis partly as a result of social strife and partly on account of the general breakdown of institutions and social relations. It is the process that has given rise to a lot of violence taking different forms-violence against women, children, dalits, adivasis or indigenous people, ethinic groups, linguistic and religious minorities and so on. The ruling classes not only are incapable of handling such problems but becoming a part of the growing brutality.

Of the many violations of human rights that can be listed none is worse than povery, the mother of all human rights violations. The horror of poverty was highlighted in a message by U.N. Secretary General Kofi Annan "How many times have we said that it (poverty) was incompatible with human dignity. But billions of people are still trying to survive on less than Rs.130 a day, with no drinking water, health care or access to education, still denied the jobs that would help them escape their impoverished state, and thus still deprived of some of their most basic rights".

Freedom of an individual which is the postulate of human right, can have no meaning so long as the poor in the country do not have their economic conditions improved and the discrimination based on privilege do not become mere memories instead of becoming more and more aggressive as time passes on.

According to planning commission official figures over 260 million still live below the poverty line in India. Being poor as Amartya Sen has urged, is not just about low income, low consumption and low calorie intake, the criteria that policy makers use to count the poor. Rather it is a lack of access to essential things required for a decent living, health, education, economic opportunities, security and social respect. 1.5 million children die each year before seeing their first birthday and nearly 50% of children aged 0-35 months are underweight or stunted. The intensity of poverty in parts of India is equal if not worse than that in Africa. There are more poor people in 8 states of India than in the 26 countries of sub-saharan Africa.

Granting that Human Rights touch on the most sensitive areas of an individual's relationship to his society and his state, how best can we enforce these rights at the national level?

The rights to be protected should be stated in precise legal language and in terms appropriate to their application to individual cases. A machinery has to be set up to ensure effective protection of these rights. Any person who alleges violation of any of the fundamental rights should have easy access to courts without political interference, and such judicial protection to be effective must be exercised by an independent and objective judiciary neither subject to political pressures nor the object of political patronage. The scope of Judicial control should be clearly defined in order to avoid any conflict between the judiciary and other organs of the state.

There must be adequate protection for the right of the individual against the abuse of administrative power. Judicial protection in such cases is not adequate and a specialized institutions to deal with such abuse should be set up. An essential feature of this institutions should be that it must have legal competence to investigate individual complaints unimpeded by official and political consideration and must provide an effective and cheap remedy where rights have been infringed or denied.

It is wrong to treat human rights merely as a legal or constitutional concept to be solved by courts and lawyers. They have an ethical and spiritual content representing the very basic values of human civilization. Education should among other things be directed to make people fully conscious of their rights, to promoting among them at the same time, a sensitiveness to the rights of others, to inspiring them with a determination to secure and protect those rights at all costs and to stimulating in them a desire to exercise willingly the responsibilities which these rights entail.

At the same time, it is essential to build a strong public opinion against erosion of human rights. The media can play an effective role in building up public opinion. In the ultimate analysis, human rights cannot be secured without the active support of a vigilant and enlightened public opinion.

The book 'Human Rights in a changing world' has grown out of the deliberations of a national seminar on Human Rights sponsored by the University Grants Commission and organized by the Department of Political Science of NSS College Pandalam under the chairmanship of Dr. P. Sukumaran Nair who has edited this volume. The participant of the seminar includes legal luminaries, social scientists, senior administrators, outstanding journalists and reputed social activists. The 30 papers published in this volume presents a holistic view of human rights with special reference to the Indian situation. The various dimensions of human rights have been discussed threadbare by the experts in these papers. The papers cover a wide spectrum from conceptualization of human rights to protection of human rights. All the papers presented at the seminar were later revised in the light of the discussions that took place following the presentation and ably edited by Dr. P. Sukumaran Nair. The papers are scientifically classified into four major sections. Papers dealing with the conceptualization of human rights are included in Section I, while Section II carries papers related to the challenges facing human rights and human rights movement. In Section III are included papers dealing with environment and human rights while papers discussing protection of human rights find their place in section IV. The papers included in this volume present a Kaleidoscopic picture of human rights to the readers. A reading of the book will give one a fairly correct perspective on the problem of human rights in a fast changing world. The book, a rare collection of scholarly papers will definitely be a valuable addition to the existing scanty literature on human rights. By going through the pages of the book, one gets a synoptic view of the concept of human rights which ultimately determines man's relationship with the state and society. It is a must read for any one genuinely concerned with man's life, liberty and pursuit of happiness, the major concerns of human rights.

With immense pleasure, I commend this valuable book to a wider audience.

Thiruvananthapuram
25th January 2011

**Prof. (Dr) K. Raman Pillai**
Former Dean, Faculty of Social Science
University of Kerala

# ACKNOWLEDGEMENTS

This edited volume entitled "Human Rights in a Changing World" has grown out of a UGC sponsored National Seminar organised by the Department of Political Science, N.S.S. College, Pandalam, Kerala. Infact this academic venture is the result of a collaborative effort of several people. At the very outset I am thankful to the University Grants Commission for providing financial assistance without which we would not have been able to organise this Seminar.

I am greatly indebted to each of the distinguished contributors to this volume who have been very responsive and helpful in making their contributions. I would like to thank Dr. G. Jayakumar, former Principal, N.S.S. College, Pandalam, for his unfailing help and assistance to conduct the Seminar. I am also extremely thankful to our present Principal Dr. G. Madhukumar, for his academic pursuits and for lending a helping hand to publish this volume. My special thanks are also due to Prof. R. Prasannakumar, Secretary, N.S.S. Colleges' Central Committee, Changanacherry, for his generous help.

My respected Professor, K. Raman Pillai, former Dean, Faculty of Social Science, University of Kerala, has been a constant source of encouragement to me and helped at various stages to bringout this publication. He has written 'Foreword' to this volume. I am greatly indebted to him.

My heartful gratitude is also due to my colleagues for their active co-operation and unending support. Among them Dr. D. Pradeep, Prof. T. Ramani, and Prof. P.B. Anil of the Department of Political Science and Prof. Jaishree Vijayakumar, Prof. P. Harikrishna (Senate Member, University of Kerala), Dr. K.B. Jagadeesh (Secretary, PTA), and Dr. K.G. Padmakumaran Nair have been very active and strived hard to make the Seminar successful. I am thankful to my students whose hard work resulted the fruitful end of this academic exercise.

I would like to express my heartfelt sense of gratitude to Dr. R.K. Sureshkumar, Head, P.G. Department of Political Science, University College, Thiruvananthapuram for his immense help during the editing of this volume. I am also thankful to Stalin.T, Hometech, Thiruvananthapuram, for typing the manuscript. My sincere thanks also due to M/s. Kalpaz Publications, Delhi for publishing this volume in record time. Last but not the least, I am thankful to P. Maheswaran Nair and P. Anilkumar, my wife Indira Devi and children Aswin and Jyotsna for providing me with all possible helps during the compilation of this collection of papers.

Dr. P. Sukumaran Nair

# LIST OF CONTRIBUTORS

1. **Prof. (Dr) N.K. Jayakumar** - Vice-Chancellor, National University of Advanced Legal Studies (NUALS), Kochi, Kerala.
2. **Prof. (Dr) J. Prabhash** - Professor in Political Science and Pro-Vice-Chancellor, University of Kerala.
3. **Prof. (Dr) Muzaffar Assadi** - Professor, Department of Political Science, University of Mysore, Karnataka.
4. **Dr. R. Sreekantan Nair** - Associate Professor of Political Science, VTMNSS College, Dhanuvachapuram, Neyyattinkara, Kerala.
5. **Dr. P.S. Vijaya Natharaj** - Associate Professor & Head, Department of Political Science, S.N. College, Chempazhanthi, Kerala.
6. **Prof. (Dr.) P. Narasaiah** - Former Professor of Public Administration, B.R. Ambedkar Open University, Hyderabad (AP).
7. **Dr. K.C. Sreekumar** - Visiting Fellow, Department of Politics and International Relations, M.G. University, Kottayam, Kerala.
8. **Dr. P. Suresh Kumar** - Associate Professor, P.G. and Research Department of Economics, Government College, Attingal, Kerala.
9. **Dr. S.S. Sreekumar** - Associate Professor of Political Science, J.N.Government College, Andaman, Port Blair.
10. **Dr. S.R. Jitha** - Associate Professor in Political Science, S.N. College, Ala, Alappuzha District, Kerala.
11. **Dr. K. Jayaprasad** - Associate Professor, P.G.Dept. of Political Science, S.N. College, Kollam, Kerala.
12. **Ms. R. Ashitha** - Research Scholar, M.G.University, Kottayam.
13. **Ms. T. Ramani** - Associate Professor in Political Science, N.S.S.College, Pandalam, Kerala.
14. **Ms. Ardra Manasi** - doing Integrated Masters in Development Studies, Dept. of Humanities and Social Sciences, IIT Madras.
15. **Dr. D. Pradeep** - Associate Professor of Political Science, N.S.S. College, Pandalam, Kerala.
16. **Dr. Raju Abraham** - Associate Professor of Political Science, M.A. College, Kothamangalam, Idukki District, Kerala.
17. **Shri B. Madhusoodanan Nair** - Assistant Professor of Political Science, N.S.S. Hindu College, Changanacherry, Kottayam District, Kerala.
18. **Dr. P.S. Panikkar** - Human Rights Activist, 'Janajagratha', and a former Professor of Political Science, N.S.S. College, Nemmara, Palghat, Kerala.

19. **Dr. K.M. George** - Professor of Economics, Govt. Law .College, Kozhikkode, Kerala.
20. **Dr. P. Rajendran Nair** - Associate Professor, P.G. Department of Economics, N.S.S. College, Pandalam, Kerala.
21. **Shri Reinhart Philip** - Research Scholar, Department of Politics, Central University, Pondicherry.
22. **Shri. Panicker Harisankar** - doing 5th Year Integrated Masters in Development Studies, Dept. of Humanities and Social Sciences, IIT, Madras.
23. **Dr. R. Rajeevan** - Associate Professor of Political Science, N.S.S. College, Nilamel, Kollam District, Kerala.
24. **M.S. Vidya Nair** - Assistance Professor of Political Sciences, All Saints College, Thiruvananthapuram, Kerala.
25. **Shri P. Faziluddin** - Renowned Journalist and formerly State Information Commissioner, Kerala.
26. **Prof. (Dr.) G. Rajasekharan Nair** - Principal, Government Law College, Ernakulam, Kerala.
27. **Shri K. Padmakumar, IPS** - I.G. of Police, (Intelligence SBCID HQ), Thiruvananthapuram, Kerala.
28. **Dr. K. Alexander** - Associate Professor, P.G.Department of Politics and Public Administration, St. John's College, Anchal, Kerala.
29. **Shri B.R.P. Bhaskar** - Veteran Journalist and Social Activist.
30. **Dr. P. Sukumaran Nair** - Associate Professor and Head, Dept. of Political Science, N.S.S.College, Pandalam, Kerala.

# INTRODUCTION

## P. Sukumaran Nair

Discourses on Human Rights have become a veritable wave on the Global plane today from the lips of newscasters, politicians, academics, jurists, commentators and the activists. It recognises the inherent dignity and fundamental freedoms of all human beings irrespective of sex, caste, colour, religion and region. Disregard and violations of human rights have resulted in disastrous consequences to humanity. Human rights when protected by rule of law ensures peace and order in society and establishes justice, liberty and equality. In the present day world, awareness about human rights is inevitable to maintain people-friendly relations and establishing cordial relations among nations. In fact, human rights are natural and intrinsic rights to which all human beings are entitled to enjoy in the absence of which one can not live as a human being. No one has any right to take them away; on the contrary it is the duty of all to respect and protect the rights of each other.

The concept of human rights have been in existence ever since the days of river valley civilizations. During the course of the Babylonian Civilization, Hammurabi, the first law giver in history, has collected, codified and categorised the existing customs in the Babylonian Society in the form of law and placed them in front of a famous temple at Babylon for the information of the public. This inscribed version of law known as "Hammurabi's Code" exemplifies the spirit of Human rights. Similarly reference to human rights can also be found in the judicial rulings of the ancient Israeli Sanhedrin banning torture and limiting the case of capital punishments, the islamic legislation on rights of women and also in the vedic scripts. Dharma in the vedic period provides a code of conduct and rules for morality in the form of righteousness and propriety of actions for the society.

Issues relating human rights viz. offences, punishment etc. can be found in Manusmriti of Manu, the great epics the Ramayana and the Mahabharata and Arthasastra of Kautilya. Manu warns in Manusmrithi: "the King should protect and support all his subjects without any discrimination in the same manner as the earth supports all living beings". In Ramayana, Lord Rama exhorted his brother Lakshmana not to use a weapon of war which could destroy the entire humanity because such mass destruction was forbidden in ancient law of war.

Kautilya in his treatise Arthasastra stressed the need for civil, legal and economic rights and asserts "that the happiness of the subjects lies in the happiness of the King and what is beneficial to the subjects is his own benefit." According to him, "the King shall provide the orphan, the dying, the infirm, the affected and helpless with maintenance, he shall also provide subsistence to mothers as well as children whom they give birth to." During this period the welfare of the people was given top priority and welfare of the subjects was deemed as welfare of the rulers.

The intellectual formulations to the modern notion of human rights can be traced from the writings of the Greek and the Roman Philosophers. The celebrated Greek Philosophers - Socrates, Plato and Aristotle - devoted their attention to the concept of natural justice, equality and non-arbitrariness. The Greek philosophers believed that laws in conformity to recognised human values should be the final sovereign and this notion might have influenced the evolution of human rights in the past.

Human rights were earlier recognised by the Society as natural rights. In philosophy, the idea of natural rights of man was developed by Stoic philosophers. The Stoics first developed the theory of natural law and by virtue of which explained the nature of human rights which according to them are rights that every individual possess as a human being.

The Stoics moulded a cosmopolitan philosophy based on the principles of equality of all and universal application of law. Based on the Stoic conception of natural law, the Romans framed a code of legal rules for administration of justice. It may be observed from the writings of Greek and Roman Philosophers that they had given to their citizens freedom of speech, equality before law, right to vote, right to be elected to public office, right to trade and right of access to justice.

In the Middle Ages, the concept of human rights developed during the ancient period received a setback mainly from St. Thomas Aquinas, a foremost philosopher and theologian of the Roman Catholic Church and Machiavelli, the tough-minded ex-chancellor of Florence. While Aquinas justified the practice of slavery thereby refuting human rights notions, Machiavelli opposed the concept of natural law and favoured absolute monarchy.

The Social Contract theorists - Thomas Hobbes, John Locke and Jean Jacques Rousseau - made an attempt to link the theory of social contract with the theory of natural law. They derived the idea of social contract to explain the relationship between individual and society.

The 'Twelve Articles of European History' (1525) are considered to be the first record of Human Rights in European history. The Twelve Articles were part of peasants demands raised towards the Swabin League in the German peasant war in Germany.

The Magna Carta (1215) provided a break through in the evolution of the modern concept of human rights. This document has been considered as the fountain of their liberty by the British. This great charter signed by King George guaranteed political liberties to the English under pressure from the rebellious Barons. This document granted freedom from imprisonment or from dispossession of property and from prosecution unless the lawful judgement by the law of the land.

The two major revolutions of the 18th century viz., the American war of Independence and the French Revolution have played a vital role in the development of human right concept and to establish certain legal rights. The war of Independence of Americans and their determination to overthrow the imperial Government actuated them to make the declaration of independence on July 4, 1776. Through this Virginian declaration, Jefferson attacked not only the Divine right of Kings to rule but also vehemently attacked/criticised a Government which did not reflect the will of the people. The document says: "We hold these rights to be self-evident, that all men are created equal, that they are endowed by their creator with certain inalienable rights, that among these are life, liberty and pursuit of happiness.... it is the right of the people to alter or abolish it and institute new government." The Americans made their claim for independence on the basis of inalienable rights of man, popular sovereignty and the right of revolution. The American Bill of Rights, the first ten amendments to the U.S. Constitution (1791) also fulfils the spirit of human rights. The Virginian Declaration of Rights (1776) encoded into law a number of fundamental Civil Rights and freedom.

Declaration of independence adopted by the French National Assembly (1789) gave a new impetus to political thinking vis-a-vis developing the concept of human rights. Rousseau's prophetic words - liberty, equality and fraternity - through which he intellectually influenced the French Revolution were recognised as the essence of human civilization by the French National Assembly. On August 26, 1789, the French National Assembly declared, "Men are born free and equal in rights...." It is the bounden duty to preserve and protect natural rights of men and they are liberty, property, security and resistance to oppression.

The French Declaration of Rights of man includes a number of other rights too, viz.

- All men are born and remain equal in their rights.
- All men are equal before law
- All men should have freedom from arrest, and
- All men are innocent until they are proved guilty.

No doubt the French Declaration of Rights of man is an important mile stone in the development of the concept of human rights.

The notion of human rights was in vogue in the 18th century through the writings of Thomas Paine and William Lloyd Garrison. In his the Rights of Man, (1991-92) Thomas Paine defended the French Revolution and espoused Republicanism. Through Garrison's 'The Liberator' (1831) he was trying to enlist the readers to the great cause of human rights.

Amidst these developments, the concept of Universalisation of human rights has become a focal point of discussion at the international level. In 1929 Institute of international law adopted a declaration of international rights of man recognizing the right to life, liberty and property irrespective of nationality, race, region or sex. Added to that the oppressive and exploitative practices followed by the totalitarian regimes under Benito Mussolini and Adolf Hitler also favoured the deliberations of Universalisation of Human rights. Under the Nazi and Fascist rule individuals were deprived of their civil and political rights and persecuted them on the ground of their race or religion. These atrocities in turn caused global concern for the protection and promotion of human rights. Another contributing factor favouring the concept of universalisation of human rights was the Bolshevik revolution (1917) of Russia. The Russian revolution reiterated the belief that economic and social rights were as important as civil and political rights.

The beginning of the 20th century witnessed the emergence of many groups and movements with the intention of transforming social change over the issue of human rights. In Western Europe and North America, Labour Unions brought about laws granting workers right to strike, establishing minimum working conditions and forbidding child labour. Further, these movements in many countries including India succeeded in driving out colonial masters from the colonies.

The issue of 'human rights' has entered the arena of world Politics following II World War Charters and conventions. In the two global wars heneous and shocking crimes were committed, human values were undermined thereby adversely affecting the dignity of the individual. Hence the aftermath effects of the war induced the international community to secure and protect the human rights of people all over the world. The Dumbarton Oaks Conference (1944) decided to promote of Human rights and the UN General Assembly had been authorised to perform the same through its main organ Economic and Social Council (ECOSOC). The first documentary reference to human rights could be seen in the UN charter which declared that "We the people of UN determined to reaffirm faith in human rights in the dignity, and worth of the human person, in the equal rights of men or women". Subsequently the UN General Assembly adopted the Universal Declaration of Human Rights on December 10, 1948 as a message of undeniable importance. Article I of UDHR provides: "All human beings are born free and equal in dignity and rights. They are endowed with reason and conscience and should act towards one another in a spirit of brotherhood". Further, ECOSOC established a committee to prepare a report and give recommendation on an International Bill on human rights. The Bill consists of (i) The Universal Declaration of Human Rights (1948), (ii) International Covenant on Economic Social and Cultural rights (1966), (iii) International Covenant on Civil and Political rights (1966) and The Optional Protocol (1966).

From the above, it is obvious that the genesis of human right principles lies in the very dignity of the human beings.

As far as our country is concerned, India also has had a long tradition of struggle for human rights. In India, the pre-independence movement was launched as a movement for civil liberties and became an offshoot of the freedom struggle. During the independence struggle, the leaders who lead the struggle adhered to the principles of democracy and civil liberties.

The Constitution of India which came into existence on 26th January, 1950 bears the impact of Universal Declaration of Human Rights. The framers of the Constitution of India were influenced by the concept of human rights and accordingly they showed great respect for human rights and fundamental freedoms. The Preamble to the Constitution of India resolves to secures to all its citizen Justice, Liberty and Equality. Further, it promotes among them all 'Fraternity' assuring the dignity of the individual. The dignity of the individual is the basic principle underlying Universal Declaration. The UDHR comprises civil and political rights and Economic, Social and Cultural rights. While Civil and Political rights are incorporated in Part III (Fundamental Rights) of the Constitution, Part IV contains Social and Cultural rights in the name of Directive Principles of State Policy.

The Union Parliament has enacted the protection of Human Rights Act on 28 September 1993. The Act provided for the constitution of a National Human Rights Commission, Human Rights Commission in States and Human Rights Courts for better protection of Human rights and for matter connected there with or incidental thereto. The Act defined 'Human Rights' to mean the rights relating to life, liberty, equality and dignity of the individual guaranteed by the constitution or embodies in the international covenants and enforceable by the courts in India. With the setting up of the National Human Rights Commission in India (NHRC), the then Prime Minister made a statement about his government's commitment to uphold human rights. To quote him, "We must send a clear message that we do not tolerate violation of Human Rights". He said further, "there is need to identify the weakness, the gaps between pronouncements and action, and between legislation and its implementation".

It is a fact that the horizon of human rights is expanding day by day and the people all over the world are able to enjoy their basic rights and assured of dignified existence. But it cannot but be stated that the human rights and human right movements confronts a lot of challenges in the way of protecting these rights of the people.

The problems like social disharmony, societal violence, restrictions on democratic rights, violation of rights of women, police and bureaucratic delays and excesses, impact of terrorism and revolutionary groups, economic globalization etc. really cause hardships in the way of enjoying these rights. Globalization poses some challenges in the path of human rights. The uncontrolled market forces due to globalisation really threatens social and cultural rights of the people. There are also chances of increasing unemployment and poverty when wealth is accummulated in the hands of MNCs. Amidst its intense desire to accummulate profits, the MNCs have been restructuring their operation on a global scale with the result that unemployment, underemployment etc. affects severely among the countries of the third world.

The papers included in this volume were presented at a National Seminar on 'Human Rights in a Changing World' organised by the Department of Political Science, N.S.S. College, Pandalam, with the financial assistance of the University Grants Commission. The papers presented are edited after revision and are classified into four parts, Part I deals with *Conceptualising Human Rights in the Global Context*; Part II discusses *Challenges facing Human Rights and Human Rights Movements, Environment and Human Rights* are the concerns of Part III and Part IV deals with *Protection of Human Rights*.

## I

Five papers are included in Part I - Conceptualising Human Rights in the Global Contexts. In an attempt to conceptualise human rights in the global context, Prof. N.K. Jayakumar in his paper on "Human Rights: From Conceptualisation to Realisation" maintains that continuous engagement of the academic community with human rights and a stream of intellectual discourses generated by it would serve in a significant way to add new dimensions to the concept of human rights. To him, the task of teachers in this is very important as they can act as a bridge between the academia and the society. After surveying the evolution and development of human rights, he points out that the challenge of the 21st Century is to provide effective and legislative implementation through local, regional and global action. Dovetailing Gandhian perspective with Marxian approach to human rights, he expressed that Gandhiji's faith in dignity and worth of every human being made him a crusader for human rights throughout his life. The insights of Karl Marx on power relations based on economic factors had large impact on human rights discourse. Discussing the various aspects of globalization and human rights, he observes "unless we are able to strike a balance between a purely economic view of growth and a more normative concern with overcoming human suffering and inequality, the future of human rights will be in peril"

The nature and impact of globalization/neo-liberalism on human rights is a hot topic in contemporary discourse on human rights, argues J. Prabhash, in his paper entitled "Human Rights in a Globalised World: Market Friendly Rights Vs. People Friendly Rights, A Theoretical Construct". The Central argument of his paper is based on the left perspective - while contesting the propensity of economic liberalisation in materializing economic well-being, profit motive associated with it furthers all sorts of exploitation ultimately leading to the denial of even basic rights to the marginalized social groups. To him human rights normativity depends on the stability of democratic order, particularly the extent of democratic control over state power. The entire human rights discourse today has been appropriated by the ideological right which has been using it simultaneously to serve its interest and at the same time deny its blessings to the marginalised sections. Conscious attempts are needed to reverse the trend and right the wrongs in the emergent paradigm of human rights. He calls for resisting economic globalization and neo-liberal policies and advocates the need, to strengthen democratic culture at the pores of the civil society and for this NGOs and social movements, progressive political parties etc. have a very important role to play.

Prof. Muzaffar Assadi in his paper "Discourse on Human Rights: Narratives Beyond 'Political" has argued that most of the time human rights discourse is wrapped in the politics of the state, international institutions and global politics. It is in this context, one has to ask the question as to the possibility of creating universal theory or discourse on human rights. It is true that human rights discourse has created many myths, however, they can be contested. The paradigm that has been created in the post-globalisation period is known as market driven Human Right Paradigm. However there are problems inherent in actualising human rights through this paradigm. To him, in the midst of dislocation, dispossession, mal-nutrition, increasing poverty, disparity, homeless, shrinking, urban spaces and ambiguous State, the argument of creating new human rights paradigm becomes increasingly difficult. Therefore, he argues that for detailing human rights discourse we need to go beyond, "Political".

Dr. R. Sreekantan Nair makes an important contribution in his paper titled "Debating Human Rights; Discourse and Discord". To him, the most important challenge in the development of human rights is how best to realise direct and genuine participation of the masses and otherwise marginalised groups and sectors in the development of human rights discourse. It is important to continue to exert efforts that effectively and consistently provide access to these groups, not only to make their voices be heard but also to directly influence and shape the discourse. The continuing development of human rights discourse should be encouraged, says Nair, with the primary objective of recognizing and realizing, through human rights, the inherent dignity of each and every human being. Unless and until there takes place a debate/discourse, the contradictions within and outside could not be sorted out. As such, discourse and discord on human rights is very much relevant in any society at any point of time.

Dealing with "Roots of Human Rights Principles: A scan of the Sacred Texts" Dr. P.S. Vijaya Natharaj discusses the role of classical religious sources in strengthening human rights. The roots of modern concept of human rights could be traced back to the days of human civilization. The earliest concept of Right was that of natural right, following natural right leaders of French revolution coined the concept Rights of Man. All religious texts reaffirm the fact that rights are to be enjoyed when duties and obligations enforced by Government is obeyed or performed. He concludes his enquiry by submitting that the message of human right is propagated through the doctrine of 'Dharma' in Hinduism, 'Love your neighbour as thyself' in Christianity, 'spirit of brother hood' in Islam and 'relational origination' in Buddhism.

## II

Twelve papers pertaining to Challenges facing Human Right and Human Rights Movements are brought under Part II. Prof. Panjala Narasaiah's paper on "Human Rights for Good Governance and Quality Life: A Success Story" is a case study of AndraPradesh State Human Rights Commission. He discusses how APHRC has successfully performed its task for betterment of human rights. The APHRC has made several recommendations to the government on various aspects of the life of citizens ranging from Marriage Laws to Environment laws. Discussing the secret of success, he points out that it is viewed as a "better protector" of the Human Rights. Its efforts to translate Human Rights from a dream to reality are well recognized. In his opinion the press and electronic media are giving due publicity to the activities of the Commission whenever orders are being passed in sensitive matters and matters of social importance resulting in awareness in general public about their valuable rights. That people are reposing faith and confidence in the commission in an increasing manner is evident from the fact that the number of cases have increased manifold from nearly 3000 to 35000 within a short span of 4 years of its existence.

In many countries throughout the world human rights are not protected to the extent to which they are protected in the United States, observes, Dr. K.C. Sreekumar in his paper "The Civil Rights Movement : A Glorious chapter in Human Rights in the U.S". According to him, the origin of Civil Rights Movement was partially accidental and partially deliberate. The civil rights movement brought to light the problem of poverty prevalent among the African Americans and forced the policy makers to enable them to come out of that predicament. As a result, the very society that looked down upon the African Americans as a liability became aware that they are an asset and that they have a natural right to be treated as equal to any other section of the American Society. Like many other movements started in the U.S, the Civil Rights Movement also has its impact on other nations. How far the Civil Rights Movement has influenced the modern Indian Dalit Politics is a topic worth researching, he observes. He concludes his paper reminiscing his interview with the then Illinois Senator, Barack Obama, a decade back, who is now the occupant of the highest office of the United States of America.

One of the fundamental aspects of human rights perception is its relation with economic forces. Infact, there is a two-way relationship between economic progress and human rights, argues Dr. P. Sureshkumar, in his paper "The Dynamics of Human Rights and Economic Development". The strengthening of the economic base of a community liberate it from the urges of basic necessities and requirements which enable it to pursue qualitative change in its discourse. This normally entails, a clamour for more individual freedoms and liberties giving way for the formulation of series of individual rights and privileges culminating in the emphasis on human rights. He points out that the West which has set out for an economic adventure found the human rights dear as it enabled them to satisfy their natural urge on the one hand and the very human rights equipping them for further economic progress on the other. He emphasized that human rights link with economic development is a crucial element for the effective enjoyment of it human rights.

Dr. S.S. Sreekumar in his paper "Implementing Human Rights: A Third World Perspective" discusses the problems of the third world countries and how these cause hindrances in the way of implementing human rights. Based on his conceptual and theoretical framework, he lists the problems of third world countries like eradication of poverty, unemployment, illiteracy, emergence of international terrorism, globalisation, lack of tradition of human rights, corrupt and incompetent governments, ethnic divisions etc. as the reasons for having poor record of human rights in these developing countries. According to him, the need of the hour is to devise rational approach to the promotion of human rights in the countries of the third world. Implementation of humanrights should be action oriented rather than conference-oriented. Practical approach has to be adopted to make human rights meaningful. A vibrant civil society can help both in developing and improving human rights protection.

In "Bureaucracy and Human Rights under Liberalization" Dr. S.R. Jitha contends that Bureaucracy being the instrument of state is the forerunner in the protection of human rights. It is the duty of bureaucracy to understand the problems of the people and to create a balanced socio-economic and political environment so as to enable the citizens to lead a meaningful life. The state is the most important protector of human rights. Quoting relevant articles from the Universal Declaration, Jitha opines that the role of bureaucracy in the protection of human rights is manifold and multi-dimensional. In her view Laws, Declarations, Conventions and Protocols do not solve the problems and what is required is proper implementation. The responsibility of bureaucracy in developing societies is to get things done without delay. Being the servants of the people, the civil servants should preserve the country's cultural, ethnic and traditional values, and at the same time ensure the people's peace and prosperity for the enjoyment of basic human rights.

Dr. K. Jayaprasad's paper on "Terrorism, Human Rights and Civil Society Movements in India" refers to civil society movements as he holds that the defense of human rights and fundamental freedoms should be ensured by the civil society along with the political society. In this paper, he analyses the attitude of civil society movements in India towards terrorism and violation of rights by non-state actors. In his opinion human rights violations by the state are successfully challenged by these groups. But violations by the non-state actors including terrorist and fundamentalist groups are neglected by these forums. Consequently, both domestic and cross border terrorism which threaten the sovereignty of the country and fundamental freedoms of innocent citizens are not properly debated by the civil society. Also many terrorist groups and fundamentalist movements sponsor human right forums as a shield to resist the state action. The Civil Society movements and human rights activists have failed to highlight the fundamental values of human rights and the inherent dignity of all individuals.

In her paper "Tackling the Menace of Terrorism: Human Rights Approaches and Perspectives" R. Ashitha underscores the measures adopted by the two major democracies of the world: India and USA in tackling the menace of terrorism. All types of political systems are involved in the task of addressing the menace within the framework of their own ideological and legal premises. Terrorism pose natural threat to human rights, human security development and even the notions of social justice. She observes that in tackling the menace of terrorism measures adopted by India and USA reveal the level of democratic maturity of these countries. It is high time that while tackling the menace of terrorism the democratic countries should uphold human rights values and spirit as the only way to address terrorism in a durable and effective way.

T. Ramany in her paper "Women and Human Rights" makes an attempt to link women and Human Rights and critically examines the violation of rights of women in general and India in particular. The large body of international covenants, agreements and commitments about human rights gives women political leverage and a tenable point of reference. Indian women at the end of the 20th Century would argue that they still have a long way to go to attain gender justice. Women's education and political action have altered, India's social and political landscape. Women have moved from being objects of legislation to initiators. A general awakening has begun and it cannot be permanently suppressed.

Focusing on human right violations against women during armed conflicts, Ardra Manasi, in her paper titled "Gender Dimension of Armed Conflicts: Violation of Rights of Women" examines how women are more affected and the disadvantageous position they enjoy in the mainstream society. She tries to focus on how armed conflicts can negatively affect women's reproductive rights. Many national and international agencies are trying in their (best) capacity to translate women's rights into a tangible reality. But it should be noted that women need to be empowered to assert their basic rights. Humanitarian relief as a model of intervention or legalistic and formalistic human right mechanism can fail if they are externally imposed. She concludes her paper by supplementing that we need to acknowledge the voice of those who have been directly victimised by the conflict to come up with a feasible solution that will operate on the premises of their true needs, as voiced by them.

In "Right to Education in India: The Concept and Context" Dr. D. Pradeep discusses various measures taken by the Central Governments to impart free and compulsory education in India with special emphasis to the Right to education and its varying ramifications in the Indian context. The Right to education is recognised as a human right by the UN and is understood to establish an entitlement of free and compulsory primary education for all children. He examines how RTE Act can meaningfully work in the Indian context and suggests that the rural development and panchayat raj departments would need to accelerate poverty reduction programmes so as to free children from domestic chores and wage earning responsibilities. State governments should ensure that the Panchayat Raj institutions can perform their function within the frame work of RTE Act. Similarly the National Rural Health Mission must take up school health programmes to vulnerable groups and sports department should look after for the overall physical, social, emotional and mental development of the child. Unless these measures are followed effectively, the Right to education Act would loose much of its spirit and content in the Indian Context.

Right to Information is a fundamental right and it is the oxygen for democracy, says Dr. Raju Abraham in his paper "The Right to Information Act, 2005 and Human Right". The RI Act is a landmark legislation of Indian Parliament for the enhancement of democracy, human rights, transparency accountability and good governance, if it is implemented in the true spirit of the law. Around 85 states in the world have enacted right to information laws. Universal Declaration of Human Rights, International covenant on civil and political rights and Universal Declaration on Democracy accepted the importance of the freedom of information. The Supreme Court of India from time to time interpreted article 19(1) of the constitution which uphold the freedom of speech and expression, to implicitly include the right to receive and impart information. In India, only 11 percent of the relevant age group are studying in the higher education institutions, he points out. Without the active involvement of these educated youth, the practical regime of right to information cannot be fulfilled.

B. Madhusoodanan Nair in his paper on "Sex Workers Movement for Rights: Need for Civil Society Intervention" discusses the sex workers, movement which had been quite widespread in the 1970's and the response of the civil society towards sex workers rights. According to him, one of the significant issues is the emergence of a social movement for sex workers. The functioning of these movement have not been vibrant in taking up various issues such as socio-economic and political rights of the workers or providing better working conditions or medical facilities. He points out that the state and political institutions, state institutions like police and other agencies turn a deaf ear to the cause of sex workers. The human rights violations are severe in the case of sex workers and he suggests that it is high time that the civil society and human rights organisations take proactive attitude towards the sex workers and their rights. The gap created by the state in taking up sex workers rights should be filled in by the civil society.

### III

Just as human rights advocates have tended to place only civil and political rights on to their agenda, environmentalist have tended to focus primarily on natural resources preservation without addressing human impacts of environmental abuse.

In Part III of the book papers relating Environment and Human Rights are included. Prof. P.S. Panikkar in his paper "Environmental Agitations and Human Rights Violations in Kerala" discusses two agitations that took place in Kerala wherein large and small groups of individuals fought against environmental degradation and consequent human rights violations. After discussing Plachimada Anti-Coca Cola struggle (2002-2009) and Kanjikkode Railway Coach Factory Eviction Struggle (2009), he accuses authorities of the State Government and district administration who dubbed this struggle as one against development, prompted by Tamilnadu lobbies and outsiders". He argues that People's resistance and struggle are the only way out for solving their problem. He maintains that the ultimate victory, achieved through Gandhian means of Satyagraha would really be a feather in the cap for people's struggle against an insensitive, arrogant and callous officialdom and government.

Dr. K.M. George's paper titled "Pharmaceutical Patents and Human Rights" examines patents rights in the light of human rights. This has become unnecessary because of the increasing tendency of harmonization of patent laws of nations and the World Trade Organization's mandatory requirement of TRIPS compliance of patent laws by its member-nations. The analysis is made especially in the context of laws relating to pharmaceutical patents in India. The paper is structured in three parts, Part I deals with human rights and aspects of health, and Part II with pharmaceutical patents. Part III examines pharmaceutical patents and human right.

In his paper on "Enviornmental Degradation by MNCs and Human Rights violations", Dr. P. Rajendren Nair examines how big business concerns of both developed and devolping countries engaging in ruthless exploitation of nature's endowments for making profit cause unaccountable damage to environment. By producing dangerous products and disposing its waste to water, air and land they are engaged in violation of human rights. The domestic laws of many states fail to impose adequate human rights duties on corporations. Since MNCs always operate at transnational and sometimes in complicity with states, it is essential that international law plays an active role in regulating their activities. The existing international framework of corporate accountability is inappropriate, for dealing with MNCs, he observes. As such, it is necessary to construct a strong international mechanism to reconceptualize the guiding principles and approach of international law vis-a-vis MNCs.

Reinhart Philip in his paper "Commodification of Water, Human Rights Issues and MNCs" discusses commodification of water and Human Rights Violations. By commodification of water MNCs are denying the right of common man to the free gift of nature. Every where, observes the scholar, the harmful effects of commodification and excessive pricing are on the poor. Nature has provided water free of cost; pricing that water is a crime against the nature. He fears that all the corporates are exploiting, polluting, diverting and depleting the well springs of the world for their profits. Civil Society involvements have shown effective in curbing corporate human rights abuses. Taking into account the success attained in the different parts of the world through citizens struggle and civil society's intervention, he concludes that people's struggle for water rights around the world are increasing as it has become clear that when the people rise up, Government's will be forced to come out of their servitude and MNCs will be forced to bend their knees.

Panicker Harishanker's paper titled "Climate Change and Subsistence: A case for Human Rights" looks at how climate change has affected the entire humanity and especially the most vulnerable in the developing world. The paper not only examines how rights have been violated with respect to the climate change, but also how a human rights perspective to the debate on climate change can bring about new perspectives that are not captured by the present views. He argues that a human rights perspective to the debate will automatically bring about an emphasis on the intra-generational equity, crucial for sustainable development and human rights of the most vulnerable.

In "Tribal Land Alienation in Kerala: Its Human Rights Implications" Dr. R. Rajeevan maintains that both fronts that ruled Kerala (LDF & UDF) did very little to enforce the tribal protection laws effectively in the state. Consequently basic human rights of those people were continuously violated. According to him, even after all the struggles against land alienation, the tribal lands are still susceptible to large scale encroachment. The judiciary (both the Supreme Court and High Court) through their verdicts accused the State Government for its lack of concern in carrying out the distribution of lands to the tribals with in the stipulated time. The cultural leaders of Kerala and the print media too expressed their concern for their tribal fellows. Despite these efforts, the State Government seems to turn its face away, from the real issues of tribal land alienation which has become one of the serious instances of the violation of human rights of the most marginalized among its subjects, he observes.

## IV

Machineries intended to protect and promote human rights- both governmental and non-governmental agencies like the World body, the Fourth Estate, the Judiciary, Police and NGOs are dealt with in the seven papers included in the last part of this book titled Protection of Human Rights

In her paper "Role of United Nations in Promoting Human Rights" Ms. Vidya Nair states that the global human right regime involves widely accepted substantive norms; authoritative multi-lateral standard setting procedures, considerable promotional activity, but very limited international implementation that rarely goes beyond mandatory reporting procedures. There is no significant international enforcement. In the age of Globalization, Protecting and promoting human rights is imperative. Globalization has been both an impediment to the development of international human rights and a stimulus, she observes. UN human rights work must be based more on increasing emphasis on human values, with the norms and standards being more and more internationalized within societies rather than being seen as something imposed from outside. This requires a bottoms-up, introspective approach, rather than top-down and finger pointing one where everyone jumps at the violation of others for getting the problems with in.

P. Faziluddin in his paper on "The Fourth Estate as the Watch Dog of Human Rights: Some Reflections", observes that one of the most distinguishing traits of Democracy is its regard for the rights of others. Illustrating instances based on Kerala, he points out that violations of Human rights are taking place on the main streets of Kerala on a massive scale. And day after day media in Kerala goes on acting deaf and dumb on this. The media goes on celebrating the big success or massiveness of the rallies and demonstrations totally eclipsing the cruel violations of basic Human Rights they inflict on the general society. To that extent, the media has become passive participatory accomplies in these violations since they go about without taking serious notes of them, he pointsont.

In his paper "Enforcement of Human Rights: of Judiciary" Dr. G.Rajasekharan Nair examines the pro-active role of judiciary in maintaining human rights. Discussing the Jurisdiction of the Supreme Court and High Courts on the basis of notable case laws concerning this, he discusses the enforcement of human rights through judicial activism. He points out that India has always taken pride as being the world's largest democracy and being governed by rule of law. When compared to other two organs of governance, the judiciary more particularly, the Supreme Court of India can claim to have made some success in the way of protecting human rights. The Supreme Court of India has became a torch bearer and in that capacity it has turned out to be the saviour of the people inside the country but also earned the respect of the counter parts in other countries. In the realm of public interest the Supreme Court of India by its pro active role has become a fore runner.

In an ideal world where everybody respects everyone else's human rights, there will be no need for a police force. However, such a situation exists only in the realm of dreams..., observes K. Padmakumar IPS in his paper "Human Rights and Policing in a Plural Democracy". The Primary function of a police force in a democracy is the protection of Human Rights. He maintains that it is the primary duty of the police service in a democracy to ensure that, every individual is able to live with dignity and is able to enjoy the inalienable human rights to the maximum practical extent possible. When a law is violated to implement a law, the law enforcement agency loses the moral authority to implement laws. One of the major factors which threatens the enjoyment of human rights in a plural democracy is corruption and police force has a vital role in combating this evil. Police service in a plural democracy needs to respect the society it tries to serve. It should not consider themselves as having an exclusive responsibility to fight crime and keep public order totally relying on their own man powered weapons. On the contrary they must realise that they are partners in a social progress and they need to be in constant dialogue with other partners forming part of government, social organizations, local authorities, leaders of public opinion and the general public.

Dr. K. Alexander in his paper on "Police and Human Rights in Kerala: Need for Reform" underscores that a vide gap is visible between the perceptions of the people and the performance of police in Kerala. Reports appearing in the media shows that police are violators rather than protectors of human rights. As the horizon of human right is expanding, so the crime rate is also expanding with the result that the atrocities of the police is also increasing. Hence police are more feared than respected. He contends that the crying need of the hour is reforming our police to make them acceptable to the people and to make the people accept their police. He maintains that in distinguishing between reforming the police and modernization of the police force, the civil society has to be alive and should strive to mobilize public opinion demanding police reform, if they would like their police to be the guardian of human rights.

In "Role of NGOs in Human Rights Defence" B.R.P. Bhasker, a veteran social activists, points out that a vibrant society is one that has a body of civic and social organizations that are not under the control of the State or of powerful political and commercial interests and take up public causes. In the field of human rights, the role of NGO is particularly important as governments or their agencies often become violators of the very rights they are committed to protect and promote vast sections of the people who are illiterate and ill-informed, and that makes it easy for rights violators to act with impunity. Against this background human rights education assumes importance and this task is primarily performed by NGOs. Emphasizing the work done by various NGOs like Amnesty International, PUCL and other professional NGOs, he brands that these Non-Governmental organisation have made a major contribution to the cause of human rights by extensively documenting cases of violation. This role cannot be entrusted to anyone else.

Dr. P. Sukumaran Nair in his paper on "Non-Governmental Organisation (NGOs) and Human Rights: Its prototypical Role" examines the role of NGOs in furthering the cause of human rights. After discussing the various NGOs functioning at International level and National level, he points out that NGO's have been successful in attracting peoples committed to work for the cause of human rights. NGOs prototypical role in furthering human rights can be grouped into three viz., by setting standards, documenting violations and lobbying for effective enforcement. NGO's have been playing a crucial role in upholding human rights. It is time that Governments all over the world should realise the important role played by the NGOs in protecting Human Rights and fundamental freedoms. For the smooth functioning of NGO's, Government should desist from imposing unnecessary restrictions on the legitimate functioning of NGO for the protection of human rights, he opines. For effectively performing the task both NGO's and Governmental mechanisms should work hand in glove in furthering the cause of human rights.

# 1

# HUMAN RIGHTS: FROM CONCEPTUALISATION TO REALISATION

**N.K. Jayakumar**

Continuous engagement of the academic community with human rights and a stream of intellectual discourses generated it serve in a significant way to add new dimensions to the concept of human rights. Such discourses by keeping the debate on human rights always alive and in the limelight help raise awareness and awakening in the society vis- a- vis the major concerns of human rights. While emphasising the relevance and importance of academic discourses on human rights we must by no means be understood to convey a wrong notion that human rights are merely a matter of academic interest. On the other hand the practical realisation of human rights, ours as well as those of others, is of much more importance. The complimentarily of the academic and practical aspects of human rights must set the right tone for academic deliberations on human rights. The task of teachers in this process is very important because they can act as a bridge between the academia and the society. It is for them to ensure that a culture of human rights is fully and visibly embedded in young minds across the country.

The process of realization of human rights involves identification, specification and concretization of human rights through legal provisions. Each of these components presents complex problems at every stage. Since identification of human rights norms is not possible unless there is some consensus on values, this takes us to the rhetoric of human rights. The basic question that is posed is what the basis of human rights is.

The idea of human rights originates from a belief in the inherent dignity and worth of every human being. It naturally follows that certain things ought not to be done to any human being and certain other things ought to be done for every human being. In that sense the idea of human rights operates as a fundamental moral limit on how we may live our lives. At another level, the idea of human rights imposes some limits on State power and also obligates the State to do certain things.

The question has persistently been raised as to whether the basis of human rights is religious of secular. While some maintain the position that the faith in the inherent dignity and worth of all human beings originates from religion, there are others who vehemently argue that human rights can and must survive independent of religion, and try to establish the secular basis of human rights. The truth may lie somewhere in between these two extreme positions. A re-conciliation between the divided realms of human rights, religion and secularism is indeed possible and necessary.

David Sidorsky of Columbia University proposes that the term human rights denotes two different but not inconsistent functions.

(i) Notion of human rights as 'universal norms or standards that are applicable to all human societies'

(ii) Idea that 'all individuals, solely by virtue of being human, have moral rights which no society or State should deny.'

James Nickel of Arizona State University is of the view that compliance with human rights is mandatory. Such rights are properly viewed as independent because they 'exist and are available as standards of justification and criticism whether or not they are recognized and implemented by the legal system or officials of a country'.

A survey of the evolution and development of human rights reveals that the achievements of 20th century provided the normative architecture of human rights. Now, the mission of the 21st century is to provide effective and legitimate implementation via local, national, regional and global actions.

## Jurisprudence of Human Rights

The modern concept of human rights is most frequently attributed to natural rights discourse, although some argue that human rights are more accurately conceived of as positive social constructs rather than as principles arising out of natural or moral norms. Any jurisprudential inquiry into human rights cannot ignore the divide between the natural law and positive law schools. The natural law school built upon the concept of natural rights has inspired most of the historic events and documents such as the French Revolution, Declaration of the Rights of Man, American Declaration of Independence, and the American Bill of Rights, which paved the way for an international jurisprudence of human rights. However, subsequent events placed more emphasis on incorporating human rights in national constitutions and laws and establishing statutory mechanisms for enforcement of human rights, undoubtedly under the influence of the positive law approach. It is better to remember that both these approaches have contributed to strengthen the idea of human rights and its realisation.

It is also necessary to examine the relevance of human rights to the idea of justice. Human rights may be seen as ethical pronouncements, with distinct political content. They may be treated as an invitation to initiate fresh legislation, rather than relying on what is already seen as legally installed, or as a template for new laws that would be enacted to legalise human rights across the world.

The renowned jurist H.L.A/Hart rightly points out that recognition of human rights can inspire fresh legislation; but relevance of human rights does not lie exclusively in determining what should 'appropriately be made the subject of coercive legal rules.'

The ethics of human rights can be made more effective through a variety of interrelated instruments and a versatility of ways and means. This is one of the reasons why it is important to give the general ethical status of human rights its due, rather than locking up the concept of human rights prematurely within the narrow box of legislation – real or ideal.

Amartya Sen examines the idea of freedom and its relevance to human rights in his classic work *The Idea of Justice*. He draws a distinction between the 'opportunity aspect' and the 'process aspect' of freedom – i.e., substantive opportunities and the actual processes involved in a person's freedom. For the opportunity aspect, the idea of 'capability' – the real opportunity to achieve valuable functioning's – would typically be a good way of formalising freedoms. But issues related to process aspect, demand that we go beyond seeing freedoms only in terms of capabilities. (Eg. Denial of due process, whether the outcome could be expected to be different or not). Amartya Sen concludes that the violation or non-realization of the freedoms underlying human rights are bad social realizations.

According to Charles Beitz, human rights play 'the role of a moral touchstone – a standard of assessment and criticism for domestic institutions, a standard of aspiration for their reform, and increasingly a standard of evaluation for the policies and practices of international economic and political institutions'

## Cultural Relativism

The conceptualisation and internationalisation of human rights, especially in the latter half of the 20th century, projected human rights as a western concept. This Euro-centric approach equated the universality of human rights with the domination of Western values over other cultures which had no respect for human rights. Academic discussions and human rights courses seem to have accepted that the concept of human rights is mainly a contribution of the West.

But this is really a distortion. In fact every culture contains certain ideals and policies which respect human rights. It is equally true that every culture also contains certain beliefs and/or practises antithetical to human rights. While such aspects in Islamic or Hindu Culture have been magnified and projected as the core of that culture, similar elements in the Western culture, like slavery and racial discrimination, have been presented as aberrations.

Amartya Sen observes that some human rights notions can be traced through centuries of Asian thought, religion, philosophy and culture. Buddhism attaches great importance to the notion of freedom which is also reflected in the early Indian tradition from which Buddhism emerged.

The relevance of Gandhian perspective on human rights is that it shows us how to blend tradition with modern values of human rights. Gandhiji's deep faith in the dignity and worth of every human being made him a crusader for human rights throughout his life. Gandhiji's public life, as we know, started with his open challenge of apartheid in South Africa.

According to Makau Mutua, the notion of universality of human rights is merely an imposition of western values and many Asian and other non-western value systems emphasise community development, order and discipline over individual rights and freedoms. The western-centric attitudes and concepts of the rights discourse imported to the developing world are not necessarily applicable regardless of nationality, geography, culture or political institutions. The correct approach, therefore, seems to be to develop the concept of human rights within the understanding of a specific people's culture, community and traditions.

The theme of cultural relativism vs universality of human rights continues to be one of the primary and ongoing concerns of human rights discourse even today.

## Categorisation of Human Rights

We are familiar with the categorisation of human rights into the first, second and third generation human rights. The first generation is generally understood to signify civil and political rights. It was once believed by an influential section of human rights theorists that only civil and political rights genuinely deserve to be recognised as human rights. Subsequently, however, the second generation human rights, viz., economic, social and cultural rights, gathered momentum, vastly expanding the domain of human rights. Today we have the third generation human rights which are known as collective or solidarity rights over- shadowing the first two generations of human rights. These rights include the right to self-determination, right to development, right to participate and benefit from common heritage of mankind and right to a healthy environment. They pose the increasingly complex challenge of addressing the need to preserve the natural environment, while simultaneously promoting development to meet the basic needs of humanity.

While such a categorisation of human rights may be necessary in some contexts for the purpose of analysis and discussion, it is important to remember that they are mutually interdependent and one generation of human rights does not supersede the other.

Another categorisation of human rights divides them into derogable and non-derogable human rights. Most of the human rights are not absolute and permit some derogation especially in the interest of protecting the rights of others. The important questions here are:

(i) Who has the power to derogate?

(ii) On what grounds and in what circumstances is derogation permissible?

(iii) To what extent derogation is permissible?

The fact that we accept some human rights as derogable in nature should not lead to a situation where, in the name derogation there is a total negation of the right. In situations of emergency and when confronted with terrorism, legal systems tend to enact legislation substantially curtailing human rights. The impact of such measures on human rights must engage the attention of activists as well as academics.

**Internationalization**

The most significant step in the internationalisation of human rights was the adoption of the Universal Declaration of Human Rights (UDHR) on December 10, 1948. Although non-binding as a legal document the UDHR has produced tremendous impact on all legal systems and on the subsequent development of human rights jurisprudence. It is considered as the first general international acknowledgement of the 'inherent dignity and of equal and undeniable rights of all members of the human family as the foundation of freedom, justice and peace in the world.'

The UDHR was followed by the International Covenant on Civil and Political Rights and the International Covenant on Economic Social and Cultural Rights, which are legally binding international instruments. Both these documents may be considered as elaborations of the principles enumerated in the UDHR. While civil and political rights have been unquestionably accepted as constituting the core of human rights, doubts have been expressed about the status and realisation of economic, social and cultural rights.

Linking these rights and the third generation human rights, Brian Barry observes that UDHR has implications – and very important ones – for the international community as a whole, not just for individual states. Barry goes on to identify what he argues are the implications of this momentous recognition: 'If governments simply do not have the means of supplying everyone with such things as adequate nutrition and housing, pure drinking water, sanitation and a generally healthy environment, education and medical care, then the wealthy counties, individually or in any combination have an obligation to ensure that, by one means or another, the resources are forthcoming'

**Marxist Approach**

The insights of Karl Marx into power relations based on economic factors had large impact on the human rights discourse, especially in respect of economic and social rights. Marx regarded the natural rights approach to human rights as idealistic and ahistorical and rejected the idea of inalienable human rights.

The Marxist approach believes that Law reflects the power relations of society. It is the expression of the ruling class, interested in the preservation of the social structure. Like society as a whole, the legal order is based on ownership relations. The State, in order to operate effectively, has to create the illusion of representing the interests of the whole of society. But in fact it does only represent the economic interests of the ruling class, maintaining the actual social structure. Even when, due to social progress, the law may seem autonomous, it remains an expression of actual economic power relations. The barriers of real freedom are, therefore, to be found within the structure of society itself.

The Marxist approach challenges the idea of human rights, based on the freedom and equality of all human beings. As long as the structure of society is not a structure of real freedom and equality, human rights will only reflect the existing power relations of the society. Marxism does not reject the idea of human rights, but questions its implementation. As long as there is no change in the societal structure itself, the idea of human rights will remain a mere ideology.

**Globalization and Human Rights**

Globalisation results in disempowerment of the State and reveals a tendency towards de-territorialisation of political authority and identity.

Widespread acceptance of efficiency and competitiveness as criteria for assessing economic performance is another hallmark of the philosophy of globalisation. International institutions become vulnerable to manipulation and control by political forces responsible for some of the worst forms of injustice, including patterns of domination, exploitation and victimization. In such a scenario, concerns of global justice move from a war-peace axis to poverty, inequality, environmental protection and social, economic and cultural rights.

The policies of globalisation exert mounting pressures on government to reduce expenditure on public goods such as education and health. Conditionality of loans administered by World Bank, International Monitory Fund etc. insists that a governmental recipient does not use public resources for poverty alleviation and social distress, but rather to build a high-growth economy. As a result of these policies of globalisation material inequality is on the rise, in spite of improvement in aggregate economic wellbeing, making the rich richer and the poor poorer. What we find is economic growth v. social equality Dilemma. Unless we are able to strike a balance between a purely economic view of growth and a more normative concern with overcoming human suffering and inequality, the future of human rights will be in peril.

Moves to uphold social and economic rights by direct state action are seen as generally dangerous to the maintenance of cultural and political rights because of their tendency to consolidate power in the State and to undermine individualism. This view rejects any commitment of responsibility to those who are economically and socially disadvantaged and has the effect of de facto narrowing of the broad scope of human rights.

Effective implementation of human rights depends upon internalising the enforcement process – i.e., taking human rights seriously at home. Such seriousness depends both on a citizenry that is committed to human rights culture and a government that is willing to apply human rights standards as vigorously within its own borders as it is in its foreign policy.

Until the emerging global market forces supported by the philosophy of economic liberalisation and globalisation can be regulated on the basis of human and environmental priorities, the dynamics of trade, investment, and growth are likely to gravely jeopardise the mission of human rights to protect those who are most at risk economically, socially, politically and culturally. This is the challenge posed to a community of academics engaged in the pursuit of human rights as a continuing and interactive process.

# 2

# HUMAN RIGHTS IN A GLOBALIZED WORLD: MARKET FRIENDLY RIGHTS VS PEOPLE FRIENDLY RIGHTS, A THEORETICAL CONSTRUCT

**J. Prabhash**

## 1. Introduction

The nature and impact of economic globalization/neo-liberalism on human rights is a hot topic in contemporary discourse on human rights. As in other issues here also the academic community is divided between those who argue about its beneficial implications for human rights and others whose arguments run the contrary direction. The first school – this may be roughly called as the neo-liberal perspective on human rights–bases its argument and seeks justification for it on the supposed ability of 'liberalised economic relationships to improve economic and social well-being of the people' [Stephens, 2010:237] and the global integration of Human Rights Movements and universal dissemination of information about rights' transgression, thanks to the developments in the field of Information and Communication Technology [Ishay, 2004:348]. Thus the protagonists of this school speak about globalization with a human face or, human rights oriented globalization [Baxi, 2006:239]. The latter perspective – broadly the left perspective – while contesting the propensity of economic liberalization in materializing economic well-being, argues that profit motive associated with it furthers all sorts of exploitation – social, economic and political – ultimately leading to the denial of even basic rights to the marginalized social groups. The central argument of this paper is based on this left perspective.

Needless to say, human rights 'normativity' depends on the stability of democratic order, particularly the extent of democratic control over state power. People themselves should be the arbiters of their life and destiny is the foundational principle of democray. All these in their turn depend on the authenticity of representation and robustness of the constitutionally guaranteed democratic rights[1]. That in an electoral democracy, elected representatives ought to have organic linkage with the constituency they represent has been a long accepted fact. For, the articulation of the voices of suffering entails act of representation [Baxi, 2006:6].

Only in such a situation the ruling dispensation could be forced to reflect popular aspirations on all vital issues concerning state craft and govern in the beneficial interests of the public. This enables the state to emancipate itself from the clutches of the dominant sections of the society and gain real power to convert the constitution and the rights it guarantees into a testament of social redemption.

A healthy civil society and a strong public sphere provide an enabling environment for the above. A civil society to be healthy has to be democratically constituted and should have enough space to ensure social pluralism and informed debates on social issues. To be more precise a democratic civil society is different from a bourgeois conception of civil society which is nothing but market writ large with its consumers, investors and vendors calling shots and money mediating social relations. From a human rights point of view, on the other hand, it should simultaneously perform the task of preventing deviations in the exercise of state power and, at the same time, lent voice to the voiceless[2]. It is worth noting here that the historic mission of human rights is to give vent to human sufferings, to make it visible and to ameliorate it [Baxi, 2006:6]. Civil society while playing host to this, also strengthens dialogical spaces leading to the establishment of a vigorous public sphere.

A democratic order based on this enables the marginalized social groups to attempt at transcending their marginality through strategies of mobilization, contestation (of state power) and representation. It is true that at times such attempts may attain only partial success or may even be futile. It is also true that powerful forces in society may find new methods for coping with new challenges to their domination and new elements may arise to enforce their power [Mohanty, 2006-2007:45]. Still, the fact that there is adequate space in the system to resist oppression/marginality/exploitation and to critically engage with the existing social order, however limited it is, is in itself a great relief for the common man, particularly the victims of human rights violations. While all these are true at the theoretical level, doubts are expressed today about the potential of even democracies to realize human rights in the context of economic globalization.

## II. Globalization and Marketisation of Governance

It needs reiterating that economic globalization is not merely an economic process relating to the movement of capital, or goods and services among nations. While it encompasses all these, it signifies much more – a comprehensive socio-economic, cultural and political project capable enough to redefine the relationship between state and citizen in such a way that they (citizens) hardly matter in actual governance process. All crucial decisions relating to public policies are decided by investors and International Financial Institutions (IFI's). The key idea in the neo-liberal theory of governance is, therefore, to treat the state as merely one player in the market game, at best a facilitator with authority and power to maintain the social order so that market can flourish [Krishna Kumar, 2008:9]. This is what the Indian Prime Minister Man Mohan Singh has described as 'free-market democracy' where democracy is not about people but all about market.

This 'marketisation' of governance/democracy has dire consequences as for as human rights are concerned, atleast on three counts: as public policies become market centric, state priorities will naturally get redefined from popular well-being to that of protecting the interest of market forces; this entails not only denying people certain socio-economic rights but even curtailing their basic political and civil rights; and ultimately these two factors cumulatively lead to the redefinition of the very concept of human rights and democracy.

Economic growth per se is the major thrust of a market friendly paradigm of development. Towards this end it calls upon the state to free as many spaces for capital as possible by fully pursuing the 3-Ds of contemporary globalization: de-regulation, de-nationalization and disinvestment [Baxi, 2006: 248]. This not only cripples the public sector but, in the name of economic growth, unleashes the private sector to exploit natural and human resources with little respect either for environment or social interest or even for the constitution and laws of the country. The Bhopal gas tragedy in India is a classical example which proves beyond doubt the extent to which corporate houses can plunder a nation and its people and still get away with it unpunished. Interestingly, as these houses amass huge fortunes, their tax commitment to the public exchequer get slashed and they may even enjoy total tax holidays. The MNCs and their Indian subsidiaries functioning in the Special Economic Zones (SEZs) in this country and elsewhere offer the best example of the inverse relationship that exists between profit and tax.

One important side effect of the above is that effective surplus in the hands of the government to utilize for critical social sectors is reduced drastically. Even a casual glance at the budgetary provisions relating to education, public health, public distribution system, poverty alleviation, rural and urban development, housing etc. shows how public spending, both in real terms and as a percentage of GDP, is shrinking to abysmally low levels that the state has only a token presence in many of these areas. All these in some important ways mark the end of the processes and regimes of human rights oriented redistributionist governance practices in ways that convert the mandate of 'progressive realization of socio-economic and cultural rights of the people into an ongoing cruel hoax' [Baxi 2006:248].

### III. Shrinking Human Rights Base

On the obverse side, a different trend is also discernible – governments are over spending to strengthen external security and law and order machinery. This becomes essential as the state and the ruling classes get themselves alienated from the masses in the face of growing socio-economic contradictions and increasing social tensions consequent on this [For an informed debate on this see, Peterson etal., 1999; and Lorzen, 2001]. To put it differently, a neo-liberal state, as it has to be extra conscious to offer maximum protection to investors, has to be ever prepared to let lose a reign of terror on its own people at the biding of these forces [Baxi, 2006:252]. And the only way to achieve this is to strengthen its coercive apparatus so that it could be used to preserve the security of the capitalist classes while depriving ordinary working people of security and other human rights [Ishay, 2004:286]. A neo-liberal state is thus a 'hard and soft' state simultaneously, soft towards global capital and hard towards its own ordinary men and women.

From a human rights ankle, the Hard State is more dangerous than the Soft State[3] for the latter denies the people even basic civil and political rights. This is done in umpteen number of ways: direct and indirect; perpetuating police atrocities; registering false cases; awarding punishments on dubious grounds etc. More important than this, however, is the propensity of the state to drag into the perimeter of crimes a wide spectrum of political opinion, political sympathy and political activity through extraordinary laws enacted in the name of tackling seditious activity, terrorist activity, and activity prejudicial to nation's territorial integrity and unity [Balagopal, 2006-07:2]. As such containment of popular struggles has the twin consequence of curtailing basic democratic rights of the people and de-politicizing the governance process, for it is through agitations and organized protests that people create politics of their own by which alone they could articulate their interests and force the government of the day to take note of them.

Under duress of such far reaching changes in every conceivable aspect of democratic governance, human rights lose their human face. While the democratic notion of human rights stands for crafting a socio-political order which will atleast ensure basic human needs, the neo-liberal paradigm has little respect for this or the human individual or collective rights of the marginalized. For instance, it has little or no space, for the stateless, the refugees, the massively impoverished human beings, the indigenous people of the world, people living with disabilities, children and women [Baxi, 2006:2]. It has little regard for labour legislations or humanitarian laws in general. The emergent paradigm, therefore, insists upon the promotion and protection of the collective human rights of global capital, in ways which 'justify' corporate well-being and dignity even when it entails continuing gross and flagrant violation of human rights of actually existing human beings and communities [Baxi, 2006:234].

Interestingly neo-liberalism always and everywhere argues the need for a borderless world, a world which is flat to borrow the words of Thomas Friedman. But paradoxically this flatness or borderlessness is meant only for the investors, Multi National Corporations (MNC's) and big business. The world is thus flat for the free movement of global capital and black money. Upendra Baxi neatly summarises the situation thus:

> The principal point concerning the end of the nation-state then, in the dominant perspective, is the creation of a borderless world for global capital, even though it stands cruelly bordered for the violated victims subject to practices of the politics of cruelty, even barbaric practices of power. Myanmar is thus borderless for Uncoal though not for Aung San Suu Kyi and the thousands of Burmese people she symbolizes. India is borderless for Union Carbide and Monsanto but not for the mass disaster-violated Indian humanity. Ogoniland is borderless for shell but becomes the graveyard of Human Rights and justice movements led by Ken Saro Wiwa [Baxi, op.cit., 2006:247].

It is clear that this concept of freedom has brought with it a corresponding notion of human rights which is at odds with the subaltern perspective on the subject. Not only that the new paradigm hardly harbours any holistic vision about human rights, but it totally submerges even the legitimate human right aspirations of the masses within the overall quest of the global capital for profit. Interestingly it even appropriates the language of rights and uses it in the service of business. Thus, today, one hears much about the right of an investor/entrepreneur to exploit natural resources over the inalienable rights of the common people for safe drinking water, healthy environment and sustenance or his (investor/entrepreneur) right to layoff labourers and subject them to inhuman service conditions – whether it is denial of trade union rights or right to minimum leisure or adequate wages.

In this scheme of things, therefore, every right guaranteed by international instruments of human rights or democratic constitutions is interpreted in a manner that it fits into the neo-liberal conception of state and society. Take for instance, the transformation that has taken place for as simple a right like speech and expression. It has been corporatized in such a manner that commercial free speech trumps the earlier forms of human rights to freedom of speech, expression and associational activity of the individual [Appadurai, 1997; Burawoy etal., 2000]. The world has, thus, entered the era of corporatisation of human rights or 'corporate human rights'. This has reached a situation in which human rights production, distribution and consumption have only a limited or no future outside the practices of this ideology [Baxi, 2006: 240].

## IV. Towards Conclusion

The entire human rights discourse today has thus been appropriated by the ideological right which has been using it simultaneously to serve its interests and at the same time deny its blessings to the marginalised sections. Therefore, from the vantage point of the common man the challenges to human rights from the champions of this ideology (neo-liberalism) is as imminent as those which emanate from terrorist groups, perhaps to a higher degree from the former than the latter as the impact of the ideology they represent is much more comprehensive than the other. In fact this has created a serious cleavage in rights discourse between the politics of human rights and the politics for human rights and has resulted in privileging the former over the latter. While the former insists that human rights belong as much to individual human beings as to economic collectivities, the latter argues for the primacy of human rights of human beings over the human rights of technoscience capital, entailing the consequence that trade-related market-friendly human rights remain 'secondary' to the universal human rights of human beings [Baxi, 2006:253]. Further, as already stated, modern tendency is to take this cleavage to a different plane and settle it in favour of market-friendly human rights.

As such, conscious attempts are needed to reverse the trend and right the wrongs in the emergent paradigm of human rights. There is a lot of talk today about 'globalisation from below' which represents the actions of social actors, such as grassroot NGOs, that join forces to address human rights abuses, inequality and underdevelopment [Cox, 1999; Falk 1995; and Linda, 2004:215]. However, the capability of such movements to establish cross-national linkages is yet to be proved and hence the proof of their effectiveness remains largely in the realm of imagination.

This is not to underestimate contemporary relevance of these movements, but only to emphasize that their potential for resisting neo-liberal practices is limited. It is worth remembering that such practices have to be fought at multiple levels of which globalization from below is just one. Another and a much more significant level is to make resistance towards economic globalization and neo-liberal policies a constituent element of the commonsense of their victims–marginalized social groups – and strengthen democratic culture at the pores of the civil society so that civil society itself could be emancipated from the grip of the bourgeoisie. This is also the best way to make it (civil society) creative. And here, more than Non Governmental Organizations and social movements, progressive political parties – by virtue of their spread, reach and popularity and ideology – have a very important role to play.

### Notes and References

1. It may be noted that there is a fundamental difference between civil liberties and democratic rights. The former connotes only legal and

political rights–freedom of expression and association, right to vote, safeguards against arbitrary arrest etc. The latter, on the other side, includes not only these civil liberties but also right to minimum wage, tribal right to forest resources, rights of women in employment, and right to education, to name a few. In short taken together these two represent rights in all their four dimensions, socio-economic, political and cultural [For an influential formulation on this read, Mohanty, 2006-07:44; Balagopal, 2006-07:4-5].

2. In this sense it comes nearer to what is termed as a 'creative society'. It refers to that stage of development of a society in which hitherto subdued contradictions become manifest and active, and oppressed groups seek remedies to their sufferings [for details see Mohanty,2001].
3. According to Gunnar Myrdal a Soft State lacks the power of disciplining practices of politics and governance. It is, thus, an effete entity unable to fulfill any of its major social welfare roles. Its softness stand constituted by the profiles of politics and state-formation marked by a conspicuous lack of discipline [For details see Myrdal 1972; Baxi, 2006 and Kelsey, 1995]. This, however, does not mean that a Hard State performs any major social welfare role. The nomenclature simply means that such a state is capable of exercising tight control over the society and implementing its decision with an iron hand. No doubt, it is predominantly dictatorial in nature.

Appadurai, Arjun (1997), *Modernity at Large: Cultural Dimensions of Globalization,* New Delhi: Oxford University Press.

Balagopal, K (2006-2007) 'The Human Rights Movement: Its Context and Concernes', Indian *Journal of Human Rights*, Vols. 10 &11, Nos. 1& 2.

" " (2008-09), 'The Constitution and Social Movements', *Indian Journal of Human Rights* Vols. 12-13, Nos. 1 & 2.

Baxi, Upendra (2006), *The Future of Human Rights*, New Delhi: Oxford University Press.

Burawoy, Michel etal. (eds.) (2000), *Global Ethnography: Forces, Connections and Imagination in a Post-modern World,* Berkeley: University of California Press.

Cox, Robert (1999), 'Civil Society at the Turn of the Millennium: Prospects for an Alternative World Order', *Review of International Studies*, Vol. 25, Nos. 3-28.

Falk, Richard (1995), *On Humane Governance: Toward a New Global Politics,* University Park: Pennsylvanian State University Press.

Ishay, Micheline R (2004), the History of *Human Rights: From Ancient Time to the Globalization Era*, New Delhi: Orient Longman.

Kelsey, Jane (1995), *The New Zealand Experiment: A World Model for*

*Structural Adjustment,* London: Pluto Press.

Krishna Kumar (2008), *'Partners in Education', Economic and Political Weekly,* Vol. XLIII, No. 3.

Linda, Butenhoff (2004), 'Localizating Human Rights in an Era of Globalization, the Case of Hong Kong' in Mahmood Monshipouri, Neil Engleheart, Andrew J Nathan and Kavita Philip (eds.), *Constructing Human Rights in the Age of Globalization,* New Delhi: Prentice Hall.

Lorenz, Edward C (2001), Defining Global Justice: *The History of US International Labour Standards Policy,* Notre Dame: Notre Dame University Press.

Mohnty, Manoranjan (2006-07), 'Human Rights in a Creative Society: Challenges of Appropriation', *Indian Journal of Human Rights,* Vols. 10& 11, Nos.1&2.

Myrdal, Gunnar (1972), *Asian Drama: An Inquiry into the Poverty of Nations,* New York: Pantheon.

Peterson, Dean R, F.Wunder and Harlan L. Mueller (1999), *Social Problems of Globalization in the Twenty First Century,* New Jersey: Prentice Hall.

Stephens, Julie Harrelson (2010), 'Achieving Human Rights: The Globalization Debate' in Rhonda L Callaway and Julie Harrelson Stephens (eds), *Exploring International Human Rights,* New Delhi: Viva Books.

# 3

# DISCOURSE ON HUMAN RIGHTS: NARRATIVES BEYOND "POLIITICAL"

**Muzaffar Assadi**

For the past one decade or so human rights issues have become major concern of policy makers, international agencies/institutions, global politics as well as the States. These concerns are the reflections of the way- paradigm shift has taken place in the realm of politics, as well as the realm of economy. No State at present can underestimate the importance of human rights discourse as well as the agenda- this has become an essential, obligatory and indispensable component of politics of the States. This is because of the fact that human rights discourse has become the barometer, a gauge, indicator to understand the strength of a Modern Democratic State. This does not mean that the agenda of pushing human rights agenda is complete, it is still remained as incomplete project of the States too. This is where the paradox of human rights discourse lies.

It is a fact that the contemporary discourse on human rights does not feel comfortable with a division" of human rights into "three generations" (Assadi: 2010). Incidentally growth of human rights have been divided into three generations or phases: first generation of rights are those which seek to uphold political as well as civil rights, second generation of rights are those which seek to defend social and cultural rights and finally is the third generation- it is a set of new rights particularly defended or upholded by different identarian social groups including social movements. Incidentally all these generations have given rise to new twist to the human rights discourse. However it is a fact that these generations of rights have come under severe contestation for the simple reason that social, political as well as cultural rights are many a time overlap with each other making it difficult to divide the human rights into neat and clear-cut categories.

Secondly human rights discourse is also not comfortable with the division of human rights into "hierarchical" one. (Eva Ernabm: 2005) This has brought the issues of "primacy of one human rights over another". It is argued that determining the primacy" of human rights is not always an easy task given the inherent problematiques of identifying the importance of human rights at a particular situation. For example can we say that political rights are more important than economic one in a situation of absolute inequality or absolute uneven development? The structuring and division of rights "hierarchical" has become the major concern for many developing as well as undeveloped countries. Many of the human rights proponents of the developing or underdeveloped world would unambiguously argue in favour of deconstructing the "hierarchy"- for them economic rights are primary over political one, even sometime they would prefer preserving cultural rights at a time when they are threatened by the global capital than the political one. This is quite contrary to the developed world- for them political become primary over economic one, including cultural one.

Third one is the "obligation" perspective. This is one of the recent perspectives that have made the political agencies such as the State to actualise or realise the human rights agenda. In other words it put the onus on the State to implement the international agreements or spirit of different covenant including UN declaration on human rights in toto. In this politics the State has been made the major and a responsible agency in the event human rights are violated- in fact the State has the obligation to protect, Defend and uphold human rights. However the problem becomes acute when political regimes play opposite role and thereby it involve in series of human rights violations and abuses. It is also true that too much stress has been given to the State, which, in the final analysis has undermined the role that the other agencies have been playing in violating human rights- One of the agencies involved in the series of human rights violation is the global capital and capitalism mediating through World Bank, or IMF. In fact one can not overlook the past history of global capital and capitalism in perpetuating human rights violations under the carpet of Colonialism and Imperialism. The best example is the way Colonialism introduced new forms of diseases in the colonized world and succeeded in wiping out native population without resorting to war. Small pox, Malaria, plague came through colonial rule. In the Canary Islands, the entire native population of Guancheas were wiped out during 16th century. In Australia small pox killed half of its population. Disease like Measles killed more than half of the population of Fiji Island in 1875. However in other countries like India it created conditions for structural incapacity including the fact that during the colonial period many cities such as Murshidabad became a depopulated city and that famine became a recurring phenomenon, India lost billions of people during colonial rule. Are such trends continued, re-enacted or recurring phenomenon under the grab of neo-liberalism or globalisation is one question one needs to address. For example the way global capitalism is violating human rights can not be glossed over. This obviously proves that human rights issues have become a terrain of contestation, a terrain of debate as well as terrain of conflict. At the same time one can not overlook the fact that it creates series of myths.

**Myths About and of Human Rights**

One of the myths that has been perpetuated and reproduced in the realm of human right discourse is that it is a modern phenomenon, limited and linked to western civilization. This is but overlooking the presence of human rights discourse, or agenda in the philosophical history of Orient as well elsewhere. In fact it is not modern in the strict sense of the term, as it is now an established fact that history is replete with examples of upholding, as well as attempt to institutionalize human rights as State Policy. Best example is the famous Cyrus Cylinder of Cyrus the Greatest during the 6th century B.C. This cylinder is known as the first human rights document in history. This cylinder gave the citizens freedom to practice religious belief, including the fact that it abolished practice of slavery. Incidentally the attempt to legalize human rights issues were taken up during the reign of Ur –Nammu the King of Ur during 2050 BC. Codification was further done during the reign of Hammurabi during 1780 BC. Even the Great Ashoka was not far behind in advancing civil rights during his reign. Nonetheless, human rights in the imagined history were inbuilt in the recognization of different cultural practices, philosophical discourses as well as right to dissent. However modernity as well as modern civilization although gave new direction to the politics of human rights discourse, which does not mean modernity itself was solely responsible for its growth.

As a corollary to the first myth, the second myth tries to argue in favour of uniformity as well as universal application without any ambiguity. The argument that human rights can be applied uniformly and without ambiguities has been challenged and contested in recent past. Many a time it creates paradoxical situation, wherein groups have contested the claims of universalism These happens at the time of conflicts between two contending parties such as Palestine and Israel society- the latter constructed its own theory of human rights vis-a-vis the Palestinian people.

The third myth is that all the countries which have signed or have become part of UNHRD or its various covenants would always adhere to it without any reservation by providing basic human rights. This is not true always. Many countries have failed even to provide basic human rights. The classic case is the Arab world, as many Arab countries have denied its citizens the basic rights of political expression, voting rights, right to assemble. Arab world has the lowest freedom score, as per the UNDP report. This is the case even with many African countries too. However what is missing in this discourse is that when rights are denied through other mechanism such as Patent Rights or regimes, a discreet silence is observed in human rights discourse-no one would rise the larger implication of such a denial- in fact the Patent Regimes would take away the basic rights to live, basic right to produce as well as basic right to cultural practice. This is where human rights discourse need to go beyond "political" one to envelop "economics".

One more myth is that human rights are too individualistic in nature. More than giving primacy to common good they give primacy to individual good. It is true that there are some rights which are absolute in nature which can not be taken away from the individuals, however there are large number of issues which are for the common good- the rights of the communities, cultural rights, even the right to development all points towards the fact that human rights discourse can go beyond the individual rights.

Further it is argued that human rights issues are too political in nature than social and economic. This is because of the primacy given to the political nature of rights. It is in this politics that the State is often viewed and seen as the site to reclaim, contest and debate over rights. Since State is an agency to implement and defend human rights, bound by the international agreements, it becomes imperative to look upon the State. Too much focus on the State has undermined the presence of other agencies in accentuating or violating human rights. The role that the MNCs played or the globalization played in different forms can not be glossed over. Even the entry of new social movements in various parts of the world definitely has increased the spaces for contestation.

**Market and Neo-Liberal Project of Human Rights**

One of the questions quite often asked is whether the human rights discourse is a larger project of democratization. (Thomas L. Friedman: 1999). Is it a neo-liberal project? It is true that the human rights issues received increasing focus immediately after the collapse of Soviet Union and the subsequent "triumph of capitalism". It came through the mediation of international institutions particularly World Bank or UN. Initially it came as a political project to expand the democratic spaces throughout the world, particularly to those countries which were reeling under authoritarian regimes including former communist countries. This was on later date expanded to include other countries whose human rights records were treated as "poor" in nature. Terms such as "democratic deficit" were often used or employed to measure the degree of democratization as well as degree of freedom enjoyed by the citizens. This was compounded by the deconcentration of political power or what is called decentralization so as to reflect upon the increasing participation of citizens as an autonomous category in the democratization as well as the politics of the country.

However one can not overlook the Market Driven Human Rights Paradigm operating within the larger neo-liberal political project. With the market becoming primacy in the neo liberalism, it becomes imperative that market become the champion of and the site of human rights –as it provide spaces for creating set of new rights akin to market. At the same time it is true that Market created New Social Categories, who are autonomous and heterogeneous but linked to larger market. The Mall, the Departmental stores, Beauty Parlours, Big Bazars, became the symbol of New Market as well as site of New Human Rights- the right to Enter, Right to Bargain, Right to Alternatives, Right to Exit, Right to Choose were seen as New Rights which were hitherto denied to the citizens under theTop Down regimes. Needless to say that, it was argued that such New Rights of the Market would translate into political one. However the question remains as to the extent of such transformation taking place in the realm of politics.

## Globalization and Defining / Redefining Rights

If globalization has created spaces for larger market to enter and thereby create a situation of Market Driven Human Rights Paradigm, at the same time it also created conditions for series of human rights violations and abuses in different forms. There is no single way that the Globalization is entering into the private sphere of citizens (Anthony Giddens: 2000) In fact globalization has created more confusion, as there are no single perspective about it. Many argue however that globalization is nothing but integration of local economy with larger economy, it is part of late capitalist development, (Leslie Sklair: 2000) it is nothing but withdrawal of Sate from the realm of social welfare, it is a post-modern phenomenon etc. Even there are no agreement about the way globalization is entering into public as well as private sphere: some would argue that it is entering through cultural forms, others would argue that it enters through the means of market, or even through symbols too.

However the problem is quantifying the way globalization is dislocating population from the realm of every day life practices. (Atty Cecilia Jimnz: 1998) This is apparent when globalization dislocate population from their cultural sphere. This is what Polanyi calls; "Avalanche of Social Dislocation" (Karl Polanyi: 1944). Globalization mediates through cultural industries, such as departmental stores, malls, beauty parlours, mobiles, including Fast Food. In fact cultural dislocation through the cultural industries takes places either violently and passively.

It is true that globalization has created conditions for larger number of people to loose their livelihood. The crisis that the globalization created in different spheres made many social categories to become victims. One of the social category who became victim were farmers (Assadi: 2010a). As a result large number of farmers committed suicide. This crisis also compounded by the new forms of capitalist development that the globalization initiated in the sphere of agriculture- new technology employed in the sphere of agriculture such as new seed technology Bt. cotton, Bt. Rice including Golden Rice further aggravated the crisis. It is estimated that in India alone more than two lakh farmers have committed suicide between 1990s and 2000s, however this phenomenon is not limited to India alone, Suicide is reported in such countries as Australia, UK, even US. In India suicide, as a protest or as a reaction to globalization, initially began in Andhra Pradesh and, later on spread to such other states as Kerala, Karnataka, Maharashtra and Punjab. Interestingly suicide is not reported from BIMARU states such as Bihar, Madhya Pradesh, Rajasthan and Uttar Pradesh as these states have not integrated totally into the global market. The highest number of suicide is reported in the state of Maharashtra and Andhra Pradesh followed by Karnataka.

Globalization had two important effects on agriculture, Large amount of lands producing food grains were converted into commercial cropping areas, leading to the fall in per capita availability of food as well as calories available to each person.This is apparent in the arguments of Vandana Shiva, "during 1979-81 and 1992-1993, calorie intake declined by three percent in Mexico, 4.1 percent in Argentina, 10.9 percent in Kenya, 10.0 percent in Tanzania, 9.9 percent in Ethiopia. In India, the per capita cereal consumption declined by 12.2 for rural areas and 5.4 percent in urban areas" Further she argues that "As soon as trade was liberlised from 1991, within a few years eight millions hectares of food growing lands were converted to exportable crops leading to fall in per head food grains output" (Vandana Shiva: 2006). This has given rise to a new campaign to make food as one of the fundamental rights in India; the civil society initiative particularly PUCL earlier resulted in the implementation of Rural Employment Guarantee Scheme, however, the Right to Food campaign is yet receive attention of the State.

Secondly, the agriculture sector has come under increasing threat with the Patent regimes that the globalization has introduced, including the fact that it has introduced Intellectual Property Rights at the grass root level. The earlier debate on Basmati rice, Neem, Jamun etc points towards the fact that the farming sector has become vulnerable to global capital. Patent regimes have taken away the right to produce, sell, and exchange the seeds. At the same time bio-diversity has become the victim of appropriation by the global capital, it is argued that with the globalization MNCs have been appropriating bio-diversity in different parts of the world at an alarming rate. This has helped them to monopolise over initially on consumption or food later on every day life practices. It is now established fact that three to four MNCs are controlling nearly 80-85 per cent of global food production. Similarly same numbers of companies are controlling 90% of wheat production. This kind of monopoly has had two effects on different social categories: one, different social categories have become the victims of knowledge appropriation, secondly, they have been trapped in the large market sphere and in the process they have lost many of their traditional and historical rights- such as the right to keep the traditional seeds, right to preserve the seeds, right to disseminate traditional knowledge, right to exchange seeds or bio-diversity etc.

Globalization has introduced new form of dislocation in different parts of the world leading the loss of land, livelihood, as well as cultural practice.

This came through the mediation of new form of development paradigm that the globalization introducing. One of the best examples is Special Economic Zones. This practice came although initially from China, for the purpose of earning foreign exchange, however other countries also emulated in due course, India is not exception to it. Till date more than 500 Special Economic Zones have come into existence or have been approved in India, however they have become the symbols of "States within States" as well as the symbol of New Capitalism. Even they have become the symbol of human rights abuses-as these zones do not follow any labour laws, even they are allowed to have Private Security force. Meanwhile they have dislocated millions of people, including farmers, tribals, dalits from their land for the purpose of Special Economic Zones. The lands have been acquired using old, colonial act- the Land Acquisition Act of 1894 (amended recently). Even some of the states have amended the Land Reforms Acts to suit the global capital. Karnataka state is one such state. During 1997, it amended the land reforms act, wherein it allowed acquisition of any amount of agricultural land for the purpose of public good. All these have created situation of constant conflict between the State on the one hand, masses on the other. It is here the political apparatus faces a peculiar problem of defending or protecting the rights of the masses at a time when they have come under serious threat. The incident in Singur, Mangalore, Raigarh etc. have become the symbol of contestation.

Human Rights have received another twist with the privatisation of natural resources. In many parts of the world, natural resources such as water, minerals, etc. have been privatized. One of the major contested area is the privatization of river water, including drinking water. The privatisation of river water has gone against the natural rights of tribals, fishermen, villagers. This is obvious in the case of privatization of Sheonath River, even the privatization of ground water has opened up flood gates to the entry of global capital into the rural areas. The case of Plachimada, Shivagangai are some best examples. Interestingly privatization of mineral resources has created multiple situations: contestation over natural resources by the tribes, situation of conflict and situation of radical politics emerging or growing. The best example is the growth of naxalites in Chattisgarh, or in Kudremukh region in Karnataka. Even the growth of Chiapas in Latin America can not be glossed over. It is here right discourse becomes problematiques: how to define the rights. Who should decide the rights of the masses? Should the masses compromise with the political apparatus on the issues of rights?

### Challenging World: Beyond "Political"

One of the arguments quite often advanced is that human rights agenda can only be realized through the mediation of the State. However the problem that one confront while detailing human rights issues is characterising as well as defining the nature of the State-both democratic and non-democratic State. Given the fact that when States acts differently at different time vis-à-vis human rights issues, it becomes difficult to comprehend and decide about its nature. Indian State is a classic case- one side it has made human rights issues part of school curricula and has established Human Rights Commission, and the other Institutions such as Human Right Cells, Human Right Courts etc. That does not mean that different agencies of the State adhere to uphold human rights- this is where the mismatch becomes apparent. Secondly problem become acute when Democratic State failed to respect, uphold human rights both within and outside its purview. It is a paradox that Democratic States have become the forerunners in human rights violation The US for example claims to be the greatest Democratic country; however it has poor human rights record both at the domestic level as well elsewhere at the global level. The former argument is apparent in the following:

*In 2008, US residents experienced 4.9 million violent crimes, 16.3 million property crimes and 137,000 personal thefts, and the violent crime rate was 19.3 victimizations per 1,000 persons aged 12 or over, according to a report published by the US Department of Justice in September 2009). In 2008, over 14 million arrests occurred for all offences (except traffic violations) in the country, and the arrest rate for violent crime was 198.2 per 100,000 inhabitants... In 2009, a total of 35 domestic homicides occurred in Philadelphia, a 67 percent increase from 2008. In New York City, 461 murders were reported in 2009, and the crime rate was 1,151 cases per 100,000 people. San Antonio in Texas was deemed as the most dangerous among 25 US large cities with 2,538 crimes recorded per 100,000 people. The murder rate rose 5.5 percent in towns with a population of 10,000 or fewer/. Most of the United States' 15,000 annual murders occur in cities where they are concentrated in poorer neighbourhoods (China Daily: 2010).*

This is true of other countries too. Thirdly, there are other set of States which are either called "Failed States" or "Near Failed States" whose human rights records are dismal, depressing bleak and beyond redemption. There are nearly 19 countries which have been treated as "alerts" – Somalia, Chad, Iraq, Afghanistan, Pakistan, Haiti, and East Timor. They scantly respect the human rights including the fact that they are known for sustained human flights, internal displacement, massive movement of refugees, group paranoid, delegitimization of State etc. In many places the inter ethnic war within the state has, increased the violation of human rights particularly of women, children. – Children have been employed in war zone as soldiers of the army. Numbers of such cases are increasing every year- in Africa alone 120,000 child soldiers are employed. This is half the total soldiers of the globe. War has made 4-5 million children disabled, 12 million homeless more than 1 million orphaned or separated from their parents; 10 million psychologically traumatized.

It is true that no two States at the global level could able to address the issues of globalization uniformly and equally. Some of the States have integrated into the Global Market. Some of them on the other have agreed upon to introduce or implement the required changes desired by the global capital. Such trends in many places have led to dislocation, dispossession, and deprivation of local population from their land, culture, social set up etc. Incidentally globalization in many places has become hydra headed project of development, even has made States too meek and weak before global capital. States incidentally have been reduced to "Silent Spectator" in the midst of series of human rights violations perpetrated by the global capital. There are reasons why such trends have become a fact. .This is because of the fact that global capital is more powerful both in its reach as well as its ideology than the States in developing world. Even their total capital, some time surpasses total GDP of many countries. Take the case of such companies as Kentucky Fried Chicken, Coca Cola, Wall Mart Cargil, Monsanto etc. It is true that the total revenue earned by one company such as Wall Mart whose total revenue of $ 408.204-8 billion(2010)_ is equivalent to the GDP of more than forty African countries. Similar is the case of other companies such as Exxon Mobil ($ 301.4 billion in 2009) Shell ($278.188 billion in 2009) Coca Cola (US$ 24,0888.0 millions in ( 2006). Many of these companies are known for violating national laws, environmental laws in many countries. Even company such as Cargil or Monsanto are known for such violations- these companies are notoriously known for suing farmers for violating Patent Laws or Intellectual Property Rights.

Interestingly different States have not able to checkmate the entry or presence of global capital in their midst, given the fact that Global capital is too powerful to contain. Meanwhile while entering into different part of the world, the global capital as well as globalization creates some myths. One of the myths is that it is a panacea for every problem, including the poverty and backwardness of the developing as well as the underdeveloped world. In fact the increasing poverty is one of the major causes for the abuse of human rights throughout the world. (Vandana Shiva, 2001) Global poverty, by using conventional methods has grown over the decades. In fact UN is now contemplating to give new dimension to calculate poverty. The Report on the World Social Situation 2010 maintains that poverty can not be understood by income criterion alone, it is much more "multifaceted, multi-dimensional and volatile" and suggested that "other non-income dimensions, such as education, health and environmental deficits, and social exclusion" be considered in the poverty equation (UN :2010) Further it argued that

"The number of people living in extreme poverty [may have fallen from] 1.9 billion to 1.4 billion people between 1981 and 2005, however, if China is taken out of the calculation, this number actually increased from 1.1 billion people to 1.2 billion people." In addition it is observed that in several countries of sub Saharan Africa, Latin America, the Middle East and northern Africa and central Asia, the actual poverty level had increased during 1981 and 2005.

On the contrary in India the official calculation states that people living below the poverty level has come down from 36.1 per to 26.1 Over the decade, however the argument of poverty gets defeated when we refer to different committee reports. Tendulkar Committee for example recently came out with the argument that 37.7 per cent of people live below the poverty line, as on 2004-05, using cost of living index. It is in this context that argument of "panacea" gets defeated, and, also the fact that increasing poverty becomes an instrument of and for series of human rights abuses, wherein poor, women, marginalized, minorities become the victims.

Corollary to the previous argument, the increasing crisis in the realm of food or hunger, urban space, cleaner water, and environment also adds to the human rights abuses in different parts of the world. The recent food riots (Peter Krauth: 2010) in Bangladesh, Pakistan, Haiti, Mozambique, Egypt, and some parts of India particularly in West Bengal reflects the growing food crisis, although food riots have come down, they may resurface at any point of time. In fact, in 2008, itself UN's World Food Programme had warned of a "silent Tsunami" in the realm of hunger sweeping different parts of the world because of inflated or soaring prices, "it was a warning that the world's poor were being squeezed as increasingly higher portions of their family incomes were being spent on the food they required for their very survival." (Peter Krauth 2010). This also reflects the failure of the States to address the issues of hunger, poverty; it also reflects the failure of public distribution system in different parts of the world.

Further one can not overlook the increasing disparity between the rich on the one hand and the poor on the other. (Robert Weissman: 2003) The Globalization, in fact more than becoming "panacea" has accentuated the disparity as well as differences. It is estimated that in the year 2000 one per cent of the super rich controlled 40 per cent of the global asset. Similarly ten per cent of the global rich controlled 85 per cent total asset during the same period. It is a paradox that "400 highest income earners in the United States make as much money in a year as the entire population of 20 African nations-more than 300 million people" (Robert Welssman: 2003). "The richest 10 percent of the world's population's income is roughly 117 times higher than the poorest 10 percent". Such increasing gap deprives has larger effect on the politics: the series of conflicts would translate into Political riots.

However increasing number of masses into the bandwagon of poverty reflects that poor are the creation of global development (Gray C. Hufbaur: 2001) paradigm initiated from above than from below. New Paradigm of Development has deprived the poor many things: water, house or shelter, health including the nutritious food for survival. It is estimated that in 2006 alone more than 36 million died of hunger, mainly due to malnutrition. The UN Special Rapporteur on Right to Food, Jean Ziegler in his report argued that in the year 2006, mortality due to malnutrition accounted for 58% of the total mortality. In India alone there are 217 million population, as per the FAO estimate, living as: undernourished". Similar is the case of increase in the homeless-in 2005 it was estimated that 100 million people around the world were homeless people. At the same time nearly 884 million people are deprived of safe drinking water. Such global trend definitely goes against the basic human rights: increasing poverty deprive the poor the rights to decent life, right to cleaner water, including the fact that it deprives poor the right to have nutritious food.

It is difficult to construct an universal, clearcut theory on Human Rights in the midst of large number of population being excluded from the realm of development, including the fact that large number of people have become the victims of New Development Paradigm initiated by the globalization and global capitalism. This has led to large number of civil society groups, including the New Social Movements, contesting, disputing the claims of globalization and the subsequent arguments about, or of expanding the Human Rights. Such contestation will continue in the years to come. This is where we need to go beyond "political" to understand human rights discourse as well as agendas.

## References

Assadi, Muzaffar (2010): *Preface, Indian Journal of Human Rights and Social Justice,* Volume 4, No 1-2 January-December 2010.

Assadi, Muzaffar, (2010a): 'Path of Development and Politics in Karnataka', in R.S.Deshpande and Saroja Rao, (ed): *Agrarian Crisis and Farmer suicide, Sage ,* New Delhi 2010.

Chaina Daily, (2010): *US Human Rights Record in 2009,* November 28.

Ernabm, Eva(2005): *Human Rights and Democracy: Discourse Theory and Global Rights Institutions,* Stockholm University, Sweden.

Friedman, Thomas L (1999). *The Lexus and the Olive Tree,: Understanding Globalization,* Cairo: international Publishers.

Giddens Anthony (2000): "Globalization", BBC Reith Lectures,
(http://www.Ise.ac.uk/Giddens_99/week!.htm)

Hufbaur, Gray C (2001). Globalization Facts and consequences, Institute for International Economics, http://www.iie.com/papers/hufbaur1000.htm

http://www.un.org/en/development/desa/news/social/world-social-situation-2010.shtml

Krauth, Peter (2010) Food riots to return, Fertiliser War intensifies March 10 http://www.commodityonline.com/news/Food-riots-to-return-Fertiliser-War-intensifies-26322-3-1.html

Jimnz Atty Cecilia (1998) Contemporary Human Rights Discourse: A Continuing Challenge, *Philippines International Review Pilot issue,*

Polanyi, Karl (1944) the great transformation, *The Political and Economic Transformation of our Time,* Bostom, Beacon Pub.

Sklairm Leslie (2002) *Globalization-Capitalism and its Alternatives,* Oxford University press.

Shiva,,Vandana (2001) *Violence of Globalization,* the Hindu (New Delhi, India ) March25,

Shiva, Vandana, (2006), Seeds of Suicide: *The Ecological and Human Costs of Seed Monopoly and Globalization of Agriculture,* New Delhi Navadanya,

Weissman, Robert(2003) *Grotesque Inequality Corporate Globalization and the Global Gap Between Rich and Poor Multinational Monitor magazine,* July / August.

# 4

# DEBATING HUMAN RIGHTS; DISCOURSE AND DISCORD

**R. Sreekantan Nair**

## Introduction

The concept of human right has been evolving through centuries old debates and discourses carried out by Philosophers and Scholars all over the world. However it has been repeatedly seen that the regions where the debate was hectic and active, equally produced more healthy and active democratic advancements and developments. The advancement made by the western societies in terms of human rights culture and democratic vibrancy is a point worth arguing here. At the same time, more or less corresponding to the same argument, in other parts of the world as well, there existed different levels of discourse subject to the maturity of their own democratic system. However, the entire discourse took a definite shape and steady course only after the establishment of the UN and its relative interferences and involvements. That is the member states are bound to respect and oblige the UN and its positions and postures with regard to the propagation and protection of human rights culture. This makes the provisions of Universal Declarations of Human rights [1948] and the two significant Covenants very decisive ones. That is no civilized state can, [legally and morally] supersede the said provisions on reasons, whatever may be, for its violations.

Over the past five decades, the concept of human rights has received much attention from the international community of states, social and political movements and non-governmental organisations, among others. It has been the subject of debate and controversy, and has seen positive development as well. The present status of the concept of human rights can be seen mainly through international law, which contains a vast array of customs and legal standards found in declarations and treaties directly or indirectly relating to human rights. All have direct bearing on national jurisdictions which should implement human rights. Most important, they have direct implications on the lives of human beings everywhere, especially in providing a basis for people to take charge of their lives.

Indeed, human rights are now part of political discourse, be it at the national or international level. This includes their recognition as "relevant" in the formulation of foreign policy as well as economic programs. Significantly, the concept of human rights has increasingly been integrated into the agenda of different social, political and economic movements of various peoples around the world. Moreover, with the end of the Cold War, such movements increasingly refer to human rights in their respective struggles.

Ever since the establishment of the state as the primary authority in the rule of the people, the concept of human rights has evolved as the basic claim of the ordinary citizen against his/her state against mistreatment and misrule. Today, this has also developed as the obligation of the state to protect its citizens, including the vulnerable and the marginalized. Moreover, states have come to be obliged not only not to oppress their people, but to ensure that their people are not oppressed by other groups as well.

The basic enunciation of these rights is seen in the UDHR provisions and its two main covenants: the International Covenant on Economic, Social and Cultural Rights (ICESCR) and the International Covenant on Civil and Political Rights (ICCPR). These three documents compose the International Bill of Human Rights. At present there are also a number of other treaties and covenants which expand on rights found in these basic documents. Examples are the Conventions on the Rights of the Child, on the Elimination of All Forms of Discrimination against Women, against Torture and Cruel and Inhuman Treatment, among others.

Other declarations and conventions still being drafted address specific human rights issues such as the rights of indigenous peoples and disappearances. Regional treaties on human rights also exist in different parts of the world, except the Asia-Pacific region. All these international agreements contain structures and systems which allow the international community to monitor states' compliance on human rights obligations towards their people and others found in their territories. The effectivity of these systems is still very much in debate, but provides the only permanent system by which the international community can scrutinize a state's behavior with regard to its own people.

Furthermore, a vast array of 'soft law' exists in the forms of UN General Assembly resolutions, 'codes of conduct', guidelines, etc. — all of which pertain to the regulation of state behavior and which later may lead to 'hard law'. At all these levels and stages, there are various degrees of involvement by different actors—states, personalities, social and political movements, economic blocs, non-governmental organisations—in the formulation of these many forms of human rights standards, and to their acceptance or recognition by the international community. Last but not least, international custom has developed many human rights norms (e.g. genocide as crime against humanity) which have come to be accepted by the international community.

**Human Dignity and Rights**

Human dignity is increasingly recognized as the basis for human rights protection. The recognition of human dignity has led to the recognition that human dignity pertains to all human beings, regardless of race, sex, political opinions, religious orientation, etc. This is essentially the core of the principle of the universality of human rights. The universality of human rights simply means that all human beings, by virtue of their being human, have the same rights everywhere, all the time. A human being from one part of the world does not have any less right than another from a different part of the world.

Indeed, the universality of human rights is a fundamental principle that has been theoretically accepted by the international community (as recently as the 1993 Vienna Declaration and Plan of Action). Nevertheless, it is still consistently challenged. The primary conceptual challenge comes from a number of Asian and African states, which have put forward the concept of 'cultural relativism' as justifying the different treatment of their respective citizens. The concept of 'cultural relativism', as promoted by these states, is based on the existence of different religions, traditions and philosophies which have distinct world outlooks on the place of the person within his/her society and in relation to authority, civil or otherwise. In recent months, the 'universality' of the UDHR itself has been challenged by an Asian state as being non-reflective of the cultural specificities of different traditions. In both cases, 'cultural relativism' is used as a justification or facade for human rights violations. This kind of 'cultural relativism' has been rejected by many social movements, human rights NGOs and academicians active in the human rights field. These actors put forward an alternative concept of 'cultural relativism' as a means for enriching human rights discourse. In other words, different religions, traditions and philosophies around the world should be the source of never-ending enhancement of human dignity and development of human rights worldwide. At present, numerous rights NGOs, institutes and academic centers are doing research in this area. Moreover, the challenge to re-draft the UDHR is widely seen as a retrogression on the promotion of human dignity and human rights worldwide.

Another concept often used as a foil to the universality of human rights, is that of 'non-interference in internal affairs', cited by many states opposed to international monitoring of its performance on human rights. This concept is based on the idea that state sovereignty preserves to the state power over its citizens, to the exclusion of other forces. In recent years, however, major exceptions have been recognized, including the proposition that the state cannot claim sovereignty for the oppression of its people. Thus, gross violations of human rights have increasingly been seen as warranting scrutiny, criticism and even joint action by the international community.

Despite the political and economic vested interests of international powers, the view that state sovereignty and its attendant claim of non-interference cannot be cited to block international criticism of a state's commission of human rights violations, has gained adherence even among progressive social and political peoples movements. One counter-proposition put forward is that 'sovereignty' should be regarded as 'state responsibility' for the general welfare and guarantee of human rights of its peoples. But for this concept to be realised in actuality and not used as just another smokescreen for the commission of human rights violations, international monitoring and the cooperation of the international community of states and other actors is essential.

Notwithstanding the above debate, differences in the needs and situations of specific groups of people have also been recognised as entitling special consideration in the protection and promotion of rights. These groups of peoples are those regarded as vulnerable and/or marginalized, thus needing special protection by the state and by groups of people, and whose rights require special action against further discrimination or oppression. Thus, some human rights instruments deal with special groups such as children (Convention on the Rights of Children) and prisoners (guidelines on the treatment of prisoners).

All in all, human rights can be seen as having a moral basis (human dignity) that has developed into legal claims on the part of the human being, and into obligations on the part of states. Such a process is still continuing amidst attempts to prevent the advancement of human rights by various actors for different reasons. Mostly, the evolution of different standards and struggles for their implementation especially at the local and international levels involve dynamics between the state and individuals or groups of individuals. These dynamics are usually negative, involving contradictions between a political or economic authority, exemplified by human rights violations by government agents, and legitimate dissent by its population. But there have been instances where such dynamics have been positive, exemplified by cooperation between a state and its citizens in promoting human rights.

With human dignity as the basis for their existence, human rights exist prior to the state's legal recognition of its obligations. The international community and the people can therefore morally hold the state accountable for its human rights performance. With a state's acceptance of its human rights obligations under international law (primarily through ratification of treaties) and under national law (through domestic legislation), the state can be held legally accountable. The same thing was debated and discussed by many at various point of time and in each time most of the philosophers had come up with new theory to substantiate their arguments. The debate over dignity and rights originated from the theoretical questions.

**Theoretical Positions**

The earliest direct trace to human rights might be found in the notions of 'natural right' developed by classical Greek philosophers, such as Aristotle, but this concept was more fully developed in modern times by Thomas Aquinas. It was Thomas Aquinas, the early Christian philosopher, who initiated the discussion on modern school of natural law. He had maintained the position that it was that part of perfect law which could be divined though the application of human reason. That is, for several centuries Aquinas' conception held sway: there were goods or behaviours that were naturally right (or wrong) because God ordained it so. What was naturally right could be ascertained by humans by 'right reason' – right thinking.

The natural law philosophy stipulated that each individual's issues in life were determined by God and all are subject to the authority of God. Such a position deliberately placed individual away from the authority of state and Monarchy. Thus the natural law theory placed the individual with in the frame of natural rights. Otherwise, the theory argued that each individual was autonomous with in the personal domains. Natural law was thus closely tied with god and theistic in its nature and content. But this theory was opposed from many other rational stand points. The first of its kind came from Grotius, who headed the positivist law tradition.

This limitation was however a major block to the rational development of natural law. The Dutch Jurist, Hugo Grotius undertook the mission of separating the natural law from its theistic connections and tried to make it a part of secular rational thought. Grotius took the position that it was possible to rationalize the existence of natural law. Hugo Grotius further expanded on this notion where he propounded the immutability of what is naturally right and wrong. According to him natural law was the basis of all positive law or written law. Equally he argued that all rules were ascertainable by the application of 'right reason' and did not depend on any superior force [God] for its validity. Such a rational position to law was appealing to the subsequent scholars. Thus the application of 'right reason' was crucial enough to liberate the individual from the fetters of god.

The Grotian position on natural law was prevalent during the 17th century and it got transferred in to natural rights. Individual rights was thus deriving straight from the natural right theory which subsequently conditioned the debate over the questions of rights during the 17th and 18th centuries.

Rational thinking did marvel in the overall course of development of the world. Its end result was Reformation which could shake the ecclesiastical authority and it did argue for new bases of natural right. Thomas Hobbes (1588-1679) posed the first major assault in 1651 on the divine basis of natural right by describing a State of Nature in which God did not share any role. Thomas Hobbes argued for rights, but only in very restricted terms. To him, Rights were limited to the material right to life of the individual (possibly the individuals own right to peace and physical security). Hobbes, by the way was also committed to the idea of absolutizing and centralizing the state's power.

Significantly, Hobbes also made a crucial leap from `natural right' to`a natural right'. In other words, there was no longer just a list of behavior that was naturally right or wrong. In this context, his argument was that there could be some claim or entitlement which was derived from nature. In Hobbes' view, this natural right was one of self-preservation. Though Hobbes is considered to be one of early modern thinkers to attribute to the very notion of rights, his negative identification of rights, as it lacks co-relative rights of others do not place him in the humanist tradition, which places rights in the rights-discourse family of the liberal thought.[1]

With the preservation of all their fellow human beings, subsequently it was John Locke (1632-1704) another English philosopher who expanded the concept of rights. He took up the doctrine of natural rights and made it part of individual liberty and freedom. Lock believed in God-given rights based on human dedication and effort. He encouraged landless farmers to claim the earth that they had cared for and tilled, as they had contributed much from their own bodies into it. He called such a right a "natural right"... Not only did he argue for individual private property, but he also argued that "Man is a being to be preserved as much as possible and is widely acknowledged to have argued that people ought to be concerned.

Locke argued that individual was bestowed with three basic rights –right to life, liberty and property. These rights are inherent with individual as the gift of nature and so those rights could not be taken away by the state, under any circumstances or compulsions. Explaining the state of nature ,he further clarified that due to the inconveniences crept in to the life of individual in the particular stage, man entered in to an agreement called social contract whereby this inalienable rights were transferred to the sovereign, the ruler. This transfer itself was a conditional one that in case the ruler violates the natural rights of the individual, they [the individuals] were free to replace the ruler with a better ruler who respects the natural rights.

The social contract theory of Locke was an explanation to the Glorious revolution of 1688. Otherwise, Locke was legitimizing the replacement of King James 11 for his blatant violations of his subjects. Unlike the earlier thinkers, when it comes in the context of Locke, his theory had a direct bearing on empowering the individual. The Lockian theory reiterated that the individual was an autonomous being capable of exercising choice and that more importantly he indirectly emphasized that the legitimacy of a state depends not only on the will of the people, but also upon the government's willingness and capability to protect the natural rights of the individuals[2].

The Lockian proposition had a profound impact on the subsequent theoretical formulations of a good number of thinkers, who constructed the very same proposition from different stand points. The theory had a direct bearing and role in setting the meaning and implications of American war of independence and French Revolution.

Subsequently, it was Edmund Burke who wrote a stinging attack on the French Declaration's assertion of natural rights, in which he argued that rights were those benefits won within each society. The rights held by the English and French were different, since they were the product of different political struggles through history. In this context Burke was attempting to differentiate the cultural and historical contexts of rights and maintain the position that right is evolved with in the particular society.It is rightly pointed out that Burkes intention was to picturise the modern governments as a convenience that would restrain the members of a society, satisfy their wants and ensure the upholding of a natural hierarchical social order in which the notion of natural rights was moraly and politically false[3]. In this way, Burke was questioning the very Lockian tradition and highlighted the view that natural rights could not be translated in to civil and political rights.

Soon after the attacks on the French Declaration, Thomas Paine wrote a defense of the conception of natural rights and their connection to the rights of a particular society. In The Rights of Man, Paine made a distinction between natural rights and civil rights, but he continued to see a necessary connection between the two concepts. In his own words;

*Natural rights are those which appertain to man in right of his existence. Of this kind are all the intellectual rights, or rights of the mind, and also all those rights of acting as an individual for his own comfort and happiness, which are not injurious to the natural rights of others. Civil rights are those which appertain to man in right of being a member of society. Every civil right has for its foundation, some natural right pre-existing in the individual, but to the enjoyment of which his individual power is not, in all cases, sufficiently competent. Of this kind are all those which relate to security and protection*[5].

In his view, Natural rights are those which appertain to man in right of his existence. Of this kind are all the intellectual rights, or rights of the mind, and also all those rights of acting as an individual for his own comfort and happiness, which are not injurious to the natural rights of others. Civil rights are those which appertain to man in right of being a member of society. Every civil right has for its foundation, some natural right pre-existing in the individual, but to the enjoyment of which his individual power is not, in all cases, sufficiently competent. [Thomas Paine, The Rights of Man, p. 68.]

Thus postulating more from the Theories of Locke and rejecting the rationale of Burke , Paine tried to emphasise the version of welfare -rights .This is very much evident from his minimalist view of Government where he stood for the re distribution of wealth to those who had lost the fruits of their labor .In fact he was rightly assessed that his contribution to natural-rights tradition was not as an innovator but as a populiser who made the tradition accessible. [Freeden, Michael, p. 18].

Not only that the theories of J.J. Rousseau, and Immanuel Kant emphasize the moral and legal imperatives of Lockean position, Infact these thinkers took their theoretical propositions from the traditions of natural law and natural rights.

J.J. Rousseau substantiated the position that natural law conferred inalienable sovereignty on the citizens. This implied that whatever rights were derived from natural law were rested with the people which could be identified as General will. The central concept in Rousseau's thought rest with "liberty," and most of his works deal with the mechanisms through which human beings are forced to give up their liberty. At the foundation of his thought on government and authority is the idea of the "social contract," in which government and authority are in a mutual contract. Such a contract implies that the governed agree to be ruled only so that their rights, property and happiness be protected by their rulers. Once state fails to protect the interests of the ruled, the social contract is broken and the ruled are free to choose their own alternative governments. Really, it was a moral booster to the individual and his concept of rights which Rousseau had articulated well in his theory of social contract.

Rousseau's first argument was that civilization had corrupted human beings[6]. For Rousseau, the natural moral state of human beings is to be compassionate; civilization has made us cruel, selfish, and bloodthirsty. In the Discourse on Inequality, Rousseau also argued that civilization has robbed us of our natural freedom. While semi-civilized humanity looked to itself for its values and happiness, civilized human beings live outside themselves in the opinions and authority of others. The price of civilization, in his view, is thus human freedom and human individuality. In reality, the difference is, that the savage lives within himself while social man lives outside himself and can only live in the opinion of others, so that he seems to receive the feeling of his own existence only from the judgment of others concerning him.

In the *Discourse on Inequality*, Rousseau had tried to explain the human invention of government as a kind of contract between the governed and the authorities that governed them. The only reason human beings were willing to give up individual freedom and be ruled by others was that they saw that their rights, happiness, and property would be better protected under a formal government rather than an anarchic, every-person-for-themselves type of society. He argued, though, that this original contract was deeply flawed. The wealthiest and most powerful members of society "tricked" the general population, and so installed inequality as a permanent feature of human society. Rousseau argued, in The Social Contract, that this contract between rulers and the ruled should be rethought. Rather than have a government which largely protects the wealth and the rights of the powerful few, government should be fundamentally based on the rights and equality of everyone. These ideas were essential for both the French and American revolutions.

In fact, Rousseau was trying to figure out a way to maximize individual liberty while preserving order, obedience, and harmony in society. In this sense, he was really the first Enlightenment thinker to articulate the contractual basis of rights. Rights, or principles of individual autonomy or liberty, are not magical entitlements that come from heaven into this world the moment you pop out of the womb nor are they inscribed in our DNA. Rights and liberties are social contracts. You have rights and individual liberties 'because the rest of society agrees that you have those rights and liberties. 'If you don't have a right or liberty, then you must convince everyone to give you that right or liberty. For Rousseau, natural human beings are born completely self-sufficient and self-governing; social human beings are dependent and restricted. Thus he rationally proves that rights and liberties that social human beings get are derived from a general social agreement.

Further reinforcement of natural rights came with Immanuel Kant's writings latter in the 17th century that reacted to Hobbes' work. In his view, the congregation of humans into a state-structured society resulted from a rational need for protection from each other's violence that would be found in a state of nature. However, the fundamental requirements of morality required that each treat another according to universal principles. Kant's political doctrine was derived from his moral philosophy, and as such he argued that a state had to be organized through the imposition of, and obedience to, laws that applied universally; nevertheless, these laws should respect the equality, freedom, and autonomy of the citizens. In this way Kant, prescribed that basic rights were necessary for civil society.

In the general flow of discourse he triggered a new concept – categorical imperative. This is an absolute moral good which is identifiable in the exercise of virtuous will by all rational individuals. The concept implies that individuals are obliged to develop their rational capacities and employ them for the promotion of the happiness of others.

According to Kant, the categorical imperatives operates on three levels. First of all it specifies universal act of duty on all individuals. Secondly, it provides systematic rules for determining these duties. Thirdly, it specifies the relation between freedoms and duties. In view of Kant, in a society of rational, self determining individuals rights would emerge as a consequence of the application of categorical imperative.[7]

Most of the themes expressed by Kant remain highly prominent in contemporary philosophical justifications of human rights. Foremost among them are the concept of equality and the moral autonomy of rational human beings. Kant bestows upon contemporary human rights' theory the ideal of a potentially universal community of rational individuals autonomously determining the moral principles for securing the conditions for equality and autonomy. Kant provides a means for justifying human rights as the basis for self-determination grounded within the authority of human reason. Kant's moral philosophy is based upon an appeal to the formal principles of ethics. For Kant, the determination of any such goods can only proceed from a correct determination of the formal properties of human reason and thus do not provide the ultimate means for determining the correct ends, or object, of human reason. Kant's moral philosophy begins with an attempt to correctly identify those principles of reasoning that can be applied equally to all rational persons, irrespective of their own specific desires or partial interests.

Thus Kant attaches a condition of universality to the correct identification of moral principles. He argues that the basis of moral reasoning must rest upon a condition that all rational individuals are bound to assent to. Doing the right thing is thus not determined by acting in pursuit of one's own interests or desires, but acting in accordance with a maxim which all rational individuals are bound to accept. This is what he terms as the categorical imperative .Kant argues that this basic condition of universality in determining the moral principles for governing human relations is a necessary expression of the moral autonomy and fundamental equality of all rational individuals. The categorical imperative is self-imposed by morally autonomous and formally equal rational persons. It provides the basis for determining the scope and form of those laws which morally autonomous and equally rational individuals will institute in order to secure these very same conditions. For Kant, the capacity for the exercise of reason is the distinguishing characteristic of humanity and the basis for justifying human dignity. As the distinguishing characteristic of humanity, formulating the principles of the exercise of reason must necessarily satisfy a test of universality; they must be capable of being universally recognized by all equally rational agents. Hence, Kant justifies the formulation of the categorical imperative.

Thus by the intervention of the positivists law has become an autonomous field of scientific enquiry. Such an autonomous identity of the topic was further developed by John Austin who said that law becomes valid only when it comes from the commands of the sovereign. At the same time the positivist interpretation of law was subject to criticism. The main contention was that it places no moral constraints on the rules adopted by states and individuals are constraint to enjoy those rights which are granted upon them.

The dichotomy between natural law theory and positivist arguments continued further. The positivist school tried to maintain the position that the existence and contents of rights could be derived only from the laws of the state. This new focus did reflect the scientific tempo of empiricism which subsequently did help the process of enlightenment in Europe.

David Hume raised the dichotomy between the two positions and argued that inquiry in to social phenomena could be divided in to two distinct categories, first, the category of facts which could be proved to exist empirically and which could be demonstrated to be true or false. This was the 'is' Second, there was the category of morality which could not be proved to exist objectively and about which people might have legitimate differences of opinion. This was the 'ought'. According to Hume it was only the 'is'-those matters which were empirically provable –that formed the basis of valid scientific enquiry. This had the consequences of severing the discussion of morality from the analysis of legal systems. Once this had been done, natural law appeared to be simply an argument about which moral position was better than another. Furthermore, while natural law failed to demonstrate how a systematic legal system could be constructed from its precepts, positive law took as its starting point the existence of formal legal systems. The position of Hume was well articulated by Bentham who represented the Utilitarian school of thought.

The Utilitarian school took the position that human existence was dominated by pleasure and pain. The position of humanity could be improved, Jermy Bentham argued, by increasing the amount of pleasure and decreasing the level of pain. This otherwise demanded the theory of 'greatest happiness to the greatest number'. The aim of utility is thus maximizing happiness to maximum number of people. In his critique on natural law he said; 'Right, the substantive right, is the child of law: from real laws come real rights; but from laws of nature, fancied and invented by poets, rhetoriticians, and dealers in moral and intellectual poisons come imaginary rights, a bastard brood of monsters, `gorgons and chimeras dire'[8]

Just like Hume, Bentham also, thus tried to separate law from the natural law tradition to an autonomous domain of scientific spirit and tempo.

Now taking away the discussion from the question of morality and legality, even with in the ruled there is a big question of majority and minority divide. If the question of Jermy Bentham's theory of Utilitarianism is accepted, what about the rights of minorities? This prime concern looks at Utilitarianism with a reservation. The arguments are the Utilitarian theorists did not consider the rights of the Minorities or their concerns. The question is what about their rights and positions in a majoritarian rule? This pertinent question is leveled by two critics of utilitarian theory-Dworkin and Nozick.

Nozick argues that the minimal state is constituted by a group of men and women, the basis of which is certain moral precepts. His contention is that depriving the rights of men state can not have more authority more than that of a night watch man. Certain basic moral rights like right not to be killed, assaulted, robbed, or defrauded and right to acquire, retain and dispose of property etc. are also prevailed in the minimal state. Any wrong action violates the corresponding rights of the individuals. There fore the role of minimal state is limited to that of a watchman; that is punishing those who violates the moral limits of the state. More over, if the state moves beyond these limits by any other welfare mechanisms that would tantamount to the encroachment upon the rights of the individual.[9]

Dworkin also comes forward with his concept of minimalist state. To him state is a necessity. But it should not encroach upon the individuals. His intention was to provide a theory which would maximize the liberty of all the individuals. This proposition he makes by accepting the minimal role of the state, that is by rejecting the arguments of anarchists that maximum liberty is possible only in a context of a situation without state. Along with the arguments of these anti utilitarian's, Rawls argues that justice is a way of distributing the rights, duties, benefits and burdens among individuals with in society. He contents that every person is inviolable and that even the welfare of society can not displace this inviolability. In his words;"... in a just society liberties of equal citizenship are settled; the rights secured by justice are not subject to political bargaining or to the calculus of social interest"[10]

Rawls starts his analysis from the same pattern of social contract theory, where all persons are bestowed with equality. At the same time each one is endowed with about his or her own qualities or attributes. Veil of ignorance. According to him, the Rational individual who is ignorant of their own potential will choose two principles of justice. The first principle is that every one has an equal right compatible with the same system for others. The second principle is that social and economic inequalities are to be organized so that they are to the greatest benefit to the least advantaged and so that they provide a system of equal access to all and equality of opportunity[11]. In short, according to Rawls, theory of distributive justice, all social primary goods such as liberty and opportunity, income and wealth are to be distributed equally, unless an unequal distribution in effect become effective to the disadvantaged sections of the society. Thus Rawls concludes that liberty is the pre-eminent right and that all other rights are subsidiary to it[12].

Following the economic reforms in USA by President Roosevelt called the New Deal, a number of Jurists started considering the new methods of attempting to explain the functions of law with in a complex industrial society. For most among them was Karl Llewellyn and Roscoe Pond whose main aim was to identify law and its functional mechanisms. Since they are committed more to empirical particularities, they did not offer any specific theory of rights. Rather, they believed that rights are the end products. In this regard, Pound devised a prescription for the validation of human wants, human demands and social interest through the process of social engineering[13]. Within the sociological tradition, these authors tried to identify law and their task was to 'discover what law does rather than what law is'. Karl Llewellyn, infact ascertained that the law is little more than putty in the hands of a judge who is able to shape the outcome of a case based on personal biases. Both believd that the response of the judges on a particular case could bring more profound impact on the society than the law itself.

Like other legal realists, Mc Dougal and Lasswell argue that demand for the satisfaction of human rights derive from broad based international sharing of values. These values are manifested by demands relating to such social goods as respect, power, enlightenment, well- being health, skill, affection and rectitude. All these values contribute towards the super value of human dignity. The concept of super value of human dignity may not suit to all the industrial societies, but it tend to represent an idea upon which a large core of consensus could be secured. Such identification of common goals provides evidence of a minimum shared values within the larger world community. This is what all the major human rights instruments reflect and insist for.

Any basic discussion on rights without referring to the Marxian school of thought would be meaningless. Marx approached rights more from a scientific basis, rather than making any speculative assumptions and presumptions. He totally rejects the idea of law of nature postulated by the earlier thinkers on the ground that all those theories were idealistic and unhistoric. According to him, rights were bourgeois concepts and a product of bourgeois-capitalist society, desined to maintain and re-enforce the pre-eminent position of the ruling class. His only positive argument on right is that in the early stages of communist state, rights have an important role to play in the transformation of society.

Marx denounced rights as a fabrication of bourgeois society. This rejection comes from ground that the individual was divorced from his or her society. According to him rights were needed in capitalist states in order to provide protection from the state. In the Marxist view of society, an individual is essentially a product of society and, ideally, should not be seen in an antagonistic relationship where rights are needed[14]. The Marxian argument is that individuals significance in the society is due to his / her role as a social being. Individuals use respective abilities to satisfy the ones own needs. But owing to the capitalist hold of means of production, the individuals are gradually alienated, whereby they fail to satisfy their needs.

According to Marx the true potentials of human beings can be realized only if they are enabled to return to their true nature as social beings. Such a situation is possible in a communist society. This requires a historical transformation and in the final stages of the process the state will whither away. Before the withering away of state the communist party will act as the vanguard of the revolution, where by it takes care of the state and its institutions for the smooth conduct of the transformation. In such a context there emerges the Marxist concept of rights. Marx does advocate individual right at this stage of transformation. But permits only legal rights which is supposed to guarantee the transformation from the communist state to a communist society. Thus these rights can only be social and economic since they are directed towards the reduction of the means of production to common control.

The Marxian logic is that once the transformation takes place, and a communist society is established, the need for rights disappear. In such a context each individual will develop free relationship with the other. Hence

Marxian argument says that rights are tools to achieve a particular end. Once the end [transformation] has been achieved, the tools are no longer nodded and be disposed of. There fore Marx claims that rights have no eternal value.

Apart from these theoretical differences there are attempts to catogorise rights in to different streams of thought. This is based on different approaches.

**Varying Approaches**

A popular approach to human rights is the so-called 'three- generations' approach, which describes the incremental recognition of different kinds of human rights as contained in the two main human rights conventions. The first generation pertains to civil and political rights; the second to economic, social and cultural rights; and the third to so-called 'peoples' or group rights, including environmental rights and rights of indigenous peoples.

This approach to human rights, although popular, underlines the traditional division between civil and political rights on the one hand, and economic, social and cultural rights on the other. In the same vein, it emphasises the difference between individual rights and group or peoples' rights. This is understandable, since the generational approach to human rights has evolved with the historical development of international human rights discourse over the decades, mainly in Western circles. Here, development in the substance and content of specific human rights concentrated mainly on individual, civil and political rights, notwithstanding the emphasis given by the erstwhile 'Eastern bloc' to economic and cultural rights.

The usefulness of the generational approach can be seen in describing the historical development of the recognition as well as the elaboration of the contents of the said categories of human rights. Its validity lies more in recognizing that there may be differences among human rights: civil and political rights on one hand and economic, social and cultural rights on the other; as well as individual rights as compared to group rights, at least for theoretical purposes and specialization. However, it docs not contribute much for analytical purposes, nor to the development of international human rights discourse. In fact, the generational approach to human rights unduly emphasizes differences among the categories of human rights, rather than promotes their indivisibility and interdependence.

Indeed, the indivisibility and interdependence of human rights is a concept that is slow of recognition and acceptance. It pertains to the basic idea that a person is a whole being who cannot be 'divided'; the elements of his/her existence cannot be separated from one another if that person is to live a 'full life.' Thus, a person is not a mere biological being, nor a purely political animal, nor a simple social person, etc. All the elements that make a person's life worth living (personal, intellectual, religious, political, economic, social, etc.) can only be appreciated in a holistic manner. Thus, the human rights that flow from his/her being an indivisible person are also indivisible. The interdependence of human rights is emphasized further by the proposition that the promotion or fulfillment of one right is dependent on another.

In both cases, the indivisibility and interdependence of human rights are two intertwining ideas that feed on each other, meaning one set of rights cannot be given importance while another is not respected or is violated. If a human person is indivisible and the various elements of his/her life are inseparable, it is ideal that all his/her rights are respected and promoted all the time.

Another approach to human rights, the 'hierarchy of rights' approach, posits a hierarchy of rights among the different categories: civil and political rights versus economic, social and cultural rights; as well as individual versus group rights. Among the many variations of this approach is the superiority of one set of rights over another based on importance. Many Asian states hold that economic rights are more important than civil and political rights, and that the rights of society are more important than individual rights. These arguments have been consistently rejected by the international human rights NGO community, based on the twin concepts of indivisibility and interdependence. Another variation is the primacy of rights that are 'justiciable', mainly civil and political rights, because of the alleged differing nature among the categories of human rights. Again, the international NGO community has stated that this is a fallacy. The justifiability of rights as known presently is entirely dependent on the discourse on human rights and its further development, not on the differing nature of human rights.

Last but not the least is the distinction between 'fundamental' human rights and other human rights. Fundamental rights are also called basic rights, elementary rights or supra-positive, i.e. rights whose validity is so fundamental to the international community that they exist regardless of their acceptance by the state (e.g. rights against racism and slavery), and thus consist of minimum standards. Such a distinction, which necessarily implies a hierarchy of rights, goes against modern thinking of human rights as a 'single package' and indivisible. In addition, there have been no consistent agreements on clear criteria for deciding what are fundamental rights, the positions of the various actors depending on their respective vested interests. Neither do attempts to distinguish fundamental rights from other rights contribute to the more pressing problem of implementation.

Indeed, a recent approach that has been developed by an international NGO is what one can call the 'obligations' approach. This approach emphasises that the differences between various human rights are differences in application and degree in specification. At the same time, it places the full onus of the practicability of implementation of human rights on the state. It thus demystifies human rights theorising by placing discourse on the level of how human rights can be actualised and when they are violated.

The 'obligations' approach to human rights flows from the generic obligation of the state to fully realise a human right, which necessarily implies that the state is obliged not to violate that human right. Further, the generic obligation contains three categorical obligations:

1. The obligation to respect obliges the state not to deprive a human being of a right s/he is exercising. Thus, a person's right to life is respected by the state by not executing him/her; his/her right to housing is respected by the state by not demolishing his/her community.
2. The obligation to protect obliges the state to prevent third parties from depriving a person from a right being exercised. Thus, the state should guarantee that a person's right to freedom of assembly is not curtailed by another group wanting to disperse it; the state should assure that the right of indigenous persons to their ancestral land is not disturbed by multinational companies.
3. The obligation to fulfill obliges a state to ensure the realisation of a right where it is not attained. Thus, the state should ensure that prison conditions are humane by, for example, building adequate facilities; the state should ensure the provision of free education at least in primary school.

The 'obligations' approach reveals the existence of a spectrum of rights, the implementation of which does not depend on the category a certain right ostensibly belongs to; neither does it depend on any claim of differences between rights according to nature, political orientation or importance. This approach therefore can be useful in pinpointing where a human rights violation is being committed and how a state can implement a certain right. School.

A challenge in the development of human rights discourse has grown complex as well as wide enough to allow many different groups and sectors, aside from the traditional community of states, to contribute to the development and implementation of human rights norms. This should be undertaken in a way that is relevant to the world's present conditions, including the emergence of new actors (i.e. multinational companies) that have a direct bearing on human rights implementation. Moreover, the development of technology has advanced in a way that there is a present challenge on how to maximize information technology to influence the shaping of human rights Policy School.

The most important challenge is how to best realise direct and genuine participation of the basic masses and otherwise marginalised groups and sectors in the development of human rights discourse. It is important to continue to exert efforts that effectively and consistently provide access to these groups, not only to make their voices heard but also to directly influence and shape the discourse. Human rights violations are, after all, committed at the level of local communities and usually on individuals fighting for their rights and on marginalized peoples. The victims of human rights violations, especially, should have significant and strong input. Finally, an important consideration in this basic challenge is the continuing efforts to empower peoples to struggle for their rights in a way that contributes to liberation from oppression and to the building of genuine peoples' democracies.

Thus, the continuing development of human rights discourse should be encouraged with the primary objective of recognizing and realizing, through human rights, the inherent dignity of each and every human being. Unless and until there takes place a debate /discourse the contradictions with in and out side could not be sorted out. As such, discourse and discord on human rights is very much positive in any society at any point of time. This implies that if we do not open the discourse on rights we are not entitled to enjoy its fruits fully. The debate and discourse taken place over the last decade on GLBTS and their victory is a strong point of indication.

## Notes and References

Scott Davidson, Human Rights, [Buckingham: Open University Press; 1993] P. 26.

1. Michael Freeden, Rights, [Delhi: World view Publications; 1998], p. 12
2. Scott Davidson, no.1, p.28
3. Michael Freeden, n.2, p17.
5. Thomas Paine, *The Rights of Man*, [New York: Penguin Books, 1985,] p. 68.
6. See Rousseau, Discourse on the Moral Effects of the Arts and Sciences in 1750.
7. Scott Davidson, no.1, p.30.
8. Jeremy Bentham, "Anarchical Fallacies; being an examination of the Declaration of Rights issues during the French Revolution", in Jeremy Waldron (ed.), *Nonsense Upon Stilts: Bentham, Burke and Marx on the Rights of Man*, New York: Methuen, 1987, p. 69].
9. Scott Davidson, no.1, p. 32.
10. [J. Rawls, A Theory of Justice [Oxford: Clarandon press, 1971], p. 28.
11. Scott Davidson, no.1, p.35.
12. For a comparative analysis of liberty and justice see; Amartya Sen, in equality Reexamined, [New Delhi; O.U.P; 2008], pp. 73-87.
13. Anuradha Kumar, Human Rights Global perspectives, [Delhi:Sarup and Sons; 2002], p. 22.
14. See Karl Marx, "On the Jewish Question", Jeremy Waldron (ed.), Nonsense upon Stilts in Theories of Rights, (Oxford; Oxford University Press, 1984).

- Dworkin, Ronald. *Taking Rights Seriously*, (London: Duckworth, 1978).

- Finnis, John. *Natural Law and Natural Rights*, (Oxford; Clarendon Press, 1980)
- Freeman, Michael. *Human Rights: An Interdisciplinary Approach*, (Cambridge: Polity, 2002).
- Jean-Jacques Rousseau, The Social Contract, Maurice Cranston (trans.), Baltimore: Penguin, 1968.
- Jones, Peter. *Rights*, (Basingstoke; Macmillan, 1994).
- Mackie, J.L. *Ethics: Inventing Right and Wrong*, (Harmondsworth; Penguin, 1977).
- Nickel, James. *Making Sense of Human Rights: Philosophical Reflections on the Universal Declaration of Human Rights*, (Berkeley; University of California Press, 1987).
- Waldron, Jeremy. *Theories of Rights*, (Oxford; Oxford University Press, 1984).

# 5

# ROOTS OF HUMAN RIGHTS PRINCIPLES: A SCAN OF THE SACRED TEXTS

**P.S. Vijaya Natharaj**

The essence of the concept of Human Rights is as old as human civilization but it first assumed a global significance only in the modern age, particularly in the wake of French Revolution which gave rise to the famous slogans liberty, equality and freternity. During the ancient and medieval periods, the concept human rights was not known to all. The King or the authority was considered to be the source of all power, rights and privileges. Rights thus existed in the state authority. In the modern times the concept underlines that every human being, by virtue of his being a human, is entitled to enjoy certain basic conditions of civilized life, irrespective of the socio-economic and political system he lives in.

Human Rights are basically derived from the principle of Natural law and hence they are universal in character. Many of the constitutional rights of the modern period are similar to those of the principles of human rights, yet there are differences. The constitutional rights are granted to the individuals by virtue of their citizenship in a country while human rights exist as an universal law irrespective of the nature of government or political or legal systems. Human Rights thus could be generally defined as those rights which are inherent in nature and without which one can not live as a human being with dignity. The expression refers to the international law and order relating to the development of the status of an individual. To be specific, human rights are "inherent and inalienable that are to be guaranteed to an individual by virtue of being a human being and that these rights are necessarily to ensure the dignity of every person irrespective of race, religion, nationality, language, sex or any other factor". Human Rights are nothing but a demand for a pure social justice in all fields of life, the application of the same in all jurisprudence, in all elements and in all administration. It is the duty of the state to uphold, promote and protect them in accordance with the existing law of the land.

The content and meaning of Human Rights have changed over a period of time and continues to change with the influence of times. Hence it is rather difficult to define it exactly. According to Bosanquet, it is "a right as a claim recognised by the society and enforced by the state". David Selby says "Human Rights pertains to all persons and are possessed by everybody in the world because they are human beings. They are not brought or inherited nor are they created by any contractual undertaking". From the writings of various scholars, one can understand human rights on three grounds – human nature, human dignity and the existence of a good society. Combining all the features, Plano and Olton have stated that "human rights are those rights which are considered to be essential for the survival, existence and personality development of a human being". It is also clear that human rights, whether recognised or not, belong to all human beings, all the times and in all the places.

Universally human rights are divided into three generation's rights, as classified by Louis B. Sohan. The first generation human rights comprise of those rights which are described as 'Civil and Political Rights' as enumerated in the International Covenant on Civil and Political Rights. The rights included in this part are : right to life, right to personal liberty, right not to be subjected to slavery, right not to be subjected to torture or inhuman or degrading treatment or punishment etc. This generation rights also include privacy and respect for family life, freedom of expression, freedom of thought, conscience and religion, the right to peaceful assembly and association, and the right to participate in the government of one's own country. This civil and political rights are concretized in the form of Magna Carta, the American Declaration of independence and the French Declaration of Rights of man and citizens.

The second generation rights as enumerated in the 'International Covenant on Economic, Social and Cultural Rights' includes the right to social security, the right to adequate standard of living, the right to food, clothing and housing, the right to be free from hunger, the right to highest attainable standard of physical and mental health, the right to education, the right to take part in cultural life of the community and the right to enjoy the benefits of scientific progress and its applications. These rights are considered to have originated along with the Russian Revolution of 1917 and the Paris Peace Conference of 1919. The Paris Peace Conference emphasised the concept of social justice and proclaimed that "peace can be established only if it is based on social justice".

The third generation rights speak of the rights of the people or community in a collective sense. This generation rights include the right to self-determination, the right to development, the right to international peace and security and the right to a satisfactory environment, the rights of women, children, prisoners, refugees, and other disabled and physically challenged, dalits and other weaker sections, minorities etc. While comparing these three generation rights, one can understand that the first generation rights require the state to refrain from interfering in the exercise of the rights by individuals. While in the case of second generation rights, the stress is that it is the duty of the state to adopt measures which will positively support the individual in securing standards of social security, social justice, opportunities to education and health care etc. The third generation rights require the involvement of international community as a whole as Article 23 of the African Charter says that "All people shall have the right to National and International Peace and Security".

**Sources of Human Rights Principles**

The genesis of human rights in a structured form and in a legalistic way are not older than the World War II, though the concept of individual rights and humane treatment are as old as the doctrine of natural rights founded on the natural law. The earlier Greek Stoics school of thought held the view that 'universal working force pervades all creation and that human conduct therefore, should be judged according to, and brought into harmony with, the law of nature'. The western philosophy of "the rights of man' had been highly influenced by the Stoics thought. The writings of medieval christian thinkers like St. Augustine, St. Thomas Acquinas and later, Hugo Grotius, Thomas Hobbes, John Locke, Rousseau, Montesquieu, Voltair etc. stressed the humaneness of human being and tried to prove the superiority of natural law. The idea of natural rights of man was strengthened by religious and social factors. Freedom of conscience and belief came to be formulated which led to the freedom of religion in later days.

Unlike Thomas Hobbes's view, John Locke was of the opinion that men in the state of nature was in a state of paradise, peace, and goodwill. His theory of social contract gives importance to the individual and his rights. The views of John Locke and others during the middle age had a tremendous influence on the western scholars during 18th and 19th centuries. The Glorious Revolution of 1688, Bill of Rights of 1689, Pennsylvania Declaration of 1776, Maryland Declaration of 1787, New Homisphere Declaration of 1783, The American Declaration of Independence 1787, the Massachusetts Declaration of 1789 etc. are some of the important break through that derived the rationale of the idea of Locke. However, it was the Magna Carta of 1215 that enjoys the status of a milestone in the history of the evolution of the concept of human rights, even though around 200 years prior to this when King Conrad II had issued a charter determining the rights of the parliament in 1037 AD and King Alfonso had accepted the Principle of Habeas Corpus in 1188 A.D.

The Europeans are said to be the pioneers in acknowledging the concept of Human rights. In the 19th century, the Convention for the betterment of the conditions of the sick and the wounded on the battlefield demanded that slavery which denied the rights of the individual for centuries should be abolished. Accordingly the black people of America were granted voting right in 1870. The end of World War I enlightened the world with the idea of human dignity. The League of Nations promised to secure fair and humane conditions of labour for men, women and children. The end of World War II encouraged many philosophers to voice their concern against aggression and loss of life and property. They asserted that only an affective international institution can protect human rights of ordinary and innocent people. The Atlantic Charter of 1941, the Tehran Declaration of 1943, the United Nations Conference at San Francisco 1945 etc. spelt out the necessity of promoting and preserving human rights and freedom.

It was at The San Francisco Conference that the United Nations Charter was drafted. In the Conference, the Preparatory Commission of the United Nations recommended the establishment of a commission on Human Rights to the Economic and Social Council. The United Nations General Assembly in its first session in 1946 considered a draft Declaration of Fundamental Human Rights and Freedom as proposed by the Economic and Social Council. Thus on 10th December 1948, Universal Declaration of Human Rights (UDHR) was adopted with 30 Articles. The Declaration defines Civil and Political Rights; Economic Social and Cultural Rights. Right to development, right to pollution free environment, and right to peace etc have added a new dimension to the concept of human rights. Roughly after two decades, the U.N. General Assembly promulgated two International Covenants in 1966 namely International Covenant on Economic, Social and Cultural Rights; (ICESCR) and International Covenant on Civil and Political Rights (ICCPR). The Vienna Declaration adopted on June 25, 1993 by the World Conference on Human Rights declared, "Human Rights and Fundamental Freedom are the birth rights of all human beings".

Humanitarian ideas become a policy in India from the beginning of the 19th century. The abolition of Sati (1829), Slavery (1811) and Female Infanticide (1830), and the introduction of Widow Re-marriage (1856) and the Prohibition of Child Marriage (1929) etc. are the notable legislations during the British Rule for the protection of the rights of women. A series of labour legislations were enacted for the protection of the rights of the working class such as Workers Compensation Act 1923, Trade Union Act 1926, Industrial Dispute Act 1947, Minimum Wages Act 1948 and the Indian Factories Act 1948 etc. The Motilal Nehru Committee Report 1928 enumerated the following rights such as (a) Personal liberty, (b) Freedom of conscience, profession and practice of religion, (c) Right to free elementary education without distinction of caste or creed in the matter of admission in any educational institution, (d) Equity for all citizen before law and (e) Equity of rights to all citizen in the matter of access to use of public roads, public wells and all other places of public resort.

The Constitution of India has taken care of the human rights, human dignity and fundamental rights through Articles 12-35. Directive Principles of State Policy - Articles 36-51 and Fundamental Duties - Article 51A. The human rights principles enumerated in these Articles are equality before law, civil and political rights, economic and social rights, religious – educational and cultural rights, and the rights of minorities, women and other weaker sections and so forth. To ensure human rights of the minorities and other weaker sections the Constitution has created many right protection bodies such as Minorities Commission, Women's Commission, Scheduled Castes and Scheduled Tribes Commission etc. The enactment of Protection of Human Rights Act 1993 provides for the constitution of National Human Rights Commission and the State Human Rights Commissions.

It is not correct to assert that the roots of human rights ideology and principles can only be found in modern western cultures. The classical sources of Hinduism, Confucianism, Buddhism, Islam, Judaism and Christianity have provided quite high standards of human social conduct, social values, and socio-political rights and duties. All these religion-based cultures and their philosophies are based on the ethics of humanity. In the Indian context, the Vedas, the Upanishads, the Bhagavad Gita, Manusmriti, Kautilya's Arthasastra etc have revealed certain moral and ethical code of conduct in social life. Ofcourse none of these religious traditions speaks about human rights and none has assumed an exemplary human rights record over the centuries as acknowledged in the documents of the modern age. Their sacred texts and canons say much about commandments and obligations, which individuals and communities to follow, than their liberties and rights. However, each sacred book has produced a number of building blocks of a comprehensive theory and law of a religious human rights today i.e. conscience, dignity, liberty, equality, reason, tolerance, love, responsibility, justice, mercy, righteousness, accountability etc. Each tradition has developed its own internal system of legal procedures and structures for the protection of rights.

### Human Rights Principles in Hinduism

A precise definition of Hinduism is rather hard to formulate since the beliefs and practices of the Hindus vary widely. However the most common meaning is assigned to a geographic reference and is to mean all the natives of the Indian sub-continent. It is a favourite dictum that Hinduism is not a religion but a whole way of life, covering a vast range of human activity. Yet, Hinduism is generally accepted as a religion. It is not an organised one, and it has no real founder, no founding date, no hierarchy of priests, no standard sacraments and no rites of initiation etc. Hinduism is the oldest of the world's major religions. It evolves from the Vedic religion of ancient India. Both the

Vedas and the Epics form the core of Hindu philosophy. The Epics were the stories describing the Hindu approach to life. The most popular Epics are the Ramayana and the Mahabharata. In the Mahabharata is found the Bhagavat Gita, called the Bible of Hinduism owing to its popularity. Its theme is detached action : doing one's duty without the desire for reaping its fruit. According to Hinduism, all the creatures go through cycles of rebirth or samsara after which liberations or moksha is attained. The principle of Karma determines a being's status within the cycle of rebirth

The word 'Hindu' has come to denote the great and rich religion of Arya Vedic Varnashrama Dharma of antiquity. As Nehru in his Discovery of India, quoted "The use of the Word 'Hindu' in connection with particular religion is a very late occurrence. The old inclusive term was Arya Dharma". He further explained that the word Hindu is clearly derived from Sindhu, the name for the present Indus. From the Sindhu, the words like Hindu, Hindustani, Indus and India came into being. It was the Arab invaders in later course that had given a religious colour to Hindu. The earliest phase of Hinduism is rooted in the religion of Vedas, collections of hymns, such as Rigveda, Samaveda, Yajurveda, and Atharva veda. Among the four, Rigveda is the earliest, the 1st millennium. B.C, which declares that all human beings are equal. The Atharva Veda recognises equal rights of all human beings. Since those days many Indian poets, saints and literati have upheld the principle of fundamental equality of all human beings and their rights to basic liberties.

The core concept of Hindu philosophy is Dharma which is formed from the root dhr, literally means to hold, to sustain and to maintain a thing in its being. Every form of life and every group of people has its Dharma, which is the law of being. Dharma is the first of the four personal aims (chaturvidha phala purushartha) to be realized during the course of one's life time : Dharma, artha, kama and moksha. Artha implies wealth, prosperity, reputation etc. Kama implies sensory and aesthetic fulfillment. Moksha is liberation and salvation. The primary object of one's life is aimed at attaining moksha and so he has to practice both artha and Kama with Dharma as the foundation. Happiness, prosperity and good life are to be experienced so long as they are within the frame work of Dharma which is the supreme law governing the sovereignty and the subjects, and enumerates the principles of rights, duties and freedom.

Indian culture and civilization were based on certain spiritual and ethical values termed as Dharma. It maintains stability of the social order and promotes well-being and progress of mankind. Dharma relieves one from ignorance, fear, disease and other evils, but cherishes fellow – feeling, brotherhood, amity and other good feelings. The principle of Dharma promotes, cluster of human rights, such as equality, education, religion, social security, justice, happiness etc. Dharma in the Vedic tradition is associated with many aspects of human life. There is the Dharma of an individual, Dharma of family, Dharma of the society, Dharma of a nation, Dharma of a king etc. Dharma in social life is regarded as a mode of life or a code of conduct, which regulates the works and activities of the man as a member of society and as an individual. In short, Dharma as a concept is very wide and comprehensive. It regulates the mutual obligations of the individual and the society. It stands for the establishment of harmony, peace, stability and progress in society.

The concept of 'Raja Dharma' as incorporated in Arthasastra, laid emphasise on the right of happiness and prosperity of all individuals. It is the duty of the king or ruler to protect the rights of the individual as is seen from the following verse of the Arthasastra:

"In the happiness of the people lies the kings happiness; In their welfare, his welfare, whatever is in his own interest, the king shall not consider as good: but whatever is in the interest of the people the king shall consider as good".

The Vedas which constitute the source of Dharma, emphasised the right to equality of all human being. Happiness is not possible when there is inequality. The Hindu concept of equality is understood from the following verses of Rigveda : Vedas are almost similar to Article 14 of the Constitution of India which provides that the state shall not deny any person equality before law.

*" No one is superior (ajyestasa) or inferior (akanishtasa). All are brothers (bhrataraha). All should strive for the interest of all and should progress collectively (Sowbhagyasana va vridhunu).*

However, it is unfortunates that the Hindu social order, particularly its caste system and untouchability present a direct conflict with the Dharma and its Universal human rights framework. The social, economic, religious and political governance of the Hindu society is found not on the principle of liberty, equality and dignity, which formed the basis of human rights values, but strictly on the basis of inequality and discrimination. In this context, the concept 'human right' explains a different meaning. Unlike the other human societies, the Hindu social order recognises neither the individual nor the family as the basic unit of the society. It is the caste that assumes all the significances and recognition as the primary unit of the society. The enjoyment and denial of rights and justice of an individual or family are based not on his personality or merit but on the particular caste to which he belongs.

In a hierarchical order of Hindu society, the rights and privilages accumulate only to the caste groups which are at the higher echelon of the society. In this structure, the Brahmins who are at the top of the social order enjoys special rights and privileges and are considered 'human beings'. While among the non-Brahmin categories, the untouchables are at the bottom level who are treated as 'savaged' and thereby they are unworthy to enjoy both the civic and natural rights. They are inferior social being and therefore not entitled to any individual rights. Dr. B.R. Ambedkar, the architect of Indian Constitution and later a convert from Hinduism to Buddhism held the view that the "doctrine of inequality is the core and heart of the Hindu social order". History proves that the so called untouchables or low caste Hindus have responded to their inhuman ill treatments by converting enmass to Christianity, Buddhism and to Islam. The social system and practice of religions other than Hinduism is free from caste based discrimination and follow the principle of tolerance and equality.

In order to loose the temper of the caste based rigidities among the hindus and to guarantee both the constitutional and human rights to those low caste hindus or the untouchables, the Constitution of India provides an impressive array of provisions. These provisions try to counter institutional discrimination like the restrictions of access to public places (Art. 15 (2) ), abolition of untouchability (Art. 17), the prohibition of traffic in human beings and forced labour (Art. 23), protection of the right to admission to educational institutions (Art. 29 (2) ), the promotion of educational and economic interests of SC/ST's (Art. 46) the reservation of seats for SC/ST's in Local bodies, in state legislatures, in parliament, in civil services etc. (Articles 243 D, 332, 334, 335 respectively) and the appointment of a Commission for scheduled castes and scheduled tribes (Art. 338). The minimum wages Act 1948, the untouchability (offenses) Act 1955, the protection of civil Rights Act 1976, Bonded Labour System (Abolition) Act 1976, and the SC/ST's prevention of Atrocities Act 1989 etc are the other noteworthy legal measures initiated by the government for the protection of human rights of the low caste hindu society.

**Human Rights Principles in Buddhism**

Buddhism, both a religion and a philosophy, is founded by Siddhartha Gautama during 4th century BC in north eastern India. Buddhism is one of the major world religions and takes its goal the escape from suffering, the cycle of the rebirth and the attainment of Nirvana, means extinguishing desires and passions. Buddhism was started as a reform movement in Hinduism particularly against the Hindu practices of pyramidical structure of caste system and the untouchability. Buddhism's main teachings are summarized in the four noble truths : Dukkha, Tanha, Nirodha and Marga – means sufferings, cause of sufferings, cessation of suffering and removal of desire respectively. Buddhism's two major branches – Mahayana and Theravada means 'the doctrine of the elders' and 'the Greater vehicle' respectively, have developed distinctive practices. In India. Emperor Ashoka the Great promoted Buddhism during the 3rd Century BC but it declined in succeeding centuries.

In a human rights perspective, Buddhism took a concrete step to destroy the gospel of inequality which was in practice in Hinduism. Buddha, the title in Sanskrit means 'Enlightened one' transformed attitude of respect and obedience contained in the ethnic Hindu notion of Dharma into a universal morality which protects the weak from the strong and provides common standards and rules leading to the enjoyment of liberty and equality effective.

Buddhism offers a kind of ecological view of life, under the commandment 'not to destroy any life, the rights of animals and plants are as equal as a human being'. Buddhist scholars Masao Abe writes that the concepts of human rights of human being in the western sense can not be found anywhere in Buddhist literature. In contrast, in Buddhism a human being is not grasped only from the human point of view but a part of all sentient beings or even as a part of all beings, sentient or non sentient, because both human and non human beings are equally subject to impermanency.

In Buddhism, human rights are an extension of human nature. Human nature is understood as a part of the process of 'relational origination'. In other words, the human person is a part of the interdependence of all life. When one realizes the inter dependence of all life, he comes to the conclusion that rights are fundamental not only for the people but equally for all sentient beings as well as for nature itself. Societies cease to be truly human when they cease to acknowledge that each individual's fulfillment is the purpose of the whole. And humans are free to give away their rights in furtherance of the fulfillment of the rights others.

## Human Rights Principles in Islam

Islam, a major world religion, was founded by Muhammed in Arabia in 7th Century A.D. In Arabic word Islam means "Submission" – specifically, submission to the will of one God, called Allah in Arabic. The sacred scripture of Islam is the Quran. The fundamental concept of Islam is the Shariah or law which embraces the total way of life commanded by God. The religious duties of the Muslims are summed in the five pillars of Islam, such as belief in God and his prophet, five prayers a day, giving of alms to the poor, fasting during the month of Ramadan and the Hajj or pilgrimage to Mecca at least once in a life time, barring poverty or physical in capacity. Islamic political system, law, sovereignty and the foundations of human rights etc are entirely different from those of the principles of western societies. Islamic principles of democracy and human rights are totally subservient to the Divine Law that exercises its authority in accordance with the injunctions of God and within the limits prescribed by Him.

At the time when the U.N. General Assembly approved Universal Declaration of Human Rights in 1948, the Government of Saudi Arabia opposed it on the ground that the UDHR did not acknowledge rights to be the gift of God and thereby violated Quran's Principle by ascertaining a right to change one's religion. The issue became a core point of debate for decades among the Islamic scholars. In 1980, a seminar on Human Right in Islam was organised by the University of Kuwait and that asserted that "Human Rights and Freedoms are not attributed to the nature but are considered to be gifts of God in accordance with the Islamic faith". Further the delegates affirmed that Islam's codifications of human rights constitutes "a solid foundation for an effective exercise of human rights and freedoms and protection against any infringement of them". In Islam, God given human rights are seen as the means of assuring human dignity. In his inaugural address of the seminar, His Highness, the Sovereign Emir of Kuwait affirmed that "to preserve the dignity of man, it is necessary that society guarantees him food, drink, lodging, clothing, education and employment as well as his right to express his opinion, participate in the political life of his country and to be assured of his own security and that of his kin".

Unlike the western approach of human rights that emerged from the documents of Magna Carta of Great Britain in 1215, the Bill of Rights 1689, American war of Independence, Glorious Revolution, Russian Revolution, U.N. Charter, Universal Declaration of Human Rights 1948 and the many more Covenants, Declaration and agreements of the UNO, the human rights concepts in Islam have been granted or conferred by God. No legislative Assembly in the world or any government on earth has the authority to make any amendment or change in the rights conferred by God. The rights which have been sanctioned by God are permanent and eternal. They are not subjected to any alterations or modifications. Islam has laid down some rights for man as a human being. Right to life, Right to the safety of life, Respect for the chastity of women, Right and freedom, Right and justice, equality of human beings, etc are the key components in which the Holy Quran has definite reference. Regarding the right to life, the Holy Quran Lays down:

*"Whosoever kills a human being (without any reason like manslaughter or corruption) it is as though he had killed all mankind" (5: 32) "Do not kill a soul which Allah has made sacred except through the due process of law" (6: 151). "And whoever saves life it is as though he had saved the lives of all mankind" (5:32),.*

Right to justice is a very important and valuable right which Islam has given to man as a human being. The Holy Quran also had laid down:.

*"Do not let your hatred if a man incite you to aggression". (5:3). "And do not let ill-will towards any folk incite you so that you severe from dealing justly. Be just, that is nearest to headfulnes". (5:8)*

The almighty God has laid down equality in the Holy Quran (49:13): O Mankind, we have created you from a male and female". "And we set you up as nations and tribes so that you may be able to recognize each others". This means that the division of human being into nations, races, groups and tribes is for the sake of distinction, so that the people of different sections cooperate with each others. The superiority of one man over another is only on the basis of consciousness, purity of character and high morals. God has given man this right of equality as a birth right and therefore no man should be discriminated on the ground of colour of his skin, his place of birth, and the nation in which he was born.

Islam gives its citizen the right to absolute and complete equality in the eyes of law. There is clear instruction in the Holy Quran that all muslims are equal in their rights and obligations. "The believers are brothers" (49:10). The prophet has said that "The life and blood of Muslims are equally precious". The religious brotherhood and the uniformity of their rights and duties are the base of equality in Islamic Society, in which the rights and obligation of any person are neither grater nor lesser in any way than the rights and obligations of other people.

The Holy Quran has also clearly lays down the right of the citizens to the protection of their honour. This Islamic right is indeed superior to the western law of Defamation. Islam declares blasphemy as a crime irrespective of the fact whether the accused is a man of honour or not, and whether the words used for blasphemy have actually disagraced the victim and harmed his reputation in the eyes of the public or not. This crime deserves due punishment. In the words of Holy Quran (49:11-12) "You have to believe, do not let one (set of) people make fun of another set. Do not defame one another. Do not insult by using nicknames. And do not backbite or speak ill of one another"

Islam gives the right of freedom of thought and expression to all citizens of the Islamic state on the condition that it should be used for the propagation of virtue and truth and not for spreading evil and wickedness. This right, according to Islam, is not only a right, but an obligation. One who tries to deny this right to his people is openly at war with God, the Almighty. If any government deprives its citizens of this right and prevents them from performing this duty, then it is in direct conflict with the injunction of God. Islam also gives the right to freedom of conscience and conviction to its citizens in an Islamic state. The Holy Quran has laid down injunction : "there should be no coercion in the matter of faith" (2:256). Islam encourages the other religious people to embrace Islam, voluntarily on their own choice. The converts are welcomed to the Muslim community with equal rights and privileges.

Islam has recognized the right of the needy people, seeking help and assistance. In this sense, the state has been entrusted with the duty and responsibility of looking after all those who need help and assistance. An Islamic state is therefore a true welfare state which will be the guardian and protector of all those in need. Quran has not only conferred a right to every man to seek assistance but has made Muslims to do voluntary charity i.e. Zakat which means voluntary help by the rich to those in need in the community. If there is an orphan or an aged man, if there is an invalid or poor and has no one to help him, then it is the duty and the responsibility of the state to support him.

Islam has laid down some Universal fundamental rights for humanity. Accordingly, it is not permissible to oppress women, children, old people, the sick or the wounded. The hungry person must be fed, the naked clothed, and the diseased treated medically irrespective of whether they belong to the Islamic Community or from among its enemies. Every Muslim is regarded as eligible and fit for all position of the highest responsibility in an Islamic state without distinction of race, colour or class. Islam also has laid down certain rights for the non-muslim, called dhimmis (the covenanted people) The life, property and honour of a dhimmi is to be respected and protected exactly like that of a muslim citizen. The Islamic state shall not interfere with the personal rights of non-muslims. They will have full freedom of conscience and belief and will be at liberty to perform their religious rites and ceremonies of their own way.

**Human Rights Principles in Christianity**

Christianity stems from the teaching of Jesus in the 1st century A.D. It was originally a movement of Jews who accepted Jesus as messiah. Its principal tenets are that Jesus is the son of God, He died to redeem human kind and He resurrected on the third day after his crucifixion. Bible is the sacred book of Christianity, which consists of two documents - Old Testament and New Testament. It was composed by many authors over more than a thousand years. Christianity is defined at three angles as a way of belief, as a way of worship and as a way of life' or as 1 Cor l: 13 says, it is a 'faith, hope and charity'. The Christian faith is both a conviction about God and a trust in the ways of God. It is a belief in Trinity that God is one in his "essence" and three in his "persons"- Father, Son and Holy Spirit. Also the content of Christian faith that the life, death and resurrection of Jesus Christ are the means by which God has brought about the salvation of the world. The two motives associated with the theme that Christianity as a way of worship are the knowledge of God and the services of God. The Christian worship is directed not towards man and his achievements, but towards the glory of the 'name' of God, that is God as he has revealed himself in Christ. The worship celebrates the reign of God over the world. Christianity as a way of life is noticed as a life of charity or love that is love towards God and love towards men. The greatest commandment, "you shall love the lord your God, with all your heart, with all your soul and with all your mind", and is followed by "you shall love your neighbour as yourself" is the central essence of the teaching of Christ. Love is equated with the idea of freternity and dignity.

The Bible, becomes a key resources for the Universal Declaration of Human Rights. The urgency of the need for 'world peace' immediately after the World War II, acknowledges the Christian Principle "Love your neighbour as yourself". The UDHR also upholds human dignity as Jesus taught and as implied in the creation of humanity in "God's own image". The concepts peace, justice, good governance etc. in the UDHR are inaccordance with the biblical principles. The Declaration seeks to protect the vulnerable sections from exploitations, degrading treatments and suppressions etc, which are the central theme throughout the biblical Scripture. Jesus Christ himself was a revolutionary against the social evils and the practices of injustice. There is no doubt that the modern western Principles of Human rights not only owe much to the christian traditions, but also reflect many biblical ideals.

The concept of human rights is usually assumed to be secular notion and the emergence of human rights in the philosophies of the French Revolution as a secular movement. The French Declaration of the Rights of Man and of the Citizens on August 27, 1789 was made in the presence and under the auspicious of the "Supreme Being'. The truths inherent in and safeguarded by the concept of human rights were the accountability of sovereigns to God, the divine law and the position of the church. In the Christian point of view the rights are grounded according to the value of the created order. The fundamentals of the Christian doctrine emphasizes that human being are created by God and specifically created in his likeness and on his own image. The creator can do what he likes with his created one's and they have no rights against the creator, the God. St. Paul wrote in his letter to Jeremiah that 'God is the potter and human being his pots and hence human being have no right to complain if some are selected for salvation and others are not. Human being are precious in the eyes of God, as evident from that "Good Shephered goes out for the one sheep that is lost, hunts high and low mountains for it until he brings it home to eternal life rejoicing.

In the oldtestament, Jehovah, the Lord, has dictated many laws for the people, particularly, Ten commandments. (Deuteronomy 5:7-21; Exodus 19: 1-25) These commandments are characterised as certain kinds of duties that the people are to perform. The first four commandments deal with the relationship between God and the people and other six deal with relationship between man and man. Of the ten commandments, eight dictates 'Shalt not' and the other two are advisory and command : one is a moral duty towards one's parents and the other is a command to follow sabbath day as holy. The Ten commandments reads:

*"Thou shatl have no other God before me.*

*Thou shatl not make unto thee any graven image, or any likeness of anything Thou shalt not bow down thyself to them nor save them.*

*Thou shalt not take the name of the Lord thy God in vain.*

*Remembers the sabbath day, to keep it holy. Shalt not to do any work.*

*Honour thy father and thy mother.*

*Thou shalt not kill.*

*Thou shalt not commit adultery.*

*Though shalt not steal.*

*Though shalt not bear false witness against thy neighbours*

*Thou shalt not covet thy neighbour's house, thou shalt not covet they neighbours wife, nor his manservant, nor his ox etc."*

The philosophy of tolerance and non-violence form the most important principles of the teaching of Jesus Christ. He says (Luke 6:27-31)

*" Love your enemies, do good to them which hate you*
*Bless them that curse you and pray for them which despitefully use you.*
*And unto him that smiteth thee on the one cheek offer also the other; and*

*him that taketh away thy cloak forbid not to take thy coat also.*
*Give to everyman that asketh of thee, and of him that taketh away they goods ask them not again.*
*And as ye would that men should do to you, do ye also to them likewise".*
*"--------- said unto them He that is without sin among you, let him first cast a stone at her" (John 8:7)*

Tolerance, compassion and non-violence are the central themes of these verses. Tolerance and love towards all even those who are once the enemies and evil doers are the two principles in which Christianity signifies. Christ not only taught these principles but also practiced them in his life. His crucifixion on the Cross and his appealing to the Father, the Lord, "forgive them (crucifiers), for they know not what they do" (Luke 23:34) are the notable historical evidence of the greatest tolerance and love towards the neighbours.

This is the notion that Christian ethic is more of duty, rather than of rights. The basic philosophy of Christian action is doing the Will of the Heavenly Father. This will is for the well-being and flourishing of his creatures. As man is made in the likeness of God not as a solitary individual but as a person in fellowship knit together by love, each has equal obligation of others' welfare. It also means that the creator also has responsibility for the well being of all citizens. The state has a duty to intervene to safeguard the interest of the more vulnerables, for they too are members of the whole. The Biblical God is a God of the poor, the rejected, the powerless and the sufferers, and God intervenes on their behalf so that the last shall be the first. "Blessed are you who are poor, for yours is the kingdom of God. Blessed are you who hunger now, for you shall be satisfied. Blessed are you who weep now, for you shall laugh" (Luke 6:20-21). These verses reveal the compassion of the creator towards the created particularly those who are discriminated and under privileged in society. The values given to the poor by the creator is a sign of the human rights principles in the modern period.

The position of women in church activities goes on a radical change almost on par with men in the 21st century. Until 1970s, their was virtually no record of women speaking in the churches. But since then a tremendous change has taken place in the Evangelical and Protestant churches. They are allowed to teach and preach in the churches, seminaries and Christian conventions and are allowed to hold positions as priests and Bishops. From the days of Reformation in the 16th century, women are being given a respectable position in social, political and in the religious spheres of life. But their leadership in God's work is not His orders. Apostle Paul's statement, "I suffer not a women to teach, nor usurp authority over the man" (I Tim 2:12) stood firm throughout the centuries. Man is God's delegated authority over women. However, both men and women are equally members of the spiritual body in Christ, yet God commands women to subordinate to man in the Church (I Cor. 14:33-35)

"For Adam was first formed, then Eve. And Adam was not deceived, but the women being deceived was in the transgression" (I Tim. 2: 13,14)

God made Eve out of Adam to be his help mate. Man goes out to work and the women take care of the home. A god fearing wife is an asset to her husband. "A virtuous and submissive wife is a crown to her husband (Prov. 12:4). The submission of wife to her husband is the order of the creation and as well as the order in the church which is the Kingdom of God. Christ is the head of the church. God, the father, comes top, then Christ, and below him the church (man) and then women. This is the orders set up by God which neither a man nor a woman can break. The word submission means in spiritual way, 'denying one's rights and privileges. While submission, wife's duty to her husband includes love (Titus 2:4) respect (I peter 3:1-2), assistance (Gen 2:18) purity (Titus 2:5), submissiveness (I peter 3:5) and being a good mother (I Tim. 2:15) God sees a wife's submission to her husband as an actual part of her obedience to Jesus, "as unto the Lord" (Gal. 3:28)

Right to religion is one of the fundamental principles of human rights as envisaged in the Universal Declaration of Human Rights (Article 18) and in the European Convention of Human Rights which treats freedom of religion as the basic rights of individual. Christianity spreads through missionary works right from the first century onwards. In Indian context, eventhough the Christian population constitute below 3%, the missionary organisations are multiplying. The missionary work is a network programme of action in the name of Christ through the call of the church that "either go as a missioner or send missionaries or sponsor missionaries or atleast pray for the missionaries". Christ himself commanded his disciples that "Go ye therefore, and teach all nations, baptizing them in the name of the Father, the Son and the Holy Ghost". Teaching them to observe all things whatsoever I have commanded you : and I am with you always even unto the end of the world" (Mathew 28 : 19-20). The arrival of St. Thomas, a disciple of Christ to India was on His command and mission. The command of Jesus given to His disciples became, in later course, a principle of both constitutions and human rights. Article 25 (1) of the Fundamental Rights of the Indian Constitution meaningfully guarantees "freedom of conscience, the right to profess, practice and propagate religion" Article 18 of the Universal Declaration of Human Rights, Articles 18 & 19 of the International Covenant on Civil and Political Rights, Article 12 of the American Convention of Human Rights 1969, Article 18 of the African Charter on Human Rights and People's Right 1981, Articles 26 and 27 of the Arab Charter of Human Rights 1994 etc. clearly and specifically stress that right to religion is a basic right for persons all over the world. In India the alleged threat of forced conversion from Hinduism to Christianity is to be examined in the light of the command of Jesus Christ given to His Disciples. "Go Ye therefore ... the end of the world".

To conclude, the concepts of human rights are assumed importance globally during the past few decades. Eversince the proclamation of the

Universal Declaration of Human Rights, the concept has gained currency and has become a crucial subject of debate at social, political and ethical points of view. In fact the roots of the modern concept of Human rights could be traced back from the days of the beginning of human civilization. The earliest concept of right was that of natural rights denoting those basic conditions of life without which human being would remain in under development. The natural rights confirmed individual rights and humane treatment. Following the concept of natural rights, the leaders of The French Revolution coined the concept of "Rights of Man." Natural rights were in later course re-designated as human rights only after the secularization of politics was completed in Europe as a result of the Renaissance and Enlightenment movements. Europeans are thus said to be the pioneers in acknowledging and disseminating the modern concept of human rights principles in a broader perspective.

The natural rights fell into disfavor when the concept "Universal Right" took its root. The universal concept developed with the writings of Thoreau's 'Civil Disobedience', John Stuart Mills 'Essay on Liberty' and Thomas Paine's 'The Rights of Man'. However, it is unlogic claiming that the roots of human rights principles and ideology are found only in western cultures and tradition. The role of classical religious sources in strengthening human rights roots is significant. Religious texts have provided quite high standards of human social conduct, values, rights and duties. Each religious canon has produced necessary procedures and structures for the protection of rights and dictates people to follow commandments and obligations. All the religious texts reaffirmed the fact that rights are to be enjoyed when duties and obligations enforced by God is obeyed and performed. Human rights is safe only when every one performs duties. The message is propagated through the doctrine of "Dharma' in Hindusim, 'Love your neighbours as yourself' in Christianity, 'Spirit of brotherhood' in Islam and 'relational orgination' in Buddhism.

## References

1. Ajith Fernando (2007): *Sharing the Truth in Love*, GLS Publishing, Mumbai.
2. *Britanica Ready Reference Encyclopedia*, (2005); Vol. 5, Encyclopaedia Britanica Pvt. Ltd., New Delhi.
3. Brohi. A.K., (2004): *Manushyavakashangal Islamil* (Mal.), Islamic Publishing House, Kozhikode.
4. Clarence J.T., *The Role of Women in Church Ministry*, The Christian Life Mission, Kolkata.
5. Dhananjay Vasudeo Dwivedi, (2009): "Thoughts for Human Rights in Vedic Tradition". *The Indian Journal of Political Science*, Vol. Lxx, No. 4, Oct-Dec. pp. 1021-1034.
6. John Stott (2007): *Understanding the Bible*, GLS Publishing, Mumbai.

7. Sayyid Abdul A'la Maududi, (2008): *Human Rights in Islam*, Markazi Maktaba Islami Publishers, New Delhi.
8. Sunder Raj (1986): *The Confusion called Conversion*, TRACI Publications, New Delhi.
9. *The New Testament*
10. *The Old Testament*.
11. Vijaya Natharaj (2008): "Guaranteeing Instruments of Minority Rights : Problems and Prospects", *Historia* (Thiruvananthapuram) Vol. 2. No. 2, Nov. 2008.

# 6

# HUMAN RIGHTS FOR GOOD GOVERNANCE AND QUALITY LIFE: A SUCCESS STORY [A CASE STUDY OF ANDHRA PRADESH STATE HUMAN RIGHTS COMMISSION]

**Panjala Narasaiah**

Andhra Pradesh State Human Rights commission, first of its kind at State level, was constituted by an order of the state Govt. on 28-01-2005 "as per the provisions of the Protection of Human Rights Act, 1993 (Central Act 10 of 1994) to exercise the powers conferred upon, and to perform the functions assigned to a State Commission under chapter V of the said Act". The APSHRC is an embodiment of AP State's concern for the promotion and protection of Human Rights.

### Definition of Human Rights

According to section 2(d) of the Protection of Human Rights Act, 1993 Human Rights is related to the individual's right to life, liberty, equality and dignity.

### Composition of the APSHRC

As per the PHR Act, 1993, (as Amended) the State Commission will have a

(i) Chairman who has been a Chief Justice of a High Court

(ii) One member who is, or has been, a Judge of a High Court or District Judge in the State with a minimum of seven years experience as District Judge.

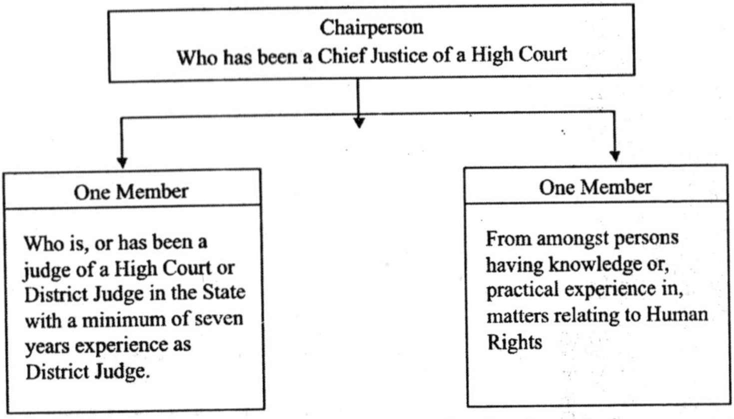


(iii) One member from amongst persons having knowledge, or practical experience in matters relating to Human Rights.

**Selection Committee**

The Chairperson (note the gender neutrality – not chairman, which is the general practice) and members are appointed by the Governor by warrant under his hand and seal on the recommendation of a committee consisting of

(a) The Chief Minister – Chairperson.
(b) Speaker of the Legislative Assembly – Member.
(c) Minister in-charge of the Department of Home, in the State – Member.
(d) Leader of the Opposition in the Legislative Assembly – Member.

There is a provision that where there is a Legislative Council in a State, the Chairman of that Council and the Leader of the Opposition in that Council will also be members of the Committee. As per the procedure the Govt. of A.P appointed a Chairperson and two members on 11-08-2005 and they assumed office on 12-08-2005.

At the time of composition of the Commission the Legislative Council was not in existence; as such the Chairman of the Council and Leader of the Opposition could not be included in the Selection Committee. The Chairperson worked as a Judge of A.P High Court and Chief Justice of Tamil

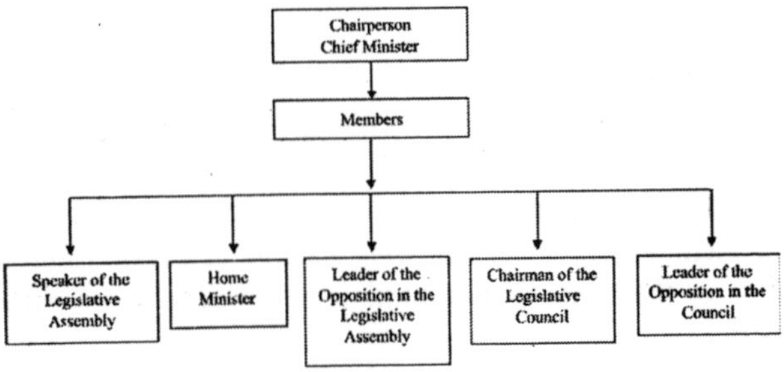

Nadu and Kerala High Courts. Another member retired as a Judge of A.P High Court. The third member was a retired District Judge. One member retired after serving for nearly 15 months on the completion of the term on 08-11-2006. Since then, the vacancy is unfilled. No human rights activist was appointed till date.

**Officers and Other Staff**

At present the commission, on the administrative side, is headed by a Secretary, as the chief Executive Officer. He is a serving District Sessions Judge. He is assisted by only 49 employees. Govt. has sanctioned an Investigation Team with full supporting staff, but nobody has been posted yet.

As per the provisions of the Act at the time of Constitution of the Commission the Govt. appointed Principal Secretary to Govt. as the Secretary of the Commission. He was withdrawn after serving the Commission for one year.

**Functions**

The functions of the Commission are listed in Chapter III of the said Act.

The Commission shall perform all or any of the following functions, namely:-

(a) inquire, suo motu or on a petition presented to it by a victim or any person on his behalf [or on a direction or order of any court], into complaint of
 (i) violation of human rights or abetment thereof; or
 (ii) negligence in the prevention of such violation, by a public servant;

(b) intervene in any proceeding involving any allegation of violation of human rights pending before a court with the approval of such court;

(c) visit, notwithstanding anything contained in any other law for the time being in force, any jail or other institution under the control of the State Government, where persons are detained or lodged for purposes of treatment, reformation or protection, for the study of the living conditions of the inmates thereof and make recommendations thereon to the Government;

(d) review the safeguards provided by or under the Constitution or any law for the time being in force for the protection of human rights and recommend measures for their effective implementation;

(e) review the factors, including acts of terrorism that inhibit the enjoyment of human rights and recommend appropriate remedial measures;

(f) study treaties and other international instruments on human rights and make recommendations for their effective implementation-;

(g) undertake and promote research in the field of human rights;

(h) spread human rights literacy among various sections of society and promote awareness of the safeguards available for the protection of these rights through publications, the media, seminars and other available means;

(i) encourage the efforts of non-governmental organisations and institutions working in the field of human rights;

(j) such other functions as it may consider necessary for the protection of human rights.

**Powers Relating to Inquiries**

The same Chapter lists out the powers relating to inquiries, which are as follows :-

(1) The Commission shall, while inquiring into complaints under this Act, have all the powers of a civil court trying a suit under the Code of Civil Procedure, 1908, and in particular in respect of the following matters, namely :

  (a) summoning and enforcing the attendance of witnesses and examining them on oath;
  (b) discovery and production of any document;
  (c) receiving evidence on affidavits;
  (d) requisitioning any public record or copy thereof from any court or office;
  (e) issuing summons for the examination of witnesses or documents;
  (f) Any other matter which may be prescribed.

(2) The Commission shall have power to require any person, subject to any privilege which may be claimed by that person under any law for the time being in force, to furnish information on such points or matters as, in the opinion of the Commission, may be useful for, or relevant to, the subject matter of the inquiry and any person so required shall be deemed to be legally bound to furnish such information within the meaning of section 176 and section 177 of the Indian Penal Code.

(3) The Commission or any other officer, not below the rank of a Gazetted Officer, specially authorised in this behalf by the Commission may enter any building or place where the Commission has reason to believe that any document relating to the subject matter of the inquiry may be found, and may seize any such document or take extracts or copies there from subject to the provisions of section 100 of the Code of Criminal Procedure, 1973, in so far as it may be applicable-

(4) The Commission shall be deemed to be a civil court and when any offence as is described in section 175, section 178, section 179, section 180 or section 228 of the Indian Penal Code is committed in the view or presence of the Commission, the Commission may, after recording the facts constituting the offence and the statement of the accused as provided for in the Code of Criminal Procedure, 1973, forward

the case to a Magistrate having jurisdiction to try the same and the Magistrate to whom any such case is forwarded shall proceed to hear the complaint against the accused as if the case has been forwarded to him under section 346 of the Code of Criminal Procedure, 1973.

(5) Every proceeding before the Commission shall be deemed to be a judicial proceeding within the meaning of sections 193 and 228, and for the purposes of section 196, of the Indian Penal Code, and the Commission shall be deemed to be a civil court for all the purposes of section 195 and Chapter XXVI of the Code of Criminal Procedure, 1973.

**Investigation**

(1) The Commission may, for the purpose of conducting any investigation pertaining to the inquiry, utilise the services of any officer or investigation agency of the Central Government or any State Government with the concurrence of the Central Government or the State Government, as the case may be.

(2) For the purpose of investigating into any matter pertaining to the inquiry, any officer or agency whose services are utilised under sub- section (1) may, subject to the direction and control of the Commission:-

- (a) summon and enforce the attendance of any person and examine him;
- (b) require the discovery and production of any document; and
- (c) requisition any public record or copy thereof from any office.

(3) The provisions of section 15 shall apply in relation to any. statement made by a person before any officer or agency whose services are utilised under sub-section (1) as they apply in relation to any statement made by a person in the course of giving evidence before the Commission.

(4) The officer or agency whose services are utilised under sub- section (1) shall investigate into any matter pertaining to the inquiry and submit a report thereon to the Commission within such period as may be specified by the Commission in this behalf.

(5) The Commission shall satisfy itself about the correctness of the facts stated and the conclusion, if any, arrived at in the report submitted to it under sub-section (4) and for this purpose the Commission may make such inquiry (including the examination of the person or persons who conducted or assisted in the investigation) as it thinks fit.

**Awareness Creation**

The existence, functions and performance of the commission are well covered by the print media and electronic media. The coverage given by the vernacular press (Telugu) is far more than the coverage given by the English press. All TV Stations broadcast programmes mainly in Telugu. As such the coverage is full. For instance, a leading Telugu daily news paper published about the commission on 12th July, 2009 a story. Thereafter the flow of victims increased manifold.

**Access to the Commission**

The commission is easily accessible to the victims. He/She can approach the commission directly or through a lawyer or an NGO. Number of complaints lodged directly by the victims are more than the complaints lodged through other means. A victim can approach the commission in person or can post a post card, send a telegram, an SMS or can call on phone also.

The Commission also takes suo motu cognizance of news published/ broadcast in news papers and Televisions.

On an average daily 250 cases are listed. There are days when 500 cases were tabled on a single day. Sometimes the commission sat upto 10 'O' Clock in the night and passed orders. On an average 50 to 60 cases are disposed off everyday.

**Justice at the Door-Step**

The Head Quarters of the Commission are located at Hyderabad, the capital of the State. The victims have no alternative but to visit Hyderabad to file complaints in person. In order to have interface with the people and to provide justice in a cost-effective and time-bound-manner, the Commission moves extensively with the people in the Districts whenever and wherever their rights are affected, abridged or violated. "These visits", the Commission observes, "are useful to it in directly understanding the human rights problems of the people, and also for appreciating the evidence submitted by them".

**Expenses, If Any**

No court fee is charged. A victim can present his / her case directly to the Commission in person. No need to engage a Lawyer.

The full Commission hears the cases in the Court Hall which is open to

**No. of Complaints Received (till the end Nov end 2009)**

| *S. No* | *Year* | *No. of Complaints* | *Increase / Decrease* |
|---|---|---|---|
| 1 | From 12-08-2005 to 31-12-2005 | 2396 | |
| 2 | 2006 | 6079 | |
| 3 | 2007 | 5568 | 511 |
| 4 | 2008 | 8165 | 2597 |
| 5 | 2009 (till the end of Nov) | 13000 | **4835** |
| | **Total** | **35208** | |

all. Thus, full transparency is maintained.

**Nature of Cases**

The Commission dealt with cases relating to medical treatment to the penniless people at the corporate hospitals, free of cost, salaries to the Govt. and private servants, pension to the pensioners, compensation to the victims of crimes, maintenance to the aged parents and infirm children, protection to the newly married couple from wrong doers. The Commission has treated the right to health as a human right on priority and right to be born healthy as an inherent human right of every child. This list is illustrative but not exhaustive.

**Some Landmark Judgments**

1. Right to Equality and Dignity (Suo Motu)

In Vurinayanapally Village of Kuppam Mandal of Chittoor District there was no education to the women, no person was allowed to wear chappals, the pregnant women are being sent out of the village to a remote place, there is no awareness about family planning and people walk barefoot even during rains and hot summer with superstitious beliefs. The case is being enquired into by the Commission.

2. Right to Health

The Commission has treated right to health as a Human Right on priority and right to be born healthy as an inherent human right of every child and has taken up the cases of muscular dystrophy and other congenital health defect cases and in that regard held hearing on 07-11-2007 and 28-06-2008 calling for the Nutritionists, Doctors and Medical Scientists for the Hearings.

3. Prevention of Child Marriages

In several cases directions were given to restrain child marriages.

In number of cases police protection was accorded to the couples who got married preceded by love affair, when they complained of threat to their life and liberty at the hands of either their parents or relatives.

In HRC. No. 161/2006 the Commission not only took effective steps in preventing child marriages at Sri Kalahasthi but also issued directions to the Government to amend the A.P. Compulsory Registration of Marriages Act, 2002 suitably and make the child marriage as a cognizable offence and also appoint marriage officers and further take necessary steps to educate the people particularly rural masses about their fundamental rights of primary education and employment guarantee.

4. Right to Life

In a gruesome murder of a prisoner in Anantapur District Jail, a direction was given to the Government to pay compensation of Rs. 5,00,000/- to his widow and to update security arrangements at the Anantapur District jail and reshuffle the entire jail staff by immediate transfers and postings. This must be the first case of its kind in the entire country which hit headlines of all the national newspapers.

Several Freedom Fighters approached the Commission as a last hope in getting their pensions by filling batch of cases. On considering their plight not the Commission has not only issued directions to the Central and State Governments but also consistently monitoring the progress in the matter with Human touch even by summoning the Principal Secretary of the State Government Revenue Department.

### Right to Dignity (by Mahila Samakhya - NGO)

When 9 Tribal Women approached the Commission through A.P. Mahila Samakhya alleging gang rape on them by the person in uniform, steps were taken to find out the truth and directions were given to the District Collector, Visakhapatnam, to provide food, clothing, shelter, employment and medical aid to the victims.

### Right to Quality Life

The Commission has also taken cognizance of the cases when it was complained that in some parts of the Hyderabad city the Human Rights of the citizens are being violated due to sound pollution on account of negligence on the part of the Pollution Control Board and Traffic Police in controlling traffic. The matters are pending enquiry.

### Good Governors

Directions are given to the authorities concerned by Suo-motu taking cognizance of news appeared in the news paper dated 10-01-2008 with regard to mis-appropriation of Government funds by the officers by manipulating records and not providing education and mid-day meals to the children of Tribals in the State of Andhra Pradesh.

It is observed that nearly 30% of the cases related to police excesses and rest cover family life, education, health, salaries, etc.

### Recommendations

The APHRC has made several recommendations to the Govt. on various aspects of life of citizens. Some of them relate to Marriage Laws, Penal Laws. Traffic Rules, Environmental Laws.

## Status

The Human Rights Commission is neither a parallel body nor established to dominate any institution or Government body or agency. It is an autonomous and independent body working for betterment of human rights and is concerned about violation of such rights.

**Compliance of the Reports**

The relationship between the Government and the Commission is cordial. It is one of cooperation rather than confrontation. Accordingly to the Commission Government is "responding positively in complying with the directions and recommendations in all the cases". However the alternative before Government is "implement or explain".

**Secret of Success**

The working of the Commission is regarded as "impressive". It is one of the better working Commissions. It is viewed as a 'better protector' of the Human Rights. Its efforts to translate Human Rights from a dream to reality are well recognized. Not only the ordinary citizens but also MLAs, MPs and Opposition parties are knocking at the door of the Commission for justice. The growing importance of the Commission is attributed mainly to the dynamic, leadership, dedicated and committed service of its Chairperson. He is a self-motivated person who constantly motivates the staff working under his able leadership. One gets the impression that 'work is worship' for him. Cent percent compliance of the Orders of the Commission by the Govt. shows the credibility and respect the Chairperson commands with the Govt. The Chairperson regards the press and the NGOs as two eyes of the Commission. "The press and electronic media are giving due publicity to the activities of the Commission whenever orders are being passed in sensitive matters and matters of social importance resulting in awareness in general public about their valuable rights". Here, in the Commission justice is done but not delayed and not denied. There is a woman behind the success of a man, is the old saying. There is a man behind the success of a woman, is the current observation. It is equally true that there is a person behind the success of any organization. That person behind the success of the AP HRC is Honorable Mr. B. SUBHASHAN REDDY.

**Conclusion**

People are reposing faith and confidence in an increasing manner in the Commission. This is evident from the fact that the number of cases have increased manifold from nearly 3000 to 35000 in the last more than 4 years of the existence of the Commission. This may be due to the fact that people have realized the importance of Human Rights and role of the Commission in protecting the same.

The Commission at present is without a library and training division. Nearly 15000 cases are pending disposal. The two members and the Secretary are over burdened due to the vacancy of the third member since last 2 ½ years.

The Commission does not have its own investigating team. It depends upon the Government officials for investigating the cases. As against a demand of 6 core budget demand, the Commission was sanctioned an amount of Rs. 97,98,000/- in the financial year 2008-09. In order to enable the Commission to discharge the functions as a facilitator and protector of Human Rights, the sanctioned 14 members may be posted without further loss of time and the budget may be increased as demanded by the Commission. In order to reduce the burden of work on the Chairperson, member and the secretary, the vacancy of another member may be filled in.

## References

1. Human rights Commissions functions in 1. Assam, 2. Himachal Pradesh, 3. Jammu and Kashmir, 4. Karnataka, 5. Kerala, 6. Madhya Pradesh, 7. Maharashtra, 8. Manipur, 9. Orissa, 10. Punjab, 11. Rajasthan, 12. Tamil Nadu, 13. Uttar Pradesh, 14. West Bengal, 15. Chattisgarh and 16. Gujarat.
2. G.O Ms. No. 48, dated 28-01-2005, Human rights cell, General Admin Dept, Govt. of A.P.
3. Ibid, Para 2.
4. Annual Report, 12-08-2009.
5. The Protection of Human Rights Act. 1993. National Human Rights Commission, Faridkot House, Copernicus Marg, New Delhi – 110 001.
6. Interviews with Chairperson, Secretary, Deputy Registrar and other staff of the Commission.
7. Press Cutting.

# 7

# THE CIVIL RIGHTS MOVEMENT: A GLORIOUS CHAPTER IN HUMAN RIGHTS IN THE U.S.

**K.C. Sreekumar**

Any person engaged in global human rights discussions would be interested in the following quote from a book on the US political system:

> "In many countries throughout the world, human rights are not protected to the extent that they are in the United States. In some nations, people are imprisoned, tortured, or killed because they oppose the current regime. In other nations, certain ethnic or racial groups are oppressed by the majority population.
>
> What can you do to work for the improvement of human rights in other nations[1]?"

What happens in other nations? Certain ethnic or racial groups are oppressed. What kind of oppression? They are imprisoned, tortured, ridiculed, ill-treated, segregated and even killed. Bywhom? The majority population. Should we understand that only the majority population can do such dastardly activities? Doesn't history tell us about powerful minorities treating hapless majorities in such manner? Then is it a thing of the past, sleeping in dreary, dusty pages of history? Before answering that should we ask ourselves the question whether we should treat these as human rights violations? If these indeed are then these are not a thing of the past but very much a part of the present. That is natural because man is an exploiting animal. From the words quoted we learn that in many countries human rights are not protected as they are in the U.S. Inherent in these words is the statement that human rights violations are more in many countries than in the U.S. Nobody is happy that human rights violations take place in many countries. But we are pleased to note that the U.S. takes particular interest in protection of human rights. However, that is not due to any revelation or sudden enlightenment of the people of that country but thanks mainly to a long drawn process of agitations by a section of the population of the U.S., especially the African Americans. Their fervent desire to live as human beings enabled them to fight for that cause and their endurance and perseverance ennobled them. Their fight for being treated as human beings, their strife for their rights, indeed is a glorious chapter in the history of the U.S., no, in the history of mankind. We are delighted by their victories but at the same time dejected by the fact that they are still forced to continue their fight. Now it is high time that we looked into the bleak past of the Blacks in the U.S. and their bold march to a bright future, the Civil Rights Movement.

**Slavery in the U.S.**

The first record of African slavery in British Colonial America was made on August 20, 1619 by the arrival of twenty captured Africans who were brought by a Dutch ship and sold as slaves at Jamestown. However, it is now believed that a Spanish explorer named Lucas Vasquez de Avllon, who founded the San Miguel de Gualdape colony (most likely located in the Winvah Bay area of present-day South Carolina) brought the first African slaves in 1526. Most of the blacks who were brought to the country during the initial stage were indentured servants (servants who were bound by contract). They were freed many years later, when the terms of their servitude contract ended. Later the 'chattel slavery' system (outright ownership of a human being and of his /her descendants was established. Almost all of the African Americans are the descendants of captive Africans who survived the slavery era. Today they are the single largest racial minority in the U.S. and they form the second largest racial group after the whites.[2] By 1775, Africans made up 20% of the population in the American colonies, which made them the second largest ethnic group after the English. There was an evolutionary growth from indentured servitude to racial slavery. There were no laws relating to slavery in the history of Virginia till 1640, in which year the courts had sentenced at least one black servant to slavery. Persons with African origins were not English citizens by birth and hence they were not covered by English Common Law. In 1656 a baptized Christian daughter of a free Englishman could win her freedom in the Virginia courts. To enslave even such people, Virginia passed in 1662 a law stating that any children of an enslaved mother would follow her status and automatically be slaves, no matter if the father was a freeborn Englishman. This was sufficient to free the white men from any legal responsibility to acknowledge or support their children. Exploitation went a step further with the Virginia Slave Codes of 1705 which defined as slaves those people imported from nations that were not Christian, as well as Native Americans who were sold to colonists by other Native Americans. By the 18th century, colonial courts and legislatures had racialized slavery, by applying it nearly exclusively to Black Africans and people of African descent, and occasionally to Native Americans.

**Brutality Towards the Slaves**

Historians of slavery in the U.S tell us that the slaves were treated in a very harsh and brutal manner.[3] The lives of slaves were regulated by legally authorized violence. Slaves were punished with a variety of objects and instruments. Some of these included: whips, being placed in chains and shackles, or in various contraptions such as metal collars, or being hanged. Weapons such as knives, guns, field tools, and objects found nearby were also used to punish them. To punish a pregnant woman, workers might dig a hole for her to rest her belly while being whipped. After whipping several slaves the overseers might direct bursting the wounds and rubbing them with turpentine and red pepper. Another report was that the overseer took a brick, ground it into a powder, mixed it with lard and rubbed it all over the slave.[4] Thick and heavy metal collars were put on slaves to remind them of their wrongdoings. Often these collars had protruding spikes that made fieldwork difficult and prevented the slave from sleeping while lying down. Louis Cain, a former slave, describes his witness to another slave being punished, "One nigger run to the woods to be a jungle nigger, but massa cotched him with the dog and took a hot iron and brands him. Then he put a bell on him, in a wooden frame what slip over the shoulders and under the arms. He made that nigger wear the bell a year and took it off on Christmas for a present to him. It sho' did make a good nigger out of him[5]". Slaves could lose their family members any moment because they could be sold by the owners. It was not unusual for enslaved black women to be raped by their owners, members of their owner's families, or their owner's friends.

During the American Revolution they fought side by side with the Englishmen to secure independence. The Atlantic slave trade helped the U.S. to have 3.5 million enslaved African Americans by 1860. At the same time there were 500,000 free African Americans. The slaves were officially freed by the Emancipation Proclamation made by the President Abraham Lincoln on January 1, 1863. During the post-war reconstruction period the African Americans could make a good degree of economic and social progress. However, such progressive endeavors of the depressed were thwarted, in the late 1890s, by the Southern states that enacted the cruel Jim Crow laws to enforce racial segregation and disenfranchisement. The noble ideals of the Revolution were thus challenged by the white enslaver and exploiter. As the Hobbesian man in the state of nature, the desolate African Americans thought about ways to overcome their predicament. We need not doubt the wisdom of the great American thinker Raymond Aron when he says in his book 'Peace and War' that turbulent eras are rich in meditation. Such a meditation led to movements to fight violence and discrimination against the African Americans, a great part of which was played by the Civil Rights Movement. However, as early as 1837 an Antislavery Convention of American Women met in New York City. Both black and white women participated in it. After a decade the women's rights movement was launched. There were other movements such as the Pennsylvania Abolition Society and the New York Manumission Society that demanded abolition of slavery. Many organizations advocating the movement of black people from the United States to locations where they would enjoy greater freedom were started during the first half of the 19th century. Thus the American Colonization Society (A.C.S.) established colony in Liberia, and enabled thousands of former African American slaves and free black people to move there from the U.S. Slavery was declared a personal sin by a religious movement led by William Lloyd Garrison. He demanded the slave owners to repent immediately and start the process of emancipation. This movement, among many other forces, could even cause the American Civil War. Even the Church split into Northern and Southern over the question of slavery[6]. While the Northern Baptists opposed slavery the Southern Baptists were for it. The Home Mission Society of the Northern Baptists declared in 1844 that a person could not be a missionary and still keep slaves as property[7]. Besides these, there were many armed uprisings by the slaves during the period between 1700 and 1859[8]. Finally the Supreme Court decision in 1857, in the Dred Scott case led to the Civil War and the Emancipation Proclamation that ensued. This peep into the history of slavery in the U.S. is helpful to understand the scenario in which the Civil Rights Movement originated and became successful in the country.

## The Reconstruction Period and the Constitutional Measures

During the Reconstruction period following the Civil War, many constitutional measures were adopted to fully emancipate and protect the slaves. The Thirteenth, Fourteenth and Fifteenth Amendments to the Constitution were made mainly for that. The Thirteenth Amendment was adopted in 1865 to forbid slavery. Nevertheless, the southern states cunningly adopted Black Codes that relegated blacks to second-class citizenship. These states held the view that this Amendment did not give the Congress the power to adopt civil rights laws. To face those objections the Congress proposed the Fourteenth Amendment, which was adopted in 1868. The equal protection clause, which prevents the states from denying to any person the equal protection of the law, was included in this Amendment. The Fifteenth Amendment (1870) states that, the right of citizens of the United States to vote shall not be denied or abridged by the United States or by any State on account of race, colour, or previous condition of servitude. The national government and most of the state governments were under the control of President Lincoln's Republican Party at the end of the Civil War. And the Party was actually controlled by a strong antislavery group called the Radical Republicans. They were instrumental in passing the Thirteenth, Fourteenth, and Fifteenth Amendments to the Constitution, known as the 'Civil War amendments'. They could force the

Congress to pass a series of civil rights acts for enforcing these amendments. They had a political intention as well. They wanted to curb the influence of the Democrats in the South with the help of the African Americans. Thus the Civil Rights Act of 1866 extended citizenship to all those born in the US and gave African Americans full equality before the law. The Civil Rights Act of 1872 made it a federal crime for anyone to use law or custom to deprive an individual of his or her rights, privileges, and immunities secured by the Constitution or by any federal law. The Civil Rights Act of 1875 declared that everyone is entitled to full and equal enjoyment of public accommodations, theatres, and other places of public amusement, and it imposed penalties for violators.

These constitutional measures were not sufficient to bring to an end racial discrimination in the country. The Jim Crow laws could effectively prevent the desired development. The Civil Rights Laws were effectively nullified by the Civil rights Cases and the case of Plessy v. Ferguson . The Supreme Court invalidated the Civil Rights Act of 1875 when it held that the discriminatory acts of private citizens were not illegal. The Court held that if "one race be inferior to the other socially, the Constitution of the United States cannot put them on the same plane[9]." The court declared that the individual invasion of the individual rights was not the subject matter of the Fourteenth Amendment. Here, it should be noted that, guaranteeing equal rights for all, the Fourteenth Amendment states that, "No state shall make or enforce any law which shall abridge the privileges or immunities of citizens of the United States; nor shall any state deprive any person of life, liberty, or property, without due process of law; nor deny to any person within its jurisdiction the equal protection of the laws." The phrase "equal protection of the laws" could be taken in its broad sense or the narrow one. In the broad sense it means that the Constitution is colour-blind and that no state is permitted to treat the whites and the blacks differently. In the narrow sense "equal protection" meant that blacks and whites had certain fundamental legal rights in common, but otherwise they could be treated differently. The Supreme Court, adopting the narrow view, decided in 1883 that it was unconstitutional for Congress to prohibit racial discrimination in public accommodations such as hotels[10]. The whites all over the country were happy about the Court decision and were ready to forget the Civil War amendments and the Civil Rights legislation. Meanwhile the proslavery groups could gain political control in the South. All these resulted in the 'separate-but-equal doctrine' which made racial segregation constitutional.

Just in the case of slum dwelling the blacks were confined to certain underdeveloped areas. They were physically prevented from having all- white neighbourhoods. Statistics of racial brutality shows that between 1882 and 1946, 4,715 people, about three-fourths of them blacks, were lynched in the US[11]. Perhaps the worst racial riot in American history was the one that took place in Detroit in 1943 over the question of housing. After the riots the African Americans were permitted to move to a Polish American section of the city. But in Chicago during the immediate post-World War II period the blacks were routed out of all-white neighbourhoods[12]. This made their social, educational and economic development almost impossible. The right to vote given to the blacks for a brief period became meaningless due to the intervention of the Southern politicians, who regained control of several state governments. President Truman took a bold stand in favour of the civil rights and appointed a Special Committee on Civil Rights. However, the recommendations of the Committee were not acceptable to the Congress. This even led to a split in the Democratic Party. Albeit the southern "Dixiecrats" deserted the Democratic Party and supported their own presidential candidate, Truman could win the election in 1948. However, it is observed that "the threat of political disunion over civil rights discouraged bold actions by presidents or Congress for about fifteen years[13]."Moreover, the fear of Communism loomed large over the society and politics of the U.S after the World War[14]. This made enacting new reforms difficult and made even the existing reforms ineffective. The whites could characterise all demands for civil rights as 'communist' and that was the most dreaded word in the U.S.

**Legal Measures**

The inequality in the treatment of the coloured people was challenged in the courts by many individuals and associations. The National Association for the Advancement of Coloured People (NAACP) helped this process in a big way. This association was formed in the year 1909 by W.E.B. Du Bois with the help of both black and white activists. It is the largest and most popular civil rights organization in the country. It took initiative in filing a series of law suits in the 1930s to admit African Americans to state professional schools. A prolonged and well planned legal struggle by the black leaders and organizations shifted the key civil-rights decisions from the legislature to the judiciary. By 1950, the Supreme Court had ruled that African Americans who were admitted to a state university could not be assigned to separate sections of class rooms, libraries, and cafeterias. In the Brown v. Board of Education of Topeka the Supreme Court unanimously decided that public school segregation of races violates the equal protection clause of the Fourteenth Amendment. Chief Justice Earl Warren found that "in the field of public education the doctrine of 'separate but equal' has no place" because "separate educational facilities are inherently unequal[15]." Thus the Supreme Court unanimously overruled Plessy V. Ferguson and thus put an end to "separate but equal". However, implementation of such a landmark decision was indeed difficult and for that also the court had to intervene. So in Brown II, the Court asked the lower courts to ensure that African Americans are admitted to schools on a non-discriminatory basis "with all deliberate speed[16]." However, such moves were resisted by the many educational institutions and even by government officials like the Arkansas governor. Noted among these was the "Southern Manifesto" signed by more than one hundred southern members of Congress. This Manifesto condemned the Brown decision as an "abuse of judicial power" and vowed to "use all lawful means to bring about a reversal of the decision." Social segregation still continued and the African Americans had to make much more organized efforts to get civil rights included in the political agenda, and to put an end to congressional barriers to making requisite legislation. This in turn required, among many other measures, mobilizing public opinion in favour of that also. The civil rights movement was a strong step toward that direction.

**The Civil Rights Movement**

Besides the causes mentioned elsewhere in this article, two noteworthy changes that took place in the first half of the twentieth century ultimately led to the successful black civil rights movement. Economic changes, especially the decline of "King Cotton" in the South, and the resultant large scale migration of the blacks from the South to the North improved their economic opportunities and enfranchisement. This in turn led to the formation of 'black community' and political organizations such as the National Association for the Advancement of Coloured People (NAACP), The Student Non-violent Coordinating Committee (SNCC), The Congress of Racial Equality (CORE), the Southern Christian Leadership Conference (SCLC), etc. These organizations could bring to the attention of the whole world the kind of racial segregation that was practised in the U.S, and project their demand for equal treatment. For placing the demand on the political agenda of the nation a long and enduring struggle was launched and this is known as the Civil Rights Movement. Its origin was partially accidental and partially deliberate.

Rosa Parks, an African American woman, made history in December 1955 by not permitting to be cowed down by the segregation laws. During a bus journey in Montgomery, Alabama was asked by the driver to vacate her seat for a white person and disobeying which the driver, using the emergency police power vested on him by the city segregation law, arrested her. She was the secretary of the local chapter of the NAACP. Because of this, her case received the attention of the leaders of her community who decided to make maximum use of the opportunity to fight the unjust system of racial segregation. Many church and civil rights groups organized a boycott of bus service in Montgomery[17]. For an entire year, African Americans boycotted the Montgomery bus line. The protest was headed by a twenty-seven-year-old Baptist minister, Reverend Martin Luther King, Jr. During the protest period, he went to jail, and his house was bombed. Blacks were harassed and black leaders were threatened with assassination. The arrest of the leaders for conspiring to interfere with business attracted the attention of the media from all over the world. This helped attract sympathy of northerners. Civil disobedience was the tactic the movement used. This helped to attract the attention of all concerned to the injustices of segregation laws. Finally, in 1956, the federal district court issued an injunction prohibiting the segregation of buses in Montgomery. The glorious era of civil rights movement thus commenced. Peter B. Levy observes that, "Rosa Park's action was to the civil rights movement what the Battle of Lexington and Concord was to the American Revolution: a shot- in this case a non-violent one- heard round the world. It set in motion a series of acts of defiance aimed at gaining full equality that grew in intensity over the course of the next ten to fifteen years[18]." The Montgomery agitation was beneficial to the blacks in many ways. The desegregation injected into them a sense of self respect because of which they began to treat themselves as first class citizens. The kind of publicity their agitation gained pointed towards the usefulness of creating world public opinion in favour of their genuine demands. This is comparable to the first successes that Gandhi attained in South Africa. There is no wonder that King adopted the same non-violent technique for his agitations.

King formed the Southern Christian Leadership Conference (SCLC) in 1957 and pursued Gandhian non-violent techniques to fight for the cause of equal treatment of the African Americans. The next decade has witnessed large number of sit-ins, freedom rides, and freedom marches by African Americans. The number of white sympathisers also increased. The contrasting image of non-violent African Americans and violent, hostile whites created strong public support for the civil rights movement.

There was no dearth of such incidents. African Americans in Greensboro, North Carolina, were refused service in a Woolworth's lunch counter. They organized a sit-in which was increasingly supported by African Americans and white sympathisers. Though white customers retaliated violently, within six months, hundreds of Woolworth lunch counters within the South started serving African American customers. There was segregation in inter-state buses and trains for a long time and this also was brought to an end by resorting to the sit-in technique by the African Americans. Nevertheless, by September 1961, more than 3,600 students had been arrested for participating in civil rights demonstrations and 141 students and 58 faculty members had been expelled by colleges and universities for their part in civil rights protests.

There were incidents connected with desegregation of schools as well. Complying with the court orders Little Rock, Arkansas, had desegregated its buses, libraries, and public parks. Out of the eligible black population nearly one-third got registered as voters. As a part of a plan to desegregate the schools nine black students were enrolled at Central High School in the fall of 1957. However, the white governor of Arkansas Orval Faubus, who was looking forward to getting re-elected, was afraid of losing the support of the pro-segregationists. Shedding his moderate garb he objected desegregation stating that the people overwhelmingly opposed it. But the NAACP was not prepared to take it like that and its lawyers approached the court which ordered Little Rock to go ahead with the desegregation plans. Instead of accepting that the Governor sent the National Guardsmen to the Central High, where nine black students were admitted, to help the whites in forbidding the black students from entering the school. One black student was almost manhandled by the white mob. President Eisenhower's interference was necessitated by the adamant stand taken by the governor and the whites. He dispatched a contingent of thousand soldiers to Little Rock to restore, as he said, "the image of America and all its parts as one nation, indivisible, with liberty and justice for all[19]." Albeit so much bold steps were taken by the very president of the nation what was the benefit that the blacks of the locality gained out of all these is our major consideration. The Little Rock and following it many other school districts closed their schools rather than permit the blacks to enter and pollute the environment. Moreover, the white students got themselves transferred to private academies which were not covered by the Brown decision. Despite court interventions to open the schools, it is on record, that, only 2.3 percent of all the southern black children attended desegregated public schools even after seven years.

**Student Participation**

Disgusted by the inability of the political and social leaders and the judicial system to put an end to the unequal treatment of the Blacks, the student community of the nation jumped on the band wagon of the Civil Rights Movement. The success of their sit-in mode of agitation on many places and occasions emboldened them to demand "freedom now!" To coordinate their activities the students formed, in 1960, the Student Non-violent Coordinating Committee (SNCC). Thousands of black students from all parts of the nation, who were dedicated and prepared to demand their due place in society, eagerly joined the new organization. Though its philosophy was initially rooted in non-violence, and the blacks and the whites working together, over the course of time, that underwent change and militancy and radicalism of its new members enabled it to stand for black power. Unthinkable as it was in the late 1960s, I would call the demand for black power, revolutionary. The electoral politics of the nation as being played by the Republicans and the Democrats helped in strengthening the SNCC as well as the black community. It was with the help of the black voters that the Democratic presidential candidate John F. Kennedy could defeat his Republican rival Richard Nixon. When Martin Luther King, Jr., was arrested a few days before the presidential election, the presidential candidates John F. Kennedy and Richard M. Nixon faced a dilemma as to whether they should support King or not. The Republican candidate Nixon, eyeing on the southern white votes, chose to ignore King. On the other hand, losing no time, Kennedy called King's wife to express his support. That was sufficient enough to cause "little short of delirium in black communities throughout the nation[20]." It was the large black majorities in key northern cities that made the difference in Kennedy's election. Though at the time of the election Kennedy promised to end discrimination in federally funded housing he didn't gave much priority to that or the other demands of the African Americans because of his need for getting support of the Southern states for his economic and foreign policies.

**Freedom Rides and the March on Washington**

A small group of African American, non-violent, activists formed an organization called the Congress for Racial Equality (CORE) during the World War II. The Journey of Reconciliation held by the CORE sought to desegregate transportation in the upper south, in 1947. Though it gained fame and momentum immediately following its formation, it gradually lost all that and became almost insignificant. However, it staged a come back in 1961 when it organized freedom rides with thirteen black and white persons who were to travel by two separate buses through the South in a desegregated manner. They were to use the rest rooms, waiting rooms, etc. also in the same manner. The violent reaction of white segregationist brought the issue into the attention of the world. Despite the President's interference the violence continued. The blacks under the leadership of Martin Luther King, Jr., faced all that in a non-violent manner.

However, protests sometimes became violent and one such incident took place in Birmingham, Alabama in the year 1963. Following that King and his followers were arrested and put behind the bars. From the jail King wrote the famous "Letter from a Birmingham Jail" in which he said that as a Christian, like the apostles and Jesus he felt compelled to carry the gospel of freedom beyond his home town. About the urgency of that he wrote, "For years now I have heard the word 'wait!' It rings in the ear of every Negro with piercing familiarity. This 'Wait' has almost always meant 'Never'. We must come to see, with one of our distinguished jurists, that 'justice too long delayed is justice denied.'... We have waited for more than 340 years for our constitutional and God-given rights. The nations of Asia and Africa are moving with jet-like speed toward gaining political independence, but we still creep at a horse-and-buggy pace toward gaining a cup of coffee at a lunch counter. Perhaps it is easy for those who have never felt the stinging darts of segregation to say, "Wait". But when you have seen vicious mobs lynch your mothers and fathers ... when you see the vast majority of your twenty million Negro brothers smothering in the airtight cage of poverty in the midst of an affluent society ... when you suddenly find your tongue twisted and your speech stammering as you seek to explain to your six-year old daughter why she can't go to the public amusement park that has just been advertised on television ... and see ominous clouds of inferiority beginning to distort her personality by developing an unconscious bitterness toward white people ... then you will understand why we find it difficult to wait[21]."

In the wake of King's release the SCLC continued the agitation vigorously and the agitators were arrested and put behind the bars, which resulted in filling the jails beyond capacity. So the Police Commissioner Eugene "Bull" Connor decided to handle the civil rights protesters brutally and he unleashed police dogs and used electric cattle prods against the protesters. The national television enabled viewers to see how the protesters were met with and that enraged many. There were 758 demonstrations in 186 cities across the South within the short span of ten weeks following the Birmingham campaign. Perhaps the culmination was the March on Washington in August 1963.This was organized under the leadership of A. Philip Randolph[22]. All important civil rights organizations took part in it and almost a quarter-million African Americans and whites participated in it and millions watched it on television. The most important speaker was Martin Luther King, Jr., who spoke of his dream: "I have a dream that my four little children will one day live in a nation where they will not be judged by the colour of their skin but by the content of their character. ... When we let freedom ring, when we let it ring from every village and every hamlet, from every state and every city, we will be able to speed up that day when all God's children, black men and white men, Jews and Gentiles, Protestants and Catholics, will be able to join hands and sing in the words of that old Negro Spiritual, "Free at last! Free at last! Thank God almighty, we are free at last[23]!"

### Legislative Measures to End the Jim Crow Conditions

These agitations resulted in the Civil Rights Acts of 1964 and 1968 and the Voting Rights Act of 1965. Out of these the Civil Rights Act of 1964 was the most far-reaching legislation on Civil Rights in modern times. It forbade discrimination on the basis of race, colour, religion, gender, and national origin. The major provisions of the Act were as follows:

1. It outlawed arbitrary discrimination in voter registration.
2. It banned racial discrimination in public accommodations (hotels, restaurants, terminals, movie theatres, etc.)
3. It authorized the federal government to sue to desegregate public schools and facilities.
4. It expanded the power of the Civil Rights Commission and extended its life.
5. It provided for withholding of federal funds from programs administered in a discriminatory manner.
6. It established the right to equality of opportunity in employment.

Title VII of the Act prohibits discrimination in employment based on race, colour, religion, gender, or national origin. The Act created the Equal Employment Opportunity Commission (EEOC), to administer Title VII.

### Enfranchisement

A skimpy 29.1 per cent of African Americans of voting age were registered in the southern states in 1960. At the same time 61.1 percent of whites had franchise. The southern stated denied the blacks the right to vote. In the 1880s the Supreme Court ruled that the states had no duty to protect black voters against white mobs. To further discourage the blacks the southern states began in 1890 to "legally" disenfranchise them by revising state constitutions. Legislations were made to impose some voting requirements such as literacy tests and special taxes on voting ("poll taxes"). For most of the blacks and a small section of the poor and illiterate whites these posed hurdles. Many state adopted the "grandfather clauses," which exempted people from literacy tests if their grandfathers had been legally registered to vote, to increase the number of white voters. Naturally this condition could exclude the blacks. However, the Supreme Court struck down the grandfather clause in 1915[24]. But the South could not be browbeaten like that. The new weapon that the southern states used was called the white primary. Since the Democratic Party dominated the South, the winner of its primary was certain to win any general election. By conducting primaries in which only whites could vote, the party effectively eliminated black political participation[25]. Such voting restrictions dramatically diminished the number of registered black voters. For example, in Louisiana, there were 130,344 black voters in 1896. The state constitution was revised, in 1898, in such a way that there were only 5'000 registered black voters in 1900 and that became 1,772 in 1916[26]. It was after paying a huge price that the blacks won the right to vote. The SNCC and like-minded organizations set up the Freedom Summer in Mississippi in which white and black volunteers helped blacks to register to vote and organize Freedom Schools. As the Democratic Party of the state was white-dominated the blacks formed the Mississippi Freedom Democratic Party (MFDP). Further, SCLC and King, Jr., organized a campaign in Selma in Alabama. The authorities faced the non-violent protests of even black teachers with much violence. Thousands of demonstrators including King were arrested and kept in jails. The march from Selma to Montgomery, organized in protest against the killing of an activist by the police, also was brutally dispersed by the authorities. The whites killed even a Unitarian minister. Nonetheless, King and his followers organized another march from Selma to Montgomery on March 21, 1965. This time, President Johnson ordered Alabama guardsmen to give protection to the marchers. The twenty-five thousand-strong march was a grand success. All these forced the President to take immediate action to enfranchise the eligible black population. He told members of Congress and a national television audience that further delay in guaranteeing the right to vote to black Americans would be intolerable. He signed the Voting Rights Act into law on August 6, 1965. Important Provisions of the Act included: (1) Suspension of the discriminatory voter registration tests (literacy tests), and (2) Authorization of federal registration of persons and federally administered voting procedures in any political subdivision or state that did electoral discriminated against a particular group.

In order to facilitate massive voter registration of African Americans and their increased political participation federal voter registrars were sent to areas, particularly in the South. Earlier in these places only less than 50 percent of the eligible population was registered to vote. This helped the process of. As early as 1966, the percentage of eligible voters registered had increased to 27.8 in Mississippi, 48.9 in Alabama, 46.7 in Virginia, 48 in South Carolina, and 43.2 in Georgia[27]. Also, there was a dramatic increase in the number of elected black officials all over the South reaching nearly 1,500 by 1970[28]. The first black political convention was held in Gary, Indiana, in 1972. The blacks who called themselves "freedom democrats" were aware about their role as the vanguard in the struggle for a new society. This substantial increase in black political power changed the perception of state and local governments as to how the black constituents should be treated. It is interesting to note that those white politicians who played the "white supremacy" card to gain political positions for a long time had to turn to the blacks now to get their electoral support.

Nevertheless, a section of the blacks disagreed with the non-violent methods pursued by King and others. They took to rioting in Los Angeles, resulting in the death of thirty-four persons and the destruction of much property. It was felt that there were differences regarding the grievances, and methods to be pursued for the ventilation of the grievances of the blacks of the north and the south. Rising up to the occasion Stokely Carmichael, the new chief of SNCC, coined the new slogan, "Black Power", which instantly replaced the old one, "Freedom Now". Rather than integrating with the whites it was the power to do things for themselves that was required by the blacks. They hoped that this would enable them to overcome notions of black inferiority and white supremacy[29]. This lead to more antagonism between the whites and the blacks and that resulted in further race-violence. So King disapproved this slogan. But the open housing marches that he organized in all-white neighbourhoods in Chicago were attacked by the whites despite the protection provided by the authorities. A section of the blacks in Chicago had no faith in the non-violent methods of King. But then this was not the case of the blacks of Chicago alone. The blacks in many parts of the country wanted to retaliate against the white violence. A section of the white supporters of civil rights movement, of course, was against such violence. In the opinion polls conducted in 1964 and in 1968 over two-thirds of the whites interviewed said that the civil rights movement was pushing too fast, had hurt the black cause, and was too violent[30]. King's demands for a legislation for open housing met with success in 1968, but only after his assassination. Meanwhile the special committee that President Johnson appointed to investigate the causes of the riots and suggest measures to prevent the occurrence of those, reported that the riots were caused by the poor social conditions of the ghetto, which were created, maintained and condoned by the white institutions. It recommended that a better society be built by a "massive and sustained effort" by the nation[31]. While the conservatives opposed the findings of the commission, people like King and Robert Kennedy supported those.

It is worth noting that the endeavour to advance civil rights through legislative action has continued to recent times. The Civil Rights Act of 1991 is the result of a two- year struggle within Congress, and between Congress and the President. This legislation is meant to refine and clarify procedures regarding enforcement of non-discrimination provisions of earlier civil rights laws. This law was necessitated by dissatisfaction with a series of Supreme Court rulings that made it more difficult to sue in job discrimination cases. Embarrassed by the court decisions civil rights leaders turned for help to Congress which was dominated by a combination of liberal Democrats and southerners who depended on the African American vote for re-election. Here also politics became the art of the possible and the Civil Rights Act of 1991 was born.

One provision of the Act deals with hiring and promotion practices, including tests that appear to be fair on their face, but when applied, have a "disparate impact". The Act holds that when an employment practice can be shown to have disparate impact, then the responsibility to justify the practice shifts to the employer, who must make obvious that the practice is required by business obligation. The Supreme Court ruling that held that it was the complainant's burden to prove that the practice was not related to business necessity[32]. The Act rejected the Supreme Court decision that the federal law applied only to discrimination in hiring and not to discrimination in dismissals, promotions, and other actions taken after an individual was hired[33]. It applied discrimination protections to actions taken after the point of being hired. The Act further enhanced the ability of those who feel they have been discriminated against in employment to seek redress in the courts and to receive compensation when their complaint of discrimination is proved valid.

One wonders whether the Civil Right cases in the U.S. would come to an end at any time. While considering a case that has been termed the Brown v. Board of Education of higher education the federal court in Mississippi ruled, in 1995, that the state's practice of historically different admission standards for the different schools to be unacceptable and ordered the state to spend more money to upgrade the black colleges. On the other hand, the Supreme Court agreed with a lower federal court ruling that overturned the University of Maryland's programme of blacks-only scholarships, in spite of the school's declaration that this programme was designed to remedy its past discrimination. Former U.S. President George Bush had to agree that, while schools in the U.S were no longer segregated by law, they were still not equal in opportunity and excellence. According to him, "Justice requires that every school teach every child in America. The habits of racism in America have not all been broken. Laws against racial discrimination must be vigorously enforced in education and housing and hiring and public accommodations[34]."

President Barack Obama is committed to expanding funding for the Justice Department's Civil Rights Division to ensure that voting rights are protected and Americans do not suffer from increased discrimination during a time of economic distress. He signed the Lilly Ledbetter Fair Pay Restoration Act to ensure that all Americans receive equal pay for equal work, on January 29, 2009. The appointment of Sonia Sotomayor as a judge of the Supreme Court in August 8, 2009 was a manifestation of his commitment to certain values, about which he is always vociferous. Much before that appointment, he expressed his views in a speech. He thought that the Constitution could be interpreted in many ways. Interpreting the Constitution in a cramped and narrow way makes the Constitution and the courts simply rubber stamps of the powerful in society. There can be another vision that makes the courts the refuge of the powerless. "And we need somebody who's got the heart — the empathy — to recognize what it's like to be a young teenage mom. The empathy to understand what it's like to be poor or African-American or gay or disabled or old—and that's the criteria by which I'll be selecting my judges[35]."

Obama made a memorable speech after signing into law the Matthew Shepard and James Byrd, Jr. Hate Crimes Prevention Act, on October 28, 2009. He said, "You know, as a nation we've come far on the journey towards a more perfect union. And today, we've taken another step forward. ... This is the culmination of a struggle that has lasted more than a decade. Time and again, we faced opposition. Time and again, the measure was defeated or delayed. Time and again we've been reminded of the difficulty of building a nation in which we're all free to live and love as we see fit. But the cause endured and the struggle continued, waged by the family of Matthew Shepard, by the family of James Byrd, by folks who held vigils and led marches, by those who rallied and organized and refused to give up, by the late Senator Ted Kennedy who fought so hard for this legislation and all who toiled for years to reach this day.

You understood that we must stand against crimes that are meant not only to break bones, but to break spirits—not only to inflict harm, but to instil fear. You understand that the rights afforded every citizen under our Constitution mean nothing if we do not protect those rights—both from unjust laws and violent acts. And you understand how necessary this law continues to be.

In the most recent year for which we have data, the FBI reported roughly 7,600 hate crimes in this country. Over the past 10 years, there were more than 12,000 reported hate crimes based on sexual orientation alone. And we will never know how many incidents were never reported at all.

And that's why, through this law, we will strengthen the protections against crimes based on the colour of your skin, the faith in your heart, or the place of your birth. We will finally add federal protections against crimes based on gender, disability, gender identity, or sexual orientation. And prosecutors will have new tools to work with states in order to prosecute to the fullest those who would perpetrate such crimes. Because no one in America should ever be afraid to walk down the street holding the hands of the person they love. No one in America should be forced to look over their shoulder because of who they are or because they live with a disability. ... We have for centuries strived to live up to our founding ideal, of a nation where all are free and equal and able to pursue their own version of happiness. Through conflict and tumult, through the morass of hatred and prejudice, through periods of division and discord we have endured and grown stronger and fairer and freer. And at every turn, we've made progress not only by changing laws but by changing hearts, by our willingness to walk in another's shoes, by our capacity to love and accept even in the face of rage and bigotry.... That is the promise of America. Over the sounds of hatred and chaos, over the din of grief and anger, we can still hear those ideals -- even when they are faint, even when some would try to drown them out. At our best we seek to make sure those ideals can be heard and felt by Americans everywhere. And that work did not end in 1968. It certainly does not end today[36]."

**Conclusion**

The African Americans made a great leap through the Civil Rights Movement in man's perpetual struggle for securing more and more human rights. It is rightly observed that by developing the civil rights movement the blacks could broaden their base of support in both elite and public opinion and thus to raise civil rights matters from a low to a high position on the political agenda[37]. The civil rights movement brought to light the problem of poverty prevalent among the African Americans and forced the policy makers to enable them to come out of that predicament. As a result the very society that looked down upon the African Americans as a liability became aware that they are an asset and that they have a natural right to be treated as equal to any other section of the American society. This is not to say that racism is completely wiped out from the nation. However, disparaging the significance of an African American being elected the President of the nation would be highly erroneous. As Prof. Robin Kelley of the University of Southern California observes "...Obama's politics of hope – his vision of uniting the nation around the creation of a caring, compassionate culture built from the "bottom up"- is actually rooted in the traditions of abolition-democracy, the ex-slaves' post-emancipation Republicanism, and Obama's own direct experience organizing the black urban poor in Chicago[38]."

Like many of the movements started in the U.S., the Civil Rights Movement also has its impact on other nations. In Britain, for example, the leaders of the racial minority communities consciously patterned their organizations, in the late 1960s and 70s, on American models. Moreover, the urban riots that rocked Liverpool, Birmingham, and London during the 1980s brought the image of those in the U.S during the 1960s in to the minds of many[39]. How far the Civil Rights Movement has influenced the modern Indian Dalit politics is a topic worth researching.

I can only conclude this paper remembering my interview with the then Illinois Senator, Barack Obama, a decade back. I was discussing with him the minority question in the U.S. politics. He was of the opinion that, at that time much remained to be done to get an equal treatment of the minorities, particularly the Blacks. However, one could not fail to notice the optimism that he had about this. It is clear that the Americans scaled the Everest as far as securing human rights are concerned by enabling an African American to be elected the President of the nation. Anybody interested in human rights would be happy about this and hopeful about the future of the minorities in the U.S.

## Notes and References

1. Steffen W. Schmidt, Mark C. Shelley, and Barbara A. Bardes, American Government and Politics Today (Wadsworth Publishing Company, New York, 1999), p. 600.
2. http://factfinder.census.gov/servlet/QTTable?
3. For details see: David Brion Davis, Inhuman Bondage: The Rise and Fall of Slavery in the New World (Oxford University Press (London, 2006).
4. George P. Rawick, "From Sundown to Sunup", Making of the Black Community 1 1972) http://en.wikipedia.org
5. Ibid.
6. For details see: Mark Noll, The Civil War as a Theological Crisis (University of North Carilina Press, Chapel Hill) 2006.
7. Department of Geography and Meteorology, Baptists as a Percentage of all Residents, 2000 (Valparaiso University, Indiana, 2000).
8. These include:
   - New York Revolt of 1712
   - The Stono Rebellion (1739) in South Carolina
   - New York Slave Insurrection of 1741
   - Gabriel's Rebellion (1800) in Virginia
   - Louisiana Territory Slave Rebellion, led by Charles Deslondes (1811)
   - George Boxley Rebellion (1815) in Virginia
   - Denmark Vesey Uprising in South Carolina (1822)
   - Nat Turner's Rebellion (1831) in Virginia
   - The *Amistad* Seizure (1839) on a Spanish ship.
9. Plessy v. Ferguson, 163 U.S. 537 (1896).
10. Civil Rights Cases, 109 U.S. 3 (1883).
11. For details, see: Gunnar Myrdal, *An American Dilemma* (New York: Harper, 1944), ch.27.

12. Peter B. Levy, The Civil Rights Movement (Greenwood Press, Westport, Connecticut, 1998), p. 5.
13. *Ibid*, p. 6.
14. *Ibid.*
15. Brown v. Board of Education of Topeka, 347 U.S. 483 (1954).
16. Brown v. Board of Education of Topeka, 349 U.S. 294 (1955).
17. Taylor Branch, "At the Crossroads of History," *Boston Globe Magazine*, Nov. 27, 1988, p. 27.
18. Peter B. Levy, op.cit. (n.10), p.9.
19. *Ibid*, p. 12.
20. Frances Fox Piven and Richard A. Cloward, *Poor People's Movements: Why They Succeed, How They Fail* (New York, Vintage Books, 1979), p. 224.
21. Martin Luther King, Jr., "Letters from a Birmingham Jail", in Peter B. Levy, *Let Freedom Ring: A Documentary History of the Modern Civil Rights Movement* (Westport, Conn.: Praeger, 1992), pp.110-14.
22. Martin Luther King, Jr., "Letters from a Birmingham Jail", in Peter B. Levy, *Let Freedom Ring: A Documentary History of the Modern Civil Rights Movement* (Westport, Conn.: Praeger, 1992), pp.110-14.
23. Taylor Branch, Parting the Waters: America in the King Years, 1954-63 (New York: Simon and Schuster, 1988), chap.22.
24. Guinn v. United States, 238 U.S. 347 (1915).
25. The Supreme Court finally acted against white primaries in 1944.
26. Paul E. Johnson, etc., American Government: People, Institutions, and Politics (Houghton Mifflin Company, Boston, 1994), p.155.
27. New York Times May 15, 1966.
28. Harold Stanley, and Richard Niemi, *Vital Statistics in American Politics* (Washington, D.C.: Congressional Quarterly Press, 1990), p.365.
29. Stokely Carmichael, "What We Want", New York Review of Books, September 26, 1966.
30. Robert S. Erikson, and Norman R. Luttbeg, *American Public Opinion* (New York: Wiley, 1973), p.49.
31. National Advisory Commission on Civil Disorders, "Report" (Washington, D.C.:GPO, 1968).
32. *Wards Cove Packing v. Antonio*, 490 U.S. 642 (1989).
33. *Patterson v.McLean Credit Union*, 491 U.S. 642 (1989).
34. William Douglas/Tom Fitzgerald; Kansas City Star May 17, 2004.
35. http://en.wikipedia.org/wiki/Barack_Obama_Supreme_Court_candidates#cite_note-7
36. Barack Obama, "This Is About Whether We Value One Another", Speech delivered on October 28, 2009, in the White House. Emphasis added.

37. James Q. Wilson, p. 548.
38. Robin D.G. Kelley, "Beyond race", Frontline, Vol. 25, No. 22, December 2008.
39. Karen O'Connor, and Larry J. Sabato, *American Government: Roots and Reform* (Allyn and Bacon, Boston, 1995), p.197.

# 8

# THE DYNAMICS OF HUMAN RIGHTS AND ECONOMIC DEVELOPMENT

**P. Suresh Kumar**

The concept of Human Rights reflect 'humanism per se' independent of all kinds of fragmentation based on economic, political and social distinctions. The rights are emanating from the potential power and possibilities of an abstract human being who by virtue of his or her status as a homosapien is entitled to enjoy a set of privileges simply for being a member of the human society. Obviously the concept is an expression of an evolving and a progressive mindset of man as a social being. The greater the concern of a society towards the human rights and its effective practices, the greater will be the transformations of the society to more democracy equality and fraternity among human beings. The modern society is increasingly concerned with the concept of human rights. However, the origin, the evolution and the development of human rights as we experience it today is not an outcome that has organically emerged in the world. In fact, it was the result of numerous struggles and fights that occurred over a considerable period of time across different parts of the world at different times. They are the historical products of fierce struggles and they are upheld only by people's vigilance and effective efforts.

That the concern for human rights was a precious preserve of the western civilization. It has been increasingly claimed that individual rights and personal freedom are the options of western civilization.

An overview of the stages occurred in the progressive realization of human rights may validate such a claim. We may look into these rights into different groups on the basis of contract and time if has been formulated. Origin of civic and personal rights and liberties were to be found in the first declaration of human rights adopted by the French National Assembly in 1789 and in the provision of Bills of Right as contained in the US constitution. These rights are now enshrined in Article 1-21 of the Universal Declaration of Human Rights. Deleneating apart from other rights the rights concerning the protection of personal integrity, including freedom of belief and religion, and the right to participate in public affairs. The sets of rights may be categorized as first generation civic and personal rights and liberties. A second generation rights are concerned with guaranteeing and safeguarding, a set of conditions enabling the citizens to exercise the first generation rights more effectively. The second generation rights include:-

The right to education
The right to work
The right to food, housing

Apart from these, there is another group viz the third generation rights. These are group or collective rights such as right to development and environmental rights. Declaration on the Right to Development was adapted by the United Nations General Assembly in 1986. It regards human person as the central subject of development, an active participant and beneficiary of the right. Right to development has viewed as an inalienable right, entitling all people to participate in, contribute to, and enjoy economic, social cultural and political development.

True that the industrial revolution has produced economic base upon which the economic needs of western society has been, by and large satisfied. The evolved productive system even has produced centers of opulence and extravagant consumption. Whatever the positive contribution the modernization process has created, it cannot ignore the kind of extensive deprivations it had caused in the world society. Such setbacks which never was confined to a specific geographical area. In fact it engulfed the majority of the population across the world particularly in the third world. Thus to say that human rights as an enlightened movement from the western geography is also to admit that the abuses of human rights emerged from the same source.

The extensive colonialisation process which was resorted to by the western powers had provided a free access to the resource base of the colonies. The hegemony initiated an unbridled appropriation of man and material from such location under this phase enabled the colonial powers to secure economic expansion through industrialization process. However, this process had devastated the local industries, destroyed local artisans and destabilized agriculture acitivities. In short, an extensive depreciation of the livelihood took place in such areas. The colonial powers structured the international division of labour according to their interests. Colonial expansion and economic retardation simultaneously occurred affecting the people in some part of the world at the cost of others. This simultaneous process has been put as 'development of development is development of underdevelopment by Gunder Frank. This has led to a conflict between development and human rights, the rights of the colonies were substantially deprived.

In this perception of human rights a fundamental aspect is its relation with economic forces. This is a two-way relationship between economic progress and human rights. The strengthening of the economic base of a community liberate it from the urges of basic necessities and requirements which enable it to pursue qualitative change in its discourse. This normally entails a clamour for more individual freedoms and liberties giving way for the formulation of series of individual rights and privileges culminating in the emphasis on human rights. The west which was set out for an economic adventure found the human rights dear as it enabled them to satisfy their natural urge on the one hand and the very human rights equipping them for further economic progress on the other.

The power of the two-way relation between development and human rights can be used as an effective strategy for a better transformation both for development and enhancing the civilisational quality of human life. It got reflected in different authoritative formulations. Thus article 28 of UDHR states that 'Everyone is entitled to a social and international order in which the rights and freedoms set forth in this Declaration can be fully realized'. Obviously the entitlement refers the material conditions prima facie required for the full and effective enjoyment of the civil rights. The UN charter in its article 55 in chapter IX explicitly stipulate the obligations of member nations to work together for 'economic and social progress and development and also for universal respect for, and observance of human rights and fundamental freedom. In 1986 the General Assembly declared development an inalienable human right. All such rights and freedoms will become meaningful if only it is bolstered up by minimum standard of living.

Thus human right is linked with economic development. It is a crucial element for the effective level enjoyment of it human rights.

Do there exist a situation or condition for the practice of development rights so that it sprout the much needed economic development further leading for the assertion and practice of human rights.

The spontaneous and independent forces available with the production systems along with the new technology provide a wide scope of development possibilities.

Given the kind of economic needs and aspirations that the world faces today, no one can deny the necessity and importance of enhancing the material productive powers of the humanity. The history of this dynamic world unambiguously point out that the productive powers of the capitalist system is amazing. The critics including Marx had realized this potential but was aware and despised the destructive and the exploitative power the unbridled capitalist growth can inflict on humanity. The evolutionary experiences of capitalism into its different epochs proved such concerns were true.

However the alternative formulation suggested and practiced as socialism has not improved the material or the ethical base of the society. In fact, both perceptions defeated the human expectations. Such failures however, never prevented the human aspirations. The clamour and search for betterment and improvement of the human life have evolved towards new perceptions, and strategies. The power of the natural, independent and spontaneous forces and entities were more relied upon. Such organic forces became more influential in human endeavors.

In the material field, the capitalism destructed many finest aspects of life of a substantial population. But in the process it has also amassed a global capital. Though much tainted it is, circumstances are now favourable that it can be used to the needs and relief of the people to improve their living conditions. The forces of globalization can be a conduit to secure a positive effect from the global capital. The scope and reach of global capital now fastly facilitated by new technology. The much needed and wanted development can proceed from the judicious conscious and balanced use of these forces.

Let us look at the new forms and varieties of human rights, at a broader level, that have been brewed and absorbed and strengthened along with the evolution of the capitalist system at its different phases. The economic power of capital became strong when it transformed its form from competitive capitalism to monopoly capitalism. This new phase of capitalism flourished through the multinational corporations (MNCs). The scope of investment, technological changes and external economics and new managerial techniques substantially raised the economic might of such corporations.

Its spread both in developed and less developed economics enhanced their productive potential tremendously. The new economic base enabled the corporations to invoke more liberal policies and practices that virtually catered to new openings for human rights. The labour class which was considered in the previous phase as unruly and non-cooperative entity were provided space in the new epoch in the form of labour participation in management. Even the conventional objective of profit maximization has been modified by the firms. The objective of the firms became more moderate and socialized such as maximization of sales, maximization of large growth, and linking objectives with social goals. Also the firms have adopted new perceptions in their functioning such as the corporate responsibility and some even started sharing environmental concerns. The functioning of the firms with such new visions have opened ways for qualitative improvement of the growth centralizing more around human values and inclusiveness. A part from such improved form of growth perceptions, it also triggered more productive potential in the third world the materialization of which go a long way to mitigate the poverty and unemployment and other deprived conditions that extensively prevailed in such economics. The major economic forces that unleash the productive powers are the agglomeration benefits and the linkages. The agglomeration effects have great power to spur and speed up growth. The inter and infra firm connectivities that an open economy can bring in elevate the size of the economic activities. The possible linkages that emerge under the new environment raises the scope of investment and efficiency leading high growth in the economies.

The globalization phase provide a much more conducive situation for strengthening the development forces in an economy. Primarily, the route to the global way for development to occur is though the inflow of foreign direct investment and special economic zones. Often the critics have severely opposed the roles of such forces in stimulating growth process. The ire against the FDI and SEZ emerge due to the kind of marginalization it creates in the host economics. We may find a conflicting realm in this sort of development experiences. However, it is essential to know the realistic premises of such antagonism against the these powerful mediums of growth propellants in a country. Whether the development process that has orchestrated in the economy is socially and economically desirable and beneficial to the whole is a crucial concern that one cannot ignore. Theoretical guidelines which go a longway to usher in and to ensure human rights through development forces are implied under different rational principles evolved by economists. The prime norms are

1. Pareto optimality concept;
2. The sustainable development, and,
3. The welfare maximization principles.

While these principles maximizes growth and welfare of the community a related question is that how to translate these norms at policy levels making effective and successful delivery points on the economy. One can say that a democratization process will emerge along with economic development. The economic development will ensure social development through which a desire and urge for more democratization will emerge. The globalization process will strengthen democracy since the integration into a global economy necessitates certain exchanges creating common goals and practices as inevitable group efforts. As such the democratization process will get strengthened though such out comes such as the popular concept of good government.

The concept of good governance has the power to value and unleash the meaningful implementation of different narratives or aspects of human rights at policy level. Broadly speaking the good governance should identify and adopt all potential means of growth. It has been critically viewed that the growth process that has occured in many developing economics are lopsided and pro-rich. However, the suggestion of inclusive growth and its implementation in different forms helped to fulfill or secure economic objectives catering to the fulfillment of many of the human rights. The good governance in a democratic set up help evolve the economic programmes more and more people centered.

# 9

# IMPLEMENTING HUMAN RIGHTS: A THIRD WORLD PERSPECTIVE

**S.S. Sreekumar**

## Introduction

### A Conceptual and Theoretical Framework

History of mankind has been associated with struggle of individuals against injustice and exploitation. The recognition of human rights is one of the manifestations of this struggle. The notion of human rights falls within the framework of constitutional law and international law. The purpose is to safeguard by institutional means the rights of human beings against violations committed by the organs of the state and thereby promote the establishment of human living conditions and all round development of human personality. The concept of human right was in rudimentary form in ancient times, in formative stage in the middle ages and fully grown in the 20th century with the formation of UN. Human rights are those rights to which an individual is entitled by virtue of his role as a human being. The use of the concept 'human rights' reveals their source – humanity, human nature, being a person or human being. As Donnelly puts it "just as legal rights have the law as their source and contractual rights arise from contracts, humanity, human nature or some such aspects of all persons would seem to be the source of human rights"(Jack Donnelly 1985:27).

Human rights include access to life, liberty, equality, food, shelter, work, leisure, education, participation in political activities and equitable distribution of power in the society. They set standards for the provision and expansion of civil, political and socio-economic rights. Again when one individual's civil, political and socio- economic rights are exhausted, he can still hope to get some relief under the umbrella of human rights. They provide moral foundations of any system of rights and akin to the concept of justice.

The origin of human rights can be traced back to the emergence of classical liberalism. Classical liberalism made a defense of principles like individualism, private property and market ethics. The ideology of classical liberalism nurtured individual liberty, his development and human progress through the functioning of the above principles. The ideas of rule of law, limited government and individualism characterised the seventeenth and eighteenth century political liberalism (Ashutosh Kumar 1992). The different variants of general political theory can be viewed as deriving theoretical foundations from one of the three types. To quote Macpherson, they are: the individualist – liberal theory whose roots are generally traced back to John Locke; the socialist theory whose roots are essentially in Karl Marx and the populist general will theory whose roots are in Rousseau (Macpherson1977:224). Many contemporary political philosophers of Rousseau like Montesquieu and Voltaire also contributed to human rights. The theory of separation of powers propounded by Montesquieu and Voltaire's attack on censorship and call for freedom of expression were crucial milestones in the evolution of human rights. The real foundation for modern human rights was laid by Immanuel Kant. Kant believed in the autonomy of the individual. Kant made human rights distinct from other rights like civil rights, international rights and cosmopolitan rights. He believed in the oneness of human rights. Thomas Paine, who followed liberal tradition of rights of man, celebrated the French and American revolutions. He believed in the sovereignty of the individual and argued for minimal interference of the state. Utilitarian thinker Jeremy Bentham's Felicific Calculus provides the basis for creation of human rights as inventions made out of necessity. To utilitarians, justice and rights are nothing but derivations of interest and desires. These rights are to be given the context to decide what is necessary to realize the maximum satisfaction (Mill1928).

Marxist theory of rights as expounded by Karl Marx and V.I .Lenin holds that rights maintained any society are the rights of the ruling class. Workers will have to overthrow capitalists and own the major means of production in order to create a new order that would protect the rights and interests of the working class. A crucial contribution to the contemporary thinking of human rights is that of John Rawls' "A Theory of Justice" (Rawls 1971). According to him, justice is the first virtue of social institutions and therefore is important for understanding human rights. Rights and duties emanate from basic institutions of society that work on principles of justice. The Libertarian theory of rights as expounded by Robert Nozick (1938-2002) gives importance to the individual. The theory maintains its faith in the natural rights of individuals. The state has no authority to engage in redistributive transfers among citizens who were originally its clients.

The issue of human rights emerged as a matter of serious concern after the Second World War. In 1948 the U.N. issued an elaborate list of human rights, known as 'Universal Declaration of Rights'. This Declaration advised its member nations to give a wide publicity of these rights in their respective countries particularly in educational institutions. This Declaration contains 30 Articles, besides its Preamble. This Declaration prohibits slavery, torture and degrading punishment, grants everyone the right to a nationality and its culture, affirms freedom of religion and right to vote; proclaim the right to such asylum in other countries to escape persecution; and prohibits arbitrary interference with one's privacy and arbitrary taking a person's property. It also emphasises that mothers and children are entitled to special care and assistance.

Besides the UN Declaration, leading nations have resolved several international compacts. These include European Convention on Human Rights (1950), International Covenant on Civil and Political Rights (1966), International Covenant on Economic, Social and Cultural Rights (1966), International Covenant on Elimination of Racial Discrimination (1966), American Convention on Human Rights (1969), Helsinki Accords (1975), African Charter on Human and People's Human Rights (1981), Convention Against Torture (1984) and the Convention on the Rights of Child (1989).

## Implementing Human Rights: Problems Facing Third World Nations

Many developing countries today have been experiencing democratic form of governance. 21st century democracy is synonym of human rights. In this context the remarks of a noted Jurist is worth mentioning. "Democracy merely may not mean majority rule: it means majority rule coupled with human rights. In the absence of human rights democracy is not possible. Liberty, freedom of dissent , rule of law and all other matters which go to constitute human rights are necessary so that democracy should be maintained"(Tarkunde 2000).

The UN Declaration 1948 inspired the newly independent states of Asia and Africa to include provisions in their constitutions. Since then efforts have been made at global level to find out ways and means to protect national interests in order to promote human welfare. However, implementation process of human rights in these nations has not been satisfactory. Earl Warren, former Chief Justice of United States had observed three reasons for this unsatisfactory situation. First, existence of fundamentally different concepts of relationship between the individual and the state. Secondly, international machinery to deal with the rights of individual citizen had been posing a challenge to traditional concept of sovereignty. Thirdly, the problem of translating specific concern with violations in one region into a general concern of all regions (Earl Warren1973).

Countries of the third world have their main concern development. Eradication of poverty, unemployment and illiteracy are chief problems facing third world nations. Implementing human rights cannot remain deprived of their basic needs of the people of developing countries. Let us examine the position of human rights in the context of third world.

Many developing countries have poor record of human rights. One can notice two reasons for this. As mentioned earlier many third world nations face the problem of poverty and ethnic tensions. Externally they face problems like support for dictatorship by the great powers and the global system. Secondly, some developing countries have been vulnerable both to military coups and to ethnic conflict. Both these are attributable to legacies of colonialism and lead to serious human right violations. Thirdly, corrupt and incompetent governments have contributed to the economic failure of many developing countries. Human rights violations are partly explained by the desire of powerful and corrupt rulers to remain in power. China, Indonesia, Iraq, Saudi Arabia, Nigeria and Zimbabwe are some of the developing countries in which power has been corrupting and corruption is one among the causes of human right violations. Fourthly, developing countries with ethnic divisions may lead to serious human right violations. The process of democratisation played a role in ethnic conflict and genocide in Rwanda. Yet another problem is that most developing countries lack tradition of human rights. The value of human rights may not be deeply embedded in the culture of the society. Even in those nations where government has ratified treaties and human rights have become part of the constitutions, this may not be a significant element of their political culture.

Further, emergence of international terrorism which affected the developing countries has threatened the prospects of human rights in these societies. With the increasing demand for self determination by many countries in the third world nations, these communities often use violence to achieve their goals. Yet another problem facing human rights pursuit in developing societies is the one relating to need of the growth of institutions and structures. In some countries appropriate mechanism for governance is lacking.

## The Asian Values Debate

In the 1990s government representatives and intellectuals from countries of South East and East Asia questioned the universality of human rights. All these nations were the colonies of West and have different cultures. They argued that human rights should be reinterpreted according to the values in their societies. Asian cultures are emphasizing community values such as social order, respect for authority, general welfare, and loyalty to the family, state and nation. Some Asian political leaders such as Lee Kuan Yew of Singapore argued that human rights are culturally biased in promoting individual freedom and general well- being. There is, however, an emerging Asian consciousness that distances itself from the perceived selfishness and irresponsibility of Western capitalism (Catriona Mckinnon 2008:203).

Asian Values argument came mainly from two countries: Malaysia and Singapore. One of the leading exponents of Asian values Dr. Mahathir

Mohamed, Prime Minister of Malaysia acknowledged that Asian Values were similar to conservative western values: order, harmony, respect for authority. This made the issue of Asian values clearer but made the debate one between liberalism and conservatism, rather than the West and Asia (Peter Burnell and Vicky Randall 2005:257).

Asian leaders and intellectuals began to assert claims of legitimate, culturally based differences that justified substantial deviation from the international interpretation of human rights norms. A focal point for this discussion was the Regional Meeting for Asia of the World Conference of Human Rights held from 29th March to 2nd April, 1993 in Bangkok. Articles in prominent Western journals began appearing with titles such as "Asia's Different Standard" (Kausikan, 1993), "Culture in Destiny" (Zakaria1994), and Can Asians Think? (Mahbubani 1998). The "East Asian Economic Miracle" which even after the crisis of 1997 remain impressive and helped to create interest in such arguments in other regions.

Human rights are treated as fundamentally universal, but substantial space is allowed for variations in implementing these universal norms. Experts in the field like Jack Donnelly described this approach to human rights as "weak cultural relativism" (Jack Donnelly) and Andrew Nathan speaks of "tempered universalism" (Andrew Nathan 2001)

## Globalization and Human Rights

Yet another factor influencing implementation of human rights in third world nations is globalization. There is considerable discussion on this matter. One view is that globalization enhances human rights leading to economic benefits and political freedom. Many believe that market mechanisms and liberalized trade will improve the standards of the people. Besides this, globalization facilitates international exchanges allowing participation in a global community. But opponents of globalization observe it as a threat to human rights. First of all, globalization hinders local decision making and democratic participation when MNCs, IMF and World Bank are involved in setting national economic and social policies. Secondly, in a globalised society, uncontrolled market forces threaten social, economic and cultural rights. Thirdly, there are chances of increasing unemployment and poverty when wealth is accumulated in the hands of MNCs.

Globalization has been opposed by a world wide protest movement expressing diverse concerns, including world poverty, environmental degradation, and human rights. The targets of this movement are primarily rich states, associations of rich states (side as GS) and Multinational Corporation (MNC). The human rights movement has recently increased its concern about the role of MNCs in human right violations. Meyer conducted an empirical study on the impact of MNCs on human rights in developing countries. He concluded that there is positive correlation between MNC investment in developing countries and human rights. However he does not deny that some

MNCs are included in human rights violation in these countries. (Meyer 1998). Globalization in some way increases inequality, drives vulnerable to the margins of survival and thereby feed religious and nationalist extremism. After the financial crisis in South East Asia at the end of the 1990s, the IMF imposed strict conditions on Indonesia that led to ethnic riots.

Briefly, the barriers to human rights implementation in developing countries are as follows. Many developing countries are poor and have to accord 'development priority' over human rights. Most of the developing countries have little power in the global economic system and hence consequently venerable to the policies of powerful states and these states are often unfriendly to human rights. Many developing countries have ethnic divisions that predispose to conflict in conditions of scarcity and consequently to repression. Corrupt and incompetent governments are common in many developing countries and human rights are explained in part by the desire of corrupt rulers to remain in power. Many developing countries have had traditional cultures wherein human rights engaged little place. Some countries have developed human right culture in a weak form.

**Suggestions**

1. General public especially from remote village areas lack awareness regarding human rights and the need for its protection. This results in tolerating excesses of other people and organizations. This is relevant in the case of marginalized sections like women, dalits and illiterates. Hence there is an urgent need to socialize the rural masses with the help and collaboration of educational institutions, and NGOs. Human rights Groups and Committees in schools and colleges and universities are to be instituted to educate the student community and public regarding the protection of their rights.
2. Agencies involved in the process of implementation have to be strengthened. For example, police personnel have to be adequately trained to deal with cases relating to human rights .In this respect the efforts undertaken by National Human Rights Commission is a promising one. The Commission has already initiated measures to prepare list of resource persons in the field of human rights. It is appropriate to organize in-service courses, seminars and workshops on human rights.
3. Human rights network has to be strengthened so that appropriate Machinery should be made available at the grass root level. In this respect it is advisable to have Advisory Committees at the grass root level to involve people in the matter.
4. Human rights cell can be constituted at various levels so as to register cases of violation of human rights. This cell also can play a positive role in generating awareness among the public regarding human right issues. Establishing monitoring cells to constantly watch the

performance in the field and respond immediately and effectively is yet another step. It is better to have this kind of cells at Taluk and District levels.

5. The role of media especially electronic media cannot be undermined in this regard. They can play a positive in this matter. For example, prominent television channels conduct investigations regarding human right violations and reveal real issues before the public which can generate discussions and deliberations.
6. Reforming the undemocratic structures, laws and policies is another suggestion for better implementation of human rights .Easy accessibility to courts, legal aid and assistance can help in smooth implementation and to have faith in the principle.
7. The governments of the third world have to give greater attention to vulnerable groups such as women, children, migrant workers minorities, indigenous communities and those with disabilities. The governments are required to be more responsive to public opinion regarding inhuman or repressive laws in force.

**Concluding Observations**

The concept of human rights which can be acceptable to modern liberal democratic societies has to fulfill two basic assumptions. First, the rights equal in an effective manner. Second, there must be the obligation on others to accept the rights of each human being.

Economic development is undoubtedly important for third world nations. But economic growth has to the accompanied by wide measure of egalitarianism, protection of the rights of workers and democratic work practices. The need of the hour is to devise rational approach to the promotion of human rights in the countries of the third world. The implementation of human rights should be action oriented rather than seminar / conference oriented. Practical approach has to be adopted to make human rights really meaningful. Laws, machinery and personnel should be accessible to the disadvantaged sections of the society. Simultaneously, there is the need for human rights conscientisation and mobilization. The task of promoting a civic- political culture and creating democratic values and norms should be left to the enlightened public in the respective countries. Although Human Rights are now well established in greater power politics the best hope of their future lies with the increasing number of grass root movements in developing societies. A vibrant civil society can help both in developing and improving human rights protection. Human rights seem to require a balance between effective states and strong civil society.

## References

Ashutosh Kumar "F.A. Hayek: Economics and Politics", Indian Journal of Political Science, Vol. LIII, No.1, Jan- March, 1992.

Andrew Nathan J: "Universalism : A Particularistic Account", in Lynda Bell et al (ed), Negotiating Culture and Human Rights, Columbia University Press, New York, 2001.

Bilahari Kausikan: "Asia's Different Standard", Foreign Policy, 92, (Fall): 24-41,1993.

Catriona Mackinnon (2008): Issues in Political Theory, Oxford University Press, New York.

Earl Warren: "It is time to Implement Declaration of Human Rights", Vol. 2 (4), 1973, JBC, 375 at 377, 1973.

Fareed Zakaria: "Culture is Desitny : A Conversation with Lee Kuan Yew", Foreign Affairs, 73, March – April, pp. 109-126, 1994.

Jack Donnelly: The Concept of Human Rights, Croom Helm, Kent, 1985.

Jack Donnelly (2005): Universal Human Rights in Theory and Practice, Manas Publications, New Delhi, p. 119.

John Rawls (1971): A Theory of Justice, Harvard University Press, Cambridge,

Kishore Mahbubani: "Can Asians Think?" The National Interest, 52, (Summer), pp. 27-35, 1998.

Macpherson C.B (1977): Democratic Theory: The Essays in Retrieval, Oxford University Press, Oxford.

Meyer, W.H. (1998): Human Rights and International Political Economy in Third World Countries, Westport, Conn: Praeger.

Mill J.S., (1928): On Liberty, World Classics, No.170, Oxford.

Peter Burnell and Vicky Randall (2005): Politics in Developing World, Oxford University Press, Oxford.

Tarkunde (2000): "Democracy and Human Rights" in S. Mehartaj Begum (Ed), Human Rights in India, A.P.H. Publishing House, New Delhi.

Viswanathan V.N: "Human Rights in a Globalized World: The Indian Experiences", Indian Journal of Political Science, Vol. LXIX, No. 1, Jan. – Mar. 2008, pp. 53-54.

# 10

# BUREAUCRACY AND HUMAN RIGHTS UNDER LIBERALIZATION

**S.R. Jitha**

Liberalization and Globalization are both part of the programme of economic reform undertaken by dozens of countries in the last decade to give a new shape and direction to their economies. This programme represents a most radical departure from the theory and practice of state intervention that had a powerful grip in the backward economies of Asia, Africa and Latin America in the post war years[1]. Liberalization is the progressive elimination of the control of the state over economic activities. It is driven by the neo-liberal idea that government involvement should be as low as possible, leaving the field to the operation of self interest driven market forces of demand and supply. Measures have been taken to make the economy more responsible to market forces. Private agents are granted freedom to make their own decisions regarding consumption, production, input choice, pricing, market lending, borrowing and investment. The growth and penetration of globalist policies have engendered a significant increase in inequity between the minority and the majority. Taxes have become increasingly regressive, government tax revenues increasingly come from waged and salaried groups while the percentage from multinational corporate capital is declining. State subsidies for multinational corporate capital grow while the share for wageworkers, pensioners, low wage families, the ill and the injured, children etc. declined[2].

India responded to the development with a reform-trinity of liberalization, privatization and globalization. The NIP of 1991 led the government to take serious initiatives in respect of policies in areas like industrial licensing, foreign investment, foreign technology policy, public sector policy and MRTP Act. All these resulted in shrinking of the role of the state and increased inter-play of private sector. The new economic policy, which entails liberalization, privatization and globalization, are redefining the role of state and administration to suit the foreign capital. The policies of LPG minimises the role of welfare state. The role of state was reduced to a facilitator rather than a regulator and a controller. The withdrawal of state from the economy allowed the free play of corporates. MNCs and TNCs became the major actors.

The greatest social crisis is in the countries that have advanced furthest in globalization. The number of workers without medical coverage, non-unionized workers and temporary or part-time workers with less or no social benefits is greatest in the US followed by the U.K. Argentina and Brazil have unemployment rates of 18 and 15 percent respectively, rates that have been multiplied with the globalization of their economics. In East European Countries living standards have fallen between 30-80 percent and in Mexico a fall of 30 percent of wage earning became evident[3]. In third world nations SAPs acted as a process of income re-concentration through cuts in social spending, corporate tax reductions and increased subsidies to corporates. In almost all nations a parallel development occurred making the rich richer and the poor poorer. Wealth began to concentrate in the hands of a few, creating gross inequality and reduction in the purchasing power of the common man.

Human Rights are those rights which are inherent in our nature and without which one cannot live as a human being[4]. In other words it can be defined as those rights which are entitled to enjoy by virtue of being a member of human species. Equality and Justice are at the heart of all human rights. It includes adequate and decent food, water, health, freedom from slavery, fair treatment under law, shelter etc. Thus, under the shadow of human rights all people are entitled not to starve, not to suffer from preventive disease, to have opportunity to better their economic condition, to have access to knowledge and information and to decide on anything that affect their life. These basic human needs and values are at the foundation of universal ideas of human rights and which is in Article (2) of the Universal Declaration of Human Rights (UDHR 1948), which states:

*"Everyone is entitled to all the rights and freedoms set forth in the Declaration, without distinction of any kind such as race, colour, sex, language, religion, political or other opinion, national or social origins, property, birth or other status. Furthermore, no distinction shall be made on the basis of the political jurisdictional or international status of the country or territory to which a person belongs, whether it be independent, trust, non self governing or under any other limitation of sovereignty[5]."*

Bureaucracy is an important instrument of the state to administer its people and to manage the affairs. It consists of officials at all levels, who are expected to carry out the day-to-day administration without any fear or favour. The duty of the bureaucracy is to understand the problems of the people and to create a balanced socio-economic and political environment, so that citizens could lead a meaningful life. Human Rights means all human beings have the right to live with dignity at all times regardless of their legal or political status. The state is supposed to be the most important protector of human rights. Human Rights are a solemn reminder that a state owes to its citizens. Bureaucracy being the instrument of state therefore is the forerunner in the protection of human rights. This can be seen while going through various articles of the Universal Declaration of Human Rights[6]:

*Government officials must be accountable for their actions through clearly formulated and transparent process, and more particularly the legitimacy of a government must be regularly established through a well-defined open process of public choice (Article 21).*

*The safety and security of citizens must be assured (Article 3 & 5); The rule of law must prevail and citizens must be protected from arbitrary or capricious actions by public authorities (Articles 7, 8, 9, 10 & 11).*

*Everyone has the right to an adequate standard of living and necessities of life which should be provided for the benefits of all citizens in an equitable manner (Articles 22, 23, 24 & 25).*

*Freedom of association and expression of opinion must be permitted and information must be readily available to ensure accountability (Articles 19 & 20).*

From this it is clear that the role of bureaucracy in the protection of human rights is manifold and multidimensional. Getting things done without delay itself is a way of protecting human rights. Justice delayed is justice denied. Laws, Declarations, Conventions, and Protocols etc. do not solve the problems, unless they are implemented promptly. The agency to implement this is the bureaucracy. The observation made by the Supreme Court should be brought to mind here, "for the ruling set-up, Public Interest Litigations (PILs) may have been the Achilles heel as they mainly highlight abject poverty and denial of rights to citizens, but the government and bureaucracy must welcome such litigation as it provides an opportunity to examine the efficacy of the policies[7]." The Bench comprising Justices Dalveer Bhandari and Mukundakam Sharma vehemently stressed on the positive effect of PILs on the social and economic justice front. The Bench said, "PILs are a challenge as well as an opportunity to the government and bureaucracy to make basic human rights meaningful to the deprived and vulnerable sections and to assure them social and economic justice, which was the signature tune of the Constitution." The observation of the court can be put in this way. The government and its officers must welcome public interest litigation because it would provide them an occasion to examine whether the poor and the downtrodden are getting their social and economic entitlements or whether they are continuing to remain victims of deception and exploitation at the hands of strong and powerful sections of the community.

We know that in the present day the influential are always going for short cuts and are trying to infringe the basic human rights of the individual, and common men are tied with red-tapism and hierarchical delay to enjoy this basic rights. Laws for the common man and shortcuts for the influential are the modern day reality. The administrative procedure is so complicated and cumbersome that the files dealing with ordinary man's problems needs to climb up and down the bureaucratic ladder.

Bureaucracy ignores the criteria to be objective and value laden. Trends have emerged like rules and regulations are modified or even ignored to suit their convenience, in such a way, that is for protecting the interest of the MNC's and the rich. Complaints of favoritism to friends and relatives or men of positions and money are the regular complaints of the people. They felt that they are not treated with due respect and failed to protect the basic human rights. This degrading situation is because of the linkage of administration with social, political and legal system[8]. In an increasingly integrated world there exists nexus between liberalization and corruption. Corruption is one of the major evils of every society and in developing societies, corruption is institutionalized and out of control posing impediment to development.

In the ecology of administration people too have accepted their destiny to be exploited by them, which resulted in corruption of different form like, Sugar Scandals, Fodder Scandal, Uniform Scandal, Urea Scandal, Telecom Scandal and the Spectrum Scandal and other types of human right violations. India Corruption Study 2007 reveals the most shameful face of corruption in India that even the poorer sections are not spared by the corrupted administrators and politicians. The study found that about one-third of below poverty line (BPL) households in the country bribed officials to avail a total of 11 services-from police to PDS (Public Distribution System). According to the survey which covered 22,728 households in all states and Union Territories, Rs. 883 crore in all were estimated to be paid as bribe by BPL households[9]. The study also points that more than half of the eligible households in North Eastern States did not have a BPL card on reasons that they could not pay bribe or have a "contact" to influence. In Bihar 80 % of the subsidized food aid to the poor is stolen[10]. Thus common men are denied of basic human rights in the hands of officials. Corruption reduces the net income of the poor and wrecks programmes related to the basic needs from sanitation to education and to health care. In a democratic society the problems of marginalized sections cannot be ignored and marginalization of any sections is a shame to democracy.

The ascendency of liberalization provided a comfortable climate for the spread of corruption. Studies show that as competition increased corruption also increased. Mikhal Drugor, states that "during the monopoly regime it was core for an unqualified firm to obtain a licence. More than that a qualified firm pays only lower bribe than an unqualified one. Experience shows that an unqualified firm more frequently obtains licence[11]." The post-liberalization government officers have realized that their decisions can make others rich. So their logic is "If greedy Indian business man can evade taxes, influence policies and make money through devious means, the government officer who moves the file can have a share of the booty." Corruption in Indian bureaucracy has now come to be accepted as a part of the machinery that governs India. Neither rules, nor regulations come on the way and illegal and impermissible transactions are carried quickly.

The disinvestment policy has made many public sector undertakings partially or totally under the control of big corporates. These include Bharat Aluminium Corporation, National Aluminium Corporation, Computer Maintenance Corporation, Indian Petroleum Corporation Limited, Videsh Sanchar Nigam Limited, Indian Tourism Development Corporation, Gas Authority of India Limited, and National Thermal Power Corporation etc. Moreover some of the profits making public sector undertakings like Bharat Heavy Electricals Limited, Maruti, ITDC, Modern Foods, etc were also disinvested[12]. The net result of disinvestment is inequality and the widening of rich-poor gap. So to ensure equity all such actions should be halted. Usually the public sectors were headed by IAS officers. These civil servants had not offered any creative criticism about this policy and there have been only a few debates among the civil servants.

The entry of the multinationals and the hefty pay and perk their executives get, are cause of concern for the bureaucrats in India. They are mainly concerned with the expectation on the possibilities of liberalization and globalization such as posting in abroad and career mobility, re-employment in International Agencies and multinationals corporations after retirement[13]. More over Government of India made compulsory foreign training for the IAS officers to cope up with the changing scenario. Govt. of India has deputed 97 Senior IAS officers for training in USA[14]. The training for the officers is given by the executives of the World Bank, IMF and other Non-Governmental Organizations. The training is for opening sectors like electricity, housing, water supply, public distribution system, education and health, to foreign investment. It is assumed that the agenda of the government is to give them training to implement the liberalization polices through civil service, whatever may be the government in power[15].

The greatest assault of globalization is the commodification of the commons. For the profit of multinationals the 'free gifts' of nature – water, air and other natural resources have been commodified and commercialized. This has undermined the basic rights and needs of common man all over the world. Through the commoditization of the commons, especially water, criminal negligence was made by the bureaucracy, not only in India but also in other parts of the world. Instead of cautioning the government about the ill effects of water privatization, what the bureaucracy has done was preparation of detailed plans for privatization. The possibility of getting money makes bureaucracy chalk out plans for water privatization. The best example of criminal negligence was the action of Department of Water Resources at Plachimada (Coco-Cola bottling plant). They have not dared to conduct inspection at the factory site, even though the fact was known that coco-cola was violating the Kerala Ground Water Act. The decision of the Panchayat Director (IAS Officer), cancelling the order of Panchayat banning licence to the company is another example[16]. Bureaucrats have not uttered a single word, when the Government sold River Ganga and River Bhavani to satisfy the corporate greed on 2003. This sale of Bhavani has been effected by the government even while the state (Tamil Nadu) is reeling under severe drought, ground water levels have reached depths of over 1,000 ft., and water riots and water-related murders have become an everyday occurrence[17].

Bureaucrats are now open in supporting multi-national corporations and the policies of liberalization. The statement of T.Balakrishnan, Principal secretary, Industries Department, openly supporting Coco-Cola, Pepsi and Tata is the recent example. Addressing a seminar organized by the Industrial Development Corporation, he commented that "it was sad that coco-cola factory at Palachimada can't be saved[18]". His argument is that as a result of the closure of the cola factory numerous job opportunities have been lost, together with a revenue loss of Rs. 500 core to the state exchequer in the form of taxes. The Principal Secretary also rose a question "why Tata has become unacceptable in Kerala alone?" To him it was because of the "will power" of the industries Department that Pepsi factory hasn't been closed[19]. Instead of speaking for the victims of the companies exploitation State principal Secretary preferred advocating the interests of the corporate. His observation was totally against not only the government's policy but also of the observation made by the court, favouring the victims.

The rise of Special Economic Zones contributed to another phase of human rights violations in India. Large tracts of lands including prime agricultural lands are being acquired for the projects, forcing thousands out of their livelihood. States where SEZs have been set up has witnessed cold-blooded murders and evacuation – Orissa, Jharkand, Maharashtra, West Bengal etc. A rational analysis of the 'land grabbing' makes it clear that in the name of development real estate scam is going on. What the governments are doing is pauperization of the local population by taking away their only practical source of income to ensure further prosperity of large business corporates. The new development strategy has familiarized a new concept "developmental terrorism" – terror for development. In the name of development innocent thousands- tribals, women, children and peasants, are being displaced of their land and livelihood. Cold blooded murders, forcible eviction, police firing, lathicharges and other gruesome practices had occurred at Singur, Nandigram, Jharkand, and Orissa in the banner of development. The site of human eviction in Orissa, West Bengal, Moolampalli in Kerala for Vallarpadam Project, etc. raises doubts about bureaucrats being the agents of corporates. No chances of humanitarian consideration have been shown in these areas. Recent example is the Kinallur issue, where the police brutally lathicharged the public, including women and children who tried to stop the survey for the proposed four-lane road. Land acquisition has been a major dispute all over India and in many cases we can see exemptions to the powerful and the rich[20]. Making the poor victims of land acquisition is grave injustice.

In modern capitalist society, private sector bureaucracy is larger than public bureaucracy. The public bureaucracy has now become the sponsors of private bureaucracy. While the public bureaucracy is funded by taxing the population, private bureaucracy is funded by sales revenue and careful investment of profits. Today unrestricted competition leads to absolute rule of the private bureaucracies over the whole world and dismembering of the public bureaucracy. The unaccountable private bureaucracy, whose sole function is to maximize the profit of the corporates' are the one making maximum damage to human rights.

Human rights today occupy top-level priority internationally as well as nationally. The general idea of human rights has today wide spread acceptance. The situation of human rights in developing societies has been complex and it intensified with the advent of globalization. Globalization has popularized the concept of human rights, but its onslaught has resulted in grave violation of human rights. In a market driven economic, it is profit that matters and not human rights. The domestic laws of many states failed to impose adequate human rights duties on corporates, which are the most horrific abusers of human rights in the modern times. In some cases we can see that the government and its agencies acting as agents of corporates.

The Bhopal Gas tragedy case brings this unholy alliance to light. For eg. In 1985 the government of India enacted the Bhopal Claims Act and took away from victims the right to represent them and vested itself with the exclusive right to represent victims. In 1989 the government agreed to a settlement with Union Carbide Corporation (UCC)[21]. The payment of compensation to victims did not, however, begin until 1992 and involved numerous problems, including payment of inadequate sums, delayed payments, arbitrary rejection or downgrading of claims. Excessive bureaucracy in the claims process led to the entry of middlemen and rampant corruption, further reducing the amount of compensation money that victims were able to finally get. Even the court's verdict in Bhopal case is disappointing. The risks posted by Carbide to Bhopal's citizens were well- known. The state environmental board had recorded the presence of poisonous gases inside the plant to be in excess of permissible limits. Journalist Jyoti Punwani reports, "The plant's union had, in late 1982, written to the Union Home Minister and State Chief Minister about the spate of mishaps inside the plant[22]. Now it is clear that all warnings have been ignored for protecting the Carbide's interest. Prominent newspapers and channels, with video clippings reported the role of government machinery in helping Warren Anderson to escape from India. As Jyoti Punwani says – "Who let Warren Anderson go? Is the wrong question. The right question is who didn't let Warren Anderson go[23]?"

History shows that bureaucracy is the only group that has not been much affected by the onslaught of globalization. So the responsibility before bureaucracy in developing societies is much higher than that in developed societies. In these societies what is need from bureaucracy is protection from petty corruption and getting things without delay. They have to root out corruption and use their knowledge, experience and political neutrality to identify the good things. They are the person to organise the rescue efforts in areas like agriculture, education, health, flood control, environment protection, railway, roads, bridges, defence and power. India should learn from the experience of other societies and has to be actively involved in the process of production and equitable distribution of wealth to ensure social security. In strengthening the social sectors the bureaucrats have to play a constructive role. Public distribution system and the health care system should be strengthened to reduce the social crisis of liberalization. They should resist the onslaught of multinationals and for that the challenge before the bureaucracy is to initiate decentralization, people's empowerment through devolution of power and encourage local self governing institutions to administer and meet collective over social needs while encouraging the market to meet the individual needs. Above all, the civil servants should keep in mind that they are the servants of society, not masters, so should aim at preserving the country's cultural, ethnic and biodiversities, traditional values, freedom, environment and at the same time ensuring the people peace and prosperity now and forever for the enjoyment of basic and human rights.

## References

1. Soumyen Sikder (2007): Contemporary Issues in Globalization, New Delhi: Oxford University Press, p. 2.
2. James Petras & Henry Veltmeyer (2001): Globalization Unmasked, New Delhi: Madhyam Books. p. 51.
3. *Ibid.*
4. Darren J Byrne (2005): Human Rights An Introduction, Pearson Education India. p. 399.
5. "The United Nations and Human Rights," New York: The UN Department of Public Information. (1995) P. 153-5.
6. Anitha Cheria, Sriprabha, Petcharamesree & Edwin (2004): Human Rights Approach to Development, Bangalore: Books for Change. P. 38.
7. Dhananjay Mahapatra, "Govt, bureaucracy must welcome PILs on right of poor: SC," The Times of India, Jan 22, 2010, 01.08 am IST.

8. Jitha S.R, (2009): "Higher Bureaucracy and Development," New Delhi: Kalpaz Publications, 2007. p. 232.
9. TII-CMS India Corruption Study, 2007. p. 8.
10. "Bihar a byword for Worst of India," The Economist <http://www.expressindia.com/news/fullstory.php>.
11. Mikhal Drugor, (2009): "Competition in Bureaucracy and Corruption." Dept. of Economics, University of Oxford, Jan. 2009. p. 2
12. Ruddar Dutt, (2006): "India's Economy," New Delhi: S. Chand & Co. Ltd., 2006. p. 242.
13. P.J. Alexander, "Role of Civil Servants in the Context of New-Economic Policy," Kerala Journal of Social Science, Vol. 1, No. 1, January-June 1996.
14. "Indian Bureaucrats to be Trained in the US," Competition Success Review, Vol. XLIII, No. 9, March 2007. p. 23.
15. J. Prabash, "Janadhipathyathinte Panakkillukkam," Kala Kaumudi Weekly (Malayalam), Vol. 33, No. 46, August 3, 2008. p. 11.
16. "Oru Deshathinte Porattam," Plachimadayile Jalachushanavum Janakeeya Prathirothavum (M), Mathrubhumi Books, 2 January, 2005. p. 27-8.
17. "Sale of River Bhavani," India Resource Center, http://www.indiaresource.org/issues/water/2003/bhavaniriver.html
18. Kerala Kaumudi (Kollam), May 25, 2010. p.1.
19. *Ibid.*
20. "Kinallur Sambhavam Daurbhagiam," (Editorial) Mathrubhumi, May 8, 2010. p. 4.
21. "DOW Chemical Company (DOW), Union Carbide Corporation and the Bhopal Communities in India The Role of the Governments of India and Madhya Pradesh." Amnesty International, http://www.amnestyusa.org/business-and-human-rights/dow-chemical/india-govt-role/page.do?id=1011389.
22. Jyoti Punwani, "Who didn't help Carbide?" Kerala Kaumudi (Kochi), June 17, 2010.
23. *Ibid.*

# 11

# TERRORISM, HUMAN RIGHTS AND CIVIL SOCIETY MOVEMENTS IN INDIA

**K. Jayaprasad**

Terrorism, Human Rights and Civil Society are the three major areas which attracted worldwide attention and debate along with Globalization in the post-cold war world order. Today the authority of the state has been limited with the maintenance of the sovereignty and integrity of the State and protection of the people. With the disintegration of the USSR and the socialist bloc, a new awareness of human rights, freedom and democracy flourished in East Europe, former Soviet Republics, Latin America, Africa and Asia. But contrary to the expectations, the world witnessed serious new challenges. Globalization and international terrorism pose a serious threat to the state sovereignty and integrity. During the cold war period, the world was divided into two power blocs. While in the era of terrorism, nation States, have been united against terrorism, but the "War on Terror" not yet succeeded. Hence this problem needs further discussion.

With the dawn of the 21st century terrorism and War on Terrorism (WOT) became the major concerns of the world. 9/11 Terrorist attack on USA changed the nature of International Politics. War on Terror resulted in serious human right violations, especially in Afghanistan and Iraq. Initially, the unipolar world emerged after the cold war offered unchallengable authority to the USA. But unlike in the Cold war period, where international peace and security sustained, the post-cold war world is always under the threat of global terrorism. Millions of people were affected by this menace. The terrorist strikes always the soft centres of the state and thus create a fear psychosis among the people. So far no nation state including the super powers can claim immunity from terrorist attacks. For example, after the Second World War, for the first time the USA was attacked. Its economic and political capitals were shaken by the Islamic terrorist groups and thousands of civilian people were killed.

It is a fact that, Islamic terrorism attained such a capability to threaten the nation states and their primary duty to protect the life and property of their citizens. In the fight against terrorism the state as well as the civil society have equal responsibility as the civilian mask always help the terrorist and fundamentalist groups. In that sense terrorists always have an advantage and the State has serious limitations.

In this paper the focus is on civil society movements, because, the defences of human rights and fundamental freedoms should be built by the civil society along with the political society. The limitations of the nation States had already been exposed with the 9/11 terrorist attack in New York (USA) and 26/11 terrorist attack in Mumbai (India).

**Decline of State Authority**

During the 20th century the emergence of Welfare State and the popularity of the Socialist model of economic development acted as an input for a big increase in the functions of the State. The State began using its sovereignty for becoming an owner of industrial establishments and a strong regulator and determinator of the economic life of the society. Subsequently, it began wielding a large amount of power over the socio-economic life of the people. However, the last decade of the 20th century witnessed the liquidation of the Socialist economic model and the consequent emergence of a strong wave of politico-economic liberalization. Globalization emerged in the sphere of international economic and trade relations and it began replacing the traditional concept of internationalism. Multinational companies (MNCs) and other Non-state actors began to reign the world.

**Human Rights and Terrorism**

The post-Cold War world order demonstrated better awareness of human rights. Many countries accepted human rights charter which set a common standard of human behaviour. Also Globalization offered new awareness and helped the new social movements, NGOs and other non-State actors. Generally human rights activists are concerned with State's encroachments on individual rights. Since globalization offered new awareness to the non-State actors and limited the role of nation states, the rights violations by these agencies also need consideration.

The emergence and development of organized terrorism as a worldwide phenomenon during the last two decades changed the struggle for human rights. Interestingly, in the post-cold war era, terrorism grew with the civil society movements. In the era of globalization on the one hand large number of civil society movements flourished along with growing human right awareness and on the other, terrorism, especially Islamic terrorism led by Al Queda and Taliban strengthened. Al Queda declared war on three States, i.e. USA, India and Israel. Among them the USA and India are two great democracies with stable constitutional order and guarantee of fundamental rights and institutional support to the protection of human rights. As a result new social movements and a large number of Human Rights organizations emerged in these two democracies.

This paper makes an attempt to analyse the attitude of civil society movements in India towards terrorism and violation of rights by non-State actors. It is a fact that, human right violations by the State are successfully challenged by these groups. But violations by the non-State actors including terrorist and fundamentalist groups were neglected by these forums. As a result, both home grown terrorism and cross border terrorism which threatened the sovereignty of the country and fundamental freedoms of innocent citizens are not properly debated by the civil society. Also many terrorist groups and fundamentalist movement sponsors human right forums as a shield to resist the State action. At this juncture, the role of civil society movements needs further discussion.

**Civil Society**

The language of Civil Society become popular on the contemporary political scene with the rise of the Solidarity movement, in Poland[1]. The concept of 'Civil Society' which was first articulated by the liberals, especially John Locke during the 17th century and Hegal in 18th century had fallen into disuse during the 19th century due to the fascination with the nation State. In the 1970's as the Socialist States began to disintegrate, intellectuals and political activists throughout the Eastern Europe invoked the image of civil society to mobilize people against the oppression of the State and the demanded liberal, social, political and economic life.

The language of civil society was picked up by the Western intellectuals to articulate their discomforts with modern society and government. In Western Europe, Civil Society was conceptualized in opposition to neo-corporatist arrangements that has brought organized labour and its parties into institutionalized patterns of governance but afforded little access to other constituencies[2].

Generally, the concept of civil society was picked up by the people's movements all over the world[3]. Civil society became a kind of aspirational shorthand for ideas of equity, participation and public fairness. Currently, the most commonly used definitions of civil society is a sphere between the family and the State where people associate across ties of kinship, aside from market and independent of the State. It includes both relatively formal array of friendship and networks of social life outside the family. It is the arena of community meetings and street corner activity, clubs and churches, 'sabhas' and 'samajas', professional associations and unions, social movements and community action groups. It is both a collection of organizations and the relatively protected space which they occupy.

**Civil Society Movements in India**

India is a unique nation credited with having most diverse and complex society with overlapping identities of religion, caste, class and region. This resulted in the formation of a variety of groups, associations and movements. We cannot compare the Indian scenario with that of Western capitalist or liberal societies. Caste, religion, ethnic and regional affiliations of social movements need to be counted. Though some of the groups act like autonomous action groups, there is an ideological commitment for its action and inaction. Another distinction of civil society movements in India is its political commitment. Overlapping of civil and political societies is an Indian reality. While discussing the civil society movements in India, Western liberal interpretations and theories have serious limitations[4].

Almost all revolutions and people's movements in the world were concerned with protection of rights of common man against authoritarianism. But with the advent of terrorism the position has changed. Citizens now have to seek protection of their human rights form the terrorists, where the state becomes mere spectator. More than sixty five thousand citizens and twenty five thousand security personals were killed by the terrorist in India since 1980. Formerly the remedy offered by the constitution in case of violation of fundamental rights acted as a safety valve to the citizen against the encroachment of State on individual rights. Both in USA and India, the judiciary entered into an activist role while protecting the fundamental rights. For example The Supreme Court of India elaborated Article 21 of the Indian constitution and included all human rights in the scope of this Article. But this judicial guarantee has no relevance when the ordinary, unarmed civilians have been struck by terrorism. The terrorists strike the soft centres of the State. Now public transport, airways, railway, markets, religious places, schools etc are not, free from terrorist threat.

For the last 30 years, India has been a laboratory of global terrorism. Not only civilians, but also thousands of security personnels were killed by the terrorists. Both cross-border terrorism and home grown terrorism affect the civilian life. Jammu Kashmir, Assam, North Eastern States, Punjab etc are terror prone States, especially by cross-border terrorism. On the other hand, there is the Maoist terrorism which has worsly affected 83 districts in nine States like Andhra Pradesh, Bihar, Catttisgarh, Jharkhand, Madhya Pradesh, Maharastra, Orissa, U.P and West Bengal. It is estimated that the Maoist presence is there in around 220 districts of the country[5]. Today, five lakh Hindu Pandits of Kashmir valley are living as refugees in Jammu region and other neighbouring States. Also thousands of Tribals are living as refugees in Chattisgarh due to Maoist terror. Only tribal populations is affected in Maoist terror attacks in Chattisgarh and Jharkand. More than five thousand tribal people were killed since 2004 due to the Maoist terror.

As far as India is concerned, the terrorists, whether Islamic or Maoist terrorists, now challenge the authority of the State. They attacked the seat of democracy, i.e. the Parliament, as well as the centres of power both political and economic. But human right groups, NGOs, the civil society movements etc are not being the target of terror. There is an unholy understanding between some of these groups and terror movements in India. Terror groups also sponsor many human rights movements. Hence, so far, there is no civil society movement which ardently opposes the terrorists groups, but they often stands in between the State and the terrorists and thus limit the state action against the terrorist groups. Hence India failed to adopt a strong preventive legislation to curb terrorism. Many of the new social movements also oppose the war on terror and they have justification for these inhuman activities of terror. For example terror strikes by Islamic groups on USA has been justified because of her imperialist policies and in India the problem of self determination in Kashmir, Hindu assertion and the demolition of Babri Masjid, Gurajat riots etc. Unfortunately this kind of justifications comes not from the terrorists, but from human right activists, civil society movements and writers like Ms. Arunthathi Roy[6], Mahashweta Devi etc. Romantic treatment of the radicals, Naxalites and insurgents may be seen in films and novels. These writers condemn their violence, of course, but they hint that it is actually an outburst of the deprived masses and pooor tribals. Besides, by equating the violence perpetrated by the State against the rebels with the latter's murderous deeds, the intellectuals tend to legitimize the terrorist violence. They keep silence when thousands of civilians are being killed, when the State takes a proactive policy towards terrorism, the civil society movements come to the forefront.

**"Justifiable Violence"**

Maoist violence has become the greatest threat to the national security of India. Like the Islamic Terrorist they have no interest in dialogue or respect to parliamentary democracy. But to a section of intellectuals the Maoists or Naxalites are "favourite radicals". Like the Fascists, the Communists in general or Maoists in particular believes in a one party State. While the violence of the fascists is seen directed at selected groups identified by their religion or race and irrespective of their social or economic status, the aggression of the Maoists is perceived to be in favour of impoverished people and directed at the State, which, in classical Marxist terms represents the oppressive bourgeoisie. This context automatically makes the violence of the Maoists more justifiable than the State[7].

So far no human right movements or civil society movements have come forward to defend the civil rights of citizens against the terrorists. Terrorism is opposed only by some section of the political society. A section of the Indian Press also takes a terrorist - friendly approach. Except one or two incidents in Punjab (by the Sikh terrorists) the terrorists, especially the Islamic Jehadi Terrorists and Maoists never targeted the press, the English press in India.

These groups often use the media to send warning messages to the people and government.

Human rights movements and civil society movements often adopt different yardsticks in assessing the terrorist attacks and communal riots. They came forward in defending the victims of Gujarat riots. But the victims of anti - Sikh riots of Delhi were neglected. Also the group which fought for the re-trial of the Best Bakery case and the Bilkis Banu case in Gujarat, came to the forefront in protecting the accused in the Parliament attack case. Today, they are with the convicts. Also, the movements which raise voice, for the displaced tribals from Narmada Project area are keeping silence on the displaced tribal population in Chattisgarh due to Maoist terror attacks. Interestingly, the case of Hindu refugees of Kashmir is not at all a major area of discussion among human right groups in India. The Tibetan refugees in India also face this kind of neglect from civil society movements in the country.

Civil Society movements in India failed to define terrorism. They failed to protect the civil rights of innocent civilians. They are against anti-terror legislations, special courts, federal investigative agency, and silent on cross-border terrorism. They failed to protect the civil rights of innocent civilians. They are concerned only with State's anti-terror activities. Hence they never demanded compensation for innocent civilian victims of terror. The Indian State failed to stop cross border terrorism and home grown terrorism. Both Maoists and Islamic terrorists were armed and funded by the neighbouring States. The State also failed to prevent the uninterrupted supply of sophisticated arms to these militants. Human right groups strongly oppose the armed intervention of the state. According to them the answer to Maoism and terrorism does not lie in the use of State violence. Due to the civil society's intervention the Government is reluctant to take a firm action. The "Salwa Judum" or people peace movement[8] failed because of the resistance of Human right groups, and the English press. They succeeded in creating a public opinion against 'Salwa Judum' experiment and availing judicial intervention against this popular resistance movement. Later, the Operation Green Hunt launched by the Union Government also failed because there was a lack of strong public opinion in favour of it. To overcome this terror, a new strategy and political will is needed.

An important matter is to be mentioned while discussing "the war on terror" in India is the poor position of security forces in India. Generally the writers and human right activists are against the State action. Police atrocities are termed as one of the reason for terrorism and escalation of violence. In India thousands of security personnels were killed by the terrorists. The brutal killing of 76 CRPF Jawans in a Maoist ambush at Dantewada on 6th April 2010 in Chattisgarh underlines the failure of soft options by the State.

Civil society movements always project police atrocities as a major reason for people's resistance. The facts reject the "State Violence" theory. For example in Chathisgarh, in 2005, 52 civilians and 48 security personnels and 26 Maoists were killed. In 2006, it was 189, 55 and 117, in 2007 95, 182, and 73; In 2008 35, 67 and 66 and in 2009 it was 87, 121 and 137 respectively[9]. Up to April 6, 2010, 133 jawans were killed in Chattisgarh[10]. While comparing the causalities among civilians (killed by the Maoists), security forces and Maoists, from 2005, to 2009 – 419 Maoists were killed; the police force lost 473 men and 458 civilians were killed by Maoists. This shows that during the last five years causalities were more in police force than the civilians or Maoists in Chattisgarh. Altogether the Maoists killed 938 people including security personnels within five years while they lost only 419 militants.

**Conclusion**

Civil Society movements in India failed to uphold the values of true democracy, secularism, freedom, accountability and concern for marginalized people that they espouse. They are mainly concerned with political, economic, sectarian or religious interests of fundamentalist groups or romantic revolutionaries. The proponents of global capital are moving effectively across civil and political society. To the Human Rights activists like Aruna Roy or Arundhathi Roy or Medha Patkar or Binayak Sen, the present day democracy in India is very nearly a fraud since it does not reflect the aspirations of the poor. This disapproval of the present system strengthens the terror groups including the Maoists. The Islamist groups or the Maoist never accept dialogue or debate. But the right activists propose dialogue and development rather than force. At the same time the terrorists groups always use weapons and reject the theory of compromise. To them it is a fight to the finish because they believe in an ideal world where there is no scope for compromise and no place for enemies, political opposition, and criticism. Just as Jihadi terror groups cannot be expected to come to terms with those who do not believe in their version of Islam, the Maoists cannot reach a settlement with a bourgeois establishment. Though the civil society movements defends terrorism for lack of development, the Maoists claim that they stood for the establishment of ideal communist State[11]. It was also evident that within two years 2008, 2009 the Maoists wrecked over 1700 schools in Chattisgarh alone[12]. This shows that they are not keen on development, but they are fighting for a political cause. In the last decade more lives have been claimed by Maoists violence than Islamic terror in India. Both the Maoist guerillas and Islamic terror groups described India as their "enemy" and conflict as a "War". Thus both internally and externally India is challenged. But the political society as well as the Civil society in India has failed to define terrorism and tackle the great menace. By using the development card the civil society movements defend terrorism as popular resistance or against religious discrimination by the majority community, while the political society is divided on petty and partisan political lines. But other civilized countries and communities across the world have made the fight against terror as an article of faith, where the political establishment has risen above party politics. The intelligentsia and administration in these societies, while remaining committed to fundamental values of democracy, have recognized the grave and extraordinary threat to civilization that terrorism constitutes, and have adequately empowered the executive, intelligence and enforcement agencies to deal with the challenge.

It is a fact that in India, the Civil Society movements and human rights activists failed to highlight the fundamental values of human rights and the inherent dignity of all individuals. They keep a closed eye towards the burning issues such as national security and terrorism. Rule of law, civil liberty, right to life and freedom from fear were neglected. Certainly, some of the civil society movements are the actors of a global network which stood for destablising the great democracy and culture.

**References**

1. Robert Putnam, "Making Democracy work civil traditions in Modern Italy", Princeton; Princeton University Press.
2. Bob Edwards and Michael Foley, "Civil Society and Social Capital Beyond Putnam", American Behavioral Scientist, Sept., 1988 – p. 125.
3. Jean Cohen and Andrew Arato, "Political theory and Civil Society", Coimbatore, MIT Press, 1992. See also Suganna Hoeber Rudolph, Civil Society and the Realm of Freedom. Economic and political weekly, 13 May, 2000 p. 1767.
4. Samuel Huntington, "The clash of civilizations and the remaking of the world order, Simon and Schuster, New York, 1996.
5. India Today, April 19, 2010.
6. Arundhati Roy – Walking with the comrades, Outlook, March 29, 2010.
7. Amulya Ganguli – Favourite radicals. The New Indian Express, Kochi, 29th Oct. 2009.
8. Salwa Judum – Peace movement or "peace hunt", it took birth in Chattisgarh in May 2005, as a State sponsored popular movement against the Maoists, which initially had the joint backing of the BJP led State government and congress leader Mahendra Karma, who was persuaded by Chief Minister Raman Singh to be its public face. The Special Police Officers, have been recruited from the ranks of the Salwa Judum.
9. Outlook, 22, Feb 2010.
10. India Today, April 19, 2010.
11. See Interview with Moist leaders, Outlook, Feb. 22 2010.
12. India Today, April 19, 2010.

# 12

# TACKLING THE MENACE OF TERRORISM: HUMAN RIGHTS APPROACHES AND PERSPECTIVES

**R. Ashitha**

## Introduction

Terrorism is today one of the greatest threats to humanity. Over the last decade the concept assumed greater dimensions, by interfering in the global political contexts as well as in the local[1]. All types of political systems are involved in the task of addressing the menace within the framework of their own idelogical and legal premises. The theme has captured a pivotal space in the modern discourse on civil society, democracy, state security, human security, human rights, welfare, development and so on[2]. Terrorism has become a factor in international relations[3]. All types of systems involved with the task of addressing the menace within the framework of their own ideological legal premises. In fact some of the authoritarian and autocratic systems could check its frequent occurrences in their own societies successfully. This has led to the presumption that terrorism is not prone to such political systems. Rather it affects liberal political systems and democracies.

As terrorism is a confusing term, it is very difficult to give a clear cut theory or definition of the term. It is highly complex phenomena and acquired multiple dimensions and assumed alarming proportions all over the world. The word however did not gain wider popularity until the late 19th century when it was adopted by a group of Russian revolutionaries to describe their violent struggle against Tsarist rule. The aftermath of the September 11 attacks and the increasing dimensions of terrorism have proved it to be a scourge of humanity.

## Definitions of Terrorism

Terrorism is used to describe different things by different people. Any article on terrorism must enter the labyrinthine debate on what terrorism means and how it is to be defined. Indeed the definitional quest has haunted the field of terrorism studies. Number of theorists have come up with different types of definitions[4]. Some of them are:

1. The unlawful use of force or violence against persons or property to intimidate or coerce a government, the civilian population, or any segment thereof, in furtherance of political or social objectives (FBI).
2. The calculated use of violence or the threat of violence to inculcate fear, intended to coerce or intimidate governments or societies as to the pursuit of goals that are generally political, religious or ideological (U.S Department of Defence).
3. Premeditated, politically motivated violence perpetrated against non combatant targets by subnational group or clandestine agents, usually intended to influence an audience (US State department).
4. The use or threat for the purpose of advancing political, religious or ideological cause of action which involves serious vilolence against any person or property (United Kingdom Government).
5. Contributes the illegitimate use of force to achieve a political objective when innocent people are targeted (Wasterhageur).
6. A strategy of violence designed to promote desired outcomes by instilling fear in the public at large (Waster Reieh).
7. The use of threatened use of force designed to bring about political change (Brias Jenkeins).
8. The deliberate, systematic murder, maiming, and menacing of the innocent to inspire fear in order to gain political ends. Terrorism is intrinsically evil, necessarily evil and wholly evil (Paul Johnson).

## Terrorism: Challenge to Democracy

Terrorism strikes at the very heart of democracy. In the first place terrorism causes serious damage to the environment of pluralism, tolerance and liberty which are the basic ethos of democracy[5]. Liberal democracy is fairly recent development that in theory it provides the ample scope for political opposition and Participation within the law. It is because they enjoy constitutional legitimacy in the eyes of the majority of their citizens that modern liberal democracies have proved remarkably resilient against terrorist campaigns by extremist political movements. Al Qaeda style terrorism poses a particular threat to democracy both indirectly by causing insecurity and directly by deeming democracy to be hectical and anti-islamic and hence a legitimate target. Terrorism undermined the cherished goal and objective of democracy.

In the fight against terror should not violate the core values of democracy and human rights. Terrorism pose natural threat to human rights, human security development and even the notions of social justice.

### Democratic Limitations on Tackling Terrorism

Democracies face major difficulties in dealing with terrorism. The limited possibilities for surveillance and detention all combine to encourage terrorist action on their soil. In dealing with terrorist threats democratic societies have to be careful to maintain the essence of their system – the rights of individual[6]. There are danger of over reaction and deciding that expedited justice is necessary. Democracies faces great dilemma. If the government yields to the terrorism they are inept and of the government over reacts to the threat and suppress civil liberties, it results in weakening democracy. Democracies need to take care in dealing with violent dissidents since the costs may include not only lives and money but potentially the loss of political liberties as well as society facing terrorist attacks may develop a siege mentality. The country may also adopt procedures to provide for detention of the suspect for lengthy period of time without the filing of formal charges, and over reaction by the government may even increase support for the dissidents. There can also be cases of rash judgments where suspects are poorly treated and confessions are coerced and other rights bypassed. It is a known fact that legal systems in democracies give suspected terrorists more rights than other system.

Looking forward to the 21st century when the awareness of man to his rights has increased, so have increased the forces that are jeoparding their realization. Towards the end of the 20th century, we are face to face with a new situation – democratic societies all over the world are under threat from terrorist activities. In such a situation Human rights become the first casuality. Citizens are forced to accept some curtailment of their rights. Freedom of movement, privacy, access to information etc. become incompatible with the state's efforts to contain and bring the conflict to an end. Citizens often complain about curfews, searches, and detentions resorted to by the state without realizing that these are being resorted to save their lives and properties. Democracy can be defended only within the law, and the minute the law is violated, democracy disappears. Human rights are aimed to preserve democracy and rights of the people to govern themselves. They were used with great effect against totalitarian regimes to liberate the people. They are found inadequate to solve the dilemma faced by democracies fighting a low intensity conflicts.

### Democracy, a Real Potential Weapon

It has been argued that democracy helps to prevent terrorism because the voting process gives people an outlet to express themselves a role filled by terrorism under repressive, undemocratic governments. Bush wanted to "change the conditions that give rise to extremism and terror". Under dictatorship responsible opposition cannot develop, and dissent is driven underground and toward the extreme[7]"

But there is "no solid empirical evidence for a strong link between democracy, or any other regime and terrorism." During the 1970's and 1980's, various terrorist organizations arose in democratic countries, including the Red Brigades in Italy, the provisional Irish Republican Army in Ireland and the United Kingdom, and the Baader meinhof Gang in West Germany. One study found that most terrorists incidents in the 1980's were committed in democracies, generally by their own citizens. There is no reason to think that Al Qaeda would be unable to recruit followers under democratic Arab governments especially of those governments fashioned policies in tune with American interests or made peace with Israel.

Between 2000 and 2003, according to the state department's annual "patterns of Global terrorism" report, 260 major terrorist incidents around the world occurred in countries classified as "free by freedom House, 119 occurred in "partly free countries", and 138 occurred in "not free" countries. (This count excludes both terrorist attacks by Palestinians on Israel, which would increase the number of attacks in democracies even more, and the September 11, 2001, attacks on the United States, which originated in other countries). This is not to argue that free countries are more likely to produce terrorists than other countries. Rather these numbers simply indicate that there is no relationship between the incidence of terrorism in a given country and the degree of freedom enjoyed by its citizen. They certainly do not indicate that democracies are substantially less susceptible to terrorism than are other forms of government.

## The Case of Two Major Democracies: USA and INDIA

In this aspect this paper focussed on the terrorist attack on the two democratic countries of the world i.e. USA and India.In the case of USA the September 11 brought many changes in the policies and programmes of US government.Within the United states the immediate post 9/11 period witnessed the enactment of number of key policies that have had a lasting impact. The central new piece of legislation were undoubtedly;

1. The USA patriot Act
2. The establishment of the Department of Homeland security ,and
3. The restructuring of the intelligence community.

### (A) The USA Patriot Act[8]

The Act increases the ability of law enforcement agencies to search telephone, mail, communications, medical, financial and other records; cases restrictions on foreign intelligence gathering within the Untied States, expands the secretary of the treasury's authority to regulate financial transactions, particularly those involving foreign individuals and entities and enhances the discretion of law enforcement and immigration authorities in detaining and deporting immigrants suspected of terrorism related acts. The act also expands the definition of terrorism to include domestic terrorism, thus enlarging the number of activities to which the USA PATRIOT Act's expanded law enforcement powers can be applied.

The PATRIOT Act has made a number of changes to US law. Key acts changed were the Foreign intelligence surveillance Act of 1978 (FISA), the Electronic Communications Privacy Act of 1986 (ECPA), the money laundering control act of 1986 and Bank secrecy act (BSA) as well as the immigration and Nationality Act. The act itself came about after the September 11 terrorist attacks on New York city and the Pentagon. After these attacks congress immediately started work on several proposed anti-terrorist bills, before the Justice Department. Finally drafted a bill called the Anti-Terrorism act of 2001. This was introduced in the House as it provide appropriate tools required to intercept and obstruct terrorism Act of 2001, and was later passed by the House as the uniting and strengthening America (USA) Act (H.R 2975) on October 12. It was then introduced in the Senate as the USA Act of 2002 where a number of amendments were proposed by senator Russ Feingold, all of which were passed. The final bill, the USA PATRIOT Act was introduced into the House on October 23.

**Controversy on Patriot Act**

The USA PATRIOT Act has generated a great deal controversy since its enactment. EPIC have criticized the law as unconstitutional, especially when "the private communications of law-abiding American citizens might be intercepted incidently". While the EFF hold that the lower standard applied to wiretaps "gives the FBI a 'blank check' to violate the communications privacy of countless innocent Americans." The EFF's criticism is more extensive they believe that the amendment "is in possible violation of the 4th amendment to the U.S Constitution" because previously if the FNI listened to voicemail illegally, it couldn't use the messages in evidence against the defendant[9].

The USA patriot Act's expansion of Court jurisdiction to allow the nation wide service of search warrants proved controversial for the EFF. They believe that agencies will be able to "shop for judges that have demonstrated a strong bias toward law enforcement with regard to search warrants, using only those judges lest likely to say no-even if the warrant doesn't satisfy the strict requirements of the Fourth amendment to the constitution".

Law governing the material support of terrorism proved contentious. It was criticized by the EFF for infringement of freedom of association. The EFF argues that had this law been enacted during Apartheid, U.S citizens would not have been able to support the African National Congress as the EFF believe the ANC would have been classed as a terrorist organization.

Another controversial aspect of the USA PATRIOT Act is the immigration provision that allow for the indefinite detention of any allies whom the Attorney General believes may cause a terrorist act. Another controversial aspect of the USA patriot act is its effect on the privacy of British Columbian citizens. British Columbia privacy commissioner raises concerns that the USA PATRIOT Act will allow the United states government to access Canadians private information, such as personal medical records, that are outsourced to American companies. Although the government of British Columbia has taken measures to prevent Untied States authorities from obtaining information, the widespread powers of the USA patriot Act could overcome legislation that is passed in Canada. Congress passed the USA patriot act in response to the terrorists attack of September 11, 2001. The USA patriot Act, commonly known as the "patriot Act", is a statue enacted by the Untied States Government that President George W. Bush signed into law on October 26, 2001.

### Opposition to Patriot Act

ACLU activists and many allies on the left and right have been making waves across the country by passing resolutions opposing sections of the patriot act that violate fundemental rights and liberties. Many parts of the contraversial law passed just 45 days after the september 11 2001 attack, with virtually no debate take away checks on law enforcement and threaten the very rights and freedoms that were struggling to protect. Many aspects of the bill increase opportunity for law enforcement and the intelligence community to return an era where they monitored and sometimes harassed individuals. In the days after September 11 federal government took to custody more than 1100 people.

### The Case of India: Legal Initiatives

### Anti-Terrorist Laws in India[10]

India earlier had certain laws to deal with terror activities. They are:

#### (a) The Terrorist and Disruptive Activities (Prevention) Act 1987

The TADA act was the first and only legislative effort by the union government to define and counter terrorist activities. It was formulated in the back drop of growing terrorist violence in Punjab which had its violent effects in other parts of the country too. An act to make special provisions for the prevention of and for coping with, terrorist and disruptive activities and for matters connected therewith or incidental thereto. The act extends to the whole of India. It applies also to citizens of India outside India.

#### Punishment for Terrorist Acts

Whoever with intent to overdue the Government as by law established or to strike terror in the people or any section of the people or to alienate any section of the people or to adversely affect the harmony amongst different sections of the people does any act or thing by using bombs, dynamite or other explosive substances or inflammable substances or lethal weapons or poisons or noxious gases or other chemicals by any other substances of a hazardous nature in such a manner as to cause or as is likely to cause death of, or injuries to, any person or persons or loss of, or damage to, or destruction of, property or disruption of any supplies or services essential to the life of the community, or detains to kill or injure such person in order to compel the Government of any other person to do or abstain from doing any act, commits a terrorist act.

The Act which was criticized on various counts by human rights organizations and political parties was permitted to lapse in May 1995 though cases initiated while it was in force continue to hold legal validity.

### (b) The Prevention of Terrorism Act 2002

The prevention of terrorism Act, enacted on March 28, 2002 replaced the prevention of Terrorism Ordinance (POTA) 2001. The act provided the legal frame work to strengthen administrative rights to fight terrorism within the country of India and was to be applied against any person and acts covered by the provisions within the act. It was not meant as a substitute for action under ordinary criminal laws.

The Act defined what a terrorist act and a terrorist is and grants special powers to the investigating authorities described under the act. Under the new law detention of a suspect for up to 180 days without the filing of charges in court was permitted. It also allowed law enforcement agencies to withhold the identities of witness and treat a confession made to the police as an admission of guilt. Under regular Indian law, a person can deny such confessions in court, but not under POTA.

### (c) The Unlawful Activities (Prevention) Amendment Ordinance 2004

After the prevention of Terrorism Act, 2002, was repealed through an ordinance, the President of India on September 21, 2004 promulgated an ordinance to amend the unlawful activities (Prevention) Act, 1967. It extends to the whole of India. Every person shall be liable to punishment under this act for every act or omission contrary to the provisions thereof, of which he is held guilty in India. Any person, who commits an offence beyond India, which is punishable under this act, shall be dealt with according to the provisions of this Act in the same manner as if such act had been committed in India.

### Punishment for Terrorist Activities

Whoever, with intent to threaten the unity, integrity, security or sovereignty of India or to strike terror in the people or any section of the people in India or in any foreign country, does any act by using bombs, dynamite or other explosive substances or inflammable substances or fire arms or other lethal weapons or poisons or noxious gases or other chemicals or by any other substances of a hazardous nature in such a manner as to cause, or likely to cause, death of, or injuries to any person or persons or loss of, or damage to , or destruction of, property or disruption of any supplies or services essential to the life of the community in India or in any foreign country or causes damage or destruction of any property or equipment used or intended to be used for the defense of India or in connection with any other purposes of the Government of the country.

Whoever conspires or attempts to commit, or advocates, abets, advises or incites or knowingly facilities the commission of, a terrorist act or any act preparatory to the commission of a terrorist act, shall be punishable with imprisonment for a term which shall not be less than five years but which may extend to improvement for life, and shall also be liable to fine.

### (d) The unlawful Activities (Prevention) Amendment Bill, 2008

The unlawful Activities (prevention) amendment (UAPA) Act, radically changes procedures for trying those accused of terrorism, extends the periods of police custody and of detention without charges, denies bail to foreigners, and the reverses the burden of proof in many instances.

The Amendments that have, Post-Mumbai been rushed through in the unlawful Activities Act make it more draconian by giving mere powers to the police to search, arrest and keep in police custody and in jail persons on mere subjective suspicion even if there is no evidence of their being involved in any terrorist acts.

The newly introduced section 43A of the act empowers an officer of a designated authority to search any premises or arrest any persons about whom he or she has "reason to believe or knows" that he or she has a "design" to commit an offence under the act.

Further, the Police officers investigating an offence under the Act have been empowered to realize any organization or any individual to furnish any information that the officer may demand for the investigation. Failure to furnish such information has been made punishable with imprisonment up to three years. The new amendments extended the maximum period for filling a charge in the relevant cases to 180 days[11].

Another amendment virtually rules out bail even during trial. It provides that an "accused persons shall not be released on bail or on his own bond. If the court on a perusal of the case diary or the report made under section 173 of the code is of the opinion that there are reasonable grounds for believing that the accusations against the persons are prime facia true. These amendments make the unlawful activities (prevention) act mere or less as draconian as POTA.

### Human Rights Violations

After 9\11, the Bush administration not only adopted the language of a war on terror, deploying troops to Afganistan to topple the Taliban and then moving on to attack Iraq it also decided to circumvent, if not entirely abandon, the criminal justice system as a means of dealing with suspected terrorist[12].

Prisoners captured in Afghanistan or elsewhere were labeled unlawful combatants; and interned without trial in a specially designed prison camp at Guantanamo Bay, Cuba. Instead of indicting prisoners suspected of terrorism for trial in the federal courts, the US government devised a system of military tribunals, which are supposed to try the suspects on the basis of evidence of their involvement in terrorism. However, very few detainees have ever had the chance of appearing before a tribunal, and the tribunals are conducted by the military, the suspect is not allowed to choose their own lawyer. Guantanamo Bay and extra– judicial procedures only do harm to the traditional reputation of the US as a champion of the rule of law and individual. Abandoning the due process under the rule of law and by violations of human rights of suspect. We betray the very value and principles are the foundation of the democracies we seek to defend. We are also corrupting our democracies and those public officials, members of the military and others who are ordered to carry out such policies. We are also perpetrating major injustice in the name of national security.

Amnesty International is concerned that the USA PATRIOT Act undermines the human rights of Americans and non-citizens, and weakens the framework for promoting human rights internationally. Combined with other post-September 11 domestic security policies, the USA PATRIOT Act becomes even more potent in its ability to erode basic civil and human rights. Even in times of crisis, it is important to preserve constitutional freedoms and human rights[13].

In particular, the USA PATRIOT Act threatens the rights protected in the U.S. Constitution and international documents, such as the Universal Declaration of Human Rights, the International Covenant on Civil and Political Rights (ICCPR), the Convention against Torture, and the Convention on the Elimination of All Forms of Racial Discrimination.

The Patriot Act breaches the First Amendment, which declares our rights to freedom of expression, speech and information. Freedom of information and individual liberty had a tremendous impact on the people in the 20th century, which allowed them to have their perceptions and examine situations from their own point of view. The Fourth Amendment should also protect us from search and seizure. Our society should deny the Patriot Act because it raises controversial issues, such as violating the Constitution and having a tremendous impact on our social lives.

One of the first reasons why the Patriot Act violates the First Amendment rights is because, as it states, "Congress shall make no law respecting an establishment of religion, or prohibiting the free exercise thereof; or abridging the freedom of speech, or of the press, or the right of the people peaceably to assemble, and to petition the Government for a redress of grievances."

These words are stated in the Constitution and they should be respected at all times. Evidently, the Patriot Act violates freedom of speech in the way that people are losing the right to say what and how they truly feel. We have to be careful with the use of words about politics or government because we can be prosecuted. To illustrate it another way, the Patriot Act violates the democratic rights of the freedom of political expression. Furthermore, the Patriot Act researches what people are saying, which makes them very careful with their vocabulary and the meaning of words they use. Even though the government cannot deny our rights to react on certain political issues, the Patriot Act restricts what we can say. These important issues bring the Patriot Act into conflict with our constitutional rights and deny us the right to act freely. "The real protection of free expression rights lies not in the words of the First Amendment. Rather, it lies in the people's willingness to appreciate and support those rights" (Dautrich & Bare, 2005). As the Nieman Reports described, the First Amendment individual liberties are based on the people and they should be able to fight for them. The First Amendment emphasizes very important issues of free speech, free press and free expression, and the Patriot Act in the way of denying people the right to freely act upon governmental and political issues ruins these.

Another way in which The Patriot Act is a controversial issue is the Fourth Amendment. The Fourth Amendment in the Constitution of the United States guarantees that: "The right of the people to be secure in their persons, houses, papers, and effects, against unreasonable searches and seizures, shall not be violated, and no Warrants shall issue, but upon probable cause, supported by Oath or affirmation, and particularly describing the place to be searched, and the persons or things to be seized."

The Patriot Act violates the Fourth Amendment in every point, which should be the concern of every person, because "it violated the Constitution by giving federal authorities unchecked power to obtain the private information" (Swartz, 2004). The Patriot Act allows the federal government to take away the property of a supposed terrorist without notice or the agreement of the judge, even though the person can be innocent. The FBI can search private records within financial institutions, which are our personal documents and should be protected and not searched by law. They can also look into personal records such as medical, phone, internet, student or library records.

Why is anybody concerned about our favorite books or movies? That should be just our own interest. The Federal Agents do not need to have or show any reasons that a person is engaged in criminal or political activity to search the person. The FBI agents do not need to prove any criminal charges against her/him. Furthermore, a person can be above suspicion. The Fourth Amendment illustrates and gives us examples of the points in which The Patriot Act violates human rights against unreasonable search that are clearly interpreted in the basic law of our state.

In addition, The Patriot Act violates the democratic structure of the state. According to Abraham Lincoln, democratic government should be, "government of the people, by the people and for the people." This description of democracy contains a message for us as human beings. Furthermore, we are people who live in a democratic society, but our rights are tightly controlled by the federal government. The Patriot Act gives the right to access sensitive information about people, which makes it a controversial issue. If this is a democratic society, then we cannot be afraid about what we say, read, or do. The Constitution is the basic law for democracy, and by violating its Amendments with the Patriot Act, we violate democracy.

In the case of personal liberties, such as private phone calls, Olmstead vs. USA alerts us to the fact that the taping of phones should be restricted. This was in the 1920s and it should be upheld in today's society. "Some of this speech that will be silenced is speech that is important to an open democracy" (Hudson, 2006). Freedom of speech in the phone call portrays an important aspect of the democracy. No matter how technology or society changes, we still should take into accounts an understanding of Constitutional law. Democracy should protect us from searches of our email or web pages, which the Patriot Act encourages, and guarantee us our private liberties to do what we please. We will always have some limitations but the government (federal agents) should not read our emails or listen to our phone calls. Otherwise, we will need to be very careful with our vocabulary and words. The Founding Fathers established our personal liberties, and democracy represents their basic laws, which are disobeyed by the Patriot Act.

People who disagree might argue that The Patriot Act was not meant to violate the privacy of the people but to protect them from the terrorism. President Bush in a 2005 speech explained that it is to protect the people. He explains, "The Patriot Act is essential to protecting the American people against the terrorists. The Act tore down the wall between law enforcement and intelligence officials so that they can share information and work together to help prevent attacks." Its intention was good in the beginning before establishing the Patriot Act, but after we examined it in real life, we see that the Patriot Act does not just violate our rights, but also prohibits new ideas. It gives the right to government officials to search financial statements, and library, movie, and business records of private persons. Moreover, the Patriot Act is in conflict with the most important rules of the United States, the Constitution.

The rights of ordinary Americans have met with challenge after the September 11 terrorist attacks. The anti-terrorism law USA Patriot Act, which took effect on October 26, 2001, provides law enforcement agencies with greater powers for investigation, including wiretapping of phone calls and Internet E-mail communications by suspect terrorists.

A Federal Court of Appeals on November 18 ruled that the Department of Justice asking for expanding its investigative powers is constitutional, and therefore should not be restricted. It aroused great concern among the American public that the DOJ would encroach upon their right of privacy in its work. Commenting on the court ruling, US House Judiciary Committee Representative John Conyers said in a statement the same day, "Piece by piece, this Administration is dismantling the basic rights afforded to every American under the Constitution." Some civil rights and electronic information organizations worried that there would have no effective protection of civil rights after the ruling. Police brutality is a chronic malady in American society. On July 6, 2002, a bystander videotaped a scene in which several white police officers at Inglewood, Los Angeles, slammed the head of a handcuffed 16-year-old black, named Donovan Jackson, on a squad car and punched him in his eyes, neck and hands. Afterwards, one police officer involved was ordered a paid leave. In contrast, the man who filmed the videotape was detained on July 10. In another incident, on July 8, Oklahoma City police officers repeatedly beat a black suspect on the ground with their batons. The suspect was pepper-sprayed twice. On September 16, police in Boston shot at a suspect car hijacker in the downtown area and wounded him seriously. The incident led to a mass demonstration against police brutality. Indiscriminate arrests are another serious problem in the United States. According to an investigation by the American Civil Liberties Union (ACLU), prosecutors declined to bring charges in 15,798 arrests in 2001, or 26 percent of the 60,412 cases they reviewed that year, the vast majority brought by Baltimore police[14].

In 2002 the number of monthly arrests increased by 15 percent over the previous year to 7,832. Prosecutors declined to charge in24 percent of the cases. Two-thirds of the cases they dropped were dropped on the day of arrest because they could not be proved in court (May 9, 2002, Sun).

Within half a year after the September 11 terrorist attacks, the FBI detained for security reasons more than 1,200 non-US nationals, mainly men from Muslim or Middle Eastern countries (Washington, Dec.10, 2002, EFE). Most of them were detained for overstaying their visas, and according to rules the detention should last for no more than 48 hours. However, many were actually held in custody for a month or more, or even up to 50 days. While in custody, they were deprived of their basic rights—making phone calls, access to a lawyer, family visits, being informed of the reasons for the detention, or challenging the lawfulness of the detention.

They were let out for exercise and air less than an hour a day. Many were handcuffed, and some were even bundled. Those falling ill could not get timely medical treatment.

### Human Rights Violations in India

Under the Terrorist and Disruptive Activities (Prevention) Act, 1987, the total number of detainees was around 76,000. Of these, 25% were dropped bythe police without charges; trials were completed in only 35% of the cases and 95% of these trials ended in acquittals. The conviction rate was less than 1.5% and there were reports of human rights violations committed by the police abusing their excessive powers under this act.

The Government of India used the events of September11, 2001, to justify legislating on terrorism once again–and the new Prevention of Terrorism Act 2002 (POTA) is similar to its predecessor in its provisions and in its implementation. There is no dearth of reports of it being abused for politically motivated arrests and torture: cases such as Mr. Vaiko, who, when a Member of Parliament and a leader of the main opposition party in the state of Tamil Nadu, was incarcerated for over a year under this law without any charges being filed in court. Many tribal women and children in the state of Jharkhand were arrested and placed in custody for long Periods under this law. Similarly, many Muslims were held under the law in the state of Gujarat after anti-Muslim riots. In India too much misuse of her own laws was questioned in Indian soil itself. There was too much hue and cry against the misuse of POTA in many contexts[15].

POTA has been a controversial piece of legislation. Analysts say it is difficult to know whether the law has been effective in curbing the threat of terrorism. There have been allegations that Muslims were being targeted under POTA. Human rights groups attacked the law for its draconian provisions which they said posed a serious threat to individual freedoms and fundamental rights guaranteed by the Indian Constitution. They said the law gave the authorities unbridled powers to deal with any suspect.

## Preserving Human Rights While Combating Terrorism

Internationally terrorism is more than a challenge to rule of law and a clear threat to the individual life and security. In the guise of fight against terrorism security is the justification used by both the democratic states to curb democratic liberties and rights, and by authoritarian states to crush demands for democratic liberties. As a result when nation states began to focus much on security and new security states began to emerge. This has given rise to new demands in the name of human security, human rights and development[16]. As a result it is the dual responsiblity of democratic government not only to protect people from death, injury, or other determent but also to maintain democratic freedoms and the rule of law. To combating terrorism there emerge detention of persons without trial ,house arrest, highly oppressive forms of detention and interrogation. When fighting terrorism the democratic societies need to demonstrate that, unlike the terrorist they value and respect human rights and democratic proceedures. History shows that it is in times of war and instability that it is most dangerous to adopt special meassures limiting freedom and granting excessive powers to the state.

Thus in tackling the menace of terrorism the meassures adopted by the two countries reveals the levels of democratic maturity of these countries. It is high time that while tackling the menace of terrorism the democratic countries should uphold human rights values and spirit .This is the only way by which such societies can address terrorism in a durable and effective way.

## Notes and References

1. Hoffman, Bruce: *Inside terrorism*, (London: Indigo, 1998)
2. Paul Wilkinson: *Terrorism and Democracy*, (USA Rout ledge, 2006)
3. Terrorism Research centre, United States, Website: www. terrorismanswers.com
4. David. J. Whittaker, ed. *Terrorism reader*, (London: Rout ledge, 2001).
5. Dr. Rema Nair, Relationship between security and democracy in combating terrorism (Geneva centre for security policy of csp, 2007)
6. Dr B.N. Pandey: Global terrorism and democratic societies (Centre *India Law quarterly* 1997).
7. F. Gregory Gauses, Can democracy stop terrorism? (*Foreign affairs*, September-October 2005)
8. www.whitehouse.gov/nsc.htm
9. Larry Abramson and Maria Gody, The patriot act key controversies (July 18, 2005).
10. Indian document on anti terror laws,www.satp.org/India/document/ actsand ordinances. (New Delhi).
11. K.G. Balakrishnan, Terrcrism, Rule of law and Human rights: *The Hindu*,16/12/08.
12. Paul Wilkinson: *Terrorism and democracy*, (USA Routledge, 2006).
13. Civil rights and The war on terror, Denial of rights : Amend the USA patriot act now *(Amnesty International Report).*
14. Nancy Baker national security versus civil liberties (*Presidential studies quarterly* Vol. 33 issue 3, 2003).
15. C. Raj Kumar, Fighting terrorism by reforming governance: *The Hindu*, 11/12/08.
16. Paul Wilkinson: *Terrorism and democracy*, (USA Rout ledge, 2006)

# 13

# WOMEN AND HUMAN RIGHTS

**T. Ramany**

The term "Human Rights" is comparatively recent in origin, but the idea is as old as the history of human civilization. Human rights are rights which individuals are entitled to by virtue of being 'human'. Human rights are the minimal rights which every individual must have against the state or other public authorities by virtue of his being a member of the human family irrespective of any other consideration. The first documentary use of the expression "Human Rights" is to be found in the charter of the United Nations, which was adopted at San Francisco on 25th June, 1945. Article I of the UN charter stated the purpose among others, is to achieve international co-operation in promoting and encouraging respect for human rights and for fundamental freedoms for all without distinction as to race, sex, language or religion. The first concrete step by way of formulating human rights was taken up by the United Nations on 10th December, 1948 by adopting the Universal Declaration of Human Rights.

Today women's rights are given more importance than any other rights in the society. Women's rights are integral to Human Rights. This paper attempts to link women and human rights and critically examine the violation of women's rights in general and in India.

**Nature of Women's Rights**

The Universal Declaration of Human Rights (UDHR) defines human rights as universal, inalienable and indivisible which are important for women's human rights. The universality of human rights, demand that the rights of women be acknowledged. The idea that human rights are universal also challenges the contention that the human rights of women can be limited.

The idea of human rights as inalienable means that it is impossible for anyone to abdicate his/her human rights since every person is accorded those rights by virtue of being human. The idea of inalienable rights means that human rights cannot be sold, ransomed, or forfeited for any reason. For decades, work to transform practices which are physically or psychologically damaging to women and that have often been "protected under the rubric of religion, tradition or culture has been particularly difficult, given both the integrity of culture guaranteed by the Universal Declaration and the history of Northern domination in much of the world. The Vienna Declaration and Programes of Action from the world conference on Human Rights held in Vienna in 1993, and the United Nations Declaration Against Women passed by the General Assembly the same year, affirmed that in cases of conflict between women's human rights and cultural or religious practices, the human rights of women must prevail.

The indivisibility of human rights means that none of the rights that are considered to be fundamental human rights is more important than any of the others more specifically that they are interrelated. That Human Rights are indivisible is important for women since their civil and political rights historically have been compromised by their economic status, by social and cultural limitations placed on their activities, and by the ever-present threat of violence that often constitutes an insurmountable obstacle to women's participation in public and political life. The idea of indivisibility has provided women with a common framework through which to emphasize the complexity of the challenges they face and to highlight the necessity of including women and gender conscious perspectives in the development and implementation of gender sensitive policies. Women have argued that political stability cannot be realized unless women's social and economic rights are also addressed and incorporated in the policy processes. Social equity cannot be generated without economic justice and this cannot happen without women's participation at all levels of political decision-making.

**The concept of Women's Human Rights**

The UDHR provides general action against discrimination on the ground of sex and in matters relating to the status of women in general. The General Assembly of UN at its 9th session, dealt with the status of women in private law, customs, ancient laws and practices affecting the human dignity of women. Article 26 of the International Covenant on Civil and Political Rights provides that all persons are equal before the law and are entitled without any discrimination of the equal protection of the law.

The Economic and Social Council established a sub-commission on the status of women. The International Women's Year (1975) was a call to men and women everywhere and to the government and non-governmental organizations to exert every effort to promote equality of men and women.

During the United Nations Decade for Women (1976-1985), women from many geographical, racial, religious, cultural and class backgrounds actively took part in efforts to improve the status of women. The UN sponsored women's conferences, which took place in Mexico City in 1975, Copenhagen in 1980, and Nairobi in 1985, were convened to evaluate the status of women and to formulate strategies for women's advancement. These conferences were critical venues at which women came together, debated their differences and discovered their commonalities and gradually began learning to bridge differences to create a global movement. In the late eighties and early nineties, women in diverse countries took up the human rights framework and began developing the analytic and political tools that together constitute the ideas and practices of women's human rights.

### The Movement for Women's Human Rights

The term "Women rights" does not refer simply to the theoretical approaches that women have used to transform human rights concepts, programs and agendas. In addition to being instrumental in the formulation of the conceptual challenges and demands levied by women, the idea of women's human rights has had immense impact as a tool for political activism. The concept of women's human rights has opened the way for women around the world to ask hard questions about the official inattention and general indifference to the widespread discrimination and violence that women experience every day.

Women's activities developed globally during and following the United Nations Decade for women, more and more women raised the question of why "Women's rights" and women's lives have been deemed secondary to the "human rights" and lives of men. Over the past decade, a movement around women's human rights has emerged posing a challenge to the limited notions of human rights. It has focused particularly on violence against women as a prime example of the bias against women in human rights practice and theory.

The United Nations World Conference on Human Rights held in Vienna in 1993 was the first such meeting since 1968, and it became a natural vehicle to highlight the new visions of human rights thinking and practice being developed by women. Since the conference represented an historic re assessment of the status of human rights, it became the unifying public focus of a worldwide Global Campaign for Women's Human Rights. The meetings held in Tunis, San Jose and Bangkok discussed the idea of women's human rights as a framework for women to articulate and collaborate around broad and similar concerns about the status of women. It also provided women with a way to elaborate on the most pressing human rights issues specific to particular political, geographic, economic and cultural contexts.

Women comntinued to lobby for the wider recognition of women's human rights at subsequent United Nations Conferences. At the International Conference on Population and Development in Cairo in 1994, Women's reproductive rights were recognized as human rights. At the Fourth

World Conference on Women in Beijing in 1995 signaled the successful mainstreaming of women's rights as human rights.

The most important international treaty specifically asddressing women's human rights is the Convention on the Elimination of all forms of Discrimination Against Women (CEDAW) which was initiated during the UN Decade for women and has been ratified by over 130 countries. Further, local women's groups have integrated the women's human rights framework into their legal literacy programs and legal strategies.

## The Contemporary Women's Movement in India

The first women's movement condemned tradition and religion for women's suffering and sought redress in education and legal change. It was the feminist leaders of the organization who recognized women as oppressed because of their sex. They constructed women as biologically, psychologically, and spiritually different from men and based their claim for representation in public life.

The UN declaration of International Women's Year and the International Women's Decade led to the appointment of the Guha Committee. Its report was to prevent the oppression and exploitation, sexual harassment and domestic violence they were now experiencing. The contemporary feminist movement emerged in the late 1970's and early 1980's.

One of the first steps taken by the leaders of this movement was to expose the "various categories of humiliation, atrocities, tortures and mass assault to which women were subjected. Towards the end of 1979, a small group of women in New Delhi published 'Manushi', a journal about Women and Society. This has now become India's premier feminist journal, treating specifically women's issues, such as sexual harassment, violence against women, in the home and as a weapon of political and social control, history and literature on women and social, political, economic issues such as communalism and public health policy.

Those women who liked this new word thrived to develop a world of their own. Sex segregation and norms of female seclusion offered them an opportunity to form their own organizations relatively free from male tutelage though not free from patriarchy. The first was feminist movement, motivated by this ideology and working through women's organizations, presented demands for women's rights.

The contemporary feminist movement, has brought women's issues to the attention of all Indians. Feminists, galvanized by endemic violence against women, developed new organizations and new institutions.

## Violation against Women's Rights

Violence against women is global and widespread and is tolerated as a social phenomenon, in institution and custom and, to some degree, in law. The widespread violence against women around the world, is based on consideration on her sex alone. Violence against women was not a new issue. Sati in the 19th century became a religious issue.

Violence against women is universal, occurring in all cultures and countries. Violence against women takes from domestic abuse and rape to child marriages and female circumcision. The former UN Secretary General Boutros Ghali, stated that violence against women seems to be increasing around the world. He focussed on the following aspects of violation.

### (a) Extent and Severity of Violence

WHO calculated there are over 1000 million girls and women in the world today who suffered violence inflicted on them by way of female genital multilation, most often between the ages of four and eight. Violence against women is often connected with their sexuality. Violence can have to do with deprivation of liberty or equality, especially as girls grow up. In many countries, girls are less valued than boys, and grow up with less food, move domestic chores and less status in the family or even sexual moleslation, from a family members. These factors can drive girls into prostitution at the age of ten or eleven.

Identifying the multiplicity of forms of violence against women suggests the universality of the problem. All forms of violence against women is an indication of the variety and severity of abuse: bettering, rape, dowry death, emotional abuse, bride burning, child sexual abuse, forced prostitution etc. Violence can be move easily carried out against women because of their lower social, economic and legal status. Women make up over half of the world's population and pereform 2/3 rds of its work, but receive one-tenth of its income and own less than one hundredth of its property.

The majority of world's poor are women - the poverty of women and their inability to participate fully in development are linked to the violence against them. Violence and abuse are factors which are keeping women from functioning independendly in the world. Women are prone to multiple disabilities in economic activity - wage discrimination, legal constraints and poor access to education and this puts them at continuing risk for exploitation and abuse.

### (b) Violence by state agencies

Throughout the world in varying degrees there is reluctance to prosecute assailants of women. Violence against women is of personal and intimate nature. The state policies reflect the basic social attitude. All citizens are equal but some (men) are more equal than others (women). Women have complained that the police tried to collude unconsciously with the culprits and feel that they should not interfere in family of the family and the dominance of the man within the family who has a right to exercise power over the woman.

## Law and Violence against Women in India

The Indian constitution has made a number of provisions for protecting the rights and dignity of a woman. Gender inequality leading to gender violence, is deeply embedded in the Indian social structure. Violence against women has been justified in cultural and religious grounds. There is also a high degree of official and social tolerance of violence against women, which has its roots in religious doctrines.

**Summing up**

Women's human rights not only teaches women about the range of rights that their governments must honor, it also functions as a kind of gestalt by which to organize analyses of their experiences and plan action for change. The human rights framework creates a space in which the possibility for a different account of women's lives can be developed. The fundamental principles of human rights that accord to each and every person the entitlement to human dignity give women a vocabulary for describing both violations and impediments to the exercise of their human rights. The large body of international covenants, agreements and commitments about human rights gives women political leverage and a tenable point of reference. And finally the idea of women's human rights enable women to define and articulate the specificity of the experiences in their lives at the same time that it provides a vocabulary for women to share the experiences of other women around the world and work collaboratively for change.

Indian women at the end of the twentieth century would argue that they still have a long way to go to attain gender justice. The issues of the moment and the unsolved problems must not be allowed to negate the victories of the past. Women's education and political action have altered India's social and political landscape. Women have moved from being objects of legislation to initiators. For many women the family no longer exercises total control over their destinies. A general awakening has begun and it cannot be permanently suppressed.

## References


- Ashok Kumar Pandey, (2002), *Emerging Issues on Empowerment of Women*, (New Delhi).
- Charlotte Bunch and Samantha Frost (2007), *Women's Human Rights: An Introduction*, (Ranchi).
- Maya Majumdar, (2005), *Encyclopaedia of Gender Equality through Women Empowerment*, (New Delhi).
- Meenakshi Malhotra (2004), *Empowerment of Women*, (New Delhi).
- K.L. Panigrahy (2006), *Women Empowerment*, (Agra).
- Susmitha Nayak Subhas C Parida (2009), *Empowerment of Women in India*, (New Delhi).
- Sushamma Sahay, (1998), *Women and Empowerment Approaches and Strategies* (New Delhi).

# 14

# GENDER DIMENSION OF ARMED CONFLICTS: VIOLATION OF RIGHTS OF WOMEN

**Ardra Manasi**

Human rights are rights inherent to all human beings. It is a 'universal'[1] concept rooted in 'moral concerns' which call for respecting the rights of another human being, irrespective of caste, national or ethnic origin, language, or religion a person belong to. Human rights are also said to be 'inalienable'[2] in the sense that it cannot be taken away by force except under exceptional situations employing due process. They can be broadly categorised as civil rights, political rights, economic, social and cultural rights. These rights are said to be 'interrelated, interdependent and indivisible.'[3] The advancement or deprivation of one right equally affects other rights. Another principle underlying human rights is the principle of non-discrimination as complemented by the principle of equality which stated in Article 1 of the Universal Declaration of Human Rights[4]: "All human beings are born free and equal in dignity and rights. Human rights entail 'both rights and obligations.' There require a strong institutional mechanism to fulfil these rights. It lies in the responsibility of states to assume obligations and duties under international law to 'respect, to protect and to fulfil human rights.' At the individual level, while we are entitled our human rights, we should also respect the human rights of others.

In 1993, in her seminal work 'Women and Human rights' (1993), Katrina Thomasevski raises a pertinent question. Does the term 'Human Rights' necessarily include the realm of women's rights? She believed that 'human' and 'rights' were perceived from a masculine view point. She cited examples like the 'French declaration of rights of man'. Thus, Tomasevski could successfully bring into limelight the need to include 'her' (and not just 'him') within national as well as international laws and conventions.

According to a report published by UN department of public information in 1996, human right violations against women occur at different realms of the society namely family, community and the state. Domestic violence, traditional practices like female genital mutilation, son preference, dowry related deaths and early marriage without the consent of the girl constitute human right violations at the family level. Rape, Sexual harassment in work places; prostitution; trafficking; and pornography are human right violations which are pronounced at the community level. There is yet another category which includes state perpetrated violations of human rights. Custodial violence, violence against women in armed conflicts, and violence against refugees and displaced women constitute this. This paper will attempt to focus in detail on human right violations against women during armed conflicts.

Women and men are distinctly affected by war. This paper tends to look at how women are more affected, considering the already disadvantageous position they enjoy in the mainstream society. Thus, the term gender enters the picture. Gender refers to the perceptions of '[5]appropriate behaviour, appearance and attitude for women and men that arise from social and cultural expectations.' This paper looks at how conflict alters this common understanding of stereotypical as well as non-stereotypical roles of women. A conflict is seemed to be composing of different stages like '[6]Run up (pre-conflict), Conflict, Peace process, Reconstruction (post conflict).' It is to be noted that human right violations against women are not just restricted to the conflict phase. Even peace may not denote the end of the armed conflict, but a time to address the structural power imbalances that caused the conflict in the first place. Thus, such a nuanced understanding is important to look at gender inequality that manifests across these stages.

## Armed Conflict and Women

There are different ways in which conflicts directly affect women. Audrey Macklin points out those conflicts greatly reduce mobility among women due to responsibility for elderly, children or disabled kin and obstacles to travel without male accompaniment.' The lack of adequate sanitation and clean water worsens women's well being. [7]Audrey Macklin describes about the plight of women in conflict stricken parts of southern Sudan as follows:

"Women fear rape by militia, rape by men who distribute aid in exchange for sex, and rape by husbands who demand that they replace dying children by producing more children who will grow up to wage the national struggle-that is if the women survive their pregnancies and the children survive to adolescence."

Conflicts also lead to shifting of gender roles. In most cases, women take up the non-stereotypical role of the breadwinner in the absence of her male counterpart in order to earn a livelihood and to save her family from the distress exacerbated by the conflict. [8]There were even extreme cases where women in Sri Lankan ethnic conflict zones took up carpentry to earn a livelihood. Conflicts are also said to have lead to states of [9]'complex emergencies', quoting the language of humanitarian specialists. It refers to the 'combined combustible effects of poverty, gender discrimination, economic crisis, armed violence, environmental devastation, social and political disarray, and massive displacement.' All these factors reinforce each other to form a 'catastrophic web.'

Conflict leads to the violation of reproductive rights of women which in turn affects their will to assert economic and political rights. Sexual violence against women and forceful sexual slavery demanded from refugee women are clear cut examples of violations of reproductive rights of women. [10]Reproductive rights can be summarised as:

- Right to basic health, reproductive health and family planning measures.
- Right to be free from sexual violence and exploitation.
- Right to be free from any cruel, inhuman or degrading treatment/ punishment.

## [11]Impacts of Conflicts on Women

### 1. Forced Displacement

UN defines forced displacement as the "clearest violation of human, economic, political and social rights and the failure to comply with inherent humanitarian laws.' It is disheartening to note that UN Refugee convention of 1951 doesn't recognize the rights of internally displaced persons.Global statistics points towards the fact that over the last decade, the number of refugees has increased from 15 million to 22 million. About 20 to 25 million IDPs (Internally displaced persons) fall outside the 'international definition of a refugee.'Displacement is often viewed as a 'temporary or transitory phenomenon.' However, experience in countries such as Peru, Sri Lanka, Somalia and Sudan shows it is actually a 'prolonged process.'

Giorgio Agamben, the Italian philosopher considered refugee camps as '[12]absolute bio political spaces.' He made a distinction between Zoë and bios, basically drawing from Greek traditions. Zoe was defined as "simple fact of living common to all living beings" while Bios was defined as a "way of living proper to an individual or group." He believed that in a refugee camp, individuals are in a 'state of exception' where they lead a 'bare life' (Vita nuda) and are stripped of every possible rights, which includes even 'rights to have rights' and dignities of a citizen.'

There are many ways in which forced displacement directly affects the rights of women. It leads to instances of increased physical and emotional violence against them. On the economic front, it reduces their access to resources which pushes them into the vicious cycle of poverty. In many cases like in Sri Lanka, women trade sex for a livelihood, when they are widowed and abandoned. This earns them the title of 'bad mothers or bad women.' Thus, many women also dread the social ostracism that follows from this. Also, as we have already seen, conflicts in many cases call for a shifting of gender roles. But it is a crucial question to be addressed whether it necessarily leads to greater autonomy for women. It can also mean greater vulnerability with respect to their reproductive rights.

**2. Gender Based Violence**

Sexual violence against women constitutes the major chunk of gender based violence. Rape is often used as a 'weapon of war' as cited in the cases of Rwanda and Bosnia. For example, up to 500,000 women were raped at gunpoint, in Rwanda in 1994. Sexual violence has also become a weapon of 'ethnic cleansing', as seen in Bosnia-Herzegovina and Kosovo, where rape was used by Serbian police and paramilitary forces to punish women belonging to the Kosovo Liberation Army (Human Rights Watch 2000). Also, sexual service to army personnel in exchange of food and protection lead to unwanted pregnancies among women. Many women were dragged into prostitution for the sake of earning a livelihood during the conflict phase.

Mc Ginn et al found that 'fertility rates declined and rates of unsafe abortions and maternal mortality ratios went up during the intense phases of the conflict.' It was observed that unsafe abortions constituted 25-30% of maternal deaths among refugees compared with 13% of such deaths worldwide. Studies conducted in Rwanda and Sierra Leone found sexual favours were often demanded in exchange for food, which led to an increase in the number of women's sexual partners (Benjamin 2001). This can be supplemented with the fact that there is higher incidence of HIV infection and as well as other sexually transmitted infections (STIs) in conflict zones, calling for greater attention with respect to women's physical health and psychological condition Also, food scarcity and inequalities in food distribution are exacerbated during periods of armed conflict, render women and girls more susceptible to malnutrition (UN 2002).

**Major Challenges and Possible Solutions**

The major challenge ahead lies in the proper implementation of various laws as well as conventions pertaining to the rights of women. There is no dearth of laws per say when it comes to the realm of women's rights. [13]UN Charter (1945),UN Universal Declaration of Human rights(1948), CEDAW (Convention on the elimination of all forms of discrimination against women-1979), UN Vienna Declaration-1993,Beijing Declaration and platform for action(1995), Windhoek Declaration: Namibia plan (2000), and the UN Security council Resolution 1325 on women, peace and security(2000) exclusively acknowledge the rights of women. It is to be recognised that women experience armed conflict in diverse ways as 'victims, survivors, leaders and peacemakers.' In consonance with the ideals of UN Security

Council Resolution 1325 on Women, Peace and Security, [14]the following suggestions/solutions can implemented.

### (1) DDR- Disarmament, Demobilization and Reintegration

It is commonly perceived that women are mere victims of a conflict. But it is to be noted that there is another category comprising female combatants who take up non-stereotypical roles during a conflict. It is also equally important to focus on how they are incorporated into the main stream society during the post conflict phase. DDR aims at re-integrating ex combatants back into the society. This is illustrated in point 13 of the UN Security council resolution which calls for all 'those involved in the planning for disarmament, demobilization and re-integration to consider the different needs of male as well female ex combatants and to take into account the needs of dependants.'

### (2) Increase Funding to Specialized Services and SOPs to Prevent Sexual Violence

Specialized services mainly include counseling and medical infrastructure that should cater to the needs of victimized women in the post conflict zones. Also, we observe that sexual violence has reached alarming proportions in conflict zones, mainly employing it as a weapon of war. Standard operating procedures (SOPs) should be formulated to prevent sexual violence against women during conflicts. This can include measures like continuous monitoring and patrolling of conflict hit zones by trained staff to prevent the occurrence of such abuses.

### (3) Involve Women in Peace Process and Negotiations

Generally, women are excluded from such measures leading to peace building and finally, men end up formulating policies that affect women too. Also, there is a need to involve women's organizations in decision making within legal and political structures.

### (4) Gender Mainstreaming and Context Specific Interventions

Gender mainstreaming refers to the 'process of assessing the implications for women and men in any planned action, including legislation, policies or programme.' The ultimate goal of mainstreaming is to achieve 'gender equality.' The administration of post-conflict Rwanda has emerged as a good practice example of gender mainstreaming. Continuous efforts have been made to ensure 'gender cuts across all policies and priority areas.' This is even reflected in the formulation of budgets which appear to be gender sensitive. The gacaca in Rwanda which was a traditional, communal judicial system that was re-introduced to relieve the burden on the national courts gave room for women judges apart from their male counterparts.

In short, this paper has tried to focus on how armed conflicts can negatively affect women's reproductive rights. This in turn can have an equal bearing on their capacity to assert their other rights-be it political or economic or cultural. Many national as well as international agencies are trying in their best capacity to translate women's rights into a tangible reality. But it should be noted that in the first place, women need to be empowered to assert their basic rights. '[15]Humanitarian relief as a model of intervention' or '[16]legalistic and formalistic human right mechanisms' can fail if they are externally imposed. Thus, we need to acknowledge the voice of those who have been directly victimised by the conflict to come up with a feasible solution that will operate on the premises of their true needs, as voiced by them.

## Notes and References

1. International laws under UNHR-http://www2.ohchr.org/english/law/
2. International laws under UNHR-http://www2.ohchr.org/english/law/
3. What are human rights(UNHR)- http://www.ohchr.org/en/issues/Pages/WhatareHumanRights.aspx.
4. The universal declaration of human rights: http://www.un.org/en/documents/udhr/index.shtml.
5. Gender approaches in conflict and post conflict situations - UNDP Manual.
6. Rosalind P Petchesky, 'Conflict and Crisis Settings: Promoting Sexual and Reproductive Rights', Reproductive Health Matters 2008;16(31):4–9.
7. *Ibid.*
8. Jennifer Hyndman and Malathi de Alwis, Beyond Gender: Towards a Feminist Analysis of Humanitarianism and Development in Sri Lanka, Women's Studies Quarterly, Vol. 31, No. 3/4, Women and Development: Rethinking Policy and Reconceptualising Practice (Fall - Winter, 2003), pp. 212-226
9. Rosalind P Petchesky, Conflict and crisis settings: promoting sexual and reproductive rights, Reproductive Health Matters 2008;16(31):4–9
10. Displaced and Disregarded: Refugees and their Reproductive Rights-Briefing paper-Centre for reproductive rights.
11. These are the major impacts listed in the overview report on gender and armed conflict, Institute of development studies, University of Sussex authored by Amani el Jack.
12. Internet Encyclopedia of Philosophy on Agamben
13. International laws under UNHR-http://www2.ohchr.org/english/law/
14. Gender approaches in conflict and post conflict situations - UNDP Manual.
15. Rosalind P Petchesky, Conflict and crisis settings: promoting sexual and reproductive rights, Reproductive Health Matters 2008;16(31):4–9.
16. *Ibid.*

# 15

# RIGHT TO EDUCATION IN INDIA: THE CONCEPT AND CONTEXT

**D. Pradeep**

## Introduction

The Government of India introduced a new Act –The right to education act. As such the act has triggered a series of new discussions and debates nation wide. A close perusal of the act itself reveals that it is a revolutionary step taken by the UPA Government. However, such a step could not be seen as an isolated move, rather it should be read along with the series of efforts taken by various central governments at different periods of time ,since independence. The present paper would like to look in to the various measures taken by the central governments to impart free and compulsory education in India, where special emphasis would be given to the Right to education and its varying ramifications in the Indian context.

India has a long history of stretching back to the ancient urban centres of learning. The Nalanda University was the oldest university-system of education in the world. However, by the advent of British Imperialism, Western education became ingrained into Indian society. In free India the division of powers put the responsibility of education both under the central and state governments control. Though India has made a huge progress in terms of increasing primary education, attendance rate and expanding literacy to approximately two thirds of the population, her improved education system is one of the main contributors to the economic development of the nation. At the same time much of the progress in education has been credited to various private institutions. The private education market in India is estimated to be worth $40 billion in 2008 and will increase to $68 billion by 2012. However, India continues to face multi-faceted challenges. Despite growing investment in education, 35% of the population is illiterate and only 15% of the students reach high school. As of 2008, India's post-secondary high schools offer only enough seats for 7% of India's college-age population, 25% of teaching positions nationwide are vacant, and 57% of college professors lack either a master's or PhD degree. As of 2007, there are 1522 degree-granting engineering colleges in India with an annual student intake of 582, 000, However, these institutions face shortage of faculty and concerns have been raised over the quality of education in an alarming way.

With the advent of British rule, a section of Westernized elite was versed in the Western system of education which the British had introduced. This system soon became solidified in India as a number of primary, secondary, and tertiary centres for education cropped up during the colonial era. Between 1867 and 1941 the British increased the percentage of the population in Primary and Secondary Education from around 0.6% of the population in 1867 to over 3.5% of the population in 1941. However this was much lower than the equivalent figures for Europe where in 1911 between 8 and 18% of the population were in Primary and Secondary education.

Following independence in 1947, Maulana Azad, India's first education minister envisaged strong central government control over education throughout the country, with a uniform educational system. However, given the cultural and linguistic diversity of India, it was only the higher education dealing with science and technology that came under the jurisdiction of the central government. The government also held powers to make national policies for educational development and could regulate selected aspects of education throughout India which included a series of initiatives.

**Earlier Central Initiatives**

The central government of India formulated the National Policy on Education (NPE) in 1986 and also reinforced the Programme of Action (POA) in 1986. The government initiated several measures like the launching of DPEP (District Primary Education Programme) and SSA (Sarva Shiksha Abhiyan, India's initiative for Education for All) and setting up of Navodaya Vidyalaya and other selective schools in every district, advances in female education, inter-disciplinary research and establishment of open universities. India's NPE also contains the National System of Education, which ensures some uniformity while taking into account regional education needs. The NPE also stresses on higher spending on education, envisaging a budget of more than 6% of the Gross Domestic Product. While the need for wider reform in the primary and secondary sectors is recognized as an issue, the emphasis is also on the development of science and technology education infrastructure. All these efforts were taken with a view to universalizing education in the country.

### 1. Primary Education

The Indian government lays emphasis to primary education up to the age of fourteen years [referred to as Elementary Education in India.] As part of this program the government has also banned child labor in order to ensure that the children do not enter unsafe working conditions. However, both free education and the ban on child labor are difficult to enforce due to economic disparity and social conditions. 80% of all recognized schools at the Elementary Stage are government run or supported, making it the largest provider of education in the Country. However, due to shortage of resources and lack of political will, this system suffers from massive gaps including high pupil teacher ratios, shortage of infrastructure and poor level of teacher training.

There have been several efforts to enhance quality made by the government. The District Primary Education Programme (DPEP) was launched in 1994 with an aim to universalize primary education in India by reforming and vitalizing the existing primary education system. 85% of the DPEP was funded by the central government and the remaining 15 percent was funded by the states. The DPEP, which had opened 160000 new schools including 84000 alternative education schools delivering alternative education to approximately 3.5 million children, was also supported by UNICEF and other international programmes.] This primary education scheme has also shown a high Gross Enrolment Ratio of 93–95% for the last three years in some states. Significant improvement in staffing and enrolment of girls has also been made as a part of this scheme. The current scheme for universalization of Education for All is the Sarva Shiksha Abhiyan which is one of the largest education initiatives in the world. Enrolment has been enhanced, but the levels of quality remain low. This further creates problem in most of the rural semi-urban areas where students enrolment is deeply interrelated with certain other socio-economic peculiarities.

### 2. Secondary Education

The National Policy on Education (NPE), 1986, has provided for environment awareness, science and technology education, and introduction of traditional elements such as Yoga into the Indian secondary school system. Secondary education covers children 14-18 which covers 88.5 million children according to the Census, 2001. However, enrolment figures show that only 31 million of these children were attending schools in 2001-02, which means that two-third of the population remained out of school. A significant feature of India's secondary school system is the emphasis on inclusion of the disadvantaged sections of the society. Professionals from established institutes are often called to support in vocational training. Another feature of India's secondary school system is its emphasis on profession based vocational training to help students attain skills for finding a vocation of his/her choosing. A significant new feature has been the extension of SSA to secondary education in the form of the Madhyamik Shiksha Abhiyan.

A special Integrated Education for Disabled Children (IEDC) programme was started in 1974 with a focus on primary education but which was converted into Inclusive Education at Secondary Stage. Another notable special programme, the Kendriya Vidyalaya project, was started for the employees of the central government of India, who are distributed throughout the country. The government started the Kendriya Vidyalaya project in 1965 to provide uniform education in institutions following the same syllabus at the same pace regardless of the location to which the employee's family has been transferred.

### 3. Tertiary Education

The university system is, in many parts of India , in a state of disrepair. In almost half the districts in the country, higher education enrolments are abysmally low, almost two-third of our universities and 90 per cent of our colleges are rated as below average on quality parameters. Paradoxically, India's higher education system is the third largest in the world, after China and the United States. The main governing body at the tertiary level is the University Grants Commission (India), which enforces its standards, advises the government, and helps coordinate between the centre and the state.

As of 2009, India has 20 central universities, 215 state universities, 100 deemed universities, 5 institutions established and functioning under the State Act, and 13 institutes which are of national importanc. Other institutions include 16000 colleges, including 1800 exclusive women's colleges, functioning under these universities and institutions.The emphasis in the tertiary level of education lies on science and technology. Indian educational institutions by 2004 consisted of a large number of technology institutes.

### 4. Technical Education

From the first Five Year Plan onwards India's emphasis was to develop a pool of scientifically inclined manpower. India's National Policy on Education (NPE) provisioned for an apex body for regulation and development of higher technical education, which came into being as the All India Council for Technical Education (AICTE) in 1987 through an act of the Indian parliament. At the level of the centre the Indian Institutes of Technology and the Indian Institutes of Information Technology are deemed of national importance. The Indian Institutes of Management are also among the nation's premier education facilities. Several Regional Engineering Colleges (REC) have been converted into National Institutes of Technology. The UGC has inter-university centres at a number of locations throughout India to promote common research, e.g. the Nuclear Science Centre at the Jawaharlal Nehru University, New Delhi.

In addition to above institutes, efforts towards the enhancement of technical education are supplemented by a number of recognized Professional

Engineering Societies like: (i) the Institution of Engineers (India); (ii) The Institution of Chemical Engineering (India); (iii) The Institution of Electronics and Tele-Communication Engineers (India); (iv) The Indian Institute of Metals; (v) The Institution of Industrial Engineers (India); (vi) The Institute of Town Planners (India); (vii) The Indian Institute of Architects, etc., who conduct Engineering/Technical Examinations at different levels(Degree and diploma) for working professionals desirous of improving their technical qualifications.

**5. Literacy**

According to the Census of 2001, "every person above the age of 7 years who can read and write in any language is said to be literate". According to this criterion, the 2001 survey holds the National Literacy Rate to be around 64.84%. Government statistics of 2001 also hold that the rate of increase in literacy is more in rural areas than in urban areas. Female literacy was at a national average of 53.63% whereas the male literacy was 75.26%. Within the Indian states, Kerala has shown the highest literacy rates of 90.02% whereas Bihar averaged lower than 50% literacy, the lowest in India. The 2001 statistics also indicated that the total number of 'absolute non-literates' in the country was 304 million.

World Bank statistics found that fewer than 40 percent of adolescents in India attend secondary schools. The Economist reports that half of 10-year-old rural children could not read at a basic level, over 60% were unable to do division, and half dropped out by the age 14. Only one in ten young people have access to tertiary education. Out of those who receive higher education, only a quarter of graduates are "employable".

**6. Private Education**

According to current estimates, 80% of all schools are government schools making the government the major provider of education. However, because of poor quality of public education, 27% of Indian children are privately educated. According to some research, private schools often provide superior results at a fraction of the unit cost of government schools. However, others have suggested that private schools fail to provide education to the poorest families, a selective being only a fifth of the schools and have in the past ignored Court orders for their regulation. In their favour, it has been pointed out that private schools cover the entire curriculum and offer extra-curricular activities such as science fairs, general knowledge, sports, music and drama. [The pupil teacher ratios are much better in private schools (1:31 to 1:37 for government schools and more teachers in private schools are female.] There is some disgreement over which system has better educated teachers. According to the latest DISE survey, the percentage of untrained teachers (paratechers) is 54.91% in private, compared to 44.88% in government schools and only 2.32% teachers in unaided schools receive inservice training compared to

43.44% for government schools. The competition in the school market is intense, yet most schools make profit. Even the poorest often go to private schools despite the fact that government schools are free.

### 7. Women's Education

Women have much lower literacy rate than men. Far fewer girls are enrolled in the schools, and many of them drop out. The number of literate women among the female population of India was between 2-6% from the British Raj onwards to the formation of the Republic of India in 1947. Concerted efforts led to improvement from 15.3% in 1961 to 28.5% in 1981. By 2001 literacy for women had exceeded 50% of the overall female population, though these statistics were still very low compared to world standards and even male literacy within India. Recently the Indian government has launched Saakshar Bharat Mission for Female Literacy.This mission aims to bring down female illiteracy by half of its present level.

The government objective for the Sarva Shiksha Abhiyan (SSA), started in 2001, is to provide education to children between 6–14 years by 2010. The programme focuses specially on girls and children with challenged social or financial backgrounds. The SSA also aims to provide practical infrastructure and relevant source material in form of free textbooks to children in remote areas. The SSA also aims at widening computer education in rural areas. SSA is currently working with Agastya International Foundation -an educational NGO - to augment its efforts in making science curriculum current and exciting. However, some objectives of the SSA, e.g. enrollment of all children under the scheme in schools by 2005 remain unfulfilled. Education Guarantee Scheme and Alternative and Innovative Education are components of the SSA.

India's minorities, especially the ones considered 'educationally backward' by the government, are provided for in the 1992 amendment of the Indian National Policy on Education (NPE). The government initiated the Scheme of Area Intensive Programme for Educationally Backward Minorities and Scheme of Financial Assistance or Modernisation of Madarsa Education as part of its revised Programme of Action (1992). Both these schemes were started nationwide by 1994. In 2004 the Indian parliament allowed an act which enabled minority education establishments to seek university affiliations if they passed the required norms.

### 8. Fiscal Initiatives

As a part of the tenth Five year Plan (2002–2007), the central government of India outlined an expenditure of 65.6% of its total education budget of Rs. 438250 million, or (Rs. 287500 million) on elementary education; 9.9% (Rs. 43250 million) on secondary education; 2.9% (Rs. 12500 million) on adult education; 9.5% (Rs. 41765 million) on higher education; 10.7% (Rs. 47000 million) on technical education; and the remaining 1.4% (Rs. 6235 million) on miscellaneous education schemes.

According to the United Nations Educational, Scientific and Cultural Organization (UNESCO), India has the lowest public expenditure on higher education per student in the world.

In recent times, several major announcements were made for developing the poor state of affairs in education sector in India, the most notable ones being the National Common Minimum Programme (NCMP) of the United Progressive Alliance (UPA) government.

The announcements are; (a) To progressively increase expenditure on education to around 6 percent of GDP, (b) To support this increase in expenditure on education, and to increase the quality of education, there would be an imposition of an education cess over all central government taxes, (c) To ensure that no one is denied of education due to economic backwardness and poverty, (d) To make right to education a fundamental right for all children in the age group 6–14 years, (e) To universalize education through its flagship programmes such as Sarva Siksha Abhiyan and Mid Day Meal.

However, even after five years of implementation of NCMP, not much progress has been done on these promises or announcements. The public expenditure on education has actually declined from around 3.23 percent of GDP in 2000-2001 to 2.88 percent in the recent times. As a proportion of total government expenditure, it has declined from around 11.1 percent in 2000-2001 to around 9.98 percent during UPA rule. A policy brief issued by [Network for Social Accountability (NSA)] titled "[NSA Response to Education Sector Interventions in Union Budget: UPA Rule and the Education Sector]" provides significant revelation to this fact. Due to a declining priority of education in the public policy paradigm in India, there has been an exponential growth in the private expenditure on education also. [As per the available information, the private out of pocket expenditure by the working class population for the education of their children in India has increased by around 1150 percent or around 12.5 times over the last decade].

### 9. Legal and Constitutional Imperatives

Article 45, of the Constitution of India originally stated:The State shall endeavour to provide, within a period of ten years from the commencement of this Constitution, for free and compulsory education for all children until they complete the age of fourteen years.This article was a directive principle of state policy within India, effectively meaning that it was within a set of rules that were meant to be followed in spirit and the government could not be held to court if the actual letter was not followed. However, the enforcement of this directive principle became a matter of debate since this principle held obvious emotive and practical value, and was legally the only directive principle within the Indian constitution to have a time limit. Following initiatives by the Supreme Court of India during the 1990s the Ninety-third amendment bill suggested three separate amendments to the Indian constitution:

- The constitution of India was amended to include a new article, 21A, which read:

The State shall provide free and compulsory education to all children of the age of six to fourteen years in a such manner as the State may, by law, determine.

- Article 45 was proposed to be substituted by the article which read:

Provision for early childhood care and education to children below the age of six years: The State shall endeavour to provide early childhood care and education for all children until they complete the age of sixteen years.

- Another article, 51A, was to additionally have the clause:

*a parent or guardian [shall] provide opportunities for education to his child or, as the case may be, [a] ward between the age of six to fourteen years.*

The bill was passed unanimously in the Lok Sabha, the lower house of the Indian parliament, on November 28, 2001. It was later passed by the upper house-the Rajya Sabha-on May 14, 2002. After being signed by the President of India the Indian constitution was amended formally for the eighty sixth time and the bill came into effect. Since then those between the age of 6–14 have a fundamental right to education. Article 46 of the Constitution of India holds that:

The State shall promote, with special care, the education and economic interests of the weaker sections of the people, and in particular of the Scheduled Castes and Scheduled Tribes, and shall protect them from social injustice and all forms of social exploitation'.

Other provisions for the Scheduled Castes and Scheduled Tribes can be found in Articles 330, 332, 335, 338–342. Both the 5th and the 6th Schedules of the Constitution also make special provisions for the Scheduled Castes and Scheduled Tribes.

**10. Right to Education**

The Right of Children to Free and Compulsory Education (RTE) Act 2009 came into force on April 2010. It is a landmark in the history of India's unprivileged masses. The Act, according to Kapil Sibal, Minister of Human Resource Development, was the result of our 100years struggle for universalizing elementary education. The Prime Minister Manmohan Singh while appealing to the states and the Union Territories to implement the Act said "I am what I am today because of education". The prime minister also stated "We are committed to ensuring that all children irrespective of gender and social category have access to education, an education that enables them to acquire skill, knowledge values and attitudes necessary to become responsible and active citizens of India".

The present Act has history in the drafting of Indian constitution at the time of independence but is more specifically to the constitution amendment that included the Article 21A in the Indian constitution making education a fundamental right. This amendment has even specified the need for a legislation to describe the mode of implementation of the same which necessitated this drafting of a separate education bill. The rough draft of the bill was completed in the year 2005.

### 1. Background

India has the worst history of denying access to knowledge to majority of its masses. For centuries a caste based Brahmin dominated feudal hierarchical system has prevailed in India. The women untouchables toiling masses and other backward class people were not allowed getting primary education. Acquiring knowledge by those sections was also considered as greatest crime and unforgivable sin. It was illustrated and justified in our ancient classics and literature. Thus our system of education was unjust, unethical, undemocratic and unproductive. Its purpose was to keep the majority of Indian masses in utter darkness-slavery, illiteracy, poverty, superstitions etc and keep them away from the main stream. The confining of the privilege of education to a small elite resulted in intellectual stagnation for centuries. This so called system of education was also unscientific as it did not provide vocational and technical knowledge in the scheme. It doesn't cultivate the qualities of self respect, reason, liberal-democratic vision etc.

This system of education was not universal in character and context as it didn't promote fraternity, sympathy and other humanitarian qualities. It was also costly and unaffordable to majority of the people. Medievalism, obscurantism, religious dogmatism etc were the other basic characteristics of pre-independence educational system of India.

The British policy of social neutrality and non-interference in India helped the domination of monarchial aristocracy, plutocracy and olygarchical elites in the field of education. The system was capitalized by the British for their successive adoption of divide and rule policy in India and prevents the awakening of masses as against it. Nevertheless the advent of the British in India and the great service of the missionaries have changed the over all system .They laid down western system of education which was resulted in renaissance in Indian society. Through education, they sowed the seeds of noble ideas like humanism, liberalism, democracy, secularism, equality etc. The British system of education was based on the policy of "occidental school" under Macaulay's leadership. It was triumphed in the field of education. He sincerely wanted that Indians should have knowledge of science and western thought.

Thus the western education laid foundation of a new type of intellectual and political life in India. This system could also have succeeded in producing enlightened citizens and later on led to the foundation of Brahma Samaj, Arya Samaj and other genuinely interested philanthropies foundations stood for universal education. In 1816-1817, Rajaram Mohan Roy founded the first English school in Calcutta. The Brahma Samaj reacted against social stagnation. Arya Samaj under the leadership of Dayananda Saraswathi (1875) proclaimed the inherent rights of all people to study the Vedas and thus devoted for universal education.After getting independence, enactment of a constitution with the objectives of democracy, secularism, socialism, justice, liberty, equality, rights etc we hoped a total change in the sphere of education in India. Our national leaders like Jawaharlal Nehru and others are committed to introduce universal, compulsory and free education at the primary level. It was prioritized in our Five Year Plans. Various committees and commissions were also appointed to radicalize the system. But the mission could have only a partial success due to adverse socio-economic situations. Children belonging to the vulnerable sections of the society had to bear the burden of looking after other members of their family and help their parents in domestic works. A substantial portion of Indian poor children are engaged in agricultural labour, Petty trades, house work and sibling care. Millions of children left out the school due to various reasons.

The Gross Enrolment Ratio (GER) in India is 21.4%. in the developed world, GER is not less than 40%. A vast gap of resources facilities and efficiencies exist between the private schools carter for the better off strata of society and the ones run by the government. Within government schools there is a vast difference between central schools and those run by Panchayats and municipalities. Private sector in school education was grown quite substantially and rapidly over the past two decades. A strong ideological lobby which favors privatization has also grown.

Shortage of qualified teachers, neglect of teachers training and poor social status of elementary school teachers also worsened the quality of our primary education. The dropout rates are very high in the elementary and secondary level mainly because of poverty. Parents engage their children for daily wages. Many of these children are formerly enrolled in a school but have either dropped out or never been there. Many others like migrant and street children live in extremely vulnerable conditions are also denied education. The poorest and most vulnerable groups are the most disempowered. Free and compulsory education for all children until they complete the age of 14 years was one of the Directive Principles of State Policy intended to be implemented within ten years of the commencement of our constitution. Only after 60 years an attempt has been made with the Right to Education Act to the entitlement of free universal education has become enforceable.

## 2. The Act

The right of children to free and compulsory education act passed by the Indian Parliament on 4th august 2009 describes the modalities of the provisions of free and compulsory education for children between 6 and 14 in India . Under Article 21 A of the Indian Constitution, India became one of the 135 countries to make education a fundamental right of every child. The Act came into force on April 2010. The right to education required as a human right by the UN and understood to establish an entitlement of free and compulsory primary education for all children, an obligation to develop secondary education for all children as well as equitable access to higher education and the responsibility to provide basic education for individuals who have not completed primary education. In addition to this access to education provisions the right to education encompasses also the obligation to eliminate discrimination at all levels of the educational system to set minimum standard and improve quality.

The right to education enshrined in the Article 26 of the UDHR and Article 14 of the international covenant of Economic Social and Cultural Right. The right to education has also been reaffirmed in the 1960 UNESCO Convention Against Discrimination in Education, First Protocol of ECHR (European Convention on Human Rights) and the 1981 Convention on Elimination of All Forms of Discrimination Against Women. The law came into effect the whole of India except Jammu and Kashmir from 1st April 2010, the first time in the history of India a law was brought into force by a speech by the prime minister.

The present act has history in the drafting of Indian constitution at the time of independence but are more specifically to the constitution amendment that included the Article 21 A in the Indian constitution making education a fundamental right. This amendment has even specified the need for a legislation to describe the mode implementation of the same which necessitated the drafting of a separate education bill. The rough draft the Bill was composed in the year 2005.

It received much opposition due its mandatory provisions to provide 25% reservation for disadvantaged children in private schools. The Sub Committee of the Central Administrative Board of Education which prepared draft bill held the provisions as a significant pre requisite of creating a democratic and egalitarian society. The Indian law commission had initially proposed a 50% reservation for disadvantaged students studying in private schools. The Act passed by the parliament on 4th of August 2009 describes the modalities of the provisions of free and compulsory education of children between 6 and 14 in India under Article 21 A of the Indian constitution. As far as a child at the time of his enrolment is unable to fight for his right, it is the society which must act on behalf of the child. It is the collective effort and commitment from the part of the state, parents and the community to ensure that children of school going age are in schools. The system of education should have been revamped on the holistic and systematic basis. The emerging global knowledge economy necessitated shift from the linier, passive, hierarchical and non participatory paradigm to dynamic vigorous and bold inclusive and integrated system focused on cultivating creativity and intellectual skills aligned to the need of this sub system of the Indian society and geared to provide vocational technical professional education required in the global work place (The Hindu, April 3).

The 11th Five Year Plan 2007-2012 allocated 19% budgetary support to The National Education Plan as against 7.7% in the Tenth Plan. According to

Kapil Sibal, the vision that was that India should be a knowledge power in the coming decade (The Hindu, April 1).

The Act also offers a framework for ensuring quality education for creating infrastructure for making available a sufficient number of competent trained teachers and for extending government funding for private schools. Well trained teachers, infrastructure and basic requirements like classroom facilities and books couldn't have been provided to majority of children. The lack of these facilities defeated the very object of the mission. The right to education goes beyond free and compulsory education to include quality education for all. Quality is an integral part of the right to education. Lack of quality is the denial of the right of the child. The Act lays down that the curriculum should provide for learning through activities, exploration and discovery. These place an obligation on us to change our perception of children as passive receivers of knowledge and to move beyond the convention of textbooks as basis of examination. The teaching learning process must become stress free and child friendly learning system. Teacher accountability system and processes must ensure that children are learning and that right to learn in a child friendly environment is not violated. The Act mandates children's right to an education that is free from fear stress and anxiety. The other important provision in the Act include provisions prohibiting corporal punishment, detention and expulsion which are the conventional notions of disciplines and control and explore alternative approaches to class room management including peer behavior, teacher child and teacher parent relationship. The direct responsibility to provide school infrastructure, trained teachers, curriculum and teaching learning material and mid day meal lies with he education department of the central and state government.

The Right to Education Act makes education a fundamental right of any child between the ages of six to fourteen and specifies minimum norms in government schools. It requires the reservation of 25% places in private schools for children from poor families. It prohibits unrecognized schools from practice and makes provisions for no donation or capitation fee and no interview of child or parent for admission. No child shall be held back expelled or required to pass a Board Examination until the completion of elementary education. There is also provision for special training of school drop outs to bring them up to par with the students of the same age. The right to education of persons with disabilities until 18 years of age also become made a fundamental right.

The Act provides for establishment of national commission for protection of child rights and state commissions for supervising proper implementation of the Act looking after complaints and protection of child rights. Other provisions regarding improvement of school infrastructure, teacher-student ratio and faculty are made in the Act.

A well coordinated mechanism is needed for inter sectoral collaboration and convergence. The finance department must provide adequate and appropriate financial allocations and timely releases of funds at all levels. The public works department should re conceptualize and re design school spaces, address issues of inclusion of children with disability through barrier free access. The department of science and technology should provide geo-spatial technologies for school mapping and location to supplement social mapping exercises at the grass root level. Programme for water and sanitation must ensure access to adequate and safe drinking water and accessible and adequate sanitation facilities especially for girls in schools. The Right to Education Act mandates that every child must be in school. These presuppose that child labour will be eliminated. The labour department must align that policies with the RTE Act so that all children participate in the schooling process regularly.

It goes without saying that the immense relevance of inclusive education, particularly of disadvantaged groups demands vibrant partnership with organizations concerned with children of all scheduled caste and schedule tribes and educationally backward minorities. We will need to set up system for equal opportunities for children with special needs.

The rural development and Panchayat Raj department would need to accelerate poverty reduction programmes so that children are freed from domestic chores and wage earning responsibilities. Equally, the state governments simultaneously should ensure that the Panchayat Raj institutions can discharge their functions under the RTE Act. The National Rural Health Mission must take up school health programme including de-worming and minor nutrient supplementation with special attention to vulnerable groups especially girls approaching adolescence. The sports department would need to build in physical education for the overall physical, social, emotional, mental development of the child. Unless these anomalies are addressed properly and systematically the Right to education act would loose much of its spirit and contents in the Indian context.

## References


- "*Science and Technology Education*". Press Information Bureau. http://pib.nic.in/archieve/ others/2007/May07/200705012.
- Kalyani Menon-Sen, *A. K. Shiva Kumar* (2001). "Women in India: How Free? How Equal?". United Nations. http://www.un.org.in/wii.htm. "22 universities across India fake: UGC". Express India.
- http://www.expressindia.com/latest-news/22-universities-across-India-fake- UGC/425697
- http://www.nsa.org.in
- http://www.indg.in/primary-education
- http://www.timeshighereducation.co.uk/hybrid.asp?typeCode=161
- Asia's Best Science and Technology Schools.
- Ferguson, Niall (2003). Empire: How Britain made the Modern World. Penguin. p. 191. ISBN 0141007540.

- "A special report on India: An elephant, not a tiger". The Economist. 11 December 2008. http://www.economist.com/specialreports/displayStory.cfm?story_id=12749735
- Journal. http://online.wsj.com/article/SB116882502361976702.html.
- http://www.atimes.com/atimes/South_Asia/FC02Df03.htm.
- http://www.dise.in/Downloads/Publication%202007-08/Rural0708/teacher_part1.pdf
- "Country Strategy for India (CAS) 2009-2012". World Bank.
- http://www.ukibc.com/ukindia2/files/India60.pdf
- "Higher education spending: India at the bottom of BRIC". Rediff. 2005. http://www.rediff.com/money/2007/feb/05edu.html
- http://www.nsa.org.in/Policybrief/2009/345NSARUBEDU1.html
- http://www.nsa.org.in/Policybrief/309NSAResearchTeam1.html
- http://www.livemint.com/2010/01/18232326/44-institutions-to-lose-deemed.html
- The Hindu.
- Blackwell, Fritz (2004), *India: A Global Studies Handbook*, United States of America: ABC-CLIO, Inc., ISBN 1-57607-348-3.
- Elder, Joseph W. (2006), "Caste System", *Encyclopedia of India* (Vol. 1) edited by Stanley Wolpert, 223-229, Thomson Gale: ISBN 0-684-31350-2.
- "Infrastructure: S&T Education", *Science and Technology in India* edited by R.K. Suri and Kalapana Rajaram (2008), New Delhi: Spectrum, ISBN 81-7930-294-6.
- India 2009: *A Reference Annual* (53rd edition), New Delhi: Additional Director General (ADG), Publications Division, Ministry of Information and Broadcasting, Government of India, ISBN 978-81-230-1557-6.
- Prabhu, Joseph (2006), "Educational Institutions and Philosophies, Traditional and Modern", *Encyclopedia of India* (Vol. 2) edited by Stanley Wolpert, 23–28, Thomson Gale: ISBN 0-684-31351-0.
- Raman, S.A. (2006). "Women's Education", *Encyclopedia of India* (Vol. 4), edited by Stanley Wolpert, 235-239, Thomson Gale: ISBN 0-684-31353-7.
- Setty, E.D. and Ross, E.L. (1987), "A Case Study in Applied Education in Rural India", *Community Development Journal*, 22 (2): 120–129, Oxford University Press.
- Sripati, V. and Thiruvengadam, A.K. (2004), "India: Constitutional Amendment Making The Right to Education a Fundamental Right", *International Journal of Constitutional Law*, 2 (1): 148–158, Oxford University Press.
- Vrat, Prem (2006), "Indian Institutes of Technology", *Encyclopedia of India* (Vol. 2) edited by Stanley Wolpert, 229-231, Thomson Gale: ISBN 0-684-31351-0.

# 16

# THE RIGHT TO INFORMATION ACT, 2005 AND HUMAN RIGHT

**Raju Abraham**

The free flow of information and ideas lies at the heart of the very existence of democracy. Central to the guarantee in practice of a free flow of information and ideas is the principle that public bodies hold information not for themselves but on behalf of the public. The international human rights NGO, ARTICLE 19, Global Campaign for Free Expression has described information as "the oxygen for democracy[1]". Article 19 of both the Universal Declaration on Human Right and International Covenant on Civil and Political Rights provide that every person shall have the right to free expression and to seek and impart information. In 1995 the Inter- Parliamentary Union assembled experts from various regions and disciplines to develop an international standard on democracy. Building on this work the Universal Declaration on Democracy was adopted in September 16, 1997. Democracy is based on two core principles: participation and accountability. Everyone has the right to participate in the management of public affairs. Likewise, everyone has the right to access information on government activities, to petition government and seek redress through impartial administrative and judicial mechanisms[2].

In 1998, the UN General Assembly adopted the Declaration on the Right and Responsibility of Individuals, Group and Organs of Society to Promote and Protect Universally Recognized Human Rights and Fundamental Freedom [the Declaration on Human Rights Defenders[3]]. Article 6 specifically provides for access to information about human rights.

Everyone has the right, individually and in association with others:

(a) To know, seek, obtain, receive and hold information about all human rights and fundamental freedoms, including having access to information as to how these rights and freedoms are given effect in domestic legislative, judicial or administrative systems;

(b) As provided for in human rights and other applicable international instruments, freely to publish, impart or disseminate to others views, information and knowledge on all human rights and fundamental freedoms

Article 6 recognizes that the right to know, seek, obtain, receive, hold and disseminate information on human rights is fundamental to the effective promotion and protection of human rights.

These provisions are, for the most part, aimed at security access to information the State holds regarding human rights and human rights abuse, as well as the right to the disseminated this sort of information. They hint, however, at a more profound obligation, one which ARTICLE 19 has long argued in favor of namely that States are under substantive positive obligation in this area, including to ensure the availability of information about human rights violations. This is signaled, for example, by the word 'know' in Article 6(a). ARTICLE 19 has for example argued that the right to freedom of expression, "long recognized as crucial in the promotion of democratic accountability and participation, also places an obligation upon Governments to facilitate the uncovering of information about past human rights violations[4]. In other words, it is not enough for individuals simply to have access to whatever information the State already holds. The State must also ensure that information about past human rights violations are readily available, including by collecting, collating, preserving and disseminating it, where necessary.

The 'right to truth' has also started to be recognized by international tribunals. In the case of Barrios Altos v. Peru[5] for example, the Inter-American Court of Human Rights took steps towards recognizing this right. It noted the strong finding of the Commission in this regard, stating:

*The Commission alleged that the right to truth is founded in Articles 8 and 25 of the Convention(guaranteeing the right to a fair trial and the right to judicial protection for human rights), insofar as they are both" instrumental" in the judicial establishment of the facts and circumstances that surrounded the violation of a fundamental right. It also indicated that this right has its roots in Article13 (1) of the Convention (guaranteeing freedom of expression), because that article recognizes the right to seek and receive information. With regard to that article, the commission added that the State has the positive obligation to guarantee essential information to preserve the rights of the victims, to ensure transparency in public administration and the protection of human rights[6].*

**The Court did not go quite so far but did note:**

*In the circumstances of the instant case, the right to the truth is subsumed in the right of the victim or his next of kin to obtain clarification of the events that violated human rights and the corresponding responsibilities from the*

*competent organs of the State, through the investigation and prosecution that are established in Articles 8 and 25 of the Convention*[7].

Universal Declaration on Democracy inter alia mentioned about the right to information. It says "the state democracy presupposes freedom of opinion and expression; this right implies freedom to hold opinions without interference and to seek, receive and impart information and ideas through any media and regardless of frontiers... public accountability, which is essential to democracy, applies to all those who hold public authority, whether elected or non-elected, and to all bodies of public authority without exception. Accountability entails a public right to access to information about the activities of government, the right to petition government and seek redress through impartial administrative and judicial mechanisms[8].

Information is public good like sunlight, clean air and drinking water. It belongs not to the state, the government of the day or civil servants, but to the public. Officials do not create information for their own benefit alone, but for the benefit of the public they serve, as part of the legitimate and routine discharge of the governments duties. Information is generated with public money by public servants paid out of public funds. As such, it cannot be unreasonably kept from citizens[9].

Right to information is an essential right for every person. It allows individuals and groups to protect their rights. It is an important guard against abuses, mismanagement and corruption. Nearly 85 countries around the world have now adopted comprehensive right to information acts to facilitate access to records held by public authorities and another fifty have pending efforts[10].

According to David Banisar there are several benefits of RTI Act. They are (i) Democratic participation and Understanding. Democracy is based on the consent of the citizens and that consent turns on the government informing citizens about their activities and recognizing their right to participate. (ii) Protecting other Rights. In India, the RTI Act, are used to enforce rations distribution by revealing that food vendors are not providing the government subsidized food items to poor people. (iii) Making Government Bodies work better. In our country, grassroots social activist groups use the RTI Act to obtain information on local public works project and reveal the amount said to have been paid at public meetings. When the public meetings were held and government officials were compelled to reveal the name and the amount of money disbursed to people the actual payment were less than the amount that had been recorded as given to people who had died and supplied to projects never completed[11].

Right to information has been seen as the key to strengthening participatory democracy and good governance. Access to information can empower the poor and the weaker sections of society to demand and get information about government policies and activities. Good governance has four elements – transparency, accountability, predictability, and participation. Transparency refers to availability of information to the general public and clarity about functioning of governmental institutions. Right to information regime opens up government's records to public scrutiny, thereby empowering citizens with a vital tool to inform them about what the government does and how effectively, thus making the government move accountable. Transparency in government organization makes them function more objectively thereby enhancing predictability. Information about functioning of government also enables citizens to participate in the governance process effectively. In a fundamental sense, right to information is a basic necessity of good governance[12].

The supreme court of India has consistently upheld the principle of a right to information. In the 1975 case of the State of Uttar Pradesh V. Raja Narain (AIR 1975 SC 865) the court said "In a government of responsibility like ours, where all the agents of the public must be responsible for their conduct there can be but few secrets. The people of this country have right to know every public act, every thing that is done in public way, by their public functionaries. They are entitled to know the particulars of every public transaction in all its bearing..... To cover with veil of secrecy, the common routine business is not in the interest of the public. The responsibility of officials to explain and to justify their acts is the chief safeguard against oppression and corruption".

The Supreme court of India in another case of People's Union for Civil Liberties V. Union of India (AIR 2003 SC 1442) held that true democracy cannot exist unless the citizens have a right to participate in the affairs of the country is meaningless unless the citizens are well informed on all sided issues in respect of which they are called upon to express their views. One-sided information, disinformation, misinformation and non-information all equally create uninformed citizens which makes democracy a farce when medium of information is monopolized either by a partisan central authority or by private individuals or oligarchy organizations. This is particularly so in a country like ours where 65% of the population is illiterate.

Recent research on the information needs of poor has confirmed that poor men and women face a series of problems in locating and using knowledge and information for their own benefit. Poor people have difficulty accessing the 'right' kind of information. Often the information is inappropriate to meet their needs, either in content (e.g.) it does not reflect their reality or in presentation (is not in their local language)[13].

In the later 1981 case of S.P Gupta Vs. Union of India, (AIR 1982 SC, 149) the Supreme Court found that right to know is implicit in the guarantee of freedom of speech and expressions found in Article 19 (1) of the constitution: a person cannot have freedom to express in the absence of knowledge. The right to information is therefore a constitutional right in India that has now been acknowledged and clarified in the Right to Information Act, 2005.

The preamble of the RTI Act, 2005 says that it is meant to provide for setting out the practical regime of the right to information for citizens to secure access to information under the control of public authorities, in order to promote transparency and accountability in the working of every public authority. Is India is able to provide for setting out the practical regime of the RTI for citizen under the present day political system.

The right to information has defined in the Act. It includes the right to inspect works, documents, records, take notes, extracts or certified copies of documents, take certified samples of materials, obtain information in form of printout, diskettes, floppies, tapes, video cassettes or in any other electronic mode or through printouts [S. 2 (j)].

The Act confers a right to information rather than just "records" or "documents". As per section 2 (f) of RTI Act, Information means any material in any form including records, documents, memos, e-mails, opinions, advices, press releases, circlers, orders, logbooks, contracts, reports, papers, samples, models, data material held in electronic form and information relating to any private body which can be accessed by a public authority under any other law for the time being in force.

All information under the control of the public authority, other than from the disclosed information under section 8 of the Act, should be given to citizens. Public Authority means any authority or body or institutions of self-government established or constituted by or under the Constitutions, by any other law made by Parliament, by any other law made by State Legislature. By notification issued or order made by the appropriate Government and includes any (a) body owned, controlled or substantially financed (b) non-Government organization substantially financed directly or indirectly by the appropriate Government [S. 2 (h)].

Public Information officers (PIOs) are required to be appointed "in all administrative units/offices as may be necessary to provide information to persons requesting it" Assistant PIOs are also to be appointed at each sub-divisional or sub-district level, and these Assistants are tasked with receiving applications and appeals and passing them on to the relevant Public Information Officers.

Most applications must be processed within thirty days, although the time limit is extended to 40 days where third party submissions are to be called for. These time limits are reduced to a more 48 hours where the information sought "concerns the life and liberty of a person." As per the Right to Information (Regulations of fee and cost) Rules, 2005, a request for to obtaining information under sub-section (i) of sections 6 should be accompanied by as applications fee of rupee ten. No application fee shall be charged for persons who are below the poverty line. If the RTI Act is implemented in the true sprite of law Indian political culture will improve substantially.

The right to information regime is a product of both 'institutions' and 'culture'. Institutions are shaped by laws and the structure of government. Culture is routed in the history and practice of government as well as in the border traditional understandings of the accountability of leaders, and what constitutes representations. Culture is often more powerful than formal arrangements, particularly in societies these are undergoing a process of democratic transition[14].

United Nations Development Programme has published a Practical Guidance Note to measure the impact of right to information Act. UNDP has identified four broad areas to measure RTI Act. They are (i) the legal regime for the right to information: (ii) implementation of right to information legislation by Government: (iii) use of the right to the information by the general public and civil society: (iv) use of the right to information by marginalized groups[15]. When we examine the RTI Act, 2005 with UNDP measurement we can say that the first measurement i.e., the legal regime for the right to information has been created by the government. But in the sphere of implementation of RTI Act, usage of RTI by the general public and civil society and the usage of this act by marginalized groups generally shows a dismal picture[16].

The effective implementations of RTI Act in India may not be fulfilled without the active participation of higher educational Institutions. As regards the enrolment of relevant age group in higher education, we have achieved rate of 11% compared to 0.7 in 1950-51 to 1.4% in 1960-61.[17] As per the World Conference of Higher Education New Dynamics of Higher Education and Research for Social Change and Development 2009, higher education must not only give solid skills for the present and future world but must also contribute to the education of ethical citizens committed to the construction of peace, the defense of human rights and the value of democracy. They are the cream of the India's society. Higher education has a social responsibility in the human development, in the defense and promotion of human rights and in democracy building in each country. It shall mould the student to a future social, political cultural leadership, and share values and, knowledge that promote social integrations[18]. Higher educations is a pillar for sustainable development, not just for training those who maintain and promote the infrastructure of democracy and justice, but also for building capacity for critical thinking, innovation and discovery.

Democracy defines a political system in which power-directly or indirectly-rests with the people. In that sense democracy implies actual participation of each individual in the decision making process. Therefore each individual should act as a responsible citizen. The key to the development of this responsibility is education and pre access to information in a pluralistic and open landscape[19]. Higher education institution have to prepare their students for the future, and they have to educate people, who are going to play an important role in shaping the future ... of the society in which they are going to work. Learning how to participate and take an active part in a democracy is a continuous process. The higher education systems are the best forms to teach and learn democracy[20].

In this context it may be very interesting to examine the report of the American Political Science Association Conference on Teaching and Learning in 2005[21]. They took the decision that political science courses need to address civic education[22] and advocate for civic engagement. It agreed that the driving legitimacy of civic education should be to raise consciousness, foster interest on social issues, and encourage participation in the public sphere. Civic engagement creates opportunities for expanding political consciousness by connecting the every day experiences of the individuals and communities with whom students come in contact to the larger, socio-economic problems of society. Students reach greater levels of understanding as they become aware of the larger problems that society faces over a long period of time. As teachers of political science our responsibility is to see that our students become politically literate: that is they acquire first hand information, with the help of RTI Act about the Socio-economic problems that will allow them to comprehend, evaluate, and analyze the world around them[23]. At the same time, as teachers of political science, it is also our responsibility that our students consider and learn the values of good citizenship and engage in the political activities in a meaningful way. Political Science Classroom thus becomes the venue for a discussion of the "Social" Problems they witnessed firsthand. This process may enhance his political socialization of our nation and enhance the political culture of our Country.

## Notes and References


1. Mendel Toby (2008): *Freedom of Information : A comparative Legal Survey,* UNESCO: Paris, P. 4
2. *Human Development Report 2002 : Deepening Democracy in a fragmented world,* Oxford University Press 2002 New Delhi P. 55.
3. Resolution 53/144, 8 March 1999.
4. Who Wants to Forget? Truth and Access to Information about Past Human Rights Violations (London: ARTICLE 19, 2000), P.5. Online at http://www.article 19.org/pdfs/publications/freedom-of-information-truth-comissions.pdf.
5. Cited in Mendal Toby, Freedom of Information: A Comparative Legal Survey 2008, UNESCO, Paris, p. 18.
6. *Ibid.*
7. *Ibid.*
8. *Universal Declarations on Democracy* : Declaration adopted without a vote by the Inter - Parliamentary Council at its 161 Session, Cairo, 16 September 1997.
9. Daruwala Maja (EdI) CHRI's 2003 REPORT OPEN Sesame: Looking for the Right to Information in Commonwealth : A Report on the International Advisory Commission of the Common wealth Human

Rights Initiative, Commonwealth Human Rights Initiative October 2003. New Delhi - 110016 p. 3

10. Freedom of Information Legislation – from Wikipedia, the free encyclopedia on 26.5.2010.
11. *Ibid.*
12. *Second Administrative Reforms Commission : First Report, Right to information : Master key to good governance* Government of India, June 2006 p. 1.
13. *Access to Information: Practice Note*, UNDP publication October 2003 p. 4.
14. Puddephatt Andrew, A Guide to measuring the Impact of Right to Information Programmes, Practical Guidance Note. Published by UNDP April 2006 p-10.
15. Ibid. pp. 9-10.
16. Central Information Commission had organized a National Convention on One Year of RTI during 13-15 October 2006. Panel No. 1 deliberated on "One year of RTI-Taking Stock - Its success and short coming" Report published by Central Information Commission"- Outcome and Recommendations of the National Conversion on 'One year of RTI' 2006.
17. Thorat Sukhadeo, Emerging Issues in Higher Education: approach, Strategy and Action Plan in the 11th Plan, The Indian Economic Journal Vol. 57, Number 1, April – June 2009, p. 35.
18. World conference on Higher Educations : Higher Educations in the Twenty- first Century: Vision and Action UNESCO, Paris 5-9 October 1998. Thematic Debate Higher Educations and society. A Student Vision working document drafted by the UNESCO Secretariat P. 6 http://www.unesco.org/educationwche/
19. Benson Obua Ogwal, All Africa Students Union (AASU) in connection with the Higher Education in the 21st Century - A student perspective: Thematic Debats: Higher Education and society : A Student Vision p. 105.
20. *Ibid.*
21. For the last 3 years American Political Science Association has been conducted annual Conference on Teaching and Learning in Political Science. Papers are available at the website of APSA- www.apsanet.org
22. Frederking Lauretta, Christopher Malone, Alison Millett, Mccarthy, 2005 APSA *Teaching and Learning Conference Track Summaries* PS Online www.apsanet.org. p. 415.
23. Civic Education is learning for effective participation in democratic and development processes at both local and national levels. It is an important means for capacity development on the societal

level by empowering people for effective civic engagement. It is essential dimension in strengthening a society's ability to manage its own affairs and is complementary to capacity development on the individual institutional levels. At the core of Civic Education are the values and principles of transparency, participation, responsiveness, accountability, empowerment and equity. Communication and Access to Information are also integral to Civic Education. For more details See- Civic Education: Practical Guidance Note United Nations Development Programme, Bureau for Development Policy, Democratic Governance Group. April 2004.

# 17

# SEX WORKERS MOVEMENT FOR RIGHTS: NEED FOR CIVIL SOCIETY INTERVENTION

**B. Madhusoodanan Nair**

The sex workers movement had been quite widespread in the 1970s. It was started as a prostitute's rights movement. Large numbers of prostitutes came out in the streets of Lyons, France to protest against the murders of prostitutes, excessive police fines and frequent arrests of prostitutes. The agitation soon spread to various parts of France when prostitutes joined the agitation and took possession of churches. In Paris prostitutes agitated for, their full rights as citizens and demanded the implementation of a tax system that would give them the right to 'retirement' benefits like every other French citizen. One of the other issues that they raised was the nationalization of sex business as public servants. The prostitutes complain that in the sex business the clients have always been in the safer side. The sex workers are always accused of creating immorality in the society. The strike went on for seven days and ended with the police invading the churches. The agitation invoked worldwide attention to the conditions under which the prostitutes worked and led to the emergence of the French collective of prostitutes and sex workers rights movement in France. Similar groups subsequently formed in England, Australia, Germany, Italy, Denmark, Canada and in major U.S cities[1].

The prostitutes movement in the U.S revolves around the issues of economic hardships. As the economic hardships grew, women across the world started to sell sex. In the U.K, the English collective of prostitutes demanded laws which punish prostitution should be aborted as the prostitutes took up this profession for their subsistence. Besides various agitations on the part of sex workers unions, numerous international conventions and platforms were organized including the International Congress of Whores

(1985 in Amsterdam and 1986 in Brussels). A number of publications by sex workers had been brought out.

Therefore, since the mid 1970s sex workers across the world have organized, demanding the decriminalization of prostitution, equal protection under the law, improved working conditions, the right to pay taxes, travel and receive social benefits such as pensions[2]. In the 1990's the sex workers rights movement widened its arena to include minority sex workers such as transgender, developing world, lesbian, gay, bisexual, heterosexual, migrants, men and woman sex workers. The minority sex workers are more secluded from the mainstream as a lot of social stigma is attached to minority sex workers. The sex workers movements continued to be seen throughout Africa, Latin America and Asia. In Mexico city the La Union Unica has organized not just sex workers but all who thrive from the sex industry including taxi drivers, hotel workers etc. The sex workers right movement has recognized the prostitution as a profession. In Australia an official sex workers union was formed in 1996 under the shadow of the Australian Liquor, hospitality and miscellaneous workers union. In Paraguay the national workers union has recognized sex workers as legitimate workers, meaning they can retire and receive full pension benefits[3].

**Sex Workers Rights: A Human Rights Issue**

The world charter for prostitute's rights was adopted in 1985 by the International Committee for prostitute's Rights (ICPR) to protect the rights of prostitutes worldwide[4]. The World charter originated from the prostitute's rights movement and culminated through the two world whores congress held in Amesterdam (1985) and Brussles (1986) which ultimately led to worldwide prostitute rights movement and politics[5].

The charter established a human rights based approach which has subsequently been further elaborated by the prostitute's right movement. In 1999, prostitutes appreciated the world charter for having "articulated a global political movement seeking recognition and social change[6]. In 2003, a writer in the journal called "Humanist" reflected that the world charter had become a template used by human rights group all over the world[7].

**World Charter for Prostitutes' Rights (1985)**

The World charter for prostitutes rights demands for decriminalization of all kinds of adult prostitution as a result of individual decisions. The World charter also states that prostitutes should be guaranteed "all human rights and civil liberties" including the freedom of speech, travel, immigration, work, marriage and motherhood and the right to unemployment insurance, health insurance and housing[8]. In addition to that the world charter addresses the issue of 'work standards' including the abolition of laws which impose separate areas for prostitution and demands that prostitutes having the freedom to choose their place of work and residence and to "provide their services under the conditions that are absolutely determined by themselves and no more else[9]. The World charter also calls for prostitutes to pay regular taxes "on the same basis as other independent contractors and employees" and to get same benefits for their taxes[10].

**European Conference on Sex Work, Human Rights, Labour and Migration**

A conference was held at Brussels, in October 2005. The conference endorsed the Declaration of the rights of sex workers in Europe and the conference was concluded at European parliament. The conference was held in the context of "increasing repressive legislative policies and state practices against sex workers across Europe[11]. The goals of the conference were to restore sex workers right back on the European agenda and change the human trafficking debate into a debate on labour, migration and human rights.

The Declaration was finalized at the conference and is based on international human rights instruments[12]. The Declaration focused on "current violations of the rights of sex workers in Europe which happen in health, and social care, housing, employment, education, administrative law and criminal justice system". It is also addressed "actions required to ensure that the rights of sex workers are respected in Europe[13].

The Declaration brought up several issues and approaches to the sex industry including those of female, male and transgender sex workers and migrant sex workers. These dimensions of sex work focused on acceptance of sex work as labour and introduction of labour rights for sex workers to the criminalization of a wide range of practices associated with sex work. The criminalization would affect the sex workers, sex workers partners or their clients. The declaration points out that the legislative activities that restrict the fundamental rights and freedoms of sex workers grow at a faster rate at local, national and international level. The Declaration states that the "many measures are in violation of the obligation of states under international human rights law to respect, promote and protect human rights of all persons within their territory, without discrimination and including the right to privacy, to a family life, to legally leave and return to one's country, to be free from torture, inhuman or degrading treatment and from arbitrary detention and in favour of the freedom of expression, information, freedom of association and movement[14]. According to the Declaration "all individuals within Europe, including sex workers" are entitled to the certain rights" which European governments are obliged to respect, protect and fulfill.[15]

**Forced Prostitution**

Forced prostitution is a form of sexual slavery that is considered more profitable than the drug trade and arms trade.[16] In some of the Scandinavian nations such as Sweden, Norway and Iceland forced prostitution is illegal. Sex workers rights advocates have argued that these laws are another form of prohibition and stigmatization that serve mainly to marginalize sex workers.[17] Sex worker's rights organizations argue that decriminalization and extension of labour rights to sex workers is more effective in ensuring their economic, mental and medical health than any form of prohibition.[18]

### Sex Workers Rights and HIV Question

Sex workers are one of the vulnerable groups who are most affected by AIDS. They are the group which are likely to be affected by HIV than the other segments of population. They are also not in a position to cope with the disease and policies and programmes to prevent AIDS. According to the strategy document sex workers are among the most marginalized and discriminated against in society and that as a result of criminalization it is often difficult to reach sex workers with interventions such as condom promotion[19]. In 2006, UNAIDS carried out a global consultation on sex work and HIV/AIDS prevention and treatment. During the consultation, sex workers and public health experts demanded better conditions for sex workers, projecting the implications of violence, police intervention and criminalization in general have on HIV prevention efforts. At the International AIDS conference in Toronto, Canada in August, 2006, the UNFPA took a rights based approach on a document on HIV and sex work. The right based approach was comprehensive and wide that includes a package of health and social service, sustainable livelihoods, respect for human rights and addressing gender concerns.

UNAIDS put a strong emphasis on measures to reduce the number of women who sell sex by motivating sex workers to give up the profession and preventing women from taking up sex work. This has been realized through a measure of wide propaganda to avoid the service of sex workers. This approach has been condemned by human rights advocates that it can increase the risk of HIV for sex workers by driving sex workers underground and restricting their ability to choose working conditions and clients.[20]

### Current Activities and Agitations by Sex Workers Around the World

In March 2000 in Britain, sex workers resorted to one-day strike in response to the decision of the government to evict the prostitutes. The prostitutes complain that police often enter the flats of prostitutes without any legal permission to do so.

In Bolivia as well, prostitutes agitated in 2007 in reaction to attacks in the city of EL Alto, where brothels were burned and sex worker were beaten up in protest against legalized prostitution.

In Canada, in 2007, many civil society groups moved against Canada's prostitution laws which threatened thousands of women involved in legal trade. Eventhough prostitution is not particularly outlawed in Canada, but all aspect of transaction are illegal.

## Sex Workers Rights: The Indian Scenario

### Sexuality and Rights

It was in the 61st session of U.N. Commission on Human Rights, for the first time, "Sexual orientation" was included in the draft resolution on violence against women. Inspite of several laws that aims to prevent human rights violations, the slow implementation of these laws in India has led to a situation where several homogenous groups such as women, lower castes and tribal populations have been sidelined. This fact is clearly reflected in aggregate provincial statistics, which show that, with few exceptions, women have significantly lower literary rates and hourly earnings rates than the men. (Dreze and Sen 1995)[21]. Among the vulnerable group, sex workers are the most affected and marginalized. Many sex workers enter the profession when they are minors, often without their consent and thereby become vulnerable to sexual violence and economic exploitation.[22]

The human rights violations and the socio-economic conditions of sex workers in India have different dimensions. These dimensions could be categorized into various segments such as legal and policy challenges, discrimination on the part of State, the HIV/AIDS debate, civil society response etc.

### Legal and Policy Challenges to Sex Workers

Despite the provision of various constitutional and legal safeguards such as article 12, 15, 23 and 32 of the constitution pertaining to fundamental rights, legislations meant for religious and ethnic minorities which includes protection of civil rights Act of 1955, protection of Human Rights Act of 1993, the National Commission for Women Act of 1990, Sections of Indian penal code etc, the condition of sex workers especially women sex workers remain poor and deplorable. The Indian State has failed to fulfill is responsibilities to protect the rights of sex workers. This has been quite evident when one examines a 1992 report by Amnesty international on human rights violations committed by the police and other state agencies in India. The Human rights commission and womens commissions have also not shown much interest to the issues of sex workers.

One of the significant legislations for protecting the rights of sex workers especially rehabilitating the sex workers is the Immoral Trafficking (prevention) Act. The Act provides for the establishment or licensing of protective homes by various provincial governments. Even though the Immoral Trafficking (prevention) Act doesn't consider sex work as illegal.[23] state agencies frequently use it for harming the sex workers. Even the rehabilitation centres which are supposed to protect the sex workers have become second brothels where their security and protection is not taken care of. The rehabilitation centres and its programmes have become ineffective, with little focus on development of marketable skills.[24] In Karnataka the sex workers had to report to the police station before their children got admitted to schools. The poor rehabilitation efforts of the government and the fact that many of the women staying at these homes/institutions perceive themselves to be used as slave labour.[25]

### State Sponsored Harassment of Sex Workers

A recent survey conducted among 300 brothel sex workers in Sangli district in Maharashtra revealed that 50% of the respondents had entered the profession at the age of 13 or less[26]. During their work life, sex workers in India are subject to frequent harassment and detention by the police[27]. A study conducted by Jacan D Cunnha found that between 1980 and 1987 more than 9000 women in sex work were arrested in Mumbai alone[28]. Later these girls are released by paying huge sum of money.

### The Sex Workers and HIV/AIDS Debate

Sexual health and reproduction rights, particularly the issue of HIV/AIDS emerged both as a central focus for the sex workers[29]. As far as common people are concerned health care professionals recommend HIV tests when symptoms of HIV/AIDS appear. For sex workers, HIV tests are recommended for a trivial illness, leading to a situation of stigmatizing the sex workers. There are situations in Mumbai and other big cities, unnecessary tests are often conducted especially among women who are suspected to have AIDS/HIV.

In a women's hospital frequented by sex workers in Mumbai, health workers took blood sample from every women seeking treatment without complaining to her purpose and nature of test which can be seen as a violation of her rights to information, privacy and security of person. It is also alleged that many customers in the red light area are affected by AIDS, HIV, because majority of the prostitutes are tested positive for HIV/AIDS. As far as the HIV/AIDS debate is concerned, there should be more and more awareness pertaining to the ways of safer sex rather than opting for a no-sex propaganda. The HIV/AIDS discourse gives it the authority to shape the discourse of sexuality language, creating communities like MSM (Men sex with Men), whose entire purpose was not to create human beings with sexual desires that need to be contextualized and understand, but as legal recipients of condom distribution programmes[30].

### Civil Society Responses to the Rights of Sex Workers

The civil society approach to the cause of workers has not been impressive in India. It may be due to the fact that sex work in India is still stigmatized and even civil society movements are carrying out low profile work. It is quite interesting that many of the social movements have emerged from the sex workers themselves. The two important communities of sex workers that have taken up the issues of sex workers are DMSC (Durbar Mahila Samanwaya committee) and SANGRAM.

The DMSC was established in the year 1995, an organization of closely 40,000 sex workers who are based in West Bengal. The DMSC emerged out of the health awareness programmes among human sex workers in Calcutta red light areas. The major focus area of the DMSC was to elevate the status of sex workers from mere trafficking to a better profession. DMSC also addressed the issues of decriminalization of sex workers and improving the lives of women sex workers. In order to invoke the attention of the civil society and political institutions, DMSC organized first national conference of sex workers in 1997. Approximately 5000 sex workers attended the conference. It was for the first time that a significant number of sex workers had assembled to raise their voice on rights and working conditions. They pointed out that women in sex work, like sex workers in other professions, had the right to demand better working conditions while remaining within the profession, and that not all women in sex work are forced into the profession[31].

One of the notable contribution made by DMSC had been in the field of health awareness and better safe sex practices, DMSC also initiated in establishing credit cooperative society aimed at giving low interest credit to sex workers who are otherwise being subjected to severe exploitation by money lenders.

The achievements of DMSC had been quite impressive over a period of its existence. In the later stage of 1990's, DMSC was able to influence the customers of sex workers to use condom. There had been significant increase in condom usage in 1998. It was due to the efforts of the DMSC that many forms of violence against women sex workers had been reduced to a great extent. The DMSC had formed a self regulatory board, mainly composed of sex workers but also member of National Human Rights Commission, the National Commission for women, and the Bar Association of India. These actions brought about some beneficial results such as efforts on the part of sex workers to be literate. The DMSC publication "The fallen" learn to raise, which presents the DMSC experience, has been widely disseminated and is often used as an advocacy tool by sex workers in India (DMSC, 1998).

SANGRAM has also been an important group established in 1992, which had been instrumental in forming two collectives of women sex work. As in the case of DMSC, the maiden venture of sangram was in the realm of HIV/AIDS prevention programmes. SANGRAM initiated a number of activities which aimed at prevention of AIDS/HIV and promotion of safer healthy sex practices such as peer education, condom promotion and creating awareness of sexually transmitted diseases. In 1996, the peer education efforts paved the way for the creation of two Veshya AIDS Muqabla Parishad (VAMP), organization of women in sex work in Maharashtra. VAMP addresses the various problems associate with sex workers ranging from community disputes, lobbying with the police, help women access government programmes, giving leadership qualities to women sex workers. SANGRAM has also taken up the issue of decriminalization of sex work. SANGRAM has sought the help of other groups from other parts of India, at various national forums.

The experience of DMSC and SANGRAM revealed the fact that the most fruitful strategies to help the sex workers have been protection of human rights of sex workers. These two NGO initiatives pointed the fact that the sex workers are no longer marginalized. NGOs are found to be effective in addressing the various human rights issues and health issues of sex workers. They are effective especially in linking the mainstream society with sex worker community.

## Conclusion

The sex workers movements unlike many other social movements and human rights movements started off very late. It was in Europe that the sex workers movements and activities had been given prominence. The sex workers agitated for fulfilling certain rights especially labour rights and retirement benefits. In many other countries the economic hardships that had paved the way for sex workers to consolidate themselves. In U.S and Britain, economic conditions were attributed for the sex workers agitation and movements. Similar kinds of movements were emerged in almost all parts of globe especially in Europe and Canada. In Canada prostitutes demanded certain laws to be scrapped which had been enacted to stop illegal prostitution. In the name of the legislation, human rights of the sex workers had been violated. In the 1990s dimension of the sex workers movements had changed to a great extent and the sex workers movements ushered its scope to include minority sex workers, lesbian, gay, bisexual, hetero sexual, migrants, men and women sex workers. Even in some developing countries in Latin America and Asia, certain movements for the rights of sex workers have been formed.

An important dimension to the rights of sex workers rights had been the question of HIV/AIDS. The HIV/AIDS has been the major challenge to sex workers. There had been very little efforts from the state agencies to address the issue of AIDS/HIV. It is an irony that plenty of legislations and policies are formulated in India for protecting the vulnerable sections of society, but their condition has not been changed much. This is particularly true in the case of sex workers. The issue of HIV/AIDS has got a catastrophic effect on the lives of the sex workers. In India, the State agencies and medical institutions has not shown much enthusiasm in creating an awareness for better health practices among sex workers. It is seen that in the pretext of diagnosing AIDS/HIV, the right to privacy of sex workers is violated in various major cities in India.

In India the sex workers have to survive in a society where there are so much of stigma attached to sex work. Even the human rights activists in India are reluctant to take up the issues of sex workers. The debate on varying dimensions of human rights and human rights practioners do not address the sufferings of sex workers. The State is an institution which is expected to protect the rights of sex workers often found to be haunting the people who sell their flesh for livelihood. The state in various contexts doesn't provide necessary information on issues such as abortion, contraception, sex work and sexual identity, resulting in drastic effects on lives of sex workers.

Against this backdrop, the civil society responses and reactions are worth analyzing. Two significant issues have been manifested in the way in which civil society responded towards sex workers rights. The first one is that a social movement for sex workers has emerged from the sex workers themselves and the second issue is that these social movements confine themselves mainly to the arena of HIV/AIDS awareness programmes. The functioning of both DMSC and SANGRAM revealed the fact that these movements have not been vibrant in taking up various issues such as socio economic and political rights of the sex workers, better working conditions, better medical facilities etc. A right-based approach is lacking on the part of the above civil society movements. However, these movements have been active in addressing core issues such as decriminalization of sex work, providing leadership qualities to women sex workers, HIV/AIDS awareness programmes etc. On the contrary the state and other political institutions turn a blind eye to the cause of sex workers. It has been found that the sex workers have been harassed by State institutions like the police and other agencies. The human rights violations are severe in the case of sex workers and these violations are forthcoming from state agencies. It is high time that the civil society and human rights organizations take proactive attitude towards the sex workers and their rights. A right based approach towards the issues of sex workers should be the priority of civil society. The gap created by the State in taking up sex workers rights should be filled in by civil society.

## Notes and Refcrences

1. Amalia Cabezos (July 28- August 4, 1999) "Hookers in the House of the Lord (http:"www.smmirrd.com/Vol. 1/issue 6/hooker.html)" Santa Monica Mirror.
2. http://www.smmirror.com/volume1/issue6/hooker.html.
3. *Ibid.*
4. Melissa Hope Detmore (2006). Encyclopedia of prostitution and sex work. p. 625. Greenwood publishing House.
5. World notes Belgium (http://www.time.com/time/magazine/ article/09171, 962548, 00. html)
6. Amalia cabezos (July 28-August, 4 1999) Hookers in the house of Lord (http://.smmirror.com/vol/issue6/hoxer.html) Santa Monica Mirror.
7. *Ibid.*

8. World charter for prostitutes' rights, 1985 (http://www.walnet.org/csis/group/ICPR-charter.html.
9. *Ibid.*
10. *Ibid.*
11. Conference 05, (http://www.sexwork Europe. Org/site/index php.
12. *Ibid.*
13. The Declaration of the Rights of sex workers in Europe (http://sexworkeurope.org/site/images/PDF/doc. brussek 2005. pdf) International committee on the rights of sex workers in Europe October 2005.
14. *Ibid.*
15. *Ibid.*
16. Israel's fight against sex trafficking (http://news.co.vk/hilmiddle-east/7070429.stm) Raffi Berg. Jerusalem (6 November, 2007) BBC News.
17. Sex workers outreach project-USA (http://www.SWOPCU.org)
18. Prostitutes Education Network (http://www.bayswan.org/peret.html)
19. Achieving universal access – the UK's strategy for halting and reversing the spread of HIV in the developing world (http://www.dfid.giv. UK/pubs/files/achieving-universal access.pdf) DFID 2007. pp. 23.
20. Timeline of event prior to and in response to the UN Guidance note on sex work and HIV, 2008.
21. Dreze and Sen, 1995.
22. Misra Geetanjali (etal), "protecting the rights of sex workers. The Indian Experience in Misra Geetanjali (ed) "sexuality, Gender, and Rights" Sage publications: New Delhi, P.222.
23. *Ibid*, p. 230
24. *Ibid*, p.231
25. *Ibid*, p. 231
26. Misra Geethanjali (etal), "Protecting of the rights of sex workers', The Indian Experience" in Geetanjali Misra (ed), "Sexuality, Gender, and Rights" Sage publications: New Delhi. PP. 222.
27. *Ibid*, p. 223
28. *Ibid*, P 223
29. "Sexual Rights and social movements in India" working paper, November 2006, FREA: New Delhi. P.14.
30. *Ibid*, p. 15
31. *Ibid*, p. 233


- AHUJA, S. 1997. *People, Law and Justice*: Casebook on Public Interest Litigation. Volume II. New Delhi: Universal Law.
- AMNESTY INTERNATIONAL. 1992. *Rape and Sexual Abuse: Torture and III Treatment of Women in Detention*. New York: Amnesty

International.

- BHARAT, S. 1999. HIV/AIDS *Related Discrimination, Stigmatisation and Denial in India*: A Study in Mumbai: Unit for Family Studies: Tata Institute of Social Sciences and the Joint United Nations Programme on HIV/AIDS.
- CENTER FOR FEMINIST LEGAL RESEARCH. 1999. Memorandum on Reform of Laws Related to Prostitution in India. New Delhi: Center for Feminist Legal Research (CFLR).
- CHOWDHURY, S, S. JANA, S. GOMATHI, S. DAS, S. MODOK, A. MAJUMDAR and M. DUTTA. 2000. 'STD/HIV Intervention Programme Calcutta'. Available in Folder of Technical Papers (from the Third West Bengal Sexual Health Conference, Calcutta, February 2000) Department of International Development.
- D'CUNHA, J. 1991. *The Legalization of Prostitution: A Sociological Inquiry into the Laws Relating to Prostitution in India and the West.* Bangalore: Wordmakers.
- DEBROY, B, 1999. 'Some Issues in Law Reform in India'. Paper presented at the conference on Governance and Development, Bonn, Germany, May.
- DREZE, J and A. SEN. 1995. *India Economic Development and Social Opportunity.* New Delhi: Oxford University Press.
- GANGOLI, G. 1998. 'Prostitution, Legalization and Decriminalization', *Economic and Political Weekly*, 33: 504.
- GOVERNMENT OF INDIA, 1950. Constitution of India. Available at http://indiacode.nic.in/coiweb.
- GRUSKIN, S and D. TARANTOLA. 2001. 'HIV/AIDS, Health and Human Rights', in P. Lamptey and H. Gayle (eds), HIV/AIDS *Prevention and Care programs in Resource-Constrained Settings: A Handbook for the Design and Management of Programs*, Washington, DC: Family Health International.
- LANDSBERG-LEWIS, I, 1998. *Bringing Equality Home; Implementing the Convention on the Elimination of All Forms of Discrimination Against Women.* New York: United Nations Development Fund for Women (UNIFEM).
- MISRA GEETANJALI (Ed) *Sexuality, Gender and Rights: Exploring* Theory and Practice in South and South east Asia.
- SAMPADA GRAMEEN MAHILA SANSTHA (SANGRAM), 1999. *Of Veshya, Whores, Vamps and Women Sangli, India*: Sampeda Grameen Mahila Sanstha.

# 18

# THE ENVIRONMENTAL AGITATIONS AND HUMAN RIGHTS VIOLATIONS IN KERALA

**P.S. Panikkar**

Large and small groups of individuals in various parts of Kerala are fighting against environmental degradation and consequent human rights violations. Depletion of natural resources like air, water, soil etc owing to industrial pollution, land use, unjust and ecologically unfriendly constructions etc are rampant in the state. As a result of it people are denied clean air, potable water land for farming, food security etc. And they are deprived of their life, liberty and properties, constitutionally guaranteed as sacred and inalienable fundamental rights. Enforcing authorities such as the police, revenue, industries and agricultural departments, PCB, Ground Water Authority, CWRDM, Geology Dept etc abet the crime. Political parties do not support their cause. The print and electronic media do not usually report their activities under the guise that they cannot stand against development. At the same time they make hue and cry on irrelevant and non-issues. Corporate agencies and capitalist forces are well organized, very powerful and they also rally against peoples' interests. Elected representatives do not champion their cause. Hence they rely on NGOs especially fighting in the social, economical and environmental fields. People's resistance and struggles are the only way out for solving their problems.

### 1. Plachimada Anti-Coca Cola struggle, 2002-2009

Plachimada is a typical agricultural village in Palakkad District which is in the rain shadow region but has a rich acquifer and is well irrigated by the Parambikulam Aliyar Project (PAP) LBC. Chitturpuzha water shed is also there. Majority of the people belong to the low income group and are adivasis. Plachimada belongs to the Perumatty Panchayat of Chittur Taluk. The Hindustan Cocacola Beverages Private Ltd. started its bottling unit there in 2000. The poor rustic people of the area were not aware of the consequences. They were mesmerized by the employment opportunities that were promised and the development it would bring to the area. But from 2001 they began to experience water scarcity. Several public and private wells got dried up and the ground water level went down due to over extraction by the company. More over, the avilable water was highly polluted and the people could not even cook rice in that water. Hence they were driven to fetching potable water from far-away places. For this purpose they were forced to employ school going children also, as a result of which dropout rates increased in the schools of Perumatty, Vandithavalam, Pattnchery etc. Now the company also started distributing the sludge to the farmers in the guise of fertilizer. It was taken to places as far away as Alathur, Kozhinjampara and even to neighbouring villages of Tamil Nadu. They even dumped it in the basin of Chitturpuzha, a tributory of Bharathapuha which is the lifeline of the people in Palakkad, Thrissur and Malapuram districts. The pollution due to this sludge reached as far as ponnani. BBC team which took the sludge and tested it state of art labs in London reported that it contained heavy metals like cadmium, lead, chromium etc which affects vital human organs like liver, kidney and heart. Later this report was confirmed by the PCB and GWA. All these factors compelled local people to form the Anti-cola struggle organisation on 22 April 2002 and launch peaceful agitation through satyagraha, fast, protest marches etc. All the activities were based/co-orinated from a small hut that was put up in front of the gate of the factory. Marches to the offices of the PCB, GWA etc were also held. At the beginning it did not get any support from any political parties or even the panchayath. The media, except Madhyamam, ignored the struggle. Soon various environmentalists, social leaders and scientists like Medha Patkar and Dr Vandana Shiva visited the place and supported the struggle. This brought mass attention and several NGOs and political parties came forward to support the stuggle. At present it has a solidarity committee comprising about 100 NGOs of the state.

After two years of the struggle Dr Sunita Narain of Centre for Science and Envionment revealed that Coca cola and Pepsi Cola contain pesticide residues much above permissible limits. Consequently in August 2006 the present government led by VS Achuthanandan prohibited the production and sale of the Colas in the state. However the High court quashed this order. In the meantime the people's agitation and the firm stand taken by the Perumatty Panchayat had forced the factory to stop production. But the losses inflicted due to over extraction of ground water (up to 15 lakh liter per day), and contamination of land and water were heavy. The negative impact on agriculture and animal husbandry were irreversible. Even during heavy monsons the people have to depend on water tankers for potable water. About

17 people had unnatural death due to illness caused by the pollution. More people have become sick. The eco system has been irreversibly damaged. The Government has miserably failed to take action against the Coca Cola company or even stop the operation of Pepsico at Kanjikkode which had also started functioning at about the same time as Coca Cola in Plachimada. Over exploitaion of water has turned the region into a draught area. And worse, the company has not even abided by the order of the Kerala High Court to provide drinking water to the people in Perumatty Panchayat.

As a result of the demand made by the agitation the government has appointed a High power committee headed by K. Jayakumar, Additionnal Chief Secetary, to study the environment and other problems created by the functioning of the company and suggest compensation to the affected people. The committee has been collecting evidence in this regard. It is expected to submit its report before 31 December 2009.

Since Silent Valley agitation, Plachimada has given an impetus to the people's resistance in India. Indeed it has rejuvenated the environment movement in the State. When the agitation started its only objective was to prevent pollution. Now it is establishing the water rights of the people also. It also demands social legislation, especially amendments to the Panchayati Raj Act, to achieve this objective and prevent plachimadas in future. The struggle has completed seven years now. All political parties in the state has supported it at one time or the other. And no one will ever argue for the re-opening of the company.

**2. Kanjikkode Railway Coach Factory Eviction Struggle, 2009**

Establishment of a railway coach factory has been a long cherished aspiration of the people of Palakkad. Late Prime Minister Indira Gandhi had initially made such an offer but later it went to Kapurthala in Punjab. Now the Central Government has again made such an offer. The State Government tried to provide 900 acres of land in Kanjikkode, comprising Mukroni, Thalapallam, Chuillipallam and Vallady areas of Pudussery Grama Panchayat. This area is inhabited by 1500 persons in 700 families/450 houses. Among them 140 families belong to the SC/ST communities. Also there are families who were displaced twice in 1972 and 1984 for developing Kanjikkode Industrial Area and NH. (The Supreme Court has ruled that a pepole can be displaced only once in their time.) These evictees were then compensated by a paltry Rs. 132/- per cent of land and they had to subsequently buy undeveloped land @ Rs. 900/- per cent. Hollow promises had also been made regarding government job to each family which was never fulfilled. The agonies of displacement has been too fresh in their minds to allow them to gracefully swallow whatever the authorities promise this time.

The paddy fields here contain rich alluvial soil and every year produce 1400 tons of paddy in double crop. The paddy produced here is also rich in quality, fragrance and weight. One measure (Para) would weight 8 kg owing to the nutrients received from the hills and forest nearby. Vallery Padasekaram (Farmer's Collective) in this area has been chosen for the food security scheme of the government. The government has also spent Rs 1.5 crores under the Command Area Development Authority (CADA). Coconut, banana and vegetables are also produced here besides 900 litres of milk per day. All in all this is an ideal example of how sustainable development should be.

This area has 8 fresh water tanks, of which one is 28 acres in area and the rest are about 5 to 7 acres each. They are unique in Kerala and they get rain water from Ayyappanmala,velancherymala and Aduppukootymala on the north western side. These tanks are scientifically connected through canals and therefore there is no spillover. These tanks have been extensively used by farmers and others for agiculture as well as domestic purposes. In addition these are the only water sources for the wildlife in the neighbouring forests.

The place is also in the catchment area of Malampuha reservoir and Korayar, a tributary of Bharathapuzha. There are several big and small watersheds and passes, including the 30km wide Palakkad Pass, the traditional gateway to Kerala. Any tampering with this delicate eco system will have far-reaching consequences.

The place lies in the lap of bio-diversity rich western Ghats. The Central Government is spending crores of rupees for the conservation of these ghats and the UNESCO is taking steps to include them in the World Heritage List.

Sufficient barren land is available in the vicinity. 520 acres of land acquired for Instrumentation Ltd is readily available. Also 3000 acres of barren land is available between Payattukattuchalla and Chullimada V V College. This land is also bounded by two railway tracks. A and B lines running between Palakkad and Coimbatore.

When the district administration started to take steps to evict the local people, they formed the Kanjikkode Railway Coach Factory Land Acquisition Action Council on 16 May 2008. It had a 54 member executive committee. A solidarity committee comprising of various NGOs was also formed. On 13 November 2008, a dharna was oraganized against the eviction, in front of the Pudussery Panchayat office. About 1000 persons participated. On 22 Februrary 2009, a Black Day was observed in the area. On 25 June 2009 a protest was organised in front of the District Collectorate. Prof. Sara Joseph, noted writer and leader of the feminist movement inaugurated the dharna which was also attended by 1000 people, mostly women. On 24 July 2009, about 1000 people under the leadership of the Action Council gheraoed the survery team which had gone to the area for surverying the land notified for acquisition. A Peoples' March was organized from Mukroni to Kanjikkode Sathrapadi on 17 September 2009. This was follow by a public meeting. Dr. P. Geetha, Writer and social activist, besides other leaders of political parties and NGOs, addressed the meeting. At an all party meeting convened by the District collector on 18/9/09, strangely the project affected people/their representatives and environmentalists were excluded. Consequently, when the survey teams reached the area once again, they were forced to retreat without being able to do any work. The Action Council stayed firm on their demand that no work, including survey of land, will be permitted until their living areas, agricultural land and the water bodies were de-notified. Meanwhile, the Union, Railway Minister also announced that no railway projects will be taken up that required eviction of people. Medha Patkar, leader of the Narmada Bachao Andholan and the National Alliance of People's Movements also intervened on behalf of the project affected people of Kanjikkode to appeal to the Railway Minister to avoid displacement in the name of development. Finally the RITES team revisited the area on 8/11/09 and approved the 400 acres of land already available with the Government. The factory less the township will come up on this land. This has been approved by the Railway Board also.

The State Government and district administration had dubbed this struggle as 'one against development, promoted by Tamilnadu lobbies and outsiders'. They had also spread lies like majority of farmers are willing to surrender their lands, 'there are no water bodies' and 'the greenery is just what is found allover Kerala's etc. Some of these lies were exposed through data gathered under the RTI Act. The authorities had tried every trick in their bag and also coercion instead of finding a just and amicable solution.

The ultimate victory, achieved through Gandhian means of satyagraha, non-co-operation and peaceful non-violent resistance is indeed a feather in the cap for people's struggles against an insensitive, arrogant and callous officialdom and government. It provides the proverbal 'light at the end of the tunnel' for those seeking to live with dignity and peace everywhere in the world.

# 19

# PHARMACEUTICAL PATENTS AND HUMAN RIGHTS

**K.M. George**

## I-Human Rights

### 1.1 International Law on Human Rights

Human rights are the minimal and inalienable rights which equally belong to every individual of the human family against the State or public authority, irrespective of any other consideration. Human rights become fundamental rights when guaranteed by constitution[1]. Written constitution is not the only exhaustive source of law, even customs or usages are legally enforceable, if they are not inconsistent with fundamental rights. The international aspect of human rights and the first attempt to codify rules to protect human rights took shape in the Charter of the United Nations (1945), the foundational treaty of the United Nations.

The preamble of the Charter states the objective of the United Nations, inter alia, as to "…reaffirm faith in fundamental human rights, in the dignity and worth of the human person, in the equal rights of …nations…, and to establish conditions under which justice… can be maintained, and to promote social progress and better standards of life in larger freedom,…"

Article 1 states the purposes of the United Nations as, inter alia, "[t]o achieve international co-operation… in promoting and encouraging respect for human rights and for fundamental freedoms for all without distinction…." Article 55 states that the United Nations "shall promote... universal respect for and observance of, human rights and fundamental freedoms for all..." As this was not legally binding, steps were taken to formulate various human rights. This led to the United Nations' adoption and proclamation of the Universal Declaration of Human Rights (1948).

The Universal Declaration - considered as the Magna Carta of mankind - that forms the paradigm for the drafting of human rights provisions of more than 30 domestic constitutions, states in Article-3 that "[e]veryone has the right to life, liberty and security of person."

The Universal Declaration sets out a common standard of achievement for all peoples and all nations, and towards that end it aims to promote respect for these rights and works to secure their universal and effective recognition and observance. Its Article 25 states:

"Everyone has the right to a standard of living adequate for the health and well-being of himself and of his family, including food, clothing, housing and medical care ... and the right to security in the event of unemployment, sickness, disability,...Motherhood and childhood are entitled to special care and assistance" [italics added].

The World Health Organization established in 1948 as an agency of the United Nations, to further international cooperation in improving health conditions, was given a broad mandate under its constitution to promote the attainment of "the highest possible level of health" by all people. It inherits the International Office of Public Health at Paris (established in 1909) and the Health Organization of the League of Nations (set up in 1923). WHO Constitution declares:

"The highest attainable standard of health as a fundamental right of every human being, without distinction of race, religion, and political belief, economic or social condition. The achievement of any State in the promotion and protection of health is of value to All. Unequal development in different countries in the promotion of health and control of disease, especially communicable disease, is a common danger. The extension to all peoples of the benefits of medical, psychological and related knowledge is essential to the fullest attainment of health. Governments have a responsibility for the health of their peoples ...." The WHO's functions under Article 2, inter alia, include promotion of maternal and child health and welfare, foster activities in the field of mental health, promotion and conduct of research in the field of health etc.

For the effective enforcement of the Universal Declaration, the UN General Assembly adopted two legally binding covenants in 1966: the Covenant on Civil and Political Rights (1966) which guarantees legally enforceable rights to individuals, and the Covenant on Economic, Social and Cultural Rights (1966) which makes it obligatory on the part of the State Parties to implement them by legislation.

Article 9 of the Covenant on Economic, Social and Cultural Rights (ICESCR) states that: "The States Parties to the present Covenant recognize the right of everyone to social security, including social insurance;" and its Article 12 recognizes "the right of everyone to the enjoyment of the highest attainable standard of physical and mental health." Towards the full realization of this right, the steps to be taken by the States include those necessary for: (a) the reduction of the still birth-rate and infant mortality and for the healthy development of the child; (b) improvement of environmental and industrial hygiene; (c) prevention, treatment and control of epidemic, endemic, occupational and other diseases; (d) creation of conditions to assure all medical service and medical attention. Also, Articles 7 and 11 "...recognize the right of everyone to ... just and favourable conditions of work which ensure ... safe and healthy working conditions; ... the right to ... an adequate standard of living." And under Article 12(b), the States Parties recognizes the right of everyone to enjoy the benefits of scientific progress and its applications. Further, Article 2 makes it mandatory on the part of State Parties to take steps to achieve progressively the full realization of the rights recognized by all appropriate means; and to guarantee the rights without any discrimination. Article 3 requires the adoption of measures to ensure the enjoyment of all economic, social and cultural rights without any sex discrimination.

Besides the above, the Convention on the Rights of the Child (1989), the Convention on the Elimination of All Forms of Racial Discrimination, the Convention on the Elimination of All Forms of Discrimination Against Women, all guarantee the right to health as a fundamental human right.The UN General Assembly Declaration on the Rights of Child (1959), reiterating in the preamble the United Nations' faith in fundamental human rights and in the dignity of human person and its determination to promote social progress and better standards of life in larger freedom proclaims the Rights of the Child in Principle 4:

"He shall be entitled to grow and develop in health; to this end, special care and protection shall be provided both to him and to his mother, including adequate pre-natal and post-natal care. The child shall have the right to adequate nutrition, housing, recreation and medical services."

The UN Convention on the Rights of the Child in its preamble, considering the United Nations' recognition of the inherent dignity and equal and inalienable rights of all members of the human family and its faith in fundamental human rights as the foundation of freedom, justice and peace in the world, sets out the civil, political, economic, social, and cultural rights of children. It is a binding treaty and its compliance is monitored by the United Nations Committee on the Rights of the Child. As of November 2009, 194 countries have ratified it. All member nations except Somalia and the United States have ratified it. Their relevant articles relating to health are considered below.

Article 6: States Parties recognize the inherent right to life of every child and that they shall ensure to the maximum extent possible the survival and development of the child.

Article 24: States Parties recognize the right of the child to the enjoyment of the highest attainable standard of health and to facilities for the treatment of illness and rehabilitation of health. ...ensure that no child is deprived of his or her right of access to such health care services...other international human rights.

Further, States Parties are obligated to take appropriate measures to diminish infant and child mortality, ensure the provision of necessary medical assistance and health care to all children, combat disease and malnutrition, appropriate pre-natal and post-natal health care for mothers, and develop preventive health care. And toward full realization of the right States Parties have to undertake to promote and encourage international co-operation, taking into consideration the particular needs of developing countries.

The United Nations International Convention on the Elimination of All Forms of Racial Discrimination (1966) guarantees the right of everyone without distinction as to race, colour, national or ethnic origin and provides under Article 5(e) (iv) among other rights the right to public health and medical care. The United Nations Convention on the Elimination of All Forms of Discrimination Against Women (1979) often called as the "International Bill of Rights for Women", was adopted by the UN General Assembly. Its Articles 10, 12, and 14, inter alia state that:

"States Parties shall ...ensure to [women] ...access to specific educational information to help to ensure the health and well-being of families, including information and advice on family planning." (Article 10).

"States Parties shall... eliminate discrimination against women in the field of health care in order to ensure...access to health care services, including those related to family planning." (Article 12).

"States Parties shall ... ensure ... that [women in rural areas] ... have access to adequate health care facilities, including information counseling and services in family planning." (Article14).

Beside the above, the United Nations Fourth World Conference on Women (1995) in its Beijing Declaration recognized the right of all women to control all aspects of their health as being basic to their empowerment, and it expressed its determination to ensure equal access to and equal treatment of women and men in health care and to enhance women's sexual and reproductive health. (Beijing Declaration, paras. 17 and 30) In its Platform for Action, it is emphasized that:

"Women have the right to the enjoyment of the highest attainable standard of physical and mental health. The enjoyment of this right is vital to their life and well-being and their ability to participate in all areas of public and private life.... Women's health involves their emotional, social and physical well-being and is determined by the social, political and economic context of their lives, as well as by biology.... To attain optimal health throughout the life cycle, equality, including the sharing of family responsibilities, development and peace are necessary conditions." (Para. 89).

While addressing the health issues of women, strategic objective was envisaged to increase women's access throughout the life cycle to appropriate, affordable and quality health care. It reaffirmed and ensured by national legislation, the right to the enjoyment of the highest attainable standards of physical and mental health of women and girls; and provided for strengthening and reorienting health services, particularly primary health care including sexual and reproductive health care, in order to ensure affordable and universal access to health services. As per it, maternal mortality had to be reduced to a minimum of 50 per cent of the 1990 levels by the year 2000 and a further one half by the year 2015, or 50 to 70 per 1,000 live births, mortality rates of infants and children under five by one third of the 1990 level or 50 to 70 per1,000 live births, and by the year 2015 infant mortality rate below 35 per 1,000 live births and an under-five mortality rate below 45 per 1,000 (Beijing Platform for Action, Para. 106 & 107).

In addition to the above, governments have made commitments to ensure the realization of the human right to health, which include commitments made at the Alma Ata Declaration on Health For All by 2000, the Earth Summit in Rio (1992), the International Conference on Population and Development in Cairo (1994), the World Summit for Social Development in Copenhagen, and the Habitat II conference in Istanbul.

The International Conference on Primary Health Care-Declaration of Alma-Ata (1978)- the famous primary health care declaration, emphasising that the gross inequality in the health status of the people particularly between developed and developing being unacceptable and promotion and protection of the health of the people are essential to sustained socio- economic development made Governments responsible to ensure primary health care for all by the year 2000.Primary health care is "essential health care which is to be universally accessible to individuals and families in the community in ways acceptable to them, through their full participation at a cost the community can afford" (Declaration II, III, V & VI)

The Earth Summit in Rio (1992) asserts that health and development are intimately interconnected and that the primary health needs of the world's population are integral to the achievement of the goals of sustainable development and primary environmental care. Some major goals it set forth were to reduce measles deaths by 95 per cent by 1995; mobilize and unify national and international efforts against AIDS, by year 2000 eliminate guinea worm disease, eradicate polio, reduce the number of deaths of children from diarrhoea by 50 to 70 per cent, effectively control onchocerciasis (river blindness), leprosy etc. (Agenda 21, Chapter 6, paras. 1 and 12).

According to the United Nations International Conference on Population and Development (1994), called the Cairo Programme in Action:

"Everyone has the right to the enjoyment of the highest attainable standard of physical and mental health. States should take all appropriate measures to ensure, without discrimination universal access to health-care services, including reproductive health care. The role of women as primary custodians of family health should be recognized and supported. Access to basic health care and health education, availability of simple cost-effective remedies should be provided" (Action Principle 8 and para. 8.6).

In the United Nations World Summit for Social Development (1995), the nations made their commitments in promoting and attaining the goals of universal and equitable access to the highest attainable standard of physical and mental health, non-discriminatory access of all to primary health care, strengthening efforts to tackle the growing HIV/AIDS pandemic and to achieve the goals of national Health-for-All Strategies. Further, at the international level commitments were made to share knowledge, experience and expertise and transfer of technology regarding health programmes that will result in endogenous capacity-building; and also to intensify and coordinate international support for education and health programmes based on respect for human dignity (Ibid Declaration-Commitment 6).

The United Nations Conference on Human Settlements - Habitat II Agenda (1996), adopted by 171 countries recognised that human health and quality of life are central to the development of sustainable human settlements. It made commitments to achieve universal and equal access to the highest attainable standard of physical, mental and environmental health, and equal access of all to primary health care; good health throughout the life-span of every child, man and woman being fundamental to ensure their participation in the social, economic and political processes of human settlements; to promote sustainable human settlements which depends upon access to food and nutrition, safe drinking water, sanitation, universal access to health-care services; creation of safe places to work and live and eradication of major diseases, particularly childhood diseases and protection of the environment. As measures to prevent ill health and disease are as important as the availability of appropriate medical treatment and care, prevention and care are placed within the context of environmental policy that would provide a holistic approach to health. (paras. 36 and 128)

The eight Millennium Development Goals (MDGs) adopted by the world leaders in the year 2000 provide a framework for the entire international community to work together towards a common end, making sure that human development reaches everyone, everywhere. They are both global and local, tailored by each country to suit its specific development needs. The targets are set to be achieved by 2015.The MDGs include three goals on health with specific targets to be achieved:

**Goal 4: Reduction of child mortality**

Target 4A: Reduce by two-thirds, between 1990 and 2015, the under-five mortality rate, i.e. from 93 children of every 1,000 dying before age five in 1990 to 31 of every 1,000 in 2015.

**Goal 5: Improve maternal health**

Target 5A: Reduce by three quarters, between 1990 and 2015, the maternal mortality ratio,

Target 5B: Achieve by 2015, universal access to reproductive health.

**Goal 6: Combat HIV/AIDS, malaria and other diseases**

Target 6a: Halt and begin to reverse the spread of HIV/AIDS,

Target 6b: Achieve, by 2010 universal access to treatment for HIV/AIDS for all those who need it,

Target 6c: Halt and begin to reverse the incidence of malaria and other major diseases.

Now consider the regional treaties on human rights. The most notable is the European Convention for the Protection of Human Rights and Fundamental Freedoms (1953), created by the Council of Europe. It recognises the universality of human rights and guarantees their legal enforceability, not only against one's own state but also against other sovereign states. The rights inter alia include the right to life under Article 2[2].

The European Commission of Social Rights (ECSR) monitors compliance of the member states to this Charter and the European Court of Human Rights bestowed with compulsory jurisdiction that pronounces judgments that are binding on Sovereign States. Besides, there is the Committee of Ministers with residual powers to deal with cases not brought before the Court.

The European Social Charter -the Council of Europe treaty- adopted in 1961 and revised in 1966 guarantees basic rights: housing, health, education, employment, social and legal protection, freedom of movement of persons and non discrimination. The enforcement machinery of the Charter is different from the European Convention of Human Rights (ECHR). Under the Social Charter, the States Parties must submit regular reports to the European Committee of Social Rights, a committee of independent experts. It scrutinizes them and gives its assessment, based on which the Committee of Ministers issues recommendations requesting States concerned to bring national law and practice into conformity with the Charter. This is in contradistinction to the ECHR which allows for individual complaints to the European Court of Human Rights. In November 1995, a system of collective complaints by international and national organisations of employers and trade unions and international non-governmental organisations was provided for in the Charter.

The American Convention on Human Rights in Article 14 states that "every person has a right to have his life respected. This shall be protected by law, and in general, from the moment of conception. No one shall be arbitrarily deprived of his life."

The NHS constitution for England lays down the objectives of the National Health Service and its guiding principles, and the rights and responsibilities of the various parties involved in health care (patients, staff, and trust boards). The NHS constitution grants patients rights which are legally enforceable and also makes other non-binding pledges. These are in the areas of access: access to treatments, medicines and screening programmes; quality of care and environment; respect, consent and confidentiality; informed choice; patient involvement in healthcare and public involvement in the NHS; and complaints and redress.

Thus, all these categorically establish that access to health is a fundamental and universal human right. "Human rights are "claims of entitlement" that arise "as of right" and are independent of external justification; they are "self evident" and fundamental to any human being living a dignified, healthy and productive and rewarding life. Human right to life is a jus cogens, non-derogable peremptory norm...[3]". And that is why specific institutions are created by the United Nations viz., the World Health Organization (1946), the United Nations Children's Fund (1946) to monitor and establish the human rights.

### 1.2. Constitution of India and Right to Heath Care

The Constitution of India provides for human rights: civil and political rights as Fundamental Rights that are justiciable under Part III; and social and economic rights like health, education, livelihoods which are not justiciable under Part IV, the Directive Principles of State Policy. The Directive Principles make a forceful appeal to the State to work towards assuring these rights through the process of governance.

Fundamental Rights prescribe the duty and obligations of the State towards its citizens. The fundamental rights enunciated under Part III of the Constitution include the right to life under Article 21 which states that:

"No person shall be deprived of his life or personal liberty except through procedure established by law."

Though Part III of the Constitution does not prescribe the right to health or healthcare as a fundamental right, by virtue of judicial interpretation of Article 21 those rights have become fundamental rights, especially since the right to health is inseparable from the right to life which implies life of a dignified human being. It covers the right for pollution free environment, medical aid, education etc. This is similar to Article 2 of the Universal Declaration of Human Rights. India having ratified the Covenant on Economic, Social and Cultural Rights (ICESCR) is obligated to take, inter alia, measures to assure health and healthcare as a right as per Articles 2 and 3. The first National Health Policy in 1982 can be considered as the first step in this direction. Article 14 of the Constitution and Article 7 of the Universal Declaration of Human Rights and Article 5 of the International Convention on the Elimination of All Forms of Racial Discrimination uphold the equality before law and equal protection of the law. Among the Directive Principles, Articles 41, 42 and 47 provide as follows:

Article 41. Right to work, to education and to public assistance in certain cases: The State shall, within the limits of its economic capacity and development, make effective provision for securing the right to work, to education and to public assistance in cases of unemployment, old age, sickness and disablement, and in other cases of undeserved want.

Article 42. Provision for just and humane conditions of work and maternity relief: The State shall make provision for securing just and humane conditions of work and for maternity relief.

Article 47. Duty of the State to raise the level of nutrition and the standard of living and to improve public health: The State shall regard the raising of the level of nutrition and the standard of living of its people and the improvement of public health as among its primary duties and, in particular, the State shall endeavour to bring about prohibition of the consumption except for medicinal purposes of intoxicating drinks and of drugs which are injurious to health.

It is to be noted that Articles 41, 42 and 47 which deal with social security, maternity benefits and health respectively were not given their due importance by the State unlike in the case of reservations for scheduled castes, tribes and other backward castes/classes under Article 46, though all of them are human rights falling under the Directive Principles. This is because of political expediency. Further, though nutrition, conditions of work and maternity relief are integral to health, the right to health is not expressly guaranteed under the Constitution as a fundamental right. But it is to be reiterated that there is substantial case law which upholds the right to health as a fundamental right, by broadly defining the Fundamental Right to Life under Article 21.

The right to health as a fundamental right sprang from litigations relating to right to pollution free environment which presupposes health and health care as fundamental rights, and secondly as the rights of Government employees to receive health care. For instance, in Municipal Council, Ratlam v. Vardhichand & Ors[4]., relating to garbage issue, the Supreme Court observed:

"The State will realize that Article 47 makes it a paramount principle of governance that steps are taken for the improvement of public health as amongst its primary duties."

In CESC Ltd. v. Subash Chandra Bose[5] the Supreme Court, holding the right to health as a fundamental right, observed:

"The term health implies more than an absence of sickness. Medical care and health facilities not only protect against sickness but also ensure stable manpower for economic development. Facilities of health and medical care generate devotion and dedication to give the workers' best, physically as well as mentally, in productivity. It enables the worker to enjoy the fruit of his labour, to keep him physically fit and mentally alert for leading a successful economic, social and cultural life. The medical facilities are, therefore, part of social security and like gilt edged security, it would yield immediate return in the increased production or at any rate reduce absenteeism on grounds of sickness etc. Health is thus a state of complete physical, mental and social well being and not merely the absence of disease or infirmity. In the light of Articles 22 to 25 of the Universal Declaration of Human Rights, International Covenant on Economic, Social and Cultural Rights and in the light of socio-economic justice assured in our Constitution, right to health is a fundamental human right to workmen. The maintenance of health is a most imperative constitutional goal whose realization requires interaction by many social and economic factors."

In State of Punjab and Others v. Mohinder Singh[6] it was held that: "It is now a settled law in India that right to health is integral to right to life. Government has a constitutional obligation to provide health facilities." In Bandhua Mukti Morcha v. Union of India[7] it was already held that the right to life includes the right to live with dignity, the right to health being essential for human existence is an integral part of the right to life. In Mahendra Pratap Singh v. Orissa State[8] it was held that people are entitled to adequate health care, that it is the duty of the Government to see that the people get treatment and lead healthy life, and that technical fetters cannot be stated as reasons for not establishing a health centre. Apart from recognizing the fundamental right to health as an integral part of the right to life, the constitutional obligation of the State to provide medical health services is also laid down in many judicial decisions.

In Consumer Education Research Centre v. Union of India,[9] the Supreme Court, while dealing with health hazards and the rights of workers in asbestos manufacturing held that the right to health and health care is a component of the fundamental right to life guaranteed under Article 21 of the Constitution. Emphasizing that Article 38(1) lays down the foundation for human rights, Article 46 directs the State to protect the poor from social injustice and all forms of exploitation, Article 39(e) requires the State to secure the health and strength of the workers, Article 42 mandates that the State should secure just and humane conditions of work, Article 43 directs that the State shall endeavour to secure to all workers a decent standard of life, Article 48-A enjoins the State to protect and improve the environment; and that Article 25(2) of the UDHR ensures an individual the right to adequate standard of living in health and medical care and that Article 2(b) ICESCR protects the right of worker safe and healthy working conditions, it observed:

"Continued treatment, while in service or after retirement is a moral, legal and constitutional concomitant duty of the employer and the State. Therefore, it must be held that the right to health and medical care is a fundamental right under Article 21 read with Articles 39(c), 41 and 43 of the Constitution and make the life of the workman meaningful and purposeful with dignity of person. Right to life including protection of the health and strength of the worker is a minimum requirement to enable a person to live with human dignity". .. [A]n industry, public or private, is enjoined to take all such action which will promote health, strength and vigour of the workman during the period of employment and leisure and health even after retirement as basic essentials to live the life with health and happiness...The right to human dignity, development of personality, social protection, right to rest and leisure are fundamental human rights to a workman assured by the Charter of Human Rights, in the Preamble and Arts. 38 and 39 of the Constitution." It held that facilities and opportunities, as enjoined in Article 38, should be provided to protect the health of the workman and that the right is available against the State and private employers.

Regarding the right to healthy environment, there are numerous judicial decisions that uphold it as a fundamental right to life. Environmental pollution as it affects health violates the right to life with dignity;[10] environmental, ecological, air and water pollution, etc. are violations of the right to health guaranteed by Article 21 of the Constitution[11]; right to pollution-free water and air is an enforceable fundamental right guaranteed under Article 21;[12] the maintenance and improvement of public health is the duty of the State to fulfill its constitutional obligations cast on it under Article 21 of the Constitution,[13] adequate and quality medical care are parts of right to health and right to life[14] are some of the decisions in this regard.

With regard to the provision of emergency medical treatment, upholding that preservation of human life is of paramount importance, it was unequivocally stated in Parmanand Katara v. Union of India[15] that "[e]very doctor whether at a government hospital or otherwise has the professional obligation to extend his services with due expertise for protecting life." On examining whether the non-availability of services in the government health centres amount to a violation of Article 21, it was held in Paschim Baga Khet Mazoor Samiti v. State of West Bengal[16] that Article 21 imposes a constitutional obligation on the State to safeguard the right to life of every person, and that the lack of financial resources cannot be cited as a reason for the State to shy away from its constitutional obligation; and that the failure to provide timely medical treatment to a person in need of such treatment results in violation of his right to life guaranteed under Article 21.

Despite the above, it is still important to have health and healthcare instituted as a right within the Constitution and/or established by a specific Act of Parliament guaranteeing the right. Ruth Roemer discussing this issue writes: "The principal function of a constitutional provision for the right to health care is usually symbolic. It sets forth the intention of the government to protect the health of its citizens. A statement of national policy alone is not sufficient to assure entitlement to health care; the right must be developed through specific statutes, programs and services. But setting forth the right to health care in a constitution serves to inform the people that protection of their health is official policy of the government and is reflected in the basic law of the land."[17]

## II – Patents

A patent is an exclusive property right granted by the government, to a person to make use of an invention or process for a specific period of time, usually 20 years. The grant of the patent, made in exchange for the disclosure of the details of the inventions with the public, provides the patentee the right to exclude others from making, using, selling, offering for sale, or importing the patented invention for the term of the patent, which usually begins from the filing date, subject to the payment of maintenances fees. Like any other property right, it may be sold, licensed, mortgaged, assigned or transferred, given away, or simply abandoned. The grant of patent protection in pharmaceutical drugs and medical technologies were/are highly disputatious. Many nations did not provide patents for pharmaceuticals, even many industrialized countries introduced it quite belatedly, for instance, United Kingdom in 1949, France in1960, Germany in 1968, Japan in 1976, Switzerland in 1977, Italy in 1978, Sweden in 1978, Spain in 1992; in 1988 WIPO listed 49 countries as not providing for patents in pharmaceutical products[18]. Patents can be granted either for process or product or for both. A process patent grants the patentee exclusive right only over the manufacturing process, not on the product itself. This means that anyone can adopt a different process to make the same product and can sell it. But in the case of a product patent different process to make the same product is expressly barred during the term of the patent, usually 20 years, without the patent holder's authorization. That is, the product patent prevents others from manufacturing, selling, distributing or importing the patented product or even its versions produced through different processes, without the authorization of the patent holder. It can be seen that while many nations granted patents only for process others granted patents both for process as well as products. This difference in the patent regime casts different socio-economic impacts. The patent rights are open to much criticism, especially in the case of pharmaceutical drugs and medical technologies because it also involves issues relating to human rights and access to health care. These are problems that require intensive study; and in this study this is done mainly with respect to the Indian context.

The history of the Indian patent laws can be traced to the Act VI of 1856 when patent law was enacted based on the British Patent Law of 1852 which granted patent rights for inventors for 14 years. After undergoing through a series of changes in the patent laws, finally in the British India, The Indian Patents and Designs Act, 1911 came into force. This Act continued its operation in the independent India till1972; though amended in 1950 and 1952 it provided for product-patents in pharmaceutical drugs. With respect to the patent law, the 1911 Act was repealed and replaced by the Patents Act, 1970, which came into force on 20.4.1972; in the case of pharmaceutical drugs it provided for patents only for process. This Act that remained in force for about 24 years had undergone through three amendments; and the third one, the Patents (Amendment) Act 2005 that came into effect on 1.1.2005, provided for the grant of patents both for products as well as process and thereby the Indian patent law became fully compliant with the Trade in Intellectual Property Rights (TRIPS) as per the mandatory requirement of membership of the World Trade Organization (WTO). The changes in the patent regime were made with definite policy implications on the production of pharmaceutical drugs and on medical technologies. In this context it becomes pertinent to analyze the changes in the Indian Patent regime upon the production of pharmaceutical drugs, on medical technologies and hence on health care.

The grant of patents being a grant of monopoly right, directly affects the allocation of resources depending on the nature of the patent (product or process), production of generics and hence the health care. The effect of changes in patent rights on medicines has to be analyzed on the basis of the jus cogens (non- derogable law) of human rights over patent rights.

## III- Pharmaceutical Patents and Human Rights

Patent right is a monopoly right granted to an innovator or inventor either for the product or for its process of manufacture. It is a trading right granted to the patentee, the trading right is a human right to trade or profession. The right to health and health care is also a human right that is recognized both nationally and internationally.

India is a State Party in the international covenants in which right to health and health care are recognized as human rights. For instance, as mentioned earlier, are the preamble, Articles 1and 55 of the Charter of the United Nations (1945); the very Constitution and Article 2 of the World Health Organization (1948); Articles 3 and 25 of the Universal Declaration of Human Rights (1948); the Covenant on Civil and Political Rights (1966) which guarantees legally enforceable rights to individuals and the Covenant on Economic, Social and Cultural Rights(1966) which makes it obligatory on the part of the State Parties to implement them by legislation, Article 2, 7, 9,11 and 12 of the Covenant on Economic, Social and Cultural Rights; the United Nations Convention on the Rights of the Child (1989), particularly its preamble, Principle 4, Articles 6 and 24; the Convention on the Elimination of All Forms of Racial Discrimination (1966), particularly its Article 5(e) (iv); the United Nations Convention on the Elimination of All Forms of Discrimination Against Women (1979) often called as the "International Bill of Rights for Women", its preamble, Articles 10, 12, and 14; the United Nations Fourth World Conference on Women (1995), especially Beijing Declaration, paras. 17, 30, 89; Beijing Platform for Action, paras. 106 &107; the Alma Ata Declaration on Health For All by 2000, particularly Declaration II,III,V&VI; the Earth Summit in Rio (1992), the International Conference on Population and Development in Cairo (1994), the World Summit for Social Development in Copenhagen, and the Habitat II conference in Istanbul.

Further, whereas patent right being a statutory right it is justiciable; the right to health and health care being human rights coming under Articles 41, 42 and 47 of the Directive Principles of the Constitution, though provide forceful policies of governance, are not explicitly justiciable. But by judicial hermeneutics the right to health and health care are regarded as fundamental human rights in our Constitution and hence becomes justiciable. The question therefore naturally arises which is more fundamental, whether patent rights or right to health and health care? To answer this question, the prevailing scenario between human right to health and access to affordable drugs has to be laid bare.

According to WHO, infectious diseases kill over 10 million people each year, and more than 90 percent of them belong to the developing countries that together account for four-fifths of the world's population[19]. The main causes are HIV/AIDS, respiratory infections, malaria, and tuberculosis. Each day, nearly eight thousand people die of AIDS in the developing world because of the lack of access to essential medicines, as medicines are prohibitively costly that has resulted from the strong protection given to intellectual property. In the developing world that account for less than 10 percent of the global pharmaceutical market, the R&D towards the health needs of their people "...has virtually ground to a standstill because drug companies in developed and developing nations simply cannot recoup the cost of R&D for products to treat diseases that abound in developing countries[20]. Of the 1,223 new drugs approved [for patents] between 1975 and 1997, approximately 1 percent (13 drugs) specifically treat tropical diseases[21]". This exorbitant rise in prices of medicines also resulted in widening the access gap between developed and developing countries.

Further, Aaron argues that patents can affect patient care in two ways: first by stretching the statutory requirements for patenting and secondly by exploiting the legal loopholes or aspects of the patent registration system to extend the period of the patents. The patent right holder can then misuse his monopoly power by limiting the options available to the patients, increase the costs of health and make cooperative research more difficult[22]. In order to maximize profits before a patent expires pharmaceutical companies adopt strategies to substitute a drug going off-patent with an under- patent drug. Another strategy is to introduce a number of drugs of more or less the same nature. For instance, Captopril, the first drug of a class of drugs called ACE inhibitors, was followed by Enalapril. Lisinopril, Ramipril, Perindopril, Quinapril, Cilazapril, Benazepril, Fosinopril etc, each one having only a marginal benefit over others. The purpose of such 'me-too' drugs is to cleverly extend the period of patents.

Besides the above, is the fact that the pricing of patented drugs is not realistic, because the companies spend more on marketing than on R &D, and most of the R & D is done through collaborations between universities and industries which got huge funding from governments. The exorbitant pricing of drugs becomes quite alarming in the case of AIDS. For instance, when US and other developed countries were charging between $10,000 and $15,000 the Indian company Cipla Ltd, could offer a cocktail of anti-AIDS drugs (lamivudine, stavudine, and nevirapine) just for an annual price per patient of US $ 350. Reacting to MNCs allegation that "Cipla is a Pirate" Yousuf Hamied, CEO of Cipla said: "The average cost of the AIDS cocktail in the west is $ 10000 to $ 15000 per patient per year - not because the drugs are prohibitively expensive to produce- they are not. It is the drug pricing structure imposed by multinational manufacturers which makes the drugs prohibitively expensive." And added that Cipla has not indulged in charity, it has made some profits. The price war triggered by Cipla had a positive effect; almost all MNCs had to reduce their prices. It is the generic from India that reined the profiteering because Indian drugs are the cheapest in the world. In 1999, the AIDS activist Darid Scondras has reported that: "On an average, drugs manufactured in India are between 1000 and 4000 percent cheaper than the same products produced in USA. The costs of medicine depend on who makes it and where it is made. In Bombay, Hyping, a sophisticated Anti hypertensive costs 7 cents a tablet, a month's supply costs about $ 4.20. In Boston it costs $44.48, more than ten times as expensive. In Boston, ranitidine costs 42cents for 150 mg. The exact product costs less than 2cents in Bombay. So in USA, even the cheap generic equivalent is marked up by 2246%."[23] Now, consider the famous Novartis case.

In 1993, Novartis filed patent for "Imatinib," a free base along with all pharmaceutically acceptable salts[24]; which was patented in US, EU and several other countries. However, it could not be patented in India, because India did not provide product patents for pharmaceuticals in 1993. Later, the company filed a patent for the beta-crystalline form of Imatinib Mesylate by formulating it into a pharmaceutically useful drug, Glivec. The claim for this polymorph was made in a "mailbox" application due to the unavailability of product patents in drugs in India until 1st January 2005. In 2005, the grant of patent was opposed by several generic drug companies and the Cancer Patients Aid Association (CPAA)) on several grounds including lack of significantly enhanced "efficacy" under section 3(d) of the Patent Act. The Patent Office rejected the patent application[25] by stating that the 'beta-crystalline form of Imatinib Mesylate' was anticipated by the 1993 US Patent No. 5521184. At the pre-grant stage it failed to establish that the patent covered only the Imatinib free base and that the beta-crystalline form of Imatinib mesylate was not obvious from a reading of the 1993 patent.

Novartis claimed that the active ingredient in Glivec (beta crystalline form of Imatinib mesylate) was more effective than the Imatinib free base, since it displayed better bioavailability properties (i.e. it was absorbed more easily into the blood) and submitted evidence showing an increase in bioavailability of up to 30%. But the Assistant Controller held that: "The present patent specification does not bring out any improvement in the efficacy of the beta crystal form over the known substances; rather it states that the base can be used equally in the treatment of diseases and in the preparation of pharmacological agents wherever the beta crystal is used." Aggrieved by this rejection, Novartis AG, along with its Indian subsidiary, Novartis India filed writ petitions in the Madras High Court[26] praying for a reversal of the Assistant Controller's order, a declaration that Section 3(d) is unconstitutional and is in violation of India's obligations under TRIPS. The Madras High Court holding that Section 3(d) is constitutional and that it does not have jurisdiction to decide on violation of TRIPS obligations, transferred the petition to the Intellectual Property Appellate Board (IPAB). Now, the matter is pending before IPAB.

Thus, the trend towards harmonisation of patent laws, especially the substantive rules of intellectual property law, across nations in accordance with the Agreement on TRIPS which aims to reduce distortion and impediments to international trade, and provide effective protection of intellectual property is causing obstacles to access to health and health care. The TRIPS compliance of the patent laws since 2005 has made the production of generics of the pharmaceuticals for which product patents were/are obtained since 1995 virtually impossible. This has made the drugs and pharmaceutical products, especially essential and life saving drugs and antibiotics, prohibitively expensive because of the lack of competition for them, particularly in developing countries and underdeveloped countries. Thus access to health care in developing countries and underdeveloped countries is adversely affected. This applies even to the people belonging to the poor strata in developed countries also. Thus access to health care has become a casualty at the cost of patents.

Now, to answer the basic question whether right to health or patent rights is primary, attention is drawn to para. 8.9 of the International Conference on Population and Development in Cairo, which reads as follows:

"Through technology transfer, developing countries should be assisted in building their capacity to produce generic drugs for the domestic market and to ensure the wide availability and accessibility of such drugs. To meet the substantial increase in demand for vaccines, antibiotics and other commodities over the next decade and beyond, the international community should strengthen global, regional and local mechanisms for the production, quality control and procurement of those items, where feasible, in developing countries. The international community should facilitate regional cooperation in the manufacture, quality control and distribution of vaccines."

Thus, a perusal of all the international covenants in which issues on health and health care are dealt with and the domestic constitutional rights and judicial interpretations as done above would lead to the conclusion that trading right cannot take supremacy over right to health. But the requirement of TRIPS compliance of the patent laws of the nations in drugs and pharmaceuticals, especially the product patent regime, lays overemphasis on trading right over right to health, and as a result the access to health has become more skewed, adversely affecting the developing countries, and even the poor in developed countries. The question whether 'health is wealth' or 'wealth is health' is to be decided by the people not by the MNCs.

## References


1. *SC Advocates on Record Association v. Union of India*, AIR 1994 SC 268.
2. See also Ireland v.U.K (1978) E.C.H.R paras. 139-40
3. Manuel Perez- Leiva, *International Law And The Right To A Healthy Environment, Ezine* Articles.com.2010.
4. Municipal Council, Ratlam v. Vardhichand & Ors., AIR 1980 SC 1662.
5. *CESC Ltd. v. Subash Chandra Bose*, AIR 1992 SC 573,585.
6. *State of Punjab and Others v. Mohinder Singh*, AIR 1997 SC225.
7. *Bandhua Mukti Morcha v. Union of India*, AIR 1984 SC 802.
8. *Mahendra Pratap Singh v. Orissa State*, AIR 1997 Ori. 37.
9. *Consumer Education Research Centre v. Union of India*, AIR 1995 SC 992.
10. *T. Ramakrishna Rao v. Hyderabad Development Authority*, 2002(2) ALT 193.
11. *Virender Gaur v. State of Haryana*, AIR 1995 (2).
12. *Subhash Kumar v. State of Bihar*, AIR 1991 SC 420.
13. *Vincent Panikurlangara v.Union of India*, AIR 1987 SC 990. See also *Unnikrishnan, J.P v. State of A.P.*, AIR 1993 SC 2178 (1993) 1 SCC 645.
14. *S.K. Garg v. State of U.P*, (1998) 2UPLBEC 1211.
15. *Parmanand Katara v. Union of India*, AIR 1989 SC 2039.
16. *Paschim Baga Khet Mazoor Samiti v. State of West Bengal*, 1996 SCC (4) 37.
17. Mihir Desai & Kamayani Bali Mahabal (Eds.), *Health Care Case Law in India* , Centre for Enquiry into Health and Allied Themes , Mumbai, August 2007, p.6
18. Julio Nogues, *Patents and Pharmaceutical Drugs: Understanding the Pressures on Developing Countries*, 4 (Working Papers, World Bank, September, 1990).
19. World Health Organization, The World Health Report, 2001, 144.
20. Bernard Pecoul et. al, Access to Essential Drugs in Poor Countries. A Lost Battle?, 281 JAMA 361 (1999) in Hoen, Ellen, TRIPS, Pharmaceutical Patents, and Access to Essential Medicines: A long

way from Seattle to Doha, *Chicago Journal of International Law*, Monday, April 1 2002, 1.

21. Patrice Trouiller and Piero Olliaro, Drug Development Output from 1975 to 1996: What Proportion for Tropical Diseases? *Intl Jl. Infect. Diseases* 61 (1999) in Hoen, Ellen, Supra, 5

22. Aaron S. Kesselheim, Intellectual Property Policy in the Pharmaceutical Sciences: The Effect of Inappropriate Patents and Market Exclusivity Extensions on the HealthCare System, 9(3) Article 33, The AAPS Journal, 2007.

23. Jayanti Vijaya Ratna. *Drug prices in India after GATT agreement*, Pharmainfo.net, 2010

24. US Patent Number 5521184 titled "Pyrimidine derivatives and processes for the preparation thereof" (filed in April 1993 and issued on May 28, 1996)

25. The PCT application claiming the beta crystalline form was filed on 16th July, 1998 and claimed a priority date of 18th July 1997

26. *Novartis AG & Anr. v. Union of India & Others*., (2007) 4 MLJ 1153.

# 20

# ENVIRONMENTAL DEGRADATION BY MNCS AND HUMAN RIGHTS VIOLATIONS

**P. Rajendran Nair**

"MNCs, the promoters of growth in developing and developed countries turns to become the abusers of human rights. Corporations carry out some of the most terrific human rights abuses of modern times, but it is increasingly difficult to hold them to account. Economic globalization and the rise of transnational corporate power have created a favorable climate for corporate human rights abusers. Their abuses are in the form of assassination, torture, kidnapping, environmental degradation, abusing public funds, violently repressing political rights, releasing toxins, destroying homes, exhaustion of resources, pollution of water, air and land by disposing harmful byproducts and chemicals which pose a threat to bio-diversity and sustainability."

Profit Oriented activities of giant MNCs throughout the world have caused undesirable change in the physical, chemical or biological characteristics of the air, water or land that can harmfully affect health, survival or activities of human or other living organisms. Economic activities of human beings have a profound impact on natural environment. Pollution has become a major threat to the very existence of mankind on this earth. It is the major challenge of our times. The Stockholm conference on Human Environment held in 1972 and Earth Summit held in June 1992 at Rio-De-Janeiro served as a catalyst to focus the attention of mankind in the deteriorating quality of life

The increasing economic development and a rapidly growing population that has taken the country from 300 million people in 1947 to more than one billion people today is putting a strain on the environment, infrastructure and the country's natural resources. Industrial pollution, soil erosion, deforestation, rapid industrialization, urbanization and Land degradation are all worsening problems. Environmental pollution is one of the most serious problems facing humanity and other life forms on our planet today.

India has been ranked among the top ten worst climate polluters of the world. While India holds the 7th position, U.S and China hold the 2nd and 3rd positions respectively. The study has been conducted by professor Corey Bradshow of the University of Adelaide's Environment Institute in April 2010. The study yielded the worst ten polluters as Brazil, U.S, China, Indonesia, Japan, Mexico, India, Russia, Australia, and Peru, in the order.

India's percapita carbon dioxide emissions were roughly 3,000 pounds (1360 kilograms) in 2007. This is low compared to China and the US, with 10,500 pounds (4,763 kilograms) and 42500 pounds (19,278 kilograms) respectively.

On March, 2010 Jairam Ramesh, Minister of State for Environment and Forests informed the Rajya Sabha that the Central pollution Control Board has done a nation wide environmental assessment of Industrial clusters based on CEPI. 43 such industrial clusters having CEPI grater than 70, on a scale of 0 to 100, has been identified as critically polluted.

A Comprehensive environmental assessment of Industrial clusters undertaken by the IIT Delhi and the CPCB, found that the environmental pollution levels in 10 major Industrial hubs had reached a very high level.

Noise levels in Urban areas of India are excessively high due to rise in population, automobiles and industrial activities. The ambient air quality of major cities and towns in the country is being monitored under National Ambient Air Quality Monitoring Programme. The monitoring results indicate that sulphur dioxide and nitrogen dioxide levels are mostly within the permissible limits whereas suspended particulate matter values are higher than the prescribed limits. This is due to vehicular and air pollution, burning of fossil fuel, and natural dusty conditions. The data on ambient water quality of rivers indicates that levels of coli form count and Biological Oxygen. Demand are generally high resulting in deterioration of water quality. Mercury poisoning results in neurological afflictions and exposure to toxic materials causes acute illness or even death.

Environmental degradation in India has been caused by a variety of social, economic, institutional and technological factors. Rapidly growing population, urbanization, industrial activities and increasing use of pesticides and fossil fuels have all resulted in a massive deterioration in the quality and sustainability of the environment.

The WHO estimates that about two million people die prematurely every year as a result of pollution, while many more suffer from breathing ailments, heart disease, lung infections and even cancer. The four reasons of air pollution are-emissions from vehicles, thermal power plants, industries and refineries. The problem of indoor air pollution in rural areas and Urban slums has increased. In India air pollution is estimated to cause 1 Lakh excess deaths and 25 million excess illnesses every year. The Govt. estimates that the cost of environmental degradation has been running at 4.5% of G.D.P. in recent years.

Vehicle emissions are responsible for 70% of the country's air pollution. Exhaust from vehicles has increased eight-fold over levels of twenty years ago. Industrial pollution has risen four times over the same period. Bangalore holds the title of being the asthma capital of the country. Studies estimate that 10% of Bangalore's 60 Lakh population and over 50% of its children below 18 years suffer from air pollution related ailments.

The Brilliant white of the Taj Mahal is slowly fading to sickly yellow. On the famous TajMahal case a very strong step was taken by Supreme Court by directing to close down 200 factories working around the Taj Mahal. In Chennai, six of the 10 top causes of death are related to respiratory disease, says Dr. D. Renganadhan, Director (In-charge), Institute of Thoracic Medicine. The levels repairable suspended particulate Matter (RSPM) or dust, in Mumbai's air have continued to increase over the past three years.

Bhopal gas tragedy was the greatest industrial disaster in the world that took place at a Union Carbide pesticide plant in the Indian city of Bhopal. At midnight on 3rd December 1984, the plant accidentally released Methyl Isocyanate (MIC) gas. Following this the death toll reached to 50,000 due to gas related to diseases. The same thing was happened in Sewri industrial area of Mumbai on July 14, 2010. Mounting air pollution affected the bio-diversity of the Nation. Studies conducted by the high attitude zoology field station of the zoological survey of India based in solan town of Himachal Pradesh have recorded a drastic fall in butterfly numbers in the western Himalayas. The population have declined more than half in just 10 years.

According to a U.N. report released on March 20, 2010 on World Water Day, contaminated and polluted water now kills more peopie than in all forms of violence including wars. According to the report- titled "sick water" 90% of waste water discharged daily in developing countries is untreated, contributing to the death of 2.2 million people a year from diarrheal diseases caused by unsafe drinking water. More than 80% of urban waste ends up in the country's rivers. River Ganga, holy to the Hindu population, is dying slowly due to unchecked pollution. River Yamuna is also not free from disaster. It is estimated that about three billion liters of waste are pumped in to Delhi's Yamuna each day. According to the Centre for Science and Environment, 70 to 80 percent of the river's pollution is the result of raw sewage.

Similarly ground water exploitation is a serious matter of concern today and legislations and policy measures taken till date by the state governments have not had the desired effect. A typical example of this grave situation is reported from Plachimada in Palakkad District of Kerala State where Coca-Cola company is extracting Lakh of liters of water per day without caring for the depletion of ground water level. It resulted in severe drought in the nearby areas and the shortage of drinking water. People of the area under the strong leadership of the late Mayilamma started agitation against the ruthless exploitation of water by the coco - cola company and the company is forced to shut down its plant in Plachimada.

Ground water quality and pollution is the most alarming environmental hazard in India. On April 01, 2010 at least 18 babies in several hamlets of Bihar's Bhojpur district have been born blind because their families consume ground water containing alarming levels of arsenic and it was confirmed by Nanda Kishore Yadav, the Health Minister of Bihar that the blindness at birth has been attributed to arsenic contamination of water. It also caused cancer of intestines, liver, kidneys and bladder and bone deformity. Gangrene and skin disorders are common among the people of this area.

Excessive use of plastic products is a major source of pollution. Deposit of plastic carry bags in the soil destroy the biological characteristics of soil. Heavy factories working in the banks of rivers deposit their waste products and water directly in to the rivers and cause heavy water pollution. The mines of Mahanadi coal fields and NTPC draw about 25 crore liters of water per day from the River Brahmani and in return they release thousands of gallons of waste water, which contains obnoxious substances like Ash, Oil, Heavy metals, grease, Fluorides, Phosphorus, Ammonia Urea and Sulphuric Acid in to the River Nandira, a tributary of River Brahmani. Due to extensive coal mining and vigorous growth of industries in the Jharkhand area the river Damodar have been badly contaminated. Amnesty International report accused the mining company Vedanta of human right abuses and damaging the environment.

Pollution due to biomedical wastes is likely to spread dangerous diseases and make atmosphere noxious to health. The death from radiation poisoning of a scrap yard worker in New Delhi has highlighted the lack of enforcement of waste disposal laws in India. India is being used as a dumping ground for hazardous waste from foreign countries. Recently twenty containers with waste goods were detained by the customs authorities. Packs of broken toys, used diapers, empty perfume bottles, used battery cells, thermocol, used aluminum foil packing materials and colored surgical gloves were found in the containers.

Pollution from e-waste is also another major problem faced by humanity. According to UNEP reports by 2020 e-waste in South Africa and China will have jumped by 200-400% from 2007 levels, and by 500% in India. India produces about 3,80,000 tones of e-waste per annum, which includes only the waste generated out of T.V. sets, mobile phones, and Pcs, majority comes from organizations. E-waste produced in India includes over 100,000 tones from refrigerators, 275,000 tones from TVs, 56300 tones from personal computers, 4,700 tones from printers and 1,700 tones from mobile phones. India imports almost 50,000 tones of e-waste yearly. It generated 330,000 tones of e-waste in 2007 and the number is expected to touch 470,000 tones by 2011.

Rising levels of p.m. 2.5 particle in air is a serious problem to humanity. If it is not regulated it will create health hazards like Asthma, lung cancer, breathing problems etc. A Survey by the Central Pollution Control Board and the All India Institute of Medical Sciences showed that a majority of people living in Delhi suffered from eye irritation, cough, sore throat, shortness of breath and poor lung functioning. India is the fifth most of any country in the world emitting Carbon. Carbon emissions have grown nine fold over the past forty years. According to the U.N. Frame Work Convention on climate change and the Kyoto protocol, the most industrialized countries are mainly responsible for causing climate change.

This part of the paper takes a look at violation of human rights by the MNCs. Here it is necessary to identify the types of human rights violated by the MNCs and how they go about deny it. MNCs can violate and have violated, a wide range of human rights - from civil and political to social, economic and cultural and could remain un accountable for their conduct by exploiting the loopholes of existing regions. Established companies like Union Carbide Corporation and Enron Corporation in India, Unocal Corporation in Myanmar, Nike and Reebok in Asia, shell Oil Company in Nigeria, Texaco in Ecuador, and Freeport- MC Maron in Indonesia are the living example of this. Human rights that MNCs have been accused of violating include human rights to life, including the right to enjoy life; freedom from torture and cruel, in human or degrading treatment; freedom from forced or slave labour; freedom from arbitrary detention or deprivation of security of person; freedom to enjoy property, freedom from deprivation of or injury to health, enjoyment of a clean and healthy environment and freedom from discrimination. One could also consider private corporate deprivations of right such as free choice in work; fairwaters, a decent living and equal remuneration for work of equal value, safe and healthy working conditions; protection of children from economic exploitation; and protection of mothers.

There exists a real possibility that MNCs violate a wide range of human rights. Such violations may occur in a variety of ways, as directly violating human rights, failing to prevent violations, remaining silent about violations or even operating in a state that violates human rights. This scenario necessarily raises the question about developing a mechanism that can enforce human rights obligations against MNCs, especially when they act in complicity with states.

In the majority of cases the victims are from developing countries. Potential victims of such countries are either ignorant about their rights, do not have means to enforce them or cannot afford a delayed determination of dispute; or the legal recourse in such countries is prone to misuse by those in positions of power. This factor again emphasizes that the sole reliance on national regulations on MNCs is bound to prove inadequate in delivering justice to the majority of victims of human rights violations by corporations.

Corporations carry out some of the most horrific human rights abuses of modern times, but it is increasingly difficult to hold them to account. Economic liberalization and the rise of transnational corporate power have created a favourable climate for corporate human right abusers. Global Exchange 2007 developed a list of some of the world's worst corporate abusers like Dow chemical, Cocacola, Caterpillar, Lockheed, philip Morris, Chevron, Dynocorp/Cse, Ford Motor Company, KBR, Lockhad Martin, Monsanto, Nestle USA, philip MorrisUSA, Pfizer, Sues-Lyonnaise Des Eaux and Wal Mart and illustrate the diverse issues as assassination, torture, kidnapping, environmental degradation, abusing public fund, releasing toxins into environment, destroying homes, discrimination and causing widespread health problems. When corporations act like criminals people have the right and the power to stop them, holding leaders and MNCs alike to the accords they have signed. Around the world-in venezuela, Argentina, India - citizens are stepping up to create democracy, and hold corporations accountable to international law.

For years the Caterpillar Company has provided Israel with the bulldozers used to destroy Palestinian homes. Despite world wide condemnation Cater pillar has refused to end their corporate participation house demolition by cutting off sales of bulldozers to the Israeli military. Peace activist Rachel Corrie was killed by a Cater pillar, D-9, military bulldozer in 2003. She was run over while attempting to block the destruction of a family's home in Gaza. Her family filed Suit against Caterpillar in 2005 charging that Cater pillar knowingly sold machines used to violate human rights.

Chevron, a Petro chemical company, is guilty of some of the worst environmental and human rights abuses in the world. From 1964 to 1992, Texaco (which transferred operations to Chervron after being brought out in 2001) unleashed a toxic "Rainforest Chernobyl" in Ecuador by leaving more than 600 unlined oil pits in northern Amazon rain forest and dumping 18 billion gallons of toxic production water into rivers used for bathing water. As a result, local communities have suffered severe health effects, including cancer, skin disorders, birth defects and spontaneous abortions. Indigenous communities have been dispossessed of their lands, and millions of hectares of rain forest have been destroyed to make way for the company's pipe lines and oil wells. Chevron is also responsible for the violent repression of non violent opposition to oil extraction. In Nigeria, chevron has collaborated with the Nigerian police and military who have opened fire on peaceful protestors who oppose oil extraction in the Niger Delta. Moreover Cheveron caused widespread health problems in Richmond, California, where one of Chevron's largest refineries is located. Processing 350,000 barrels of oil a day, the Richmond refinery produces oil flares and toxic waste in the Richmond area. As a result, local residents suffer from high rates of skin rashes, rheumatic fever, liver problems, kidney problems, tumors, cancer, asthma and eye problems.

Coca-cola, another MNC, is well known for human rights abuses. Their abuses are in the form of violent killing, kidnap and torture, water privatization health violations, environmental depletion and discriminatory practices. Between 1989-2002, eight Union leaders from coca-cola bottling plants in Colombia were killed after protesting the company's labour practices. Hundreds of other coca-cola workers who have joined the colombian Union Sinal Trainal have been kidnapped, tortured and detained by paramilitaries who intimidate workers to prevent them from unionizing. In Turkey, 14 Coca-cola truck drivers and their families were beaten severely by Turkish police hired by the company, while protesting a lay off of 1000 workers from a local bottling plant in 2005.

In India coca-cola destroys local agriculture by privatizing the country's water resources. In plachimada, Kerala, Coca-cola extracted 1.5 million liters of deep well water, which they bottled and sold under the names Dasani and Bon Aqua. The ground water was severly depleted, affecting thousand of communities with water shortages and destroying agricultural activity. As a result, the remaining water became contaminated with high chloride and bacteria levels, leading to scabs, eye problems and stomach aches in the local population. Water shortages have occured in Plachimada, Varanasi, Thane and TamilNadu as well. The Company is also guilty of reselling its industrial waste to farmers as fertilizers, despite its containing hazardous lead and cadmium.

Another MNC Dow chemical is famous for its human rights abuses. Their abuses are in the form of the creation of chemical weapons, marketing poisonous chemicals, illegal dumping of toxins in to populated areas, environmental destructions, health violations, chemical poisoning and chemical warfare. Dow chemical has been destroying lives and poisoning the planet for decades. The company is famous for the ravages and health disaster for million of Vietnamese and Dow's Napalm, a brutal chemical weapon that burned many innocents to death in Vietnam and other wars. In 1998, Dow provided pesticides to Saddam Hussain to produce chemical weapons. In 2001, DOWs inherited the toxic legacy of the worst peacetime chemical disaster in history when it acquired, Union Carbide Corporation and its outstanding liabilities in Bhopal, India.

Dow's toxic legacies of human rights abuses traverse to agricultural fields in Central America where DOW exported EPA-banned pesticide DBCP for use in banana and Pineapple crops. As a result thousands of banana workers were exposed to DBCP and became sterile.

Private security contractors have become the fastest-growing sector of the global economy during the last decade. Dyn Corp, one of the providers of these mercenary services, demonstrates the industry's power and potential to abuse human rights. Their human rights abuses causes health problems, environmental devastation and death; endangering lives; physically abusing individuals; sextraficking etc. While guarding Afghani statesmen and African Oil fields, training Iraqi police forces, eradicating colombian coco-plants, and protecting business interests in hurricane, the company devastated security of governments and organisations at the expense of many people's human rights. Dyn Corp's fumigation of Coca Crops along the Colòmbian - Ecuadorian border led Ecuadorian peasants to sue Dyncrop in 2001.

The US addiction to oil is linked with a host of human rights and environmental problems, including human rights abuses in countries such as Nigeria, Ecuador, Sudan, South Africa and Indonesia. It has pushed Indigenous people off their land and destroyed hundreds of thousands of acres of rain forests, which are home to half the planet and animal species on the planet. It has fueled wars for oil such as the war in Iraq, which has caused the death of more than 2100 US troops and an estimated 30000 to 150000 Iraq's. Among automakers, Ford motor Company is the worst. Every year since 1999, the US Environmental Protection Agency has ranked Ford Cars, trucks and SUVs as having the worst overall fuel economy of any American automaker.

KBR, (Kellogg, (Brown and Root) a subsidiary of Halliburton Corporation, is a private company that provides military support services. Notorious for its questionable book keeping, dishonest billing practices, and no-bid contracts, KBR has violated human rights on the U.S dollar. KBR provides key logistical support for war, occupation and lawful detention. The Company provides unlimited support services to US troops to continue their occupation of Iraq. KRB also constructed detention facility in Guantanamo Bay, where hundreds of detainees have languished for more than 3 years, many of whom have suffered abuse and torture.

Monsanto is the largest producer of genetically engineered seeds in the world, dominating 70% to 100% of the market for crops such as Soy, Cotton, Wheat and Corn. The Company is also one of the most egregious abusers of the human rights of food sovereignty, access to land, health violations and child labour.Monsanto is the world's leading producer of the herbicide glyphosate,marketed as 'Round up'. Round up is sold to small farmers as a pesticide but it harm crops in the long run as the toxins accumulate in the soil. Eventually plants become infertile, forcing the farmers to buy genetically modified Roundup ready seed,a seed that resists herbicide. This creates a cycle of dependency on Monsanto for both the weed killer and the only seed that can resist it. Round up ultra is extensively used as a pesticide. Exposure to the pesticide causes cancers, skin disorders, spontaneous abortions, premature births and damage to the gastro intenstinal and nervous systems. Monsanto also employs child labour. It is estimated that 12, 375 children work in cotton seed production paid by Indian and multinational seed Companies including Monsanto.

Nestle' US is another MNC engaged in human right violations. Their abuses are in the form of child labour, repression of worker's rights, aggressive marketing of harmful products, violation of national health and environmental laws. It is estimated that 109,000 child labourers working in hazardous conditions on coca farms, what is being described as the worst form of child labour. Nestle' is also notorious for its aggressive marketing of infant formula in poor countries, which may have led to the deaths of countless children who did not receive the nutrients that would have been present in breast milk. Because of this Nestl's is one of the most boycotted corporations in the world and its infant formula is still controversial. In Italy in 2005, Police seized more than two million liters of Nestl'e infant formula that was contaminated with chemical Isopropyl Thio Xanthone (ITX), a component in the packaging's ink.

According to WHO, tobacco is the second major cause of preventable death in the world. Tobacco industry claimed nearly 5 million million lives per year. Among tobacco Company's Philip Marri's is notorious. Now called Altria, it is the world's largest and most profitable cigarette corporation and maker of Malboro, Virginia slims, Parliament and many other brands cigarettes. Philip Morris is also a leader in pushing smoking with young people around the world. The company has actively targeted the world's youth by researching smoking patterns and attitudes and targeting youth as potential customers. As anti tobacco campaigns and Government regulations, are slowing tobacco use in western countries' Philip Morris has moved in to developing country market, were smoking and smoking death are mounting up. According to a study by the Harvard School of Public Health, tobacco's killing fields are shifting to the developing world and Eastern Europe where most of the world's smokers now live.

It is concluded that big business concerns of both developed and developing countries are engaging in ruthless exploitation of nature's endowments for making profit and hence causing un accountable damage to nature and its living beings. By producing dangerous products and disposing its waste to water, air, and land they are engaged in the violation of human rights. The protection of human rights is not traditionally considered a responsibility of corporations. The domestic laws of many states fail to impose adequate human rights duties on corporations. Yet MNCs are very powerful entities in the current world order. Their impact on the wellbeing of communities and individuals, including in terms of human rights is evident where ever they operate. However infringements by MNCs also occur in developed nations typically in respect of the environment, rights to privacy, consumer rights to health and information as well as freedom of association.

Since MNCs always operate at transnational and sometimes in complicity with states, it is essential that international law play an active role in regulating activities. But the existing international framework of corporate accountability is inappropriate for dealing with MNCs.Therefore a need exists to construct a strong international mechanism as well as to reconceptualize the guiding principles and approach of international law vis-à-vis MNCs. Apossible solution is to formulate a UN-WTO partnership for human rights. The partnership with active support from other international institute, the media and NGOs,would both prescribe and enforce human rights standards against MNCs. Bringing human rights issues with in the frame work of the WTO, both at the stage of negotiation and of dispute settlement, would not only help to regulate MNCs but would also provide sustainability and the people's support for the new economic order.

### References

1. Kindly David (2001): 'Human Rights as Legally Binding or Merely Relevant' in David Kinley and Stephen Bottomley (eds), *Commercial Law and Human Rights*, Aldershot, pp. 25-44.
2. Meeran, Ricsard (2000): 'Liability of Multinational Corporations-A Critical stage in the UK' in Menno Kamminga and Sam Zia-Zarifi (eds), *Liability of Multinational Corporations under International Law*. The Hague pp. 251-64.
3. Ganesa Murthy V.S (2009): '*Environmental Economics in India*', New Centray Publication, New Delhi, p. 7
4. *WHO Reports.*
5. *UN Reports.*
6. Joseph Sarah, "An Over View of Human Rights Accountability of Multinational Enterprises", In Kamminga and Zia-Zarifn p. 77.
7. Louis Henkin, *The Universal Declaration at 50 and Challenge of global Markets*, 25 Brook J 1999.
8. Commonwealth Human Research Initiative, *Human Rights and poverty eradication.*
9. *Green Peace International.*
10. *Global Exchange.*

# 21

# COMMODIFICATION OF WATER, HUMAN RIGHTS ISSUES AND THE MNCs

**Reinhart Philip**

Human Rights are the basic rights and freedom to which all are entitled. These rights are inherent to all human beings, whatever be the nationality, place of residence, sex, national or ethnic origin, colour, religion, language, or any other status. All are equally entitled to human rights without any discrimination. All these rights are interrelated, interdependent and indivisible. These rights enable a person to develop his personality and lead a decent life on earth. Right to Water forms an important element of human rights. Without water the sustenance of life on earth is a myth.

Water is a common chemical substance that is essential for the survival of all known forms of life. Water exists in solid, liquid and gaseous form and covers about 71 percent of earth's total surface. Salt water accounts 97 percent of the total water and fresh water accounts only 3 percent. Fresh water is a renewable resource, yet the world's supply of clean, fresh water is steadily decreasing. Water demand already exceeds supply in many parts of the world and with the rise in population the demand for fresh water will also increase naturally. So long as the supply is enough to meet the demand there won't be any problem. The fall in supply compared to demand creates imbalance and the problem starts there.

### Commodification of Water

The dominant development model of our time is 'economic globalization', a model of economics rooted in the belief that liberal market economics constitute the one and only one choice for the whole world. Key to globalization is commodification. New commodities are created with the expansion of markets to new geographical areas and new sectors that may not yet have been marketised. Commodification is accomplished through the deregulation of exchange mechanisms, allowing penetration of market mechanism into under-marketised spheres. Everything has become for sale, even natural resources including the commons (land, water and seed), that were once considered the common heritage of humanity. Water is one such commodity and commodification of water is considered as a direct assault on the commons.

Fresh water has gone through significant changes over the past thirty years. From an emergency storm supply in grocery stores, it is now being marketed by global corporations like Pepsi and Cola, symbolized by bottled waters hanging in front of shops. International Agencies like IMF, World Bank etc. have forced and are forcing national governments to privatize the water supplies. Public water supplies have been privatized and corporates began to gain monopoly even over local fresh water sources. Water, the free gift of nature, has been made a commodity to satisfy the corporate greed for profit.

**Commodity and Commodification in Neo-Liberal Terms**

A commodity in neo-classical economic terms is anything that can be bought and sold in the marketplace in exchange for another commodity or for money. Commodification can therefore be defined as an act, practice or policy that promotes or treats a good or service, as an article of commerce to be bought, sold or traded through market transactions. To be commodified a good or service must have the characteristics of a 'private good': it must be rival in its consumption (that is, for a private good consumption by one individual preludes consumption of the same unit by another – for example, a cup of tea) and it must be excludable (that is, people can be denied access if they do not pay – for example, admission to a theatre[1]). Private goods yield utility only to a person consuming the good, it is denied to others. Again, a private good is priced in the market and only those may be allowed the use of it who pays its stipulated price.[2]

Public goods on the other hand are those goods which can be simultaneously consumed by many in equal amounts, that is, the consumption of public good is non-rival (for example street lighting, national defence). Again public goods are not excludable (for example, TV broadcasting, and street lighting). Public goods' being non-excludable and non-rival resists commodification. The market can function only in a situation where the 'exclusion principle' applies[3], that is, where A's consumption is made contingent on paying the price, while B, who does not pay it is excluded. According to the neo-classical theory public goods and services are not likely to be provided by a private firm under market conditions because they are prone to 'free riders' making it too risky for a private firm to invest in and produce them.[4]

Services such as water in neo-classical theory lie between the two poles, neither being pure private nor being pure public. They are sometimes referred to as 'merit goods', things that would almost certainly be underprovided if left solely to market forces. Taking the case of water if there were no public sector provision, there would be some private sector provider offering services to those who could afford them (Example is the case of Britain in the 1800's). Private firms only take into account their own costs and benefits. So, socially optimum level of services providing to all is unlikely. Since the late 1970's the notion of public services as public goods has increasingly come under attack by the neo-liberalists. Their argument was that water provision must be seen as a private good that is responsive to market indicators, flexible in its demand and rival and excludable in its consumption.

Neo-liberalists not only argue that it is theoretically sound to regard public services as private goods but go so far as to consider it as an economic, social and environmental imperative. They argueat that subsidizing water as a public/merit good, leads to inefficient and unaccountable water provision, undermining its public good characteristics through waste, unresponsive behaviours and corruption. Treating water as a private good, on the other hand, creates efficient and accountable water delivery systems[5]. The upshot of the argument is that privatization and commercialization are deemed both necessary and acceptable. This argument forms the basis for a newly emerging moral discourse on privatization, which argues that market competition and commodification of services is a 'pro-poor' policy choice.

**The Path of Water Commodification**

Water the precious gift of nature covers about 71% of earth's total surface. Holding a unique place in the history of mankind, water has many distinct properties that are critical for the proliferation of life on earth. All the major civilizations like Mesopotamia, Egypt, Indus Valley etc. have flourished around rivers and river ways. The success of large metropolis such as London, Paris, New York, and Chicago etc. owes to their easy access to water. From a religious point of view water is considered as a purifier in Christianity, Hinduism, Islam, Judaism and other religions. Water plays an important role in world economy as it functions as a solvent for a wide variety of chemical substances and facilitates industrial cooling and transportation. The role of water in world economy can be understood from the statistics that it takes 10 litres of water to produce 1 litre of petrol, 100 litres of water to produce 1 kg of paper, 4500 litres of water to produce 1 kg of rice and for 1 tonne of cement, 20,000 litres of water to produce 1 tonne of steel and 40,000 litres to make a car. In United States alone, computer industry is using 1500 billion litres of water a year.[6]

According to the United Nations Environment Programme (UNEP), the total volume of water on Earth is about 1.4 billion $km^3$. The volume of freshwater resources is around 35 million $km^3$, or about 2.5 percent of the total volume. Around 30 percent of the world's freshwater is stored underground in the form of groundwater (shallow and deep groundwater basins up to 2000 metres, soil moisture, swamp water and permafrost). This constitutes about 97 percent of all the freshwater that is potentially available for human use. The Earth's atmosphere contains approximately 13,000 km$^3$ of water. The total usable freshwater supply for ecosystems and humans is about 200 000 km$^3$ of water - less than 1 percent of all freshwater resources.[7]

Though water has utmost importance and usage, the amount of fresh water available is mere and the world is running out of fresh water. Humanity is depleting and polluting the well spring of life at a startling rate. With every passing day the demand for water out spaces its utility and the demand is growing at more than the rate twice of population increase in the last century.[8] The demand for water has exceeded the supply already. Acccrding to the United Nations (UN) 43 countries in the world are currently facing water stress and scarcity and over 700 million people having no access to clean drinking water.[9] The UN Human Right to Water suggests that each person needs 20-50 litres of safe freshwater a day to ensure their basic needs for drinking, cooking and cleaning. But more than one in six people worldwide don't have access to this amount of safe freshwater. By 2025, 1800 million people will be living in countries or regions with absolute water scarcity, and two-thirds of the world population could be under stress conditions. 60 nations will be facing acute water shortage at that time.[10]

Two main reasons can be identified for commodification of water: one is its scarcity and the other it's multiple uses. The theoretical explanation for water as an economic good follows directly from Lionel Robbins' definition of economics, as "the science which studies the human behaviour as a relationship between ends and scarce means which have alternative uses."[11] Water meets these requirements: it serves a multiplicity of ends (ranging from drinking and bathing, through irrigation, recreation, and environmental use, to waste disposal), and thus satisfies the condition of "alternative uses." In many cases, water is scarce in the sense that it cannot fully satisfy all its alternative uses simultaneously.

The source of the idea of water as an 'economic good' can be cited to the 1992 "Dublin Principles" of the International Conference on Water and the Environment (ICWE). This Inter-Governmental Conference came up with "four guiding principles" for water management: (a) freshwater is a finite and vulnerable resource, essential to sustain life, development and the environment; (b) water development and management should be based on a participatory approach, involving users, planners and policy-makers at all levels; (c) women play a central part in the provision, management and safeguarding of water; and (d) water has an economic value in all its competing uses and should be recognised as an economic good[12]. The fourth principle has been elaborated by Briscoe, Economist and World Bank's Ranking Water Advisor in 1996. His thesis is that to manage water as an economic good, the value placed on it by all competing users has to balance with its 'use cost' and 'opportunity cost'. ("Use cost" is defined as the amount needed for constructing and operating the infrastructure necessary for collecting, storing, treating and distributing the water. "Opportunity cost" is a less obvious cost – that which is incurred when one user uses water and affects the use of the resource by another user). Pricing based on this balance will send the appropriate signals on how water will be best allocated, distributed and consumed. An environment of free market is where this balance can be best and most easily achieved.[13]

**The Corporate Massages**

In commodifying water and in ensuring its commercialization and privatization, the role of a global nexus consisting of International Water Agencies, International Financial Institutions and the Corporates can be seen. Among the water agencies includes the Global Water Partnership (GWP), the World Water Council (WWC) and the World Commission on Water (WCW). Though on surface each of these organizations appears to be neutral, a close look reveals that these agencies promote privatization and export of water resources[14]. Representatives of global water corporates are strategically placed at the top level of all the three agencies. Among these agencies the WWC has played a major role in commodification of water. It is an unrepresentative and undemocratic body that derives its influence from an exclusive membership of international financial institutions, large multinational water corporations, and non-governmental organizations[15]. The Council promotes extraordinarily expensive and destructive dam and water diversion projects as well as policies such as Public-Private Partnerships (PPP's) that put water services under private ownership. PPPs in Argentina, Bolivia, El Salvador, the US, and other countries have resulted in huge price hikes, water pollution, depletion and cut-offs which, in the language of the water justice movement, "deny people the right to water."[16]

Mention has to be made about the World Water Forum (WWF), an international event held every three years by the World Water Council (WWC), a policy think tank run by the World Bank; the major water corporations, such as Vivendi and Suez; and the development and aid agencies and water ministries of a number of First World governments. The World Water Council has set itself up as a kind of "Global High Command" of water. The Second World Water Forum (Hague, 2000) refused to acknowledge that "water is a human right, instead a human need"[17] and this view has been repeated at the third WWF in Kyoto, 2003. After the second WWF the WWC presented its World Water Vision calling for "full cost pricing of water." The third WWF showcased a financial plan for water funding in the global south - the report called for drastic changes in the funding of water delivery systems toward mega-dams and other projects at the expense of local sustainable technologies, and the use of public funds to protect corporate water investors against political unrest and poor profit results. Written by Michel Candessus, former head of the International Monetary Fund, the Candessus Report formed the basis for a subsequent decision to greatly increase World Bank and other regional bank funding for privatized water services in the developing world.[18] The fifth WWF (Istanbul 2009) again backed water as a human need, not as a human right, despite efforts by dissenting Latin American Countries, France and Spain to introduce the right to water. These nations were reportedly blocked by Egypt, Brazil and the United States.[19]

The main source of funding for water services, mainly in non-industrialized countries are the international lending agencies like the International Monetary Fund (IMF) and the World Bank. As a condition for loans these institutions force the domestic governments to privatize the water sector. This pattern has been followed for World Bank loans in many countries including Mozambique and Bolivia.[20] At the same time through the International Financial Corporation the World Bank provides direct capital financing to major water corporations like Suez, Vivendi. To the World Bank "giving public services away to the people leads inevitably to waste and needs a proper system of charging for water."[21] In Cochabamba, Bolivia the World Bank wrote, "No subsidies should be given to ameliorate the increase in water tariffs."[22] African Development Bank, Asian Development Bank, European Bank for Reconstruction and Development are other financial institutions supporting privatization of water services. Bilateral Investment Agreements, Free Trade Agreements and GATT, WTO Guidelines are also promoting water privatization.

### Water and Human Rights

Water is so important because of the reason that it is needed for sustaining life on earth. Right to Water forms an important part of human rights because of the same reason. No one can secure life and a decent life without access to water. The Supreme Court of India while expanding the scope of Article 21 has included "Right to Pure Drinking Water," as a key right in the Right to Life and Personal Liberty.[23] This signifies the importance of water.

The UN has recognized Right to Water as an important human right. The rationale for the emergence of the notion of water as human rights stems from the need to secure water for the poor and marginalized sections. Lack of water and sanitation clearly has an impact on the enjoyment of other human rights, such as the rights to education, health and work, which form an essential basis for poverty elimination and human development as well.

### Indicators of Water for Human Rights Approach

The UN concept of water as a human right was used as a tool for the analysis of the quality of water delivery systems. Four indicators – availability, water quality, accessibility and access to information, have been devised to measure the extent of abidance of countries to the water for human rights approach.

These indicators present a description of the condition of water sector.

- **Availibility**: Implies that the water supply is sufficient and continuous for personal and domestic uses, such as drinking, sanitation, washing, food preparation etc. The Human Right to Water suggests that each person needs 20-50 litres of safe freshwater a day to ensure their basic needs for drinking, cooking and cleaning. But in reality more than one out of every six does not have access to these.
  In Plachimada (Kerala), Grenoble (France), Cochabamba (Bolivia) etc, the water supply became inadequate because of corporate exploitation. As a result of the extraction by the Cola Company the ground water level in Plachimada drowned to that extend that for drinking water the local population had to go for miles.
- **Water Quality**: The water supplied must be clean and safe. There exists WHO Guidelines for drinking water, which guides governments to develop national water quality standards.
  Reports show that the actions of MNCs have resulted in contamination of water. In Colombia, Alberta, USA, Canada etc. this things occurred. In South Africa and in Sydney dangerous particles, bacteria, dead bodies of cats and dogs, industrial wastes etc. have been found in water tanks, belonging to the water giant Suez.
- **Accessibility**: Water, water facilities and services must be accessible to every human being. Accessibility includes both physical and economical. Physical accessibility means that water, water facilities and services must be within the safe physical reach for all sections of the population. Sufficient water should be accessible with in the immediate vicinity. Physical security should not be threatened during access to water facilities and services. In case of economic accessibility to water, water facilities and services must be affordable for all. The charges associated with securing water must be affordable and must not compromise the realization of other rights. Generally, water services are considered to be affordable when they cost no more than 2 percent of the average family income.
  After the entry of Bechtel Corporation in Cochabamba, water rates jacked up by nearly 35 percent. Families with monthly incomes of around $ 100 have seen their water bills jump up to $ 20 per month[24]. In Argentina and Manila also similar situation occurred.
- **Access to Information**: The public should have access to water data and information. This is needed for planning and sound management of water resources.
  In the case of Egypt, information is difficult to obtain due to low investment in the information industry. In the case of Jordan, reasonable information systems are in place and access to water data is feasible.

## Water, MNCs and Human Rights Violations

Corporations carry out some of the most horrific human rights abuses of modern times, but it is increasingly difficult to hold them to account. Economic globalization and the rise of transnational corporate power have created a favourable climate for corporate human rights abusers, which are governed principally by the codes of supply and demand and show genuine loyalty only to their stockholders. On issues as diverse as assassination, torture, kidnapping, environmental degradation, abusing public funds, violently repressing political rights, releasing toxins into pristine environments, destroying homes, discrimination, and causing widespread health problems, familiar companies like Dow Chemical, Coca Cola, Caterpillar, Lockheed, Philip Morris, and Wal-Mart play a big role.

The abusive behaviours of the criminal corporate are undermining the rights of the indigenous people all over the world. The 'notorious' corporates includes – Coco-cola, Suez, Vivendi, Enron, Thames Water, Bechtel, Danon and so on. The inglorious play of these corporates undermined the basic rights and needs of the common man and that is what happened in Cochabamba (Bolivia), Grenoble (France), Plachimada & Puthuserry (Kerala, India), Durban (South Africa), Ghana, Uruguay, Colombia, Canada and even in the US. Besides commodification and depletion of water these corporate, for their foul play and survival are engaging in a wide range of human rights violations such as violent killing, kidnapping and torture, health violations, environmental pollution etc.

## Water Business and MNCs

Water business is one of the most profitable businesses in the world. Like all other business the water business too is controlled by transnational corporations. According to Fortune Magazine "water promises to the 21st Century what oil was to the 20th Century." The world water market today is controlled by 10 global lords – Suez and Vivendi forms the Water Titans; Bouygues, Thames, Bechtel and Enron belongs to the II Tier; and the III Tier includes Severn Trent, Anglican Water, Kelda Group and the American Water Works Company. While Vivendi spreads over Asia, Middle East, Europe, Africa, US, Canada and Latin America, Suez controls the water markets of Asia, Middle East, Europe, USA and Latin America. The global lords have their market spread over the continents and their annual turnover exceeds Rs. 80,000$. In case of bottled waters the B 4's – Cola, Pepsi, Nestle and Danon controls the market. From water trade these companies are extracting huge profits. BBC report points that the corporations are getting a profit rise of 25 percent.[25] Bottled water is the most profitable in water trade, because of its low cost of production. The study conducted by Centre for Science and Environment shows that the total cost (excluding labour, marketing and tax) of producing 1 litre branded bottled water is Rs. 2.85 – 4.25 and the selling cost Rs. 10 – 15.[26] So the profit margin is so high in case of bottled waters.

The bottled water industry is one of the most thriving sectors in India. The market is growing at a whopping rate of about 55 per cent annually. Recent industry figures from India indicate that sales of bottled water grew from $189 million (USD) in 2003 to $599 million in 2008, a growth rate of 216 percent.[27] With this figure projected to double in the next five years India is being touted as one of the fastest growing bottled water markets in the world. The total annual bottled water consumption in India had tripled to 5 billion litres in 2004 from 1.5 billion litres in 1999. Global consumption of bottled water was nearing 200 billion litres in 2006.[28] India is the tenth largest bottled water consumer in the world. In 2002, the industry had an estimated turnover of Rs.10 billion. With over a thousand bottled water producers, the Indian bottled water industry is big by even international standards. There are more than 200 brands, nearly 80 per cent of which are local. Most of the small-scale producers sell non-branded products and serve small markets.[29]

**Human Rights Violations and MNCs**

Commodification of water itself is a violation of human rights. Because it denies the poor, access to water. Commodification and privatization of water supply system has resulted in increase of water tariffs to unaffordable rates. In Bolivia, water rates increased up to 35 percent forcing families to spend more on water than for food. The privatization of water has had a disastrous impact on the human right to clean water. French company Suez is the worst perpetrator of this abuse. The company's billions of dollars in profit come at the expense of poor people living in countries where thousands lack access to potable water. Suez has raised water rates, cut off the water of people unable to pay, refused to extend services to poverty-stricken neighbourhoods, and then threatened legal action when contracts are terminated. In Manila and Philippines, after seven years of water privatization under a Suez company (Maynilad Water) contract, water rates increased in some neighbourhoods by 400 to 700 percent.[30] In Argentina, Suez charged high consumer rates and cut off water access for citizens unable to pay, leaving those most in need without access to a life-sustaining natural resource.

Corporate exploitation also resulted in environmental degradation. Uncontrolled extraction of water has resulted in water scarcity and then pollution of water reserves. Coco-Cola is the most notorious in this case. In Plachimada, Kerala, Coca-Cola extracted 1.5 million litres of deep well water, which they bottled and sold under the names Dasani and BonAqua. The groundwater was severely depleted, affecting thousands of communities with water shortages and destroying agricultural activity. The remaining water became contaminated with high chloride and bacteria levels, leading to scabs, eye problems, and stomach aches in the local population.[31] The company extracted 15 lakh litres of water for production, leaving back 12 lakh litres of it as waste water, daily.[32] Water shortages have occurred in Varanasi, Thane, and Tamil Nadu as well. The company is also guilty of reselling its plants' industrial waste to farmers as fertilizers, despite its containing hazardous lead and cadmium.

The water supplied by these companies are also of not good quality. The Centre for Science and Environment (CSE), says it tested 57 carbonated beverages made by Coca-Cola and Pepsi at 25 bottling plants and found a "cocktail of between three to five different pesticides in all samples."[33] It was also found that the bottled waters and soft drinks (colas) contain cadmium and even pesticides in dangerous proportions. Washington DC based Environmental Working Group's Report states that, "10 popular US bottled water brands contain mixtures of 38 different pollutants, including bacteria, fertilizer, tylenol and industrial chemicals." It also stated that in many cases some of the brands had levels "no better than tap water."[34]

The MNCs also leads in abuse of workers' rights and assassinations. These companies have no hesitation in violently suppressing those who are opposing their activities. Coco-Cola, which represents the corporate symbol, is leader in this case. Global Exchange reports that, "between 1989 and 2002, eight union leaders from Coca-Cola bottling plants in Colombia were killed after protesting against the company's labour practices. Hundreds of other Coca-Cola workers who have joined or considered joining the Colombian union SINALTRAINAL have been kidnapped, tortured, and detained by paramilitaries who intimidate workers to prevent them from unionizing. In Turkey, 14 Coca-Cola truck drivers and their families were beaten severely by Turkish police hired by the company, while protesting a layoff of 1,000 workers from a local bottling plant in 2005."[35]

In Bolivia, even the state machinery has been used to suppress the agitation against privatization of water supplies. Martial laws and other black laws have been imposed to stop the people's movement. Military firing created a civil war situation in Bolivia. Leaders of La Coordiadore were arrested and many went 'missing.' Police reacted to mass protests with violence, activists were rounded up and arrested at mid night, and radio and TV programmes were shut down in mid-programme.[36]

## Conclusion

Corporate globalization has resulted in structural transformation of the world system, making MNCs the new symbols of power. The role of MNCs increased to such an extent that there is almost no area of human life that is not influenced in some way by these giant firms. The role of state declined and it became a mere facilitator of the market. The loss of power by the state resulted in concentration of power in the hands of the corporate. It is a fact that MNCs have at their disposal many tools for frustrating governmental policies, including those of guest and host government. States no longer enjoy the monopoly as violators of human rights.

The privatization of water has had a disastrous impact on the human right to clean water. By commodifying water what the corporate are doing is that they are denying the right of common man to the 'free gift' of nature. Everywhere, the harmful effects of commodification and excessive pricing are on the poor. It is not possible for the poor to spend 30 percent of their income for water. Nature has provided water free of cost and pricing that water is a crime against the nature. We can see that all the corporates are exploiting, polluting, diverting and depleting the wellsprings of the world (Third World) at a startling rate, for their profits. Government and its agencies are many-a-times and in many places acted and are acting as agents of these corporate. The action of Bolivian Government against the anti-privatization movement there, the sale of River Bhavani, Ganga and Shenoth in India etc. clearly reveals this.

Deceived by all - government and its agencies, MNCs, international institutions, the hobson choice of the common man is to organize themselves. Though it is not easy to check the power of the corporations, citizens around the world are stepping to do so and are showing much success. Civil society involvements have shown effective in curbing corporate human rights abuses. The success of La Coordiadore in Bolivia, ADES & Save the Water in France, Anti-Privatization Forum in South Africa, Plachimada Samrakshana Samiti in Plachimada (Kerala) and Save our Spring in USA brings to light these. People's struggle for water rights around the world are growing and multiplying because it has become clear that when the people rose up, Governments' will be forced to come out of their servitude and MNCs will be forced to bend their knees.

## References

1. David A McDonald & Grey Ruiters, "Rethinking Privatization," Public Services Year Book, 2006. p. 13.
2. Thomas F Pogue & L G Sgontz, "Government and Public Choice, An Introduction to Public Finance," Massachussets: Houghton Mifflin Company, 1978. P. 49.
3. Richard A Musgrave & Peggy B Musgrave, "Public Finance in Theory and Practice," New York: Mc Grew Hill Book Company, 1984. p. 47.
4. David A McDonald & Grey Ruiters, p. 13.
5. Karen Bakker, "Neoliberalizing Nature? Market Environmentalism in Water Supply in England and Wales," Annals of the Association of American Geographers, Vol. 98, No. 1, March 2008. p. 546.
6. Maude Barlow & Tony Clarke, "Blue Gold, The Fight to Stop the Corporate Theft of the World's Water," New Delhi: Left World, 2002. p. 8.
7. "Water Resources," UN Water Statistics. http://www.unwater.org/statistics_res.html.
8. "Water Use," UN Water Statistics. http://www.unwater.org/statistics_use.html.

9. "Water Scarcity," International Decade for Action, Water for Life 2005-2015, United Nations. http://www.un.org/waterforlifedecade/scarcity.html.
10. "Beyond Scarcity: Power, Poverty and the Global Water Crisis," Human Development Report 2006, New York: UNDP. p. 136.
11. Lionel Robbins, "An Essay on the Nature and Significance of Economic Science," London: Macmillan, 1932. p. 16.
12. "The Dublin Statement on Water and Sustainable Development," Dublin, Ireland: 31 January 1992. pp. 2-3.
13. John Briscoe, "Water as an Economic Good: The Idea and What it Means in Practice," Paper Presented at the World Congress of the International Commission on Irrigation and Drainage, Cairo, Egypt: September 1996.
14. Maude Barlow & Tony Clarke, p. 157.
15. Hemantha Withanage, "Water; an Economic Good or a Public Good," Environmental Foundation, Sri Lanka: Friends of the Earth. p. 2.
16. Jeff Conant, "Fifth World Water Forum Marked by Violence and Repression;" Project Censored, March 17, 2009. p. 1.
17. Maude Barlow, "The World Water Forum and Its Civil Society Opposition." https: // worldcom.nl / cgi - binmailman / listinfo / waterjustice.
18. Michel Candessus, "Report of the World Panel on Financing Water Infrastructure," 3rd World Water Forum, March 2003. p. 5-8.
19. Jeff Conant, P. 1.
20. John Shultz & Tom Kruse, "The Bolivian Water Revolts, The World Bank Letters," Bolivia: The Democracy Centre. http://www.democracyctr.org/bolivia/investigations/water/world_bank_letters.htm.
21. Maude Barlow & Tony Clarke, p. 155.
22. "Bolivia: Public Expenditure Review," World Bank, June 14, 1999.
23. Narinderjit Singh Sahni vs. Union of India (2002) 2 S.C.C. 210.
24. Maude Barlow & Tony Clarke, P. 155.
25. Toby Poston, "Are Water Profits Flowing too Freely," BBC Business Report, June 7, 2006.
26. Chandra Bhushan, "Bottled Loot," Frontline, Vol. 23, No. 7, April 21, 2006. p. 24.
27. Richard Girard, "Bottled Water Industry Targets a New Market: The Global South," Polaris Institute, Alternet, June 15, 2009.
28. "Bottled Water Industry in India." http://www.gits4u.com/water/water16.htm.
29. Chandra Bhushan, P. 23.
30. SUEZ-LYONNAISE DES EAUX, "Some of the "Most Wanted" Corporate Human Rights Violators," Global Exchange. http://www.globalexchange.org
31. M.P Veerandrakumar, "Plachimadayil Sambhavikunnathu," (M)

in *Plachimadayile Jalachushanavum Janakiya Prathirothavum*, Mathrubhumi Books, January 2005. p. 17.

32. Gagadeesh Babu, "Jalachushanam: Plachimada Mathruka," (M) Kerala Kaumudi, August 11, 2003.
33. Larry West, "Coca-Cola Charged with Groundwater Depletion and Pollution in India," Environmental Issues. http://environment.about.com/od/waterpollution/a/groundwater_ind.htm.
34. Nancy Luna, "Walmart Bottled Water Among 10 Polluted Brands, Study Finds," Register, October 15, 2008.
35. COCO-COLA, "Some of the "Most Wanted" Corporate Human Rights Violators," Global Exchange. http://www.globalexchange.org
36. Maude Barlow & Tony Clarke, p. 184.

# 22

# CLIMATE CHANGE AND SUBSISTENCE: A CASE FOR HUMAN RIGHTS

**Panicker Harishanker**

## Introduction

Humans have used science and technology to adapt the nature to our own needs and desires. This use of science and technology can be seen from two perspectives, one which is rational and objective and the other a romantic vision of nature. The former viewed the intervention of nature as inevitable and the latter considered such an action a scientific violence[1]. The dichotomy of culture vs. nature has lead man to try to dominate the nature. Although the over-romanticization of nature is as dubious as the objective view, the issue of climate change has brought out the scientific violence that humans have committed till now. There is no reason to not accept the fact that man's tweaking of nature has made the nature react in an unforeseen fashion. The implications of such a change has been so great that we have on our own discretion decided to act upon a strategy to reverse or reduce the impact of the anthropogenic changes to the climate.

Climate change has been predicted by scientists to cause severe food and water shortages. The sea-level rises that accompany the expected sea level rises will displace millions in low lying countries like Bangladesh, Maldives, etc. It is estimated that a 3-4°C increase in the global temperatures would result in 330 million people being temporarily or permanently displaced[2]. The pressures to absorb refugees in the neighbouring countries will potentially lead to conflicts. The impact will be equally on the environment as it will also affect the health of ecosystems and thereby the biodiversity of the planet. Thus, it becomes clear that climate change has the potential to be the single greatest threat to humanity in the 21st century and the future.

## Inequity and the Violation of Rights

To talk about climate change is to also talk about the survival of humanity. Addressing climate change from a human rights perspective becomes relevant. It becomes a part of the debate because of the human rights violations that occur with climate change. There are two different violations occurring here; one on an equity level (occurring between nations) and the other from an individual perspective (of the denial of basic necessities). The two violations are inter-related and are rather reinforcing. The first is in relation to power relations that create a social differential which causes the positive effects to occur at the top and the negative effects to occur at the bottom[3]. This inequity is more severe than economic inequities for the fact that while benefits are individualized, and the negative side effects become social costs[4].

The industrialization of Global North has benefited their economies while the social cost of the pollution is shared. It is estimated that the top 20% of the world population utilize 80% of the world resources, and that the rest 80% found in mostly the Global South utilize the rest. It becomes clear that climate change will have a greater impact on the developing and the under-developed world than the developed by the sheer numerical difference and the economic conditions. The second violation is with respect to mainly the poor in the developing and the underdeveloped, because climate change will adversely affect the poor rather than the rich. The lack of a resource base like the Global North means that the very subsistence of the local communities in the Global South is under question.

## Sustainable Development and Present Needs

The word 'sustainable development' has entered the modern economic as well as political thinking. As the Burtland Commission defines it, sustainable development aims at meeting the needs of the present generation without compromising the needs of the future generation[5]. The connection between sustainable development and climate change is intuitive, as climate change is a problem that needs to be tackled to ensure a sustainable development. The unprecedented changes in the climate are going to affect the future generation and their capacity to use resources. The need to care for future generations comes from two approaches; the Utilitarian and the Deontological approaches. The utilitarian approach talks about a discounted sum of well being of people over a time, it uses a discount rate to value utility in future to that of present. The utilitarian approach has been influential in the Neo-classical economics and Environmental Economics. The Kantian/Deontological approach views the right to sustainable development as a moral right of the future generation to have equal levels of well being as the present generation.

Sustainability is at the heart of any environmental thinking, as it deals with the future as well as the present .Climate change threatens the supply of resources which are imperative for the human existence. However, the problems of inequity in the present generation are not sufficiently addressed by the definition of sustainable development. Economists like Partha Das Gupta talk about the need to address the existing inequality before we can deal with larger problems of the future. Sustainability has two aspects connected to the allocation of resources, inter-generational allocation and an intra-generational allocation of resources. The predominant narrative for climate change as well sustainable development gives more emphasis on the inter-generational allocation of resources and neglect the need for an intra-generational equity in distribution or allocation of resources. Ecological economists like Krutilla also talked about the need for present needs to be addressed more importantly for the very fact that without the present generation there would not be a future generation[6]. Intra-generational allocation of resources does require us to choose a path of development and an ideal which needs to be achieved. The path thus chosen will have a direct impact on the climate change, as an adoption of a production intensive economy as the ideal will lead to more consumption and hence more emissions.

## Human Rights and Climate Change

A human rights perspective for climate change will try to bring out the problems faced the poor. It will bring out the voice of those who otherwise would have been silent sufferers of the climate change. The concerns of the poor and marginalized liked the aboriginal tribes of Australia, the poor farmers of sub-Saharan Africa will be unheard or given less importance because of they are excluded from the discourse. The worst affected will be these poor and marginalized whose rights are already in a precarious situation. The poor are therefore in a vicious circle wherein they are affected by poor access to resources, physical infrastructure, weak right protections and vulnerability to climate change related disasters[7]. The power relations of the climate change debate without a human rights perspective will be structured such that the interests of the state and international stakeholders including companies are only taken into view. Thus, the focus on the most vulnerable from a human rights perspective will ensure that a policy for climate change mitigation will be inclusive. It also brings out the need for accountability for one's action, as it is directly affecting the livelihoods and the future of another.

However, climate change mitigation talks and policies talk about physical reduction of emission levels in a carbon economy and do little or nothing to address the issue of the poor. The problem faced by states to adopt a human rights approach is that human rights are harder to enforce than a quantitative restriction on the amount of $CO_2$ released. In addition to this, states would not want a complete enforcement of human rights, as it is seen in emergency conditions (like natural calamities) that human rights become limited. It is such emergency conditions that climate change can give rise to and leave millions suffering from a lack of basic amenities. Climate change mitigation policies come under stiff opposition from the developed as well as developing countries as they are perceived to curtail the growth and development of their economies.

Developing countries point out the fact that a less restrictive policy is needed so that the poor can be ensured basic qualities of life. They bring out a distinction between the 'luxury emissions' of the developed world and the 'subsistence emissions' of the developing and the under-developed world. Therefore the emission from the exhaust of an SUV in the developed world cannot be compared to the burning of inefficient cow-dung cakes for fuel in the developing world. The argument makes sense, as it is differentiating the role of the developed and the developing as well as putting the onus on the developed world. Climate mitigation policies as some fear might restrict 'subsistence emissions' for the satisfaction of basic human rights like right to food, health, water, etc. Quantitatively, these 'subsistence emissions' are much less dangerous than the pollution caused by deforestation, transport, and energy generation. Climate mitigation policies have invariably talked about emission standards relating to industries and transport and also a search for alternative energy systems. Being a developing country does not mean that it should repeat the same mistakes as the developed world. Traditional societies have regarded nature with respect and tried to live in accordance with it, rather than modern science's tendency to tame it. Thus, climate change mitigation provides an opportunity to search for an alternate development paradigm that is less carbon intensive and the development more inclusive.

Issues of Climate change in the developed world have talked about the need to move to a less Carbon dependent economy. Fossil fuels represent a substitutable resource in the long term, and the dependence could be reduced using technology. However, it is the essential resources that we need to protect, essential resources like fresh water have no substitutes and therefore their over-use may have catastrophic impacts. Human activities has not only led to an overuse of resources, but also affected the Earth life support capabilities by exceeding its carbon sink capacities and water and carbon cycles. It had been predicted that the lack of drinking water will be the biggest headache to policy makers in the developing countries and it has proved to be so in Africa as well as South Asia.

Institutional mechanisms have to be strengthened to address the issues of intra-generational inequity as well as the problems of climate change. Technology has only been a partial answer to the problems of climate change and sustainability. It was thought that the increase in technological progress will bring in efficiency which will in turn reduce our dependence on natural resources and leave a less intensive carbon footprint. It cannot be doubted that technological progress has brought in efficiency, but unfortunately the improvements in efficiency has been offset by the increase in consumption. At the core of the problem, we find that it is not a technological problem but a behavioural one. It has been proved that human beings prefer technological solutions to behavioural ones, like preferring to buy a more energy efficient car to public transport[8]. It also shows that humans are not always as rational as they are assumed to be, a fall out of the utilitarian thinking. Political institutions have a main sway here, as their policies can not only affect behavioural choices but also public opinion. Therefore the issue of climate change poses more of a moral question of legitimate consumption versus overconsumption. It also poses an ethical issue of how we have overlooked the needs of the most vulnerable in creating a better society. Moral and ethical issues related to climate change and sustainability has to be dealt with directly and not be given false hopes in terms of technology, which brought about the problems in the first place.

**Tragedy of Commons**

The rampant industrialization has led to changes in global commons like air, water, and climate. The issue of climate change also brings about the notion of tragedy of commons proposed by Garret Hardin in 1968, where resources have been utilized indiscriminately because of the lack of accountability[9]. International law on climate change is still not enforceable and climate change mitigation plans remain to be acts of volition. However, Elinor Ostrom's (the 2009 Nobel Prize winner in Economics) work on commons show that tragedy of commons need not end in one as long as the stakeholders realize it as one[10]. Her research has shown that locals in many parts of the world have come together to form self-governing institutions to regulate the use of commons like pastures for grazing, water resources in view of a tragedy of commons. The climate change talks in Kyoto, and now in Copenhagen is in anticipation of the tragedy of commons that will result if humanity indiscriminately exploits the natural resources. However, the talks need a wider platform to bring out the need for protection of the interests of the excluded.

**Conclusion**

Climate change mitigation is about transforming the way in which we produce and use energy[11]. The policies should re-evaluate so that quantitative emissions targets are not the only point of concentration. The need of the hour is to also setup an effective accountability system that also takes into consideration trans-state actors. Positively discriminating developing countries by relaxing emission levels as compared to developed countries would not work. Multinational corporations would shift the more polluting factories (if not have already) to the developing nations and make use of the relaxed norms. Mere emission standards are not going to solve the problems created by climate change. It is not a question of just past accountability for climate change that should decide how the mitigation policies are chartered. For years now, the real problem of a behavioural change has been avoided and overlooked to provide an illusion of a simple solution of technology driven change, a case where beauty can be mistaken for reality. Policies should be a reflection of the needs and the aspirations of all sections including the vulnerable. For this, a human rights perspective is needed in addition to a scientific or an objective analysis. The question of responsibility of climate change is prolonging the debate for far too long and resulting in no action. The victims of inaction will be the poor and vulnerable and therefore the need for a broad based strategy is not only a political issue, but also an ethical issue. At stake here is not just development, but the very subsistence of 2.6 billion people who will be severely affected.

## Notes and References

1. Cini, Marcello. *Science and Sustainable Society*. 1991.
2. *Fighting Climate Change: Human Solidarity in a Divided World.* UNDP. Human Development Report 2007/2008.
3. Sachs, Wolfgang. *Climate Change and Human Rights*. Wuppertal Institute. 2008.
4. Bryne, John. Glover, Leigh. Martinez, Cecilia. *The production of Unequal Nature.*
5. *Our Common Future*. Report of World Commission on Environment and Development. 1987. United Nations.
6. Krutilla, J.V., *Conservation Reconsidered.* The American Economic Review.1963.
7. *Climate Change and Human Rights: A Rough Guide*. ICHRP. 2008.
8. Steg, Linda. Gifford, Robert. *Sustainable Transportation and Quality of Life.* Journal of Transport Geography. 2005. Vol 13. pg 59-69.
9. Hardin, G, *The Tragedy of Commons*. Journal of Natural Resource Policy Research. Vol 1. No 3. Pg 243-253 (Reprint of 1963 article).
10. Ostrom, Elinor. *Governing the Commons: The Evolution of Institutions for Collective Action*, 1990.
11. *Fighting Climate Change: Human Solidarity in a Divided World.* UNDP. Human Development Report 2007/2008.

- *Fighting Climate Change: Human Solidarity in a Divided World.* UNDP. Human Development Report 2007/2008.
- Cini, Marcello. *Science and Sustainable Society* 1991.
- *Our Common Future*. Report of World Commission on Environment and Development. United Nations 1987.
- Sachs, Wolfgang. *Climate Change and Human Rights*. Wuppertal Institute 2008.
- Bryne, John. Glover, Leigh. Martinez, Cecilia. *The production of Unequal Nature.*
- *Krutilla, J.V., Conservation Reconsidered. The American Economic Review* 1963.
- *Climate Change and Human Rights: A Rough Guide*. ICHRP. 2008.
- Ostrom, Elinor. Governing the Commons: *The Evolution of Institutions for Collective Action*, 1990

- Hardin, G., *The Tragedy of Commons. Journal of Natural Resource Policy Research.* Vol 1. No 3. pp. 243-253 (Reprint of 1963 article)
- Steg, Linda. *Gifford, Robert. Sustainable Transportation and Quality of Life*. Journal of Transport Geography. 2005. Vol 13. pp. 59-69.

# 23

# TRIBAL LAND ALIENATION IN KERALA: ITS HUMAN RIGHTS IMPLICATIONS

**R. Rajeevan**

## Introduction

"All human beings are born free and equal in dignity and rights" so announced the global declaration adopted on 10th December 1948. The U.N approved the text stating that every human had the right to life, liberty, justice and property in what Roosevelt called "a magnacarta for mankind". Years have passed since these nice words were coined. Since then enlightened philosophers, priests, politicians, teachers and preachers share, interpret and enrich it. The word has progressed a great deal since then. No men can be himself at his best without enjoying these rights.

In India, Human Rights embodied in the International covenants are being guaranteed in our constitution under Part III - Fundamental Rights. The known human history shows that the inherent character of human rights and their universal application were never recognized and practiced. The objective of this paper is to unveil the violation of the rights of the tribal sections of Kerala.

Like in other parts of the world, the tribal people in Kerala were the owners of the forests and hills. They are believed to be the earliest settlers in the land. They are generally called the 'Adivasis' implying 'original inhabitants.' They have their own customs, traditions, faith, belief, science and life style. They were politically organized, economically powerful and civilized in their own imitable ways.

They were politically controlled by the traditional modes of leadership. They enjoyed full liberty to use forest products. They cultivated various crops for their own consumption. Their diet not only contained the required calories but was balanced with ample milk, fish, fruits etc. They were free from slavery and exploitation. There were a few tribal kingdoms in Kerala and some of the tribal kings were very powerful.

In the tribal set up, private land rights were an alien concept. They had simple modes of production. Each tribal hamlet was occupied by only one tribal sect. Land and resources in the hamlet were commonly owned. It was the tribal chief with the advise of the village committee who distributed the land among the people for cultivation.

## The Colonial Period and the Violation of Tribal Rights

It was the British who for the first time adopted certain policies, which resulted in the alienation of tribal land and forest rights. The lands and forest, which the tribals enjoyed for ages was privatized by the British for plantations. Later the outsiders were allowed to come and settle in the tribal land with force and forcible consent[1]. The British also introduced the New Tax Reform with an intension to destroy the tribals in Malabar. According to this reform measure, those who used to pay tax in kind were to pay it in cash. Dileep Raj described it as a tactics to make the tribals landless and to force them to work as wage labourers[2]. Land surplus and labour shortage was the condition that prevailed during the period in North Malabar. The land policies of the British also adversely affected the tribal sections. The land policy and regulations implemented by the British through records and complicated measurement processes were totally alien to them. They were not able to understand and assimilate the new system. As a result they did not bother to get ownership deed for their land[3]. They naturally thought that they have a right to the natural resources, which constitute their environment. All these resulted in the uprootment and alienation of Adivasi population from their land. So during the British period they not only violated the basic human rights of the tribals but also denied them the basic right of right to life itself. The tribal's are today the victims of large scale human rights violations in our society.

## Tribal Rights Violation in Kerala

When India became a free nation, the leaders of India had clear vision on tribal issues. The first Prime Minister of India, Jawaharlal Nehru was famous for his pro tribal policies. His knowledge and vision on tribal issues was expressed in his famous statement that "tribal problems should be viewed in their own context, as the tribal economy cannot be separated from their cultural disposition and sovereignty. One may think that Nehru was speaking as a Prime Minister showing sympathy for poor tribal subjects, but infact he loved tribals as they were more disciplined and democratic than most other groups in India. To him they are more civilized in their own way[4].

The love and affection showered by leaders like Jawaharlal Nehru,

Mahatma Gandhi, Ambedkar etc on tribals were reflected in the Constitution of free India. The Constituent Assembly of India and its sub committee on tribal affairs had devised a structure of constitutional provision for providing legal safeguards to the tribal population living in different parts of the country. There are at least twenty articles in the Indian Constitution that provide protection directly and indirectly to the tribals. Prominent among them were included in the Sixth Schedule of the Constitution to compel the concerned state governments to take specific care of them and allow them to lead an undisturbed cultural life.

Even though the Constitution recommended positive measures for the protection of tribal rights and their development, the insensitive and biased bureaucracy and administrative machinery tried their best to violate their basic human rights resulting in large scale alienation of tribal land.

It is a truth that hills and forests constituted the main source of life and livelihood for the tribals. Land and forest rights are basic to their life. The condition of these sections separated from their land and forest could be like that of fish out of water. The free flow of immigrants to the tribal lands continued even after independence. Agricultural settlers, mainly from Central Travancore and Cochin who migrated to Palakkadu, Malabar and different parts of the Western Ghats in the 1950s was a great threat to tribal life. It should be noted that the tribals were poor, illiterate and suffered from indebtedness. Many of the immigrants had fraudulently alienated tribal land, exploiting the ignorance and innocence of these indigenous people. The absence of tribal land laws to protect their land and the lack of a vigilant governmental machinery to protect tribal rights, helped the immigrants to snatch tribal land by using various overt and covert methods.

Records say that among the tribal families in Kerala, 30% percent are landless. At the time of the formation of Kerala state, landlessness was least among tribals in Travancore and Kochi. The number of landless tribals remained low in Kottayam, Idukki and Thiruvananthapuram. The tribal sects of the region namely Kanikkar of Thiruvananthapuram, Malai Arayan of Idukki and Kottayam, Muthuvan of Idukki and Oorali of Idukki and Kottayam were the first to engage in systematic cultivation.

It was in Malabar that the number of landless tribal families was high and that too in the districts of Wayanad and Palakkadu. The Adiyas and Paniyas of the region who formed almost 27 percent of the tribal population in the state, remained landless for centuries. The large scale immigration of people especially from Travancore resulted in the tribals losing their agricultural land and hence their only means of sustenance. As the immigrants seized the tribal land through various means on a large scale, the tribals naturally became their slaves. Some of the most exploited tribal sects consisted of the Paniyas and Adiyas.

In Attappadi, immigration from the plains began in the 1950s. Within 25 years 20 percent of the tribal families in the district were rendered landless:

In the decade from 1966-1976, 44 percent of the tribal land in the district of Palakkad was seized by the immigrants. The mortaging of tribal lands too was higher in the district.

Both in the case of the cultivating land and in the case of average land possessed by each tribal family, the districts in the old Travancore-Kochi state stood ahead, while Malabar stood last.

Among the landed tribals, 62 percent of the families had an average of two acres of land in their possession. Since it was not adequate for their annual sustenance, they had to rely on labour work. It is seen that 29 percent of the tribal farmers who possess 2-5 acres of land were small scale cultivators. That is 91 percent of the agriculturists among the tribals perform other labours since the income from agriculture was insufficient for their livelihood. The percentage of families having land below 50 cents was also high in the Malabar region.

At present, the condition is worse than that prevailed thirty years back. Now more than half of the tribal population in Kerala (55.47 percent) is composed of landless agricultural labourers. The all India average is 32.99 percent. According to an estimate, the total land alienated until the end of 1996 is 80,590 hectares, of which only 440 hectares has been restored to the tribes[5].

## Land Reform Measures in Kerala

The first Communist government of Kerala (1957-59) enacted the 'progressive' land reforms law of Kerala, which was supposed to benefit the poorest and most marginalized groups like the tribals in the society. Even such a law was misused by the rich immigrants to alienate the tribals from their land. The tribals used to lease out their land for cultivation to the non tribal immigrants, who were considered tenants. According to the land reform law, the tenants would be entitled to get the land after a certain period of time and after paying nominal compensation. The rich immigrants gained the ownership of the leased land by eliminating the tribal land owner[6]. The fact that the immigrants cheated the tribals by making use of a law passed for the poor, is a clear example of how they are using political power and influence. On the other hand the tribals are neither organized nor powerful enough to resist such injustices.

The post independence development projects of Kerala also contributed much to the losing of adivasi land. The tribals lost 25924.315 hectares of land for the construction of dams, 2324.72 square kilometer for wild life sanctuaries and 182618.666 hectares for non forest purposes.

The land alienation issues of tribals were first addressed with the formation of the Dhebar Commission in 1960 by the Central government, which suggested that all lands alienated since January 26, 1950 should be restored. The R.Shankar ministry, which was then in power in the state of Kerala, has suggested to the Dhebar commission to include the tribal areas in

Kerala in the list of scheduled areas.

The Kerala Government passed the Kerala Forest Act in 1961 to protect both the forest and forest dwelling tribals. The subsection (A) of section 76 of the Act empowered the state government to formulate rules for protecting and promoting tribal interests. Accordingly the Kerala Government published the Kerala Scheduled Tribes Rules in 1964[7]. It was upheld as very beneficial to the tribal community of Kerala. It included adequate provisions for tribal development such as providing enough fertile land for cultivation free of cost, protection from the exploitation of intermediaries, adequate protection to them from exploitation etc. But a tribal belonging to Mala Araya caste and was a member of a co-operative society named 'Vana Mahasabha' challenged it in the High Court of Kerala. Actually he was becoming an instrument in the hands of vested interest who wanted to subvert the Rule. The Kerala High Court declared the subsection (A) of section 76 of the Kerala Forest Law null and void and the Kerala Scheduled Tribes Rule 1964 as illegal[8].

As a result, the migrants got ample opportunity to alienate the tribals from their land in various ways including marrying tribal girls and thereby becoming owners of tribal land. The tribals were also supplied with liquor and loans as a means of snatching their lands from them.

On the recommendation of the Dhebar commission and on its endorsement by the Centre, the CPI led Achutha Menon government unanimously passed the Kerala Scheduled Tribes (Restriction on Transfer of Lands and Restoration of Alienated Lands) Act 1975[9]. This act (KST Act 1975) was further included in the ninth schedule of the constitution to ensure that the act by itself would not be challenged in any court of law.

The KST Act 1975 was significant in that it had acknowledged the inalienability of tribal land and the need for the restoration of alienated land. However, the rules and regulations accompanying the Act were not framed for many years. It was only in 1986 that the rules operationalising the Act was formulated[10]. According to this Act, all lands alienated from 1960 to 1982 had to be restored to the tribals and all such transactions had to be nullified. It also prohibited the transfer of lands from tribals to non tribals from 1-1-1982. Despite the restriction, the transfer of lands continued without any interruption. Figures indicate that the number of landless families increased from 3549 in 1976 to 22491 in 2001, a seven fold increase despite a ban on land transfer.[11]

Till 1991 there were 8553 applications submitted for restoration of 10,177 hectares of land. Later the number of applications rose to 8879.[12] Of these the maximum number of applications has come from the districts of Palakkad (2523) mainly from the Attapadi region and Wayanad (2229).[13] At the same time applications were filed in from almost all the districts of Kerala. Only 4,524 applications were accompanied by supporting evidences (which was necessary under the KST Act 1975) and therefore found valid. Accordingly, 3,170 hectares of land had to be restored.[14] Their ignorance of the alien concept of ownership coupled with an insensitive and biased administrative machinery that trivialized the traditional rights of the tribals, contributed to a situation where the tribals were left without valid proof of ownership or enjoyment.[15]

When the KST Act 1975 became a law in the year 1986, there was much opposition from the settlers and the officials showed only a lukewarm interest in implementing it. So the government of Kerala did almost nothing for the restoration of tribal land. So in 1988, Dr. Nalla Thampi Thera filed a public interest petition seeking the intervention of the Kerala High Court on the issue. The High Court issued an order on 15th October 1993 calling for the restoration of alienated land.[16] It also ordered the government to settle all cases relating to land alienation within six months of the issue of the order.

In 1996 the UDF government, through an ordinance tried to effect changes in the 1975 Act but the then Governor failed the attempt. A little later, the LDF government also tried the same but it too failed. Since the High Court of Kerala had issued a deadline that the alienated lands had to be restored by September 1996, the LDF government passed an amendment to the 1975 Act. On 23 September 1996, the Kerala state Legislative Assembly passed the Kerala Scheduled Tribes (Restriction on Transfer of Lands and Restoration of Alienated Lands) Amendment Bill 1996[17] in the midst of opposition raised from various Human rights organizations and tribal organizations. The Bill provided legitimacy to tribal land transactions from 1960 to 1986, which was prevented in the original KST Act 1975. Accordingly the immigrants need not to restore the tribal lands occupied by them. Instead the new Bill proposed to restore equal area of land that they have lost elsewhere to the tribals along with an amount of Rs.25000 to each family. The tribal activists had made a representation to the President of India in this regard. The Bill proved to be the greatest injustice meted out by the state to its tribal subjects.

The tribal people expressed their protest in various forms. On October 4, 1996 the Ayyankali Pada detained Dr. W.R. Reddy, the District Collector of Palakkad for nearly nine hours as a sign of protest.[18] The amendment Bill which was sent to the President of India for his consent was rejected and returned by the Rashtrapathi Bhavan on March 1998.[19]

To escape from the pressure of tribal organizations and avoid criticism from judiciary, the Kerala Legislative Assembly passed "The Kerala Restriction on Transfer and Restoration of Lands to Scheduled Tribes" Bill on February 23, 1999 which was signed by the Governor of Kerala on 9-3-1999 and became a law.[20] The new Act made the KST Act 1975 invalid. According to the Act the immigrants need to return only tribal lands above 2 hectares. Lands below 2 hectares need not be given back to the tribals, instead they will be given equal area of substitute land elsewhere. The Bill further promises one acre of land to landless tribals in their own district within two years of its passing. Accordingly on 7 October 1999, the Kerala government started distributing lands to the tribals of Attappadi.[21] On 11 October 1999, the High Court of Kerala issued an order to stay the implementation of articles 5 and 6 of the Act, which allows substitute land for the alienated land.[22]

On 16 December 1999, the Division Bench of Kerala High Court which included Justice P.K. Subramanian and Justice C.S. Rajan pronounced its verdict that the Kerala government has committed contempt of court, while hearing a petition of contempt of court filed by Nalla Thampi Thera. Five more months were granted by the court to implement the KST Act of 1975. The court also warned the government that the Chief Secretary of the state will be punished in case the government fails to restore the alienated lands against which no case has been filed or no compensation has to be given, within five months. The Division Bench also made it clear that the Act of 1999 cannot pass over the Act of 1975.[23]

It is a truth that the two political coalitions the LDF and UDF did very little to enforce the tribal protection laws effectively in the state. So the basic human rights of those people were continuously violated. But they form an active support base of the political parties heading the two political coalitions. At the same time the Adivasi sections of Kerala realized this truth and they extended their support to the Naxalite movement especially in Malabar area. The Naxalite movement was strengthened mainly due to the continuous violation of the rights of dalits and tribal people of Kerala. But such movements were suppressed by the government with an iron land.

Even after this, a number of organizations and movements emerged to protect the human rights of tribals in Kerala. The most prominent among them was the Adivasi Gothra Mahasabha which came into being in 2001. It had an accidental origin. It was the outcome of many unfortunate starvation deaths among the tribals of Palakkad, Kannur and Wayanad districts in the year 2001. It demonstrated the hollowness of the achievements proclaimed by the state in terms of social micro-indicators. The organization made it clear that the tribals in Kerala have been largely kept away from the gains of the much vaunted 'Kerala Model of Development.'

The existing paradigm of development often resulted in seriously disturbing the tribal rights over their common property resources. This was possible because tribals across the state were, and are the least powerful interest group as well as the least powerful political force. On this issue, the tribals should be adequately socialized and empowered to fight for their resources – land, forest and water.

As a response to the deplorable condition of tribals, Kerala witnessed a non violent protest movement of the tribals demanding land, based on the premise that it is lack of land that lies at the root of the tribal poverty. The tribal movement was led by C.K. Janu, a young neo-literate tribal woman born to a very poor Adiya tribal family in Wayanad, who was formerly a member of the Communist Party of India (Marxist). She led the struggle under the banner of the newly floated organization known as the Adivasi-Dalit Samara Samiti (ADSS). The movement began when C.K. Janu submitted an open letter to the Chief Minister of Kerala A.K. Antony on 24 August 2001. The protest strike of ADSS by setting up tribal huts in the premises of both the Government Secretariat and the Cliff House (the official residence of Chief Minister) had attained large scale attention of the press, intelligentia, officials and the people.

This was the first tribal movement in Kerala, which showed the unity and spirit of the tribals in the state. Almost all the tribal sections participated in the struggle. It also received moral support from almost all the communities of Kerala. The news as well as the spirit of this struggle spread to the tribal belts all over the state. It revolutionalised the tribal mindset of Kerala.

In the ADSS struggle the tribals raised demands, which nobody can neglect. They demanded five acres of land for each tribal family. Land was not seen only as a commodity with exchange value or as a status symbol. But it was also seen as connected with their culture, identity and also livelihood. Janu, their leader even identified the presence of certain spiritual elements in their land and the trees which tribals worship.[24] C.R. Bijoy correctly says: "Unlike others, tribals have a special relationship and dependence on land which gives them the notion of territoriality. Their existence as communities is possible only if their inalienable right to their territories is acknowledged."[25]

The ADSS struggle was noted for its peaceful and organized nature. The researcher feels that even the leaders of the movement were not fully optimistic of conducting such a struggle so organized and peaceful. During times of the researcher's interaction with various leaders of the tribals, they also described it as a milestone in proving the capability of tribal sections to conduct such struggles in future. The volunteers stated that their leaders trained them in such a way that they could conduct similar struggles. The leadership tactics attracted the intellectuals and the administrators of Kerala. It was for the first time that the tribal issues came to the forefront of the political agenda of Kerala.[26]

On the 48th day of the strike, that is on 16 October 2001, the Kerala government agreed the demands raised by the tribals. On the basis of the agreement, it was decided to grant five acres of cultivable land to each tribal family. In case if sufficient land was not available, each of them would be then given at least one acre of cultivable land. The activists of the ADSS largely laid emphasis on the distribution of forest land in Wayanad.[27] The state government also agreed to recommend to the Centre to include tribal lands in the fifth schedule so that their land could not be alienated later. The state also assured that it would enact a law to prevent land grabbing and also make a master plan for creating jobs for their unemployed youths.

On the basis of the agreement, the government of Kerala inaugurated the first land distribution at Marayur in Idukki district on time and it was inaugurated by the then Chief Minister of Kerala, A.K. Antony in the presence of tribal leaders. The report of the Government of Kerala sent to the National Human Rights Commission (NHRC) in April 2002 states that 568 families had been provided 1,308 acres of land since 1 January, 2002, the day on which the programme was inaugurated. Only 1.06 percent of the families have been provided 2.2 percent of the identified land within the first four months of the stipulated 12 month period.[28] Since then there has not been any substantial or significant change in these figures except that the land actually allotted has been reported in the media as 1746.62 acres to 834 families. Only three percent of the promised land has been allotted in a year.[29] Also the rate of allotment has gone down drastically as only around 434 acres have been distributed from April 2002 to February 2003 as compared to the over 1300 acres in the first four months.[30] The land distribution was almost stopped then mainly due to the dispute between revenue department and forest department. Due to a number of issues the government could not distribute land to the landless tribals of Kerala.

The AGMS represented the issues to the Kerala government and tried to make the issue live through various platforms including media. After some attempts the AGMS leaders realized the fact that, the democratic and peaceful methods are not sufficient to protect the rights of tribals in Kerala. So they finalized a direct action method. On January 4, 2003 the AGMS under the leadership of C.K. Janu and M.Geethanandan entered into the deforested portions of the Muthanga and its vast Eucalyptus plantations.[31] It was a protest movement against the government of Kerala which violated the agreement that land distribution would commence on January 1, 2002 and be completed on December 31, 2002.

On February 19, 2003, the state suppressed the move through Police action. The participants of the movement including its top leaders like C.K. Janu and Geethanandan were arrested and tortured inside the jail. It is a truth that the inhuman police action and human rights violations on the marginalised sections of Kerala made serious impact on them.

Even after all the struggles against land alienation, the tribal lands are still susceptible to large scale encroachment. The high power committee constituted by the Supreme Court of India reported that about 800 acres of land out of the 7600 acres set apart by the government of Kerala to be distributed to the tribals of the state, had been encroached.[32] The High Court of Kerala too in one of its verdicts accused the state government for its lack of concern in carrying out the distribution of lands to the tribals within the stipulated time limit.[33] The cultural leaders of the state including Sukumar Azhikode, O.N.V. Kurup, Dr. K.N. Panicker, Kakkanadan, M.Mukundan, P. Valsala, Dr. Balamohan Thampi, Dr. B. Iqbal and Dr. Rajan Gurukkal expressed their concern for their tribal fellowbeings. In a joint statement, they demanded to the government to take immediate steps to distribute land to the landless tribals.[34] The intensity of the problem gets revealed when Deshabhimani daily reported that about 8000 tribals in Wayanad still remains landless.[35] Amidst all these, the state government seems to turn its face away from the real issues of tribal land alienation, which ultimately turns out to be one of the serious instances of the violation of human rights of the most marginalized among its subjects.

## Notes and References

1. Jaganath Pathy (1987): *Tribal Peasantry- Dynamics of Development*, New Delhi, Inter India Publications, P.66.
2. Dileep Raj (2003): *Thantedangal: Kerala Samooha Bhoopatam Muthanga Samarathinu Sesham* (Mal) Kottayam, D.C. Books, P.62.
3. Rajeevan. R (2006): Unveiling Injustice Towards Tribals: Kerala Scenario, *Indian Journal of Human Rights and Social Justice*, New Delhi, Vol. I, Nos. 1-2, pp. 53-61.
4. Gavit, M.H. and Attar Chand (1989): *Nehru: Tribal and Women Welfare*, New Delhi, H.K. Publishers & Distributors, P.129.
5. Government of Kerala (GOK), Department of Revenue (2001): c. *Administrative Report* 2001, Trivandrum, GOK.
6. T.V.Achutha Varyar (2003): n.1, P.47.
7. Government of Kerala (GOK) Notification No.M.S.575/64/A.D. 19-8-1964, Trivandrum GOK.
8. Judgment of High Court of Kerala (1970): KLT. 1069, Ernakulam HCK.
9. Government of Kerala, *Kerala Gazette (Extra-ordinary)* dated 14-11-1975 Notification No.673, Trivandrum, GOK.
10. Kerala Scheduled Tribes (Restriction on Transfer of Lands and Restoration of Alienated Lands) Rules 1986, *Kerala Gazette (Extra Ordinary)* 934 dated 20-10-1986 G.O.(P) No. 730/86/RD dated 18-10-1986.
11. Based on the comparison of data from the 1976 socio-economic survey of scheduled tribes and the Adivasi Master Plan Report of 2001.
12. Jose Chathukulam and M.S.John, "Issues in Tribal Development: The Recent Experience of Kerala", in Govinda Chandra Rath, (ed) (2006): *Tribal Development in India: The Contemporary Debate*, New Delhi, Sage Publications India Pvt. Ltd, pp. 182-2002.
13. Dileep Raj (2003): n.3, P.21.
14. *Ibid.*
15. K.Kunhaman (1985): 'The Tribal Economy of Kerala – An Intra-Regional Analysis', *EPW XXX No.11*, March 16, pp. 466-74.
16. *Malayala Manorama* (Kottayam) October 16, 1993.
17. The Kerala Legislative Assembly, dated 23-9-1996. Bill.No.160 Trivandrum KLA.
18. *The Mathrubhoomi*, Kozhikode, October 5, 1996.

19. K.R. Narayanan was the President of India at that time. Since he belonged to the S.C. Section of Kerala, he could understand the situation of tribals in Kerala.
20. Government of Kerala, Notification No.22363/leg.A1/98/Law dated 9-3-1999.
21. *Mathrubhoomi*, Thiruvananthapuram October 8, 1999.
22. *Ibid*, October 12, 1999.
23. *Ibid*, December 17, 1999.
24. *Madhyamam*, Thiruvananthapuram, October 28, 2001.
25. C.R. Bijoy (1999), Adivasis Betrayed: "Adivasi Land Rights in Kerala", *Economic and Political Weekly* 29 May, Vol. XXXIV, No. 22, pp. 1329-35.
26. *The Hindu*, Chennai, October 19 & 20, 2001.
27. C.K. Janu and M.Geethanandan (2001), *Adivasi Grama Panchayathum Swayambharanavum* (Mal.) Cochin, Clan n' Culture.
28. C.R. Bijoy, K. Ravi Raman, 2003. "Muthanga – The Real Story: Adivasi Movement to Recover land", *Economic and Political Weekly*, Vol. XXXVIII, No.20, May 17, 2003.
29. *Ibid.*
30. *Ibid.*
31. *Mathrubhumi*, Thiruvananthapuram, January 5, 2003.
32. *Mathrubhumi*, Thiruvananthapuram, May 1, 2010.
33. *Deshabhimani*, Thiruvananthapuram, Februrary, 20, 2010.
34. *Mathrubhumi*, Thiruvananthapuram, February 21, 2010.
35. *Desabhimani,* Thiruvananthapuram, February, 21, 2010.

# 24

# ROLE OF UNITED NATIONS IN PROMOTING HUMAN RIGHTS

**Ms. Vidya Nair**

I

## Introduction

Human Rights are rights held by individuals simply because they are part of the human species. They are rights shared equally by everyone regardless of sex, race, nationality, and economic background. They are universal in content. (Ishay: 2004:3)

In other words, human rights are the rights possessed by all persons, by virtue of their common humanity, to live a life of freedom and dignity. They give all people moral claims on the behaviour of individuals and on the design of social arrangements-and are universal, inalienable and indivisible. Human rights express our deepest commitments to ensuring that all persons are secure in their enjoyment of the goods and freedoms that are necessary for dignified living.

## Universality of Human Rights

Human rights belong to all people, and all people have equal status with respect to these rights. Failure to respect an individual's human right has the same weight as failure to respect the right of any other-it is not better or worse depending on the person's gender, race, ethnicity, nationality or any other distinction.

## Inalienability of Human Rights

Human rights are inalienable: they cannot be taken away by others, nor can one give them up voluntarily.

## Indivisibility of Human Rights

Human rights are indivisible in two senses. First, there is no hierarchy among different kinds of rights. Civil, political, economic, social and cultural rights are all equally necessary for a life of dignity. Second, some rights cannot be suppressed in order to promote others. Civil and political rights may not be violated to promote economic, social and cultural rights. Nor can economic, social and cultural rights be suppressed to promote civil and political rights.

## Realization of Human Rights

A human right is realized when individuals enjoy the freedoms covered by that right and their enjoyment of the right is secure. A person's human rights are realized if and only if social arrangements are in place sufficient to protect her against standard threats to her enjoyment of the freedoms covered by those rights. (UNDP: 2000:16)

## Roots of Human Rights Norms

Throughout history human rights projects whether-liberal, socialist, or third world in origin-have generated contradictions concerning both how to promote human rights and who should be endowed with equal human rights.

Across the centuries, conflicting political traditions have elaborated different components of human rights or differed over which elements had priority. Today, the varied meanings of human rights reflect the process of historical continuity and change that helped shape their present substance. (Ishay: 2004:3, 4)

Tracing the history of human rights norms six core controversies have shaped the human rights debate.

The first controversy: concerns the religious versus secular origins of human rights.

Each great religion contains important humanistic elements that anticipated our modern conceptions of rights. Modern ethics is in fact indebted to a worldwide spectrum of both secular and religious traditions. Thus, the concepts of progressive punishment and justice were professed by Hammurabi's code of ancient Babylon, the Hindu and Buddhist religions offered the earliest defenses of the ecosystem, Confucianism promoted mass education, the ancient Greeks and Romans endorsed natural laws and the capacity of every individual to reason. Christianity and Islam each encouraged human solidarity, just as both considered the problem of moral conduct in wartime. (Ishay: 2004:7)

Thus, Hinduism, Judaism, Christianity, Buddhism, Islam and Confucianism all assert both the dignity of individuals and peoples responsibility to their fellow humans. Hindus prohibit infliction of physical or mental pain on others. Jews support the sacredness of individuals, as well as the responsibility of the individual to help those in need. Buddhism's eight fold path includes right thought and action towards all beings. Islam teaches equality of races and racial toleration, as well as respect for all human beings. While the relative importance of these values may vary- Paul Gordon Lauren notes –"early ideas about general human rights thus did not originate exclusively in one location like the West or even with any particular form of government like liberal democracy but were shared throughout the ages by visionaries from many cultures in many lands who expressed themselves in different ways". (Karns and Mingst: 2005:416)

The second controversy revolves around the issue whether modern conception of rights is predominantly European in origin.

The developments in Europe that brought an end to the middle ages- scientific revolution, rise of mercantilism, the launching of maritime explorations of the globe, the consolidation of the nation-state, and the emergence of a middle class- these developments stimulated the expansion of western power even as they created propitious prospects for the development of modern conceptions of human rights, They intimately shattered feudalism and challenged the previously uncontested divine rights of Kings.

As Europe was plagued by religious wars putting Catholics and Protestants in a struggle to redefine religious and political structures, human rights visionaries like Hugo Grotius, Samuel Pufendorf, Emmerich de Vattel and Rene Descartes constructed a new secular language, affirming a common humanity that transcended religious sectarianism. Over the next two centuries, revolutionaries in England, America, and France would use a similar discourse to fight aristocratic privileges or colonial authority and to reorganize their societies based on human rights principles. Armed with the scientific confidence of their era, they struggled for the right to life, for freedom of religion and opinion and for property rights. (Ishay: 2004:7, 8)

Human rights philosophers from the liberal persuasion traditionally have emphasized individual rights that the state can neither usurp nor undermine. John Locke (1632-1704), among others, asserted that individuals are equal and autonomous beings whose natural rights predate both national and international law. Public authority is designed to secure these rights. Key historic documents detail these rights, beginning with the English Magna Carta in 1215, the French Declaration of the Rights of Man in 1789 and the U.S. Bill of Rights in 1791. For example, no individual should be "deprived of life, liberty, or property, without due process of law." Political and civil rights, including freedom of religion, deserve utmost protection according to liberal theories. (Karns and Mingst: 2005:417)

However, many rightly argue that the Enlightenment era in Europe did not fulfill its universal human rights promises. In the early nineteenth century, slavery continued in European colonies and in America. Throughout the European dominated world (with the exception of revolutionary France) women had failed to achieve equal rights with men, property less men were denied right to vote and other political rights, children's rights continued to be usurped. Today as was the case then we ponder over the role of the state as both the guardian of basic rights and as the behemoth against which one's rights need to be defended. (Ishay: 2004:8)

The third Controversy centers on the extent of modern liberalisms indebtedness to socialist thought.

The nineteenth century industrial revolution and the growth of the labour movement opened the gates of freedom to previously marginalized individuals who challenged the classical liberal economic conception of social justice.

Theorists influenced by Karl Marx and other socialist thinkers concentrate on those rights that the state is responsible for providing. Emerging from Marx's concern for the welfare of industrialized labor, the duty of states is to advance the well-being of their citizens, the right of the citizens is to benefit from these socio-economic advances. This view emphasizes minimum material rights that the state must provide to individuals. Individuals have the right to education, health care, social security, and housing. Without those guarantees, socialist theorists believe political and civil rights are meaningless. The socialist states of the former Soviet Bloc, as well as many European social welfare states ranked economic and social rights as highly as or more highly than political and civil rights. (Karns and Mingst: 2005:417)

Despite the important socialist contribution to the human rights discourse, the human rights legacy of the socialist and especially Marxist tradition is today widely dismissed, bearing in mind the atrocities that have been committed by communist regimes in the name of human rights. (Ishay: 2004:9)

The fourth controversy is the contentious debate on universal human rights versus cultural relativism.

One of the most intense debates within the human rights community is the one putting universalists of liberal or socialist persuasions against cultural relativists. The notions of right to self-determination, as defined by various international bill of rights, fails to specify which nationality or group should end up being favored over another when their claims conflict. More specifically there is a division between liberal and developing world rights. That division is based on the assumptions that western values are associated largely with individual civil and political rights, whereas people in developing countries emphasize rights related to the welfare of groups consistent with their cultural and religious traditions. (Ishay:2004:10,11)

In recent years, the debate over universal rights versus cultural relativism was reopened by a group of developing states, including China, Colombia, Cuba, Indonesia, Iran, Iraq etc. They argued that the principles in the Universal Declaration and other human rights documents represented western values that were being imposed on them and that the west was interfering in their internal affairs with its own definition of human rights.

The debate over universality versus cultural relativism also engages particularly sensitive issues with respect to religion, culture, women's status, protection of children, family planning, female circumcision etc. The debate also calls into question key principles, namely sovereignty and non interference in the domestic affairs of states. Acceptance of the universalist position with respect to human rights justifies interference in the affairs of others and threatens national sovereignty, while regionalization or particularization of human rights norms provides and umbrella of protection. This is one of the reasons why enforcement of human rights standards remains so problematic. (Karns and Mingst: 2005:417,419)

The fifth controversy centers on tensions between security and human rights.

Human rights must be seen, according to this view, at best as subordinate to security objectives, at worst as antithetical to security. Indeed, the emergency Patriot Act signed by President George Bush six weeks after the World Trade Centre and Pentagon attacks shows the fragility of such freedoms in times of war, as does increased support for some repressive regimes in the name of the war on terror. (Ishay:2004:12)

The sixth controversy revolves on the issue whether globalization is a boon or a bane from a human rights perspective.

Is globalization promoting or undermining human rights prospects? While there is clear evidence that globalization coincides with a widening gap between the rich and the poor within societies and between the rich and poor countries, the information age has redefined and created new spatial opportunities for human rights. With the globalization of the economy and communications and the emergence of developing post-colonial states, new rights have been added to the human rights corpus. These include rights to a healthy environment, to sustainable development, to culture, to immigration, and to political asylum.

Yet, even as rights are redefined and widened, how can we effectively protect the rights of workers and the less privileged when the state is ever more vulnerable to market pressures and more constrained in its role as a buffer against the ill effects of global economic forces? At a time when there is widening agreement that sovereignty should not protect regimes that stifle human rights, should international human rights monitoring agencies be further empowered? If so, can these agencies maintain their effectiveness when democratic forces at the national level may be weakening, nationalism is rampant and the private realm is under tighter control? (Ishay: 2004:13)

In this context, this article attempts to understand the process of institutionalizing human rights at the international level. Specifically, the role of the United Nations in the realm of human rights through standard setting, promotional, monitoring and enforcement measures are examined in the ensuing units.

## II

### United Nations and Human Rights

Intergovernmental organizations (IGO) in particular the UN and Nongovernmental organizations (NGO) have played key roles in the process of globalizing human rights. They have been central to establishing the norms, institutions, mechanisms and activities for giving effect to this powerful idea that certain rights are universal. (Karns and Mingst: 2005:419)

The UN charter adopted a broad view of human rights and placed promotion of human rights among the central purposes of the new organization. (Karns and Mingst: 2005:424)

### Human Rights and the UN Charter

The global movement of human rights is founded on and inspired by the UN Charter. The Charter was the first universal multilateral treaty to embody human rights concern in its provision. The charter is among other things, a human rights instrument. (Vijapur and Kumar: 1999:4).

The UN Charter took a major step beyond the League of Nations Covenant with respect to human rights. The Preamble reaffirmed "faith in fundamental human rights, in the dignity and worth of the human person, in the equal rights of men and women and of nations large and small".

### Human Rights were Referred Seven Times in the UN Charter.

Article 1(3) provided that, one of the four purposes of the organization is the promotion and encouragement of human rights and fundamental freedoms of all without distinction as to race, sex, language or religion. Article 13 Para 1(b) directed the General Assembly to initiate studies and make recommendations in this regard. The Economic and Social Council was given the same function under Article 62. More than any other provision of the Charter, Article 55 describes clearly and expressly the extensive purposes of the UN in the field of human rights. These included "respect for the principles of equal rights and self determination of peoples", promotion of "higher standards of living, full employment, and conditions of economic and social progress and development; solutions of international economic, social, health and related problems", and international cultural and educational cooperation; and the "universal respect for, and observance of human rights for all". Article 56 contained a "Pledge" of member states for taking joint action in cooperation with the UN for the achievement of these goals. Article 68 provides that the ECOSOC should create a permanent Commission on Human Rights. Lastly, Article 76 (c) provided that the human rights and fundamental freedoms of persons living in trust territories be encouraged. (Vijapur and Kumar: 1999:4)

## Setting Human Rights Standards and Norms

In just over fifty years, an international human rights regime has emerged that has articulated norms and standards in human rights and codified these standards in treaties, legal decisions and practices.

The UN's core role in the international human rights regime is its activity in defining and elaborating what constitutes initially protected rights. Its initial action was the Universal Declaration of Human Rights (UDHR). ( Karns and Mingst: 2005: 428)

## Universal Declaration of Human Rights (UDHR) - Significance and Provisions:

In 1946, the UN established a Commission on Human Rights (CHR) which started work on an International Bill of Rights consisting of a UDHR and the two Covenants. In the first stage of this program, the Commission, during 1946-48, drafted and recommended to the Assembly the Universal Declaration of Human Rights, which was unanimously adopted by it(as Resolution 217(III) A) on 10th December 1948.

It catalogued almost all important rights- both civil and political and economic, social and cultural rights- which were not defined in the UN charter. Though it is a non-binding instrument, it has acquired moral and legal status. It is recognized in International Law as customary law. The preamble of the Declaration points out its significant feature. It states that the individual, not the state or the government is "the foundation of freedom, justice and peace in the world." (Vijapur and Kumar: 1999:5)

Rene Cassin one of the main drafters of the UDHR identified the four pillars of the Declaration as "dignity, liberty, equality and brotherhood". The twenty seven articles of the Declaration were divided among these four pillars. Each of the pillars represents a major historical milestone. The first, covered in the first two articles of the Declaration, stands for human dignity, which is shared by all individuals regardless of race, religion, creed, nationality, social origin or sex. The second, specified in Article 3-19 of the Declaration, invokes civil liberties and other liberal rights that were fought for during the enlightenment. The third, delineated in articles 20-26, addresses rights related to political, social and economic equity and championed during the industrial revolution. The fourth outlined in Articles 27-28, focuses on rights associated with communal and national solidarity as advocated during the late nineteenth century and early twentieth century and throughout the post-colonial era. (Ishay:2004:3,4)

## UN Covenants on Human Rights

Following the adoption of the Declaration, the UN members turned towards the drafting of the rest of the International Bill of Rights. During the drafting stage, the General Assembly decided to divide the rights enumerated in the declaration into two legal instruments: (i) The International Covenant on Civil and Political Rights (ICCPR) embracing the traditional civil and political rights recognized in western societies and cultures, and (ii) The International Covenant on Economic, Social and Cultural Rights (ICESCR) to satisfy the aspirations of the socialist and third world societies. Also, an (First) Optional Protocol to the Civil and Political Rights granted right to petition to the individual. (Vijapur and Kumar:1999:13) For its effective functioning it was eventually agreed that the complaint should be looked at by a social working group. These so called 1503 procedures came into effect from 1973 onwards. However the procedures were long and cumbersome. (Luard: 1994:71, 72)

The provisions of the ICCPR were meant to be implemented immediately whereas those of the ICESCR were meant to be achieved progressively through long range education, planning and promotion. With the adoption of these Covenants in 1966 and other relevant instruments, it can be said that a solid legal foundation of human rights law has now been laid down for application at all levels of society: local, national and international.

Both the Covenants entered into force in early 1976- almost a decade after their adoption. Among all the fundamental human rights contained in these Covenants, the right of self-determination of peoples, though a collective right, has acquired the first place. This right is contained in Article 1 of both the Covenants.

## ICCPR

The ICCPR sets out the following rights(under Articles 6-27) : right to life; freedom from torture and inhuman treatment ;freedom from slavery and forced labour; the right to liberty and security; the right of detained persons to be treated with humanity; freedom from imprisonment of debt; freedom of movement and of choice of residence; freedom of aliens from arbitrary expulsion; the right to a fair trial; protection against retroactivity of the criminal law; the right to recognition as a person before law; the right to privacy ;freedom of thought, conscience and religion; freedom of opinion and expression; prohibition of propaganda for war and of incitement to national, racial or religious hatred; the right of peaceful assembly; freedom of association; the right to marry and found a family; the rights of the child; political rights; equality before the law and the rights of the minorities.

## ICESCR

The ICESCR provides a detailed list of rights (under Article 6-15) to be protected by States Parties. These include: the right to work; the right to just and favourable conditions of work including fair wages, equal pay for equal work and holidays with pay; the right to form and join trade unions, including the right to strike; the right to social security; protection of the family, including special assistance for mothers and children; the right to an adequate standard of living, including adequate food, clothing and housing and the continuous improvement of living conditions; the right to the highest attainable standard of physical and mental health; the right to education, primary education being compulsory and free for all, and secondary and higher education generally accessible to all and the right to participate in cultural life and enjoy the benefits of scientific progress.

The International Bill was expanded with the adoption in 1989 of the Second Optional Protocol to ICCPR aiming at the abolition of the death penalty. This Protocol entered into force on 11th July 1991. By August 1998, it was ratified by 33 states. (Vijapur and Kumar: 1999:13, 14)The Covenants and the other human rights treaties exemplify the standard setting character of the UN's role in Human rights.

A Convention on Genocide was drafted and the crime of genocide was defined as actions intended to destroy in whole or in part, a nation, ethnic, racial or religious group as such. A new Convention on Slavery, the slave trade and institution and practices similar to the old Slavery Convention of 1926 was adopted and came into force in 1957. Number of studies was conducted in matters regarding discrimination in education, in employment and administration. To make all the Conventions and Declarations effective in 1956, ECOSOC asked all delegations to submit every three years reports describing developments and progress achieved in their own country in the field of human rights. Another breakthrough was with the conclusion in 1966 of the International Convention on the Elimination of All Forms of Racial Discrimination. (Luard: 1994:71-72)

Other Conventions adopted by the UN over the years include subjects like women, torture, refugees, apartheid and various forms of discrimination. A list of UN Conventions and Declarations adopted over the years is given in the Table below.

**Table: UN Conventions on Human Rights**

**Charter of the United Nations**

**The International Bill of Human Rights**

- Universal Declaration of Human Rights 1948
- International Covenant on Economic, Social and Cultural Rights 1966
- International Covenant on Civil and Political Rights 1966
- Optional Protocol to the International Covenant on Civil and Political Rights
- Second Optional Protocol to the International Covenant on Civil and Political Rights, aiming at the abolition of the death penalty

**The Core International Human Rights Instruments and their Monitoring Bodies**

There are nine core international human rights treaties. Each of these treaties has established a committee of experts to monitor implementation of the treaty provisions by its States parties. Some of the treaties are supplemented by optional protocols dealing with specific concerns.

| | | Date | Monitoring Body |
|---|---|---|---|
| ICERD | International Convention on the Elimination of All Forms of Racial Discrimination | 21 Dec 1965 | CERD |
| ICCPR | International Covenant on Civil and Political Rights | 16 Dec 1966 | CCPR |
| ICESCR | International Covenant on Economic, Social and Cultural Rights | 16 Dec 1966 | CESCR |
| CEDAW | Convention on the Elimination of All Forms of Discrimination against Women | 18 Dec 1979 | CEDAW |
| CAT | Convention against Torture and Other Cruel, Inhuman or Degrading Treatment or Punishment | 10 Dec 1984 | CAT |
| CRC | Convention on the Rights of the Child | 20 Nov 1989 | CRC |
| ICRMW | International Convention on the Protection of the Rights of All Migrant Workers and Members of Their Families | 18 Dec 1990 | CMW |
| | International Convention for the Protection of All Persons from Enforced Disappearance | 20 Dec 2006 | |
| CRPD | Convention on the Rights of Persons with Disabilities | 13 Dec 2006 | CRPD |
| ICESCR - OP | Optional Protocol of the Covenant on Economic, Social and Cultural Rights | 10 Dec 2008 | CESCR |

| | | | |
|---|---|---|---|
| ICCPR-OP1 | Optional Protocol to the International Covenant on Civil and Political Rights | 16 Dec 1966 | HRC |
| ICCPR-OP2 | Second Optional Protocol to the International Covenant on Civil and Political Rights, aiming at the abolition of the death penalty | 15 Dec 1989 | HRC |
| OP-CEDAW | Optional Protocol to the Convention on the Elimination of Discrimination against Women | 10 Dec 1999 | CEDAW |
| OP-CRC-AC | Optional protocol to the Convention on the Rights of the Child on the involvement of children in armed conflict | 25 May 2000 | CRC |
| OP-CRC-SC | Optional protocol to the Convention on the Rights of the Child on the sale of children, child prostitution and child pornography | 25 May 2000 | CRC |
| OP-CAT | Optional Protocol to the Convention against Torture and Other Cruel, Inhuman or Degrading Treatment or Punishment | 18 Dec 2002 | CAT |
| OP-CRPD | Optional Protocol to the Convention on the Rights of Persons with Disabilities | 12 Dec 2006 | CRPD |

**Universal Human Rights Instruments**

In addition to the International Bill of Rights and the core human rights treaties, there are many other universal instruments relating to human rights. A non-exhaustive selection is listed below. The legal status of these instruments varies: declarations, principles, guidelines, standard rules and recommendations have no binding legal effect, but such instruments have an undeniable moral force and provide practical guidance to States in their conduct; covenants, statutes, protocols and conventions are legally-binding for those States that ratify or accede to them.

**World Conference on Human Rights and Millennium Assembly**

- Vienna Declaration and Programme of Action
- United Nations Millennium Declaration

**The Right of Self-Determination**

- United Nations Declaration on the Granting of Independence to Colonial Countries and Peoples
- General Assembly resolution 1803 (XVII) of 14 December 1962, "Permanent sovereignty over natural resources"
- International Convention against the Recruitment, Use, Financing and Training of Mercenaries

**Rights of Indigenous Peoples and Minorities**

- Declaration on the Rights of Indigenous Peoples
- Indigenous and Tribal Peoples Convention, 1989 (No. 169)
- Declaration on the Rights of Persons Belonging to National or Ethnic, Religious and Linguistic Minorities

**Prevention of Discrimination**

- Equal Remuneration Convention, 1951 (No. 100)
- Discrimination (Employment and Occupation) Convention, 1958 (No. 111)
- International Convention on the Elimination of all Forms of Racial Discrimination (ICERD)
- Declaration on Race and Racial Prejudice
- Convention against Discrimination in Education
- Protocol Instituting a Conciliation and Good Offices Commission to be responsible for seeking a settlement of any disputes which may arise between States Parties to the Convention against Discrimination in Education
- Declaration on the Elimination of All Forms of Intolerance and of Discrimination Based on Religion or Belief
- World Conference against Racism, 2001 (Durban Declaration and Programme of Action)

**Rights of Women**

- Convention on the Elimination of All Forms of Discrimination against Women (CEDAW)
- Optional Protocol to the Convention on the Elimination of All Forms of Discrimination against Women (CEDAW-OP)
- Declaration on the Protection of Women and Children in Emergency and Armed Conflict
- Declaration on the Elimination of Violence against Women

**Rights of the Child**

- Convention on the Rights of the Child (CRC)
- Optional Protocol to the Convention on the Rights of the Child on the sale of children, child prostitution and child pornography (CRC-OPSC)
- Optional Protocol to the Convention on the Rights of the Child on the involvement of children in armed conflict (CRC-OPAC)
- Minimum Age Convention, 1973 (No. 138)
- Worst Forms of Child Labour Convention, 1999 (No. 182)

**Rights of Older Persons**

- United Nations Principles for Older Persons

**Rights of Persons with Disabilities**

- Declaration on the Rights of Mentally Retarded Persons
- Declaration on the Rights of Disabled Persons
- Principles for the protection of persons with mental illness and the improvement of mental health care
- Standard Rules on the Equalization of Opportunities for Persons with Disabilities

**Human Rights in the Administration of Justice: Protection of Persons Subjected to Detention or Imprisonment**

- Standard Minimum Rules for the Treatment of Prisoners
- Basic Principles for the Treatment of Prisoners
- Body of Principles for the Protection of All Persons under Any Form of Detention or Imprisonment
- United Nations Rules for the Protection of Juveniles Deprived of their Liberty
- Declaration on the Protection of All Persons from Being Subjected to Torture and Other Cruel, Inhuman or Degrading Treatment or Punishment
- Convention against Torture and Other Cruel, Inhuman or Degrading Treatment or Punishment (CAT)
- Optional Protocol to the Convention against Torture and Other Cruel, Inhuman or Degrading Treatment or Punishment (OPCAT)
- Principles of Medical Ethics relevant to the Role of Health Personnel, particularly Physicians, in the Protection of Prisoners and Detainees against Torture and Other Cruel, Inhuman or Degrading Treatment or Punishment
- Principles on the Effective Investigation and Documentation of Torture and Other Cruel, Inhuman or Degrading Treatment or Punishment
- Safeguards guaranteeing protection of the rights of those facing the death penalty
- Code of Conduct for Law Enforcement Officials

- Basic Principles on the Use of Force and Firearms by Law Enforcement Officials
- United Nations Standard Minimum Rules for Non-custodial Measures (The Tokyo Rules)
- United Nations Standard Minimum Rules for the Administration of Juvenile Justice (The Beijing Rules)
- Guidelines for Action on Children in the Criminal Justice System
- United Nations Guidelines for the Prevention of Juvenile Delinquency (The Riyadh Guidelines)
- Declaration of Basic Principles of Justice for Victims of Crime and Abuse of Power
- Basic Principles on the Independence of the Judiciary
- Basic Principles on the Role of Lawyers
- Guidelines on the Role of Prosecutors
- Principles on the Effective Prevention and Investigation of Extra-legal, Arbitrary and Summary Executions
- Declaration on the Protection of All Persons from Enforced Disappearance
- Basic Principles and Guidelines on the Right to a Remedy and Reparation
- International Convention for the Protection of All Persons from Enforced Disappearance (not yet into force)

**Social Welfare, Progress and Development**

- Declaration on Social Progress and Development
- Universal Declaration on the Eradication of Hunger and Malnutrition
- Declaration on the Use of Scientific and Technological Progress in the Interests of Peace and for the Benefit of Mankind
- Declaration on the Right of Peoples to Peace
- Declaration on the Right to Development
- Universal Declaration on the Human Genome and Human Rights
- Universal Declaration on Cultural Diversity

**Promotion and Protection of Human Rights**

- Principles relating to the status of national institutions (The Paris Principles)
- Declaration on the Right and Responsibility of Individuals, Groups and Organs of Society to Promote and Protect Universally Recognized Human Rights and Fundamental Freedoms

**Marriage**

- Convention on Consent to Marriage, Minimum Age for Marriage and Registration of Marriages
- Recommendation on Consent to Marriage, Minimum Age for Marriage and Registration of Marriages

**Right to Health**

- Declaration of Commitment on HIV/AIDS

**Right to Work and to Fair Conditions of Employment**

- Employment Policy Convention, 1964 (No. 122)

**Freedom of Association**

- Freedom of Association and Protection of the Right to Organise Convention, 1948 (No. 87)
- Right to Organise and Collective Bargaining Convention, 1949 (No. 98)

**Slavery, Slavery-Like Practices and Forced Labour**

- Slavery Convention
- Protocol amending the Slavery Convention signed at Geneva on 25 September 1926
- Supplementary Convention on the Abolition of Slavery, the Slave Trade, and Institutions and Practices Similar to Slavery
- Forced Labour Convention, 1930 (No. 29)
- Abolition of Forced Labour Convention, 1957 (No. 105)
- Convention for the Suppression of the Traffic in Persons and of the Exploitation of the Prostitution of Others
- Protocol to Prevent, Suppress and Punish Trafficking in Persons, Especially Women and Children, supplementing the United Nations Convention against Transnational Organized Crime

**Rights of Migrants**

- International Convention on the Protection of the Rights of All Migrant Workers and Members of Their Families (ICPMW)
- Protocol against the Smuggling of Migrants by Land, Sea and Air, supplementing the United Nations Convention against Transnational Organized Crime

**Nationality, Statelessness, Asylum and Refugees**

- Convention on the Reduction of Statelessness
- Convention relating to the Status of Stateless Persons
- Convention relating to the Status of Refugees
- Protocol relating to the Status of Refugees
- Declaration on the Human Rights of Individuals who are not Nationals of the Country in which They Live

**War Crimes and Crimes Against Humanity, Including Genocide**

- Convention on the Prevention and Punishment of the Crime of Genocide

- Convention on the Non-Applicability of Statutory Limitations to War Crimes and Crimes against Humanity
- Principles of international co-operation in the detection, arrest, extradition and punishment of persons guilty of war crimes and crimes against humanity
- Statute of the International Tribunal for the Former Yugoslavia
- Statute of the International Tribunal for Rwanda
- Rome Statute of the International Criminal Court

**Humanitarian Law**

- Geneva Convention relative to the Treatment of Prisoners of War
- Geneva Convention relative to the Protection of Civilian Persons in Time of War
- Protocol Additional to the Geneva Conventions of 12 August 1949, and relating to the Protection of Victims of International Armed Conflicts (Protocol I)
- Protocol Additional to the Geneva Conventions of 12 August 1949, and relating to the Protection of Victims of Non-International Armed Conflicts (Protocol II)

Source: http://www2.ohchr.org/english/law/

These same standards are also found in national constitutions, legal documents and court cases, often referring directly the major UN standard setting documents. (Karns and Mingst: 2005:429)

**Three Generations of Human Rights Standards**

Because human rights standards have evolved from diverse traditions and over time, it is customary to refer to three generations of human rights.

**1st Generation human rights** are those associated with political and civil rights. These are clearly linked to western liberalism.

**2nd Generation human rights** build upon the socialist view of economic and social rights.

**3rd Generation human rights** centre on the idea that certain groups, including indigenous peoples, colonial peoples, women and children have collective rights such as self determination and economic and social development. Recently, some theorists have added the right to a safe environment, the right to peace and human security, and the right to live in a democracy. (Karns and Mingst: 2005:431,432)

III

**Monitoring Human Rights**

Monitoring the implementation of human rights standards requires procedures for receiving complaints of violations from affected individuals or interested groups and reports of state practice. It may also be accompanied by the power to comment on reports, make recommendations to states, appoint working groups or special rapporteurs, and vote on resolutions of condemnation. (Karns and Mingst: 2005:433)

**United Nations Human Rights Commission**

The principal body of the UN that is responsible for human rights monitoring was the Human Rights Commission established as one of the Commissions with special responsibilities set up under ECOSOC. Under it was placed a Sub Commission on Prevention of Discrimination and Protection of Minorities. (Luard: 1994:71, 72)

In 1967, the 53 member Commission on Human Rights was empowered for the first time to examine gross violations in South Africa and Southern Rhodesia. Further investigations against specific states followed, setting a new precedent for monitoring in 1970. ECOSOC Resolution 1503 authorized the Commission to undertake confidential investigations of individual complaints that suggest "a consistent pattern of gross and reliably attested violations". This procedure, however, has proved weak: the examination occurs in private and terminates with only a report to the Commission. Nonetheless, the Commission significantly expanded its activities during the 1970's creating working groups to study specific civil rights problems such as forced disappearances, torture, religious discrimination and the situation in Chile after the 1972 coup.

The Sub Commission on the Prevention of Discrimination and Protection of Mincrities also was reactivated in the 1970's. It has the advantage of being composed of independent experts and plays a key role in screening petitions from individuals and NGOs prior to consideration by the Commission. In 1999, its name was changed to the Sub- Commission on the Promotion and Protection of Human Rights reflecting its broader agenda. (Karns and Mingst: 2005:433,434)

Particularly important are the Commission's "global" or "thematic" procedures involving working groups and special rapporteurs on a wide range of topics, including disappearances, torture, summary or arbitrary executions, and most recently, human rights defenders, food, housing, and indigenous peoples. In recent years, about twenty separate thematic initiatives have been taking place at any given time. The Commission has also given considerable attention to particular vulnerable groups, especially women, children, indigenous people, minorities, displaced persons, migrant workers and human rights defenders.

The Commission also addresses human rights situations in individual countries, both in public during its annual session- situations in more than two dozen countries are discussed each year- and through the activities of country rapporteurs and representatives, who have examined situations even in high-profile countries such as Guatemala, Iran, Iraq, occupied Palestinian territories, and Burma.

The limitations of the procedures adopted by the Commission are tragically illustrated by the case of Rwanda. Rwanda was discussed confidentially under the 1503 procedure in 1992 and 1993. In addition, the report of the special rapporteur on extrajudicial executions was discussed in the spring of 1994, just before the outbreak of the genocide. In it, the special rapporteur confirmed reports of official involvement in the massacre of civilians and explicitly suggested that genocidal acts were already occurring. Nonetheless, it was not until May 25-seven weeks after the genocide began, almost a month after the Secretary General called for Security Council action, and even a week after the Security Council authorized a new peacekeeping force-that the Commission even appointed a country rapporteur. (Donnelly:2005:132,133)

The Human Rights Commission drew public attention in May 2001 when the US was voted off the Commission for the first time since the panels founding. Those who voted against the US, including some of its allies, did so because of perceived US lack of support for the UN, its continued support of Israel, and its efforts to single out China and Cuba for their human rights abuses. The Commission again drew strong adverse publicity in 2002 when Libya was elected chair, a set up that made the body's credibility questionable. (Karns and Mingst: 2005:425)

Inspite of several limitations, the Commission does serve a variety of useful roles in the area of promotion of human rights, particularly as a source of authoritative information and publicity about human rights practices in any country of the world. Furthermore its role in developing international human rights norms remains vital. In many ways the Commission is at the heart of the global human rights regime. (Donnelly: 2005:133)

## Human Rights Committee

Further initiatives in UN monitoring activities accompanied the entry into force of specific treaties, many of which required states to submit reports of their progress towards implementation. The General Assembly has established six Committees of independent experts elected by the parties to each treaty to review the reports. One of the most thorough is the Human Rights Committee designed to process state reports under the Covenant on Civil and Political Rights. It conducts open meetings, thus exposing states human rights practices and its own actions to publicity by the media. The Committee cannot take a binding decision against a persistently offending state.

In 1992, the Human Rights Committee decided to publish its general conclusions after review of states reports, thus removing the veil of secrecy. It has also appointed rapporteurs and special missions to deal with massive human rights violations in countries such as Rwanda, Georgia, Colombia, the former Yugoslavia and Democratic Republic of the Congo. (Karns and Mingst: 2005:434)

## Human Rights Council

In recent years, a serious effort to mainstream human rights in all aspects of the UN's work has started. The Report of the High-Level Panel on Threats, Challenges, and Change underscores the importance of the role of the Commission on Human Rights as the principal intergovernmental machinery responsible for human rights within the UN system. It concluded that in recent years, the Commission's capacity to perform the central mission of the United Nations to protect human rights, a mission reaffirmed by the Millennium Declaration, has been undermined due to eroding credibility and professionalism. It also recommended its reform into a new Human Rights Council. (Banerjee and Sharma: 2007:186)

The Human Rights Council is an inter-governmental body within the UN system made up of 47 States responsible for strengthening the promotion and protection of human rights around the globe. The Council was created by the UN General Assembly on 15 March 2006 with the main purpose of addressing situations of human rights violations and make recommendations on them.

One year after its first meeting, on 18 June 2007, the Council adopted its "Institution-building package" providing elements to guide it in its future work. Among the elements is the new Universal Periodic Review mechanism which will assess the human rights situations in all UN Member States. Other features include a new Advisory Committee which serves as the Council's "think tank" providing it with expertise and advice on thematic human rights and the revised Complaints Procedure mechanism which allows individuals and organizations to bring complaints about human rights violations to the attention of the Council. The Human Rights Council also continues to work closely with the UN Special Procedures established by the former Commission on Human Rights and assumed by the Council.

(http://www2.ohchr.org/english/bodies/hrcouncil/)

At present, the following actors play the most important roles in the promotion and protection of human rights: a) governments b) legislative and judicial organs of the states, c) the United Nations System, d) international and national non-governmental organizations, and e) the private sector and labour unions. (Banerjee and Sharma:2007:187)

## IV

## Promoting Human Rights

Translating norms and rhetoric into actions that go beyond stopping violations to changing long term attitudes and behaviour is the challenge of promoting human rights. These efforts have been scattered throughout the UN system and include recent activities in support of democratization as well as many economic and social programs.

UN Development activities and other operational programs of the specialized agencies have linked the language of human rights with development activities. The right to development was endorsed by the 1993 Vienna Conference on Human Rights. The World Bank's promotion of good governance includes political and civil rights. UNDP's annual Human Development Reports have increasingly focused on rights related issues, including democratization in the 2002 report. The Millennium Development Goals represent an amalgam of all the three generations of rights.

The UN has played a far more active role in Human rights promotion since the end of the Cold War. The UN has promoted democratization and associated political rights through its electoral assistance program such as in Namibia, Nicaragua, Cambodia, and Mozambique. These programs have provided aid to more than twenty countries in organizing and holding free and fair elections. (Karns and Mingst: 2005:440)

**UN Electoral Assistance in Namibia**

Namibia was the only territory formerly under League of Nations mandate that was not brought within the UN trusteeship system. In 1966, the General Assembly decided to terminate the League of Nations mandate over the territory and, the following year, the Assembly established a Council for Namibia with the ostensible purpose of administering the territory until independence would be achieved. In 1969, the Security Council recognized the General Assembly decision to terminate the mandate and the following year the Council declared that the continued presence of the South African authorities in Namibia was illegal. In 1971, the Security Council agreed with, and the General Assemble welcomed, an advisory opinion of the International Court of Justice that South Africa's presence in Namibia was illegal. South Africa, as the former mandatory power, had pledged itself to respect human rights and fundamental freedoms for all. To introduce restrictions based on national or ethnic origin constituted a denial of fundamental human rights and was a flagrant violation of the UN Charter. In 1978, the Security Council asked the Secretary-General to appoint a special representative to ensure early independence for Namibia through free elections under UN supervision and control.

Following a decision of the Security Council of 27 July 1978, the Secretary-General appointed Martti Ahtisaari as his Special Representative. South Africa and SWAPO (The South West Africa People's Organization) were to observe a ceasefire. An Administrative-General would be appointed by South Africa to work with the UN Special Representative and to maintain law and order during the transitional period. A UN Transition Assistance Group (UNTAG) would be established with both military and civilian elements, acting with complete impartiality in monitoring the cessation of hostilities and ensuring free and fair elections. This plan was approved by the Security Council in resolution 435. This became the benchmark for the Security Council's role regarding the decolonization of Namibia, though it was to take more than a decade before the Ahtisaari plan would be implemented.

It was subsequently agreed that implementation of Security Council resolution 435 would begin on 1 April 1989. An election for a constituent assembly was held in 1989. The Special Representative of the Secretary-General, with the assistance of the civilian and military personnel of the UN Transition Assistance Group (UNTAG), was to certify whether all stages of the electoral process had been free and fair.

There were 215 fixed and 143 mobile polling stations, monitored by the UN's electoral supervisors and civilian police. Just over 97 per cent of the registered voters cast their ballots for the 72 seats in the constituent assembly. SWAPO won 41 seats, the multi-ethnic Democratic Turnhalle Alliance, 21: SWAPO's strongest support was in Ovamboland, where it polled more than 90 per cent of the votes. Ahtisaari certified that the electoral process had gone smoothly and, at every stage, had been free and fair. The following February the constituent assembly adopted a constitution for Namibia. Namibia became independent and was admitted to UN membership in 1990. (Bailey: 1994:6-9, 31-35)

**The High Commissioner for Human Rights**

In 1993, the UN took the key step of creating the office of the High Commissioner for Human Rights (UNHCHR) to centralize responsibilities and provide a visible international spokesperson for human rights. (Karns and Mingst: 2005:440)

The office takes an investigation-advocacy approach. The High Commissioner has the global reach of the Commission, without its cumbersome procedures. Like the special rapporteurs, the High Commissioner may deal directly with governments to seek improved respect for internationally recognized human rights- but with the added advantage of an explicit mandate to deal with all governments on all issues. Additionally, the High Commissioner holds the office in her personal capacity, not as a representative of any State. (Donnelly: 2005:135)

The office is the focal point for the promotion of human rights: it provides advisory services to states that request them, including setting up field presences to monitor situations , it seeks to coordinate the UN system wide human rights activities and tries to rationalize and strengthen the UN machinery in the field of human rights. It supports human rights education programs. (Karns and Mingst: 2005: 440,441)

## V

**Enforcement Measures**

Of the various governance tasks in human rights, enforcement is the most problematic largely because states compliance is key and international institutions have limited capacity to compel compliance.

UN enforcement authority is found in chapter VII of the Charter. Under that provision, if the Security Council determines that human rights violations threaten or breach international peace, it has the authority to take enforcement actions. The two Cold War cases of enforcement both involved gross violations of the rights of black majorities by white minority governments one in the breakaway British colony of Southern Rhodesia and the other in South Africa. In the first case, the Security Council imposed economic sanctions, seeking to isolate the white minority regime and cause a change in behaviour. In the second, the Security Council imposed an arms embargo. The sanctions weakened the minority regimes, but did not directly change their policies nor force either government from power.

Enforcement action may also involve the use of military force. The post-Cold War era witnessed a series of unprecedented enforcement actions authorized under chapter VII to deal with ethnic conflicts that produced some of the worst human rights violations and toughest policy dilemmas for states, IGOs and NGOs. During the 1990's the Security Council and OAS imposed sanctions on Haiti to force a restoration of a democratically elected government. Ethnic conflict and massive human rights violations in the former Yugoslavia, Rwanda and Somalia also led to UN sanctions. (Karns and Mingst: 2005:444)

**UN Enforcement Measures in Somalia**

On the basis of reports from the Secretary-General, the Security Council passed a series of resolutions citing chapters VII and VIII of the Charter, calling for the provision of humanitarian assistance, imposing 'a general and complete' arms embargo, urging the Somali factions to respect international humanitarian law, to observe a cease-fire, to attend a conference for national reconciliation and unity, and [illegible]ng a UN operation in Somalia (UNOSOM) to monitor the cease fire and provide security for the movement of humanitarian principles.

These resolutions were noteworthy in two respects. First, internal conditions within a State were said to threaten international peace and security, thus providing the Security Council with a basis for taking binding decisions under Chapter VII of the Charter. Secondly, The Council expressly cited Chapter VIII of the Charter regarding regional agencies and arrangements, thus providing for cooperation with the Organization of African Unity, the League of Arab States and the Islamic Conference. In the light of the Secretary-General's report on the breakdown of law and order in Somalia, the Council condemned all violations of international humanitarian law and declared that those who ordered or committed such acts would be held individually responsible. It may be noted that an expert appointed by the Human Rights Commission 'received allegations as to human rights violations committed by the United Nations forces in Somalia'. (Bailey: 1994:84-85)

Humanitarian interventions have involved the use of UN or regional peacekeeping forces to protect relief workers, guard medical and food supplies, run convoys, shield civilians from further violence, shelter displaced people and provide safe havens.

Humanitarian interventions have been applied only selectively and not always successfully. The international community paid little attention to the brutal civil wars in Sudan, Liberia, and Sierra Leone, despite blatant human rights violations. Yet, it did choose to act in other situations, reflecting the increased importance of human rights norms in world politics. Many governments are suspicious of strengthening the UN, or any IGOs power to intervene in what many still regard as their domestic jurisdiction. Yet, the UN has set some important precedents for enforcements in the human rights field since the end of the Cold War. (Karns and Mingst: 2005:444,445)

## VI

### Conclusion

There has been remarkable progress in human rights global governance since World War II. The normative basis of international human rights has been established. Monitoring instruments are in place. Promotional activities include an expanding conception of what is considered human rights, including activities promoting women, children, refugees, and indigenous peoples, even though such activities may conflict with other societal and cultural values.(Karns and Mingst:2005:456)

The global human rights regime involves widely accepted substantive norms; authoritative multilateral standard setting procedures, considerable promotional activity, but very limited international implementation that rarely goes beyond mandatory reporting procedures. There is no significant international enforcement. Such normative strength and procedural weakness is not accidental but the result of conscious political decisions.

An international regime reflects states' collective vision of a problem and its solutions and their willingness to "fund" those solutions. In the area of human rights, this vision does not extend much beyond a politically weak moral interdependence. States are willing to "pay" very little in diminished national sovereignty to realize the benefits of cooperation. The result is a regime with extensive, coherent, and widely accepted norms but extremely limited international decision making powers-that is, a strong promotional regime.(Donnelly:2005: 135,138)

In a landmark study of the UN human rights treaty system, completed in 2001, Professor Anne F. Bayefsky comments, "the gap between universal rights and remedy has become inescapable and inexcusable, threatening the integrity of the international human rights regime. (Banerjee and Sharma: 2007:186)

Practicing human rights has, indeed, become a global enterprise. In the age of globalization protecting and promoting human rights is imperative.

Globalization has been both an impediment to the development of international human rights and a stimulus. Economic globalization has created more opportunities for MNCs to exploit cheap labour in developing countries. Economic globalization has also brought more attention to the vast economic disparities both in and between societies, disparities that undermine human rights. However, globalization of communication has meant that human rights abuses and atrocities are given widespread publicity, generating significant and often rapid responses. It has given NGOs and individuals a powerful new medium to broadcast their concerns, to create networks, and to take actions. It has created an international audience that is sensitized and ready to act on human rights issues. (Karns and Mingst: 2005:456,457)

A paradox- Globalization of Economics, Localization of Politics- bedevils the present global system. The need to conceptually reconcile and behaviourally harmonize human endeavour, within a new political culture and institutional arrangements reflecting the realities of changing times, are real. Throughout history, revolutionary moments occur when the rules that were valid for one age become obsolete and are challenged by the need for new norms and values that capture the needs of the day.(Banerjee and Sharma:2007:190)

UN human rights work must also be based more on increasing emphasis on human values, with the norms and standards being more and more internalized within societies rather than being seen as something imposed from outside. This requires a bottoms-up, introspective approach, rather than top-down and finger pointing one where everyone jumps at the violation of others, forgetting the problems within. When serious and systematic state-sanctioned violations take place, there has to be of course a process for the international community to act decisively to prevent serious atrocities being committed. In such a context, the following could be some of the critical functions of UN in the realm of human rights protection and promotion.

- Global human rights consciousness-building and education.
- Preparation of a global human rights report.
- Identification of cases of serious violations, and ways and means to improve the situation, including opportunities for introspection and self-appraisal at a more confidential level.
- Exchanging ideas on methods of redress, including sharing of best practices as well as assistance in capacity building.
- Carrying out an open process for bringing into global focus the most serious cases of persistent, systematic and state-sanctioned violations and prescribing possible sanctions.
- As a last resort, recommending decisive actions in order to exercise the responsibility to protect.

An innovative institutional mechanism, able to draw on the strengths of the government, legislature, judiciary, NGOs and the private sector for experience sharing, standard setting and norms building at the international level, and with outreach for information collection, dissemination and devolution downwards to the grassroots, could act as an effective global mechanism for a global culture of human rights. The Human Rights Council, as an upgraded version of the present Commission on Human Rights, would be a fitting exercise in enhancing the effectiveness of the UN human rights machinery to make it suitable for the 21st century world. (Banerjee and Sharma: 2007:188).

## References

Bailey, Sydney D (1994): *The UN Security Council and Human Rights*. Routledge, London.

Banerjee, Ajith M. and Sharma, Murari R (eds.) (2007): *Reinventing the United Nations*. Prentice Hall, New Delhi.

Basu, Rumki (1993): *The United Nations: Structure and Functions of an International Organization*. Sterling, New Delhi.

Diehl, Paul F. (ed.) (2005): *The Politics of Global Governance*. Viva, Mumbai.

Donnelly, Jack (2005): *Universal Human Rights in Theory and Practice*. Manas, New Delhi.

Ishay, Micheline R (2004): *The History of Human Rights: From Ancient Times to the Globalization Era*. Orient Longman, New Delhi.

Luard, Evan (1994): *The United Nations: How it Works and What it Does*. MacMillan, London.

Karns, Margaret P. and Mingst, Karen A (2005): *International Organizations: The Politics and Processes of Global Governance*. Viva, New Delhi.

Khare, Subhas Chandra (1977): *Human Rights and United Nations*. Metropolitan, New Delhi.

Perry, Michael J (1998): *The Idea of Human Rights: Four Inquiries*. Oxford, Oxford.

Rao, Digumarti Bhaskara (ed.) (2001): *Human Rights and the United Nations* (Part I). Discovery, New Delhi.

UN. 2004. *A More Secure World: Our Shared Responsibility, Report of the Secretary-General's High Level Panel on Threats, Challenges and Change*. New York, UN.

UNDP.2000. *Human Development Report*. Oxford, New York.

Vijapur, Abdulrahim P. and Kumar, Suresh (eds.) (1999): *Perspectives on Human Rights*. Manak, New Delhi.

Websites

http://www2.ohchr.org/english/law

http://www2.ohchr.org/english/bodies/hrcouncil

# 25

# THE FOURTH ESTATE AS THE WATCH-DOG OF HUMAN RIGHTS: SOME REFLECTIONS

**P. Faziluddin**

Journalism, in simple terms, is dessemination of latest information. And information both on the protection and on the denial of Human Rights is at the heart of journalism. For, democratic journalism is universally acclaimed as the guardian - angel of Human Rights.

Dissemination of information is vital to the survival of democracy for information is valued as freedom. Reliable information is real freedom. People without reliable information are people without real freedom. And so it is said that 'a democratic society without proliferation of information or without the means of seeking and acquiring information is described to be a farce or tragedy or both.

And what kind of information people are looking for? Horace Greeley of 'Tribune' used to tell his juniors: "Begin with the conception that the subject of deepest interest to the average human being is himself; next to that he is most interested in his neighbours." So what happens to his life and to the lives of others around him are always topics of deep interest to the common man.

In journalism it is said that the best of news is that which possesses the greatest degree of interest and significance to the largest number of people. Thus news is full of human affairs. And no journalist can ever afford to neglect stories of human interest and human rights.

Journalism is again considered to be "an instrument by which contemporary society orders and changes its ways towards a well-defined goal of general welfare". The American Society of Newspaper Editors declared that "the primary purpose of gathering and distributing news.... is to serve the general welfare". And general welfare can be ensured only byshow of respect to not only the lives but also the rights of one and all. Thus respect for the lives of others ie, respect for all kinds of Human Rights is the best part of good journalistic practice. That is how journalism and Human Rights become complementary.

'The Fourth Estate: Watch dog of Human Rights' is a very vast subject. Even an organization like AmnestyInternational' with national sections in 35 countries and individual membership in 75 countries and with an international secretariat of 110 people does not claim to have "the resources to undertake the comprehensive research that is needed on all countries about the Human Rights situations there. And if Amnesty International thinks like that, you can well guess the fate of the efforts of an ordinary individual who attempt to make an observation on this.

## Common Offences Against Human Rights

One of the most serious offences vis-a-vis Human Rights is the use of security forces and para-military groups as instruments of political murders. In some countries para-military forces are allowed to kidnap, torture and assassinate political opponents.

But in India, the government has not yet given cause for such allegations to be raised. Opposition parties and the press, as vigilant as always, have not yet raised any hue and cry in this respect. The government not only refrains from such misuse of the security forces, but often openly asserts that it will not use the defence forces to quell the violence perpetrated by the Naxalites in different states.

Imprisonment of political enemies, their prolonged detentions, ill-treatment of prisoners, poor prison conditions, absence of timely trial, denial of proper legal assistance, making mockery of legal procedures and other forms of brutal repression are rare in India and especially in Kerala. The government is not being subjected to accusations on most of these grounds. And the Indian Press and the Indian Media will not be lying low if and when such repressive measures are resorted to.

Government-sponsored torture is also practically something unheard of these days. The alertness that the media maintains against such violations and the reactions of the media to such violations are definitely the reasons behind such good records.

Violations of economic and social rights are subjects of repeated discussions in the media and reports subject them to quick remedial measures.

## Torture

The Universal Declaration of Human Rights, adopted by the United Nations in December 1948 states that torture is unacceptable. But torture persists and persists here also often with the knowledge of the authorities concerned.

The Indian media especially the Kerala media has been able to 'smell out' many such cases and justice was made to be extended to the victims of such cases-Many examples are there.

The declaration also affirms the right to life and states that no one shall be subjected to cruel, inhuman or degrading punishment.

But what about our police stations? Custodial deaths, police torture, late production before courts etc. are being reported. While such complaints are not few and far between, there are also reports of preferential or differential and discriminatory treatment being meted out to 'select' or political influential offenders.

Torture in family life, ie torture of wife by husband, of old parents by grown-up children, of differently abled people by close relations etc are regularly being highlighted and these reports get attention of the society focused on them.

Social ostracism / Ooruvilakku has become something unheard of now, primarily because of the splendid role played bythe media. eg: Bheemapalli case of the mid 80s.

**Fake Encounters Vis-a-Vis Terrorists**

Allegations are often vociferously raised aboutfake encounters against terrorists, especially against Islamic terrorists. Fears have been often expressed that a community as a whole is being suspected of being easily susceptible to fundamentalism and terrorism. When such fears have been expressed, the Indian media have highlighted them. Media reports have always helped to focus the attention of the government on them. Government too has acted promptly on such cases. And it is for all to see that such cries and expressions of fears are not at all heard in recent months.

Sometimes, organizations outside government control and even political parties violate Human Rights.

I have serious doubts whether the political murders and revenge murders especially at Kannur District are getting properly evaluated.

**Campus Violence**

Are the students in the campuses in Kerala free to express their opinions 'without fear'. Former UN General Secretary Day Hammarskjold said once: "Freedom from fear" could be said to sum up the whole philosophy of Human Rights."

How far are our campuses free from fear? What are the fear-creating factors there? Where fear rules, real academics suffer.

I feel media is not doing anything to dissipate the atmosphere of fear and violence in the campuses. A very well-planned and courageous campaign is needed here. Let us hope such a campaign for fear-free campuses in Kerala begins very soon.

Or what is the fun of our styling ourselves as the most literate and the most politically enlightened state if our younger generations cannot walk and talk freely in our campuses.

The Kerala society, particularly the population in the big cities and towns and more often the society in the capital city is being subjected to a special kind of Human Rights violation. In effect it is also one of the worst kinds of torture.

During Bandhs and Hartals, people are being subjected to a crude kind of enforced confinement to their homes much against there will, a totally undeserving imprisonment, a new form of house asrrest. On days of big processions, marches etc, people are being forced to suspend many of their fundamental freedoms and are being rendered incapable of using even the vital public services. Small groups, while demonstrating tread upon the fundamental rights of the vast majority.

Though such things happen repeatedly, may be that they have become almost inalienble part of the daily routine, the media has not begun to look at then as gross violations of fundamental human rights. Recently there were positive developments of the social conscientization of the destructive effects of Bandhs, but they were not carried forward to their logical ends. With the result, Kerala remains as a curious society where the rights of the vast silent majority is regularly and repeatedly being violated in the name of protecting not the fundamental but the marginal rights of a few. It never dawns on the people of Kerala that "no ones rights can be secured by the violation of the rights of others". And strangely enough the media here is giving up its time-honoured role of being a watch dog that bark at and alerts the society. Instead it becomes an unthinking and unfeeling participant/approver in this unhealthy process.

Former US President Harry S Truman once said: "In the cause of freedom, we have to battle for the rights of people with whom we do not agree; and whom, in many cases, we may not like. These people test the strength of the freedoms which protect all of us. It we do not defend their rights, we endanger our own."

In Kerala when can we hope for a movement, a popular voice that does not try to put down the dissenting and disagreeing voices, but on the other hand comes out to defend the dissent? Media occasionally does it, but I feel, very feebly only. And media should do more. It should seek to ensure that the freedoms that protect us survive all the tests that questions the strength of these freedoms.

One of the most distinguishing characteristics of Democracy is its regard for the rights of others. But in Kerala many of the democratic procedures are being practised with deadly disregard for the rights of others. And wanton abortions of Human Rights are taking place on the main streets of Kerala on a massive scale. And day after day the media in Kerala goes on acting like a deaf and dumb on - looker unable to distinguish and diagnose these sordid violations of Human Rights. The media goes on celebrating the 'big success' or 'massiveness of the rallies and demonstrations with colourful photographs and multi-column reports totally eclipsing the cruel violations of basic Human Rights they inflict on the general society. To that extent, the media has become passive participatory accomplies in these violations since they go about without taking serious note of them.

# 26

# ENFORCEMENT OF HUMAN RIGHTS: ROLE OF JUDICIARY

**G. Rajasekharan Nair**

'Human Rights' are those rights which belong to an individual as a consequence of being human. Human Rights, being the birth rights are inherent in all the individuals irrespective of their religion, caste, sex and nationality.

The provisions concerning human rights run throughout the UN charter also "like a golden thread". The Charter of the United Nations contains an affirmation of faith in the fundamental human rights, in the dignity and worth of the human persons in the equal rights of men and women. The Charter promotes and encourages respect for human rights and assists in the realization of human rights and fundamental freedoms.

The Universal Dectarationof Human Rights (UDHR) was adopted and proclaimed by the General Assembly of the United Nations on 10th December 1948. The Sixty First Anniversary of the adoption of the Universal declaration of Human Rights provides a fitting occasion for taking stock of and examining the progress achieved by the human rights movements, its meaning and significance today, the evolution of its values and norms, and its impact on the administration of criminal justice in India.

The Indian Constitution which was adopted by the Constituent Assembly on 26th November 1949 and which came into force from 26th January 1950 was greatly influenced by the above said U.N. Declaration. Since the Universal Declaration was adopted just before the Indian Constitution, the framers of Indian Constitution incorporated nearly almost all those humanrights contained in the UDHR. The Preamble of the Constitution of India proclaims and recites the solemn resolve to secure to all its citizens: Justice, Liberty, Equality and Fraternity which are the broad concepts of the

Declaration. Preamble, Part III and Part IV deals with the different aspects of human rights governed in the UDHR. The framers of the Constitution were conscious about the contents of the Declaration and therefore they gave due recognition to its provisions. In Kesavananda Bharathi Case[1] the Supreme Court observed that "The Universal Declaration of human rights may not be a legally binding instrument but it shows how India understood the nature of Human Rights at the time the Constitution was adopted"[2]. The following table indicates some of the human rights which have been incorporated in Indian Constitution:

| Name of Rights | Universal Declaration | Indian Constitution |
|---|---|---|
| Equality Before Law | Art. 07 | Art. 14 |
| Protection against discrimination | Art. 07 | Art.15(1) |
| Equality of opportunity | Art. 21(2) | Art. 16(1) |
| Freedom of speech and expression | Art.19 | Art. 19(1)(a) |
| Freedom of peaceful assembly | Art. 20(1) | Art. 19(1)(b) |
| Freedom to form Association/Unions | Art.23(4) | Art.19(1)(c) |
| Freedom of movement | Art. 13(1) | Art.19(1)(d) |
| Protection against Ex-post facto laws | Art.11 (2) | Art.20 (1) |
| Right to Life & Personal Liberty | Art. 03 | Art. 21 |
| Protection from slavery / forced labour | Art. 04 | Art.23 |
| Freedom of conscience and religion | Art. 18 | Art. 25(1) |
| Remedy for enforcement of rights | Art.08 | Art. 32 |

The Universal Declaration of Human Rights, 1948 did not categorize the different kinds of human rights but simply enumerated them in different articles.

The human rights are broadly divided into two:

(1) Civil and Political Rights and

(2) Economic, Social and Cultural Rights.

**Civil and Political Rights**

Civil rights or liberties are those rights which are related to the protection of the right to life and personal liberty. Such rights include right to life, right to privacy, freedom from torture, freedom from inhuman and degrading treatment, freedom of thought, freedom of movement etc.

Political rights are those rights which allow a person to participate in the Government of a State. For example, to vote, right to be elected, right to take part in the conduct of public affairs etc. International Covenant on Civil and Political Rights, 1966 incorporate the above mentioned rights.

## Economic, Social and Cultural Rights

Economic, Social and Cultural rights are those related to the guarantee of minimum necessities of life to human beings. In the absence of these rights the existence of human beings is likely to be endangered. Right to adequate food, clothing, housing and adequate standard of living and freedom from hunger, right to work, right to physical and mental health and right to education are included in this category of rights. These rights are included in the International Covenant on Economic, Social and Cultural Rights, 1966.

In addition to the above rights, there is another kind of rights which may be enjoyed by individuals collectively such as right to development, right to protect environment, right to self-determination etc. Such rights are referred to "Collective Rights".

The Preamble, Part III and Part IV of the Constitution of India enshrine all the known concepts of human rights. The guarantee of fundamental rights is a restraint on the State from interference, and confers a constitutional right on the individual to protect and enforce these rights. The Directive Principles cast an obligation on the State. Though these are not enforceable, the State has been made accountable for inaction and discriminatory or arbitrary actions. In India, therefore, the Constitution and the laws enable the courts to protect and enforce the several factors of human rights. The moot point is whether these provisions are ever put to use.

## Role of Judiciary and Human Rights

The role of judiciary and more particularly the Supreme Court in the protection of human rights under the Constitution, has been examined hereunder:

## Jurisdiction of Supreme Court

The system of judicial review of administrative action has been inherited from Britain. "The framers of the Indian Constitution borrowed from the United States of America the name and from great Britain the position and functions of the Chief Executive of the Union".[3] India has a hierarchical judicial system in which Supreme Court of India is the apex court. It is the final interpreter of law and the ultimate court of appeal in all Civil, Criminal and Constitutional matters. It is also the final protector of people's fundamental rights.

'Judicial review' is not only an integral part of the Constitution but is also a basic structure of the Constitution which cannot be abolished or whittled down even by an amendment of the Constitution.[4] In any democratic society judicial review is the soul of the system because without it democracy and the rule of law cannot be maintained.[5] Thus extraordinary jurisdiction of the Court under Article 32 or 136 of the Constitution cannot be taken away by legislation or principle of election or estoppel even by amending the Constitution.[6]

The Supreme Court is invested with the power of judicial review under Article 32. Article 32(1) guarantees the right to move the Supreme Court for the enforcement of fundamental rights and Article 32(2) invests the Supreme Court with the power to issue directions, orders writs for the enforcement of these rights. The right to move the Supreme Court for the enforcement of any fundamental right is itself a fundamental right and the Court has no power to refuse in its discretion to grant appropriate remedy if the violation of any fundamental right is proved.[7]

Article 136 which is in the nature of a residuary reserve power of judicial review in the area of public law lays down that the Supreme Court may, in its discretion, grant special leave to appeal from any judgement, decree, determination, sentence or order in any case or matter passed or made by any court or tribunal. Thus Article 136 does not confer a right of appeal on any party, but it confers a discretionary power on the Supreme Court to interfere in suitable cases to advance the cause of justice. Even in cases where special leave is granted, the discretionary power vested in the Court continues to remain with the Court even at the stage when appeal comes for hearing. Power under Article 136 of the Constitution, on the one hand, is an exceptional power to be exercised sparingly, with caution and care and to remedy extraordinary situations of gross failure of justice' and on the other hand, it is an overriding power where under, the Court may generously step into impart justice and remedy injustice.[8]

**Jurisdiction of the High Court**

Article 226 empowers the High Courts to issue directions, orders or writs for the enforcement of fundamental rights and "for any other purpose" also. Thus the power of judicial review of the High Courts is wider than that of Supreme Court. The words 'for any other purpose' enable the High Courts to exercise their power of judicial review for the enforcement of ordinary legal rights which are not fundamental rights. The jurisdiction of the High Court under Article 226 for the enforcement of fundamental rights is mandatory whereas for the enforcement of ordinary legal rights, it is discretionary.[9]

Article 227 empowers High Courts with the power of superintendence over administrative agencies exercising adjudicatory powers. The nature of this power is both administrative and judicial. Though the provision confers the right of superintendence over all Courts and tribunals throughout the territories in relation to which High Court exercises jurisdiction but no corresponding right is conferred upon a litigant to invoke the jurisdiction under this provision as a matter of right.

Judicial review of administrative/legislative action is a basic feature of the Constitution which cannot be taken away even by amending the Constitution.

## Locus Standi to Challenge State Actions

Locus Standi means the capacity to sue. The traditional rule governing locus standi is that only the aggrieved person can approach the court for the enforcement of fundamental right or legal rights as the case may be. The technical doctrine of 'locus standi' is being gradually widened to give it a social content in conformity with the letter and spirit of the Indian Constitution. In ABSK Sangh (Rly) V. Union of India,[10] it was held that Akhil Bharathiya Sushit Karmachan Sangh (Railway), though an unregistered association could maintain a writ petition. In Judges Transfer Case[11] a seven member bench of the Supreme Court firmly held that any member of the public havingsufficient interest can approach the court for enforcing the constitutional or legal rights of other persons and redressal for a common grievance.

## Speaking for the Majority, Bhagwati. J, Stated the Rule as Follows

*Where a legal wrong or legal injury is caused to person or to a determinate class of persons by reason of violation of any constitutional or legal right and such person or determinate class of persons is by reason of poverty, helplessness of disability or socially or economically disadvantaged position unable to approach the court for relief, any member of the public can maintain an application for an appropriate direction or order writ in the High Court under Article 226 or in case of breach of any fundamental right to this Court under Article 32. Where the weaker sections of the community are concerned such as under-trial prisoners languishing in jails without a trial, inmates of the Protective Home in Agra or Harijan workers engaged in road construction in the District of Ajmer, who are living in poverty and desolation, who are barely eking out a miserable existence with their sweat and toil, who are helpless victims of an exploitative society and who do not have easy access to justice, the Supreme Court will not insist a regular writ petition to be filed by the public spirited individual espousing their cause and seeking relief for them. The Supreme Court will readily respond to a letter addressed by such individual acting pro bono publico.*[11(a)]

In Bandhu Mukti Morcha v. Union of India,[12] "an organization dedicated to the cause of release of bonded labour informed the Supreme Court through a letter that they conducted a survey of the stone-quarries situated in Faridabad District of the State of Haryana and found that there were a large number of labour working in these stone-quarries under "inhuman and intolerable conditions" and many of them were bonded labours. The petitioners prayed that a writ be issued for proper implementation of the various provisions of the Constitution and statutes with a view to ending the misery, suffering and helplessness of these labours, and release of bonded labourers. The Court treated the letter as a writ-petition,and appointed a Commission consisting of two advocates to visit these stone-quarries and make an inquiry and report to the Court about the existence of bonded labourers.

As result of the liberalized concept of locus standi, Public Interest Litigation or Social Action Litigation (S.A.L) has emerged out in India. Public Interest Litigation means "litigation in the interest public" PIL/SAL is a socio-economic movement generated by the judiciary to reach justice to the weaker sections of the society.

SAL/PIL can be initiated by any public spirited person or group on behalf of any person or persons who because of any socio-economic disability cannot come before the court or where the right which is violated is a 'diffused' right. Thus only a genuine public-spirited persons or public spirited organization will be allowed standing on PIL/SAL. 'The term public spirited 'has been defined inAsiad case[13]. Lawyers, Professors, Social Workers, Journalists, Environmentalists etc. may be treated as public spirited person for the purpose of instituting PIL/SAL.

**Notable Case Laws**

S.P. Gupta V. President of India[14] (popularly known as Judges Transfer Case). In this case the Supreme Court entertained petitions by lawyers challenging the constitutionality of Law Minister's circular regarding transfer of Judges of High Courts and non-confirmation of sitting Additional Judges of High Courts. Standing was allowed on the ground that the independence of the judiciary is a matter of grave public concern.

People's Union of Democratic Rights v. Union of India[15] (popularly know as Asiad case). In this case the Supreme Court entertained petition from a public spirited organization on behalf of labourers belonging to socially and economically weaker sections and employed in the construction work of various projects connected with Asian Games 1982 complaining violation of various labour laws including non-payment of minimum wages and granted relief.

In people's Union for Democratic Rights v. State of Bihar[16], the Supreme Court entertained petition by a public spirited organization for compensastion on behalf of persons victim of unjustified police atrocities.

*In D.C. Wadhwa v. State of Bihar*[17] case the Supreme Court held that a professor of Political Science who is deeply interested in ensuring proper implementation of the constitutional provisions can approach the court through PIL petition against the practice of issuing ordinances on large scale to bypass legislature as being a fraud on the Constitution.

The Court allowed access to a prisoner complaining about brutal attack and assault by head warden on a fellow prisoner on the ground of class standing in Sunil Batra V. Delhi AdministrationCase[18].

*In Municipal Council, Rattlam v. Vardicham*[19] - Court held that public duties are owned not by any individual but by the public, therefore, for the enforcement of any public duty any public-spirited person will be granted standing. Supreme Court issued directions to the municipal council on a PIL petition by a citizen to construct public conveniences and drains etc. and to keep the streets clean.

*Parmanand Katara.V Union of India*[20] - On a PIL petition the Court directed the Government that every injured person brought for medical treatment should instantaneously be given medical aid without waiting for the completion of police procedural formalities in order to avoid negligent death of an accident victim.

*Vishaka v. State of Rajasthan*[21] - In the absence of a legislation the court filled in the gap giving wide directives to protect working women from sexual harassment.

*National Council for Civil Liberties v. Union of India*[22] - In this case, petition had been filed alleging that Medha Patkar and others of the Narmada Bachao Andolan are involved in subversive activities in order to obstruct developmental projects of national importance. Dismissing the petition the Court observed that it appears to be a private litigation to discredit and diffuse the agitation for rehabilitation of displaced persons from dam site.

*In D.N. Thaware v.State of Maharashtra*[23] - dismissing the PIL petition filed by a lawyer for blackmailing people and who was caught red-handed accepting blackmailing money, the Court expressed its anguish at the misuse of this strategy by unscrupulously litigants, and exhorted courts to be ruthless while dealing with such impostors.

## Enforcement of Human Rights Through Judicial Activism

Article 21 guaranteeing the cardinal fundamental right, says that "No person shall be deprived of his life and liberty except according to a procedure established by laws". Now the concept of "Life and Liberty" has been considerably expanded as a result of the beneficial interpretation of the Supreme Court and High Court is of variable content in the 'due process' concept. It denotes that the law should be 'just' but what is 'just and reasonable' is not a static or rigid concept. It varies from situation to situation and what may be regarded as reasonable in one situation may not necessarily be so in another situation.

### (1) Right to Live with Human Dignity

*Maneka Gandhi's*[24] case had a profound but beneficial impact on the administration of justice in India. It gave a new dimension to Art.21by declaring that 'right to live' is not merely confined to physical existence but it includes within its ambit the 'right to live with human dignity'. Elaborating the same view, the Supreme Court in Francis Coralie Mullin v. Union Territory of Delhi[24(a)] held that 'right to live' is not restricted to mere animal existence. It means something more than just physical survival. The 'right to live with human dignity' includes the basic necessities of life such as adequate nutrition, clothing, shelter and facilities for reading, writing and expressing, freely moving about and co-mingling with fellow human beings.

In People's Union for Democratic Rights v. Union of India[25], it was held that non-payment of minimum wages to the workers employed in various

Asiad Projects in Delhi was a denial to them of their right to live with basic human dignity, and hence violative of Art 21.

In Chandra Rajakumari v. Police Commissioner, Hyderabad[26] (AIR 1998 AP 302) it has been held that the right to live includes right to live with human dignity and decency and therefore holding of beauty contest if repugnant to decency of women it would be violative of Art 21.

**(2) Right to livelihood**

*In Olga Tellis v. Bombay Municipal Corporation*[27] (popularly known as "pavement dwellers case") a five judge bench of supreme Court ruled that the word "life" in Art 21 includes the right to livelihood also. In that case a direction of the Municipal authorities for the removal of huts from pavements and public places was challenged on the ground that their removal amounted to deprivation of right to livelihood which is included in Art.21. It was held that the impugned was constitutional since it imposed reasonable restriction in the interest of the general public. Public streets are not meant for carrying trade or business. The Supreme Court, however, took a humanistic view and directed the corporation to frame a scheme for demarcating hawking and non-hawking zones and give licences for selling goods in hawking zones. The SupremeCourt took a similar stand in a Sodan Singh v. New Delhi Municipal Committee[28] also wherein the petitioners were hawkers doing business on the pavement of roads in Delhi.

**(3) Right to Privacy**

*In R.Rajagopal v. State of Tamil Nadu*[29] (popularly known as "Auto Shanker Case") the Supreme Court has expressly held that the "right to privacy" or the right to be let alone is guaranteed by Art.21 of the Constitution. A citizen has a right to safeguard the privacy of his own, his family, marriage, procreation, motherhood, childbearing and other connected matters. None can publish anything concerning the above matters without his consent whether truthful or otherwise or whether laudatory or critical.

*In State of Maharashtrav.Madhukar Narain*[30], it has been held that the 'right to privacy' is available even for a women of easy virtue and no one can invade her privacy. Here a police inspector visited the house of one Banubai in uniform and demanded to have sexual intercourse with her. On refusing, he tried to have her by force. When he was prosecuted, he told the court that she was a lady of easy virtue. The court rejected the argument and held him liable for violating her right to privacy.

In a historic judgment in People's Union for Civil Liberties v. Union of India[31] (popularly known as "telephone tapping case") the Supreme Court held that telephone tapping is a serious invasion of an individual's right to privacy enshrined under Art.21 of the Constitution.

**(4) Right to Health and Medical Assistance**

*In Paramananda Katra v. Union of India*[32], it has been held that all doctors, whether Government or Private must extend medical aid to injured to preserve life without waiting for legal formalities. In Paschim BangKhat Mazdoor Samiti v. State of West Bengal[32(a)] the Supreme Court held that denial of medical aid by Government hospitals to an injured person on the ground of non-availability of beds amounted to violation of right to life under Art. 21 and that failure to provide timely medical treatment to a person in need of such treatment violates Art. 21 and hence the court directed to pay compensation.

**(5) Right to Members of Protective Homess**

*In Vikram Dev Singh Tomar v. State of Bihar*[33] through a public interest litigation it was brought to the notice of the Supreme Court that the female inmates of the 'Care Home, Patna' were compelled to live in inhuman conditions in an old ruined building. The Supreme Court held that the State is under duty to provide at least the minimum conditions ensuring human dignity. Accordingly the court directed the State to take immediate steps for the Welfare of the inmates".

**(6) Prisoner's Rights**

The Protection under Article 21 is available even to convicts in jails. In DBM Patnaik v. State of A.P[34] the petitioner's who were naxalites undergoing sentence in Central Jail, Vishakapatanam, contended that the armed police guards posted around the jail and the live-wire electrical mechanism fixed on the top of the jail were violative of Art.21. But the Supreme Court rejected the plea and held that such devices were preventive measures. However in Sunil Batra(1) v. Delhi Administration[35] the Supreme Court issued certain directions to the jail authorities against inhuman treatments towards life convicts. In Sunil Batra (11) v. Delhi Administration[36] it was held that the practice of keeping undertrials with convicts in jails offended the test of reasonableness under Art.21. The under trials are presumably innocents until convicted.

**(7) Right to Speedy Trial**

Speedy trial as such is not a specific fundamental right or statutory right. But the Supreme Court in Hussainara Khatoon (No.1) v. Home Secretary, State of Bihar[37] held that right to speedy trial is a fundamental right under Art 21. In Kendra Pahadiya v. State of Bihar[38(a)] several under trials had beenlanguishing in jail for eight years without trial. Here the Supreme Court emphasized the need for a speedy trialwhich is within the ambit of Art 21. The court ordered the Bihar Government to release forthwith the under-trials on their personal bonds. In Hussainara Khatoon[38] (No.2)and in Hussainare Khatan No.(3)[39] also the Supreme Court reiterated the same view. In A.R.Anthuley v. R.S.Naik[40] the Supreme Court laid down exhaustive guidelines for speedy trial of an accused in criminal trial.

**(8) Right Against Solitary Confinement**

In Sunil Batra (No.1) v.Delhi Administration[41] the question before the

Supreme Court was whether 'solitary confinement' imposed upon prisoners who were under the sentence of death wasviolative of Article 14, 19 & 21.It was held that even a prisoner under the sentence of death has the right to life until the last breach.

**(9) Right to Free Legal Aid**

In M.H.Hoskot v. State of Maharashtra[42], Supreme Court held that right to free legal aid is an essential ingredient of just, fair and reasonable procedure under Art.21. Moreover in Suk Das v. Union Territory of Arunachal Pradesh[43] the Supreme Court 'held that failure to provide free legal aid to an accused, unless refused, would vitiate the trial.

**(10) Right Against Inhuman Treatment**

In Kishore singh v. state of Rajasthan[44] the supreme Court held that the use of "third degree methods" by police is violative of Art 21 and directed the Government to take necessary steps to educate the police. The Court also held that the punishment of solitary confinement for long periods and putting bar fetters for several days on flimsy grounds must be regarded as barbarous and against human dignity.

**(11) Right Against Handcuffing**

In Prem Shankar v. Delhi Administration[45] Krishna Iyer J, delivering the majority judgment held that handcuffing should be resorted to only when there is clear and present danger of escape because handcuffing is prima facie inhuman,unreasonable and overharsh and thus arbitrary.

In sunil Guptha v. State of MP,[46] the petitioners who were social workers had staged a 'dharna' for a public cause and voluntarily submitted themselves for arrest. They were remanded to judicial custody and were taken to court from jail and back from court to jail by the escort party handcuffed. Since they had no tendency to escape from the jail, it was held that the act of the escort party was violative of Art. 21.

In Citizen for Democracy v state of Assam[47] the supreme Court has expressed serious concern over the violation of the law laid down in Prem Shankar's case against handcuffing. In the instant case, Mr. Kuldip Nayyar, an eminent journalist, in his capacity as the president of Citizens for Democracy through a letter brought to the notice of the court seven TADA detenues lodged in the hospital in the State of Assam were handcuffed and tied with long rope to prevent their movement. The court treated the letter as a petition under Art. 32 and held that handcuffing and tying with ropes to the patient prisoners who are lodged in the hospital are inhuman and violation of Art. 21. Appropriate directions were issued to limit the use of handcuffing and fetters.

**(12) Right Against Delayed Execution**

*In T V Vatheeswaran v. State of TN*[48] a two judge Bench of Supreme Court held that delay in execution of death sentence exceeding two years would be a sufficient ground to invoke the protection of Art. 21 and the death sentence would be commuted to life imprisonment. In Sher Singh v. State of Punjab,[49] the apex court endorsed this view, held that prolonged detention to await the execution of death sentence is an unjust and unreasonable procedure and the only way to undo the wrong is to quash death sentence. However the court held that this cannot be applied as a rule and each case should be decided separately.

*In Triveni Ben v. State of Gujarat*[50] a five judge bench of the supreme court has set the matter at rest and held that undue long delay in execution of death sentence will entitle the condemned person to approach the court for conversion of death sentence in to imprisonment for life, but before doing so the court will examine the nature of delay, circumstances of the case, whether the delay was due to the conduct of the convict, the nature of offence, its impact on the society etc.

**(13) Right Against Illegal Arrest, Detention and Custodial Death**

*In Jogider Singh v. State of UP,*[51] the Supreme Court has laid down guidelines governing arrest of a person during investigation, which inter-alia include"

(a) An arrested person being held in custody is entitled to inform to one friend or relative or any person having an interest in his welfare that he has been arrested; and where he is being detained (b) The police officer shall inform the arrested person when he is brought to the police station of this right (c) An entry shall be required to be made in the Diarty as to who was informed of the arrest.

In a landmark judgment in 'Nilabati Behera v. State of Orissa[52] the Supreme Court awarded compensation of Rs. 1,50,000/- to the mother of the deceased who died in police custody.

In D.K. Bassu v. State of West Bengal[53] the Superme Court has laid down exhaustive guidelines to be followed by the authorities in all cases of arrest and detention:

(a) The police personnel carrying out the arrest and interrogation should bear accurate, visible and clear identification name-tags with their designation.

(b) The police officer carrying out arrest of person shall prepare a memo of arrest at the time of arrest and such memo must be attested by atleast one witness who may be either a member of the family of the arrestee or a respectable person of the locality from where the arrest is made.

(c) A person who has been arrested or detained shall be entitled to have one friend or relative or other person known to him or havig interest in his welfare, informed as early as possible.

(d) The time, place of arrest and venue of custody must be notified to the next friend or relative of the arrestee within 8 to 12 hours of arrest.

(e) The person arrested must be aware of the right to have someone informed of his arrest or as soon as he is put under arrest.

(f) An entry must be made in the diary at the place of detention regarding the arrest of person which shall also disclose the name of the next friend or relative.

(g) The arrestee should, where he so requests, be also examined at the time of arrest, the major and minor injuries, if any present in his or her body must be recorded in the 'inspection memo' which must be signed by the arrestee and the police officer.

(h) The arrestee should be subjected to medical examination by a trained doctor within 48 hours.

(i) Copies of all documents including the memo of arrest should be sent to the Magistrate.

(j) The arrestee may be permitted to meet his/her lawyer during interrogation; though not throughout.

(k) A police control room should be provided at all district and State head quarters, where information regarding the arrest and place of custody of the arrestee shall be communicated by the officer causing arrest within 12 hours and it should be displayed conspicuously on the notice board.

**(14) Composition for Violation of Article 21**

In a judgment of far-feaching importance and Rudal Shah v. State of Bihar[54] the Supreme Court has held that the court has the power to award monetary compensation in appropriate cases for the violation of Art 21. In the present case the Supreme Court directed the Bihar Government to pay compensation of Rs. 30,000 to Rudal Shah who had to remain in jail for 14 years even after his acquittal because of the irresponsible behaviour of the state Government officials.

In Bhim Singh v . State of J.K[55] the court awarded a compensation of Rs.50,000 for the violation of Art. 21. Here the MLA was arrested and detained in police custody and deliberately prevented from attending service of the Legislative Assembly. In Saheli v. Commissioner of Police[56] the Supreme Court awarded Rs. 75,000 to the mother of a nine year old child who died in police custody.

**(15) Right Against Sexual Harassment of Working Women**

In a landmark judgement in Vishaka v. State of Rajasthan[57] the Supreme Court has laid down exhaustive guidelines to prevent sexual harassment of working women in places of their work until a legislation is enacted for the purpose. The court held that duty of the employer or other responsible person in work places or other institutions, whether public or private, to prevent sexual harassment of the working women. The petition was filed by Vishaka, an NGO working for gender equality. The immediate cause for filing the petition was alleged brutal gang rape of a social worker of Rajasthan. The supreme court directed the following guide lines:

(i) All employees, whether in public or private sector should take apropriate steps to prevent sexual harassment and he should take the following steps:

(a) Express prohibition of sexual harassment which include physical contact and advances, a demand or request for sexual favours, sexually coloured remarks, showing pornographic or any other unwelcome physical, verbal or non-verbal conduct of sexual nature. It should be noticed, published and circulated.

(b) The rules or regulations of Government and public sector bodies relating to conduct and discipline should include rules prohibiting sexual harassment and provide for appropriate penalties.

(c) As regards private employes, steps should be taken to include the aforesaid prohibitions in the standing orders under the Industrial Employment (standing order) Act 1946.

(d) Where such conduct amounts to specific offences under IPC or any other law, the employer shall initiate appropriate action in accordance with law.

(ii) The victim of sexual harassment should have the option to seek transfer.

Apparel Export Promotion Council V. A.K Chopra[58] is the first case in which the Supreme Court applied the law laid down in Vishaka's case and upheld the dismissal from service of a superior officer of the Delhi based Apparel Export Promotion Council who was found guilty of sexual harassment of a subordinate female employee at the place of work.

In Delhi Domestic working Women's Forum v. Union of India[59], the petitioner through a public interest litigation brought to the notice pathetic conditions of four domestic women servants who were raped by seven army personnel in a running train while traveling from Ranchi to Delhi. The victims were helpless tribal women belonging to State of Bihar. After making an order of compensation the following guidelines were formulated for the trial of rape cases:

(a) The complainants of rape cases should be provided with legal assistance.

(b) Legal assistance shall be provided at the police station.

(c) The police should be under a duty to inform the victim of her right to legal representation.

(d) A list of advocates willing to act should kept in the police stations.

(e) The advocates shall be appointed by the court on application by the police.

(f) In all rape trials the name of the victim shall not to be declard

(g) In accordance with Art 38 (1) to set a criminal injuries compensation Board for rape victims.

(h) Compensation for victims shall be awarded on conviction of the offender.

(i) The National commission for women be asked to frame schemes for compensation and rehabilitation of rape victims.

**(16) Right to Pollution Free Environment**

In Shriram Food and Fertilizer Case[60], the Superme Court directed the company manufacturing hazardous and lethal chemicals and gases posing danger to health and life of workmen and people living in its neighbourhood to take all necessary safety measures before reopening the plant.

In M.C.Mehta v. Union of India[61] the Sperme Court ordered the closure of certain plants polluting the river Ganga. The matter was brought to the notice of the Court by a social worker, through a public interest litigation. In Subashkumar v. State of Bihar[62] it has been held that "right to pollution free water and air is included in the right to life" under Art.21

**(17) Right to Education**

In a landmark judgment in Mohini Jain v. State of Karnatka[63] (popularly known as the "Capitation Fee Case"), the Supreme Court has held that the right to education is a fundamental right under Art 21 of the constitution. In Unnikrishnan v. State of A.P[64], the Superme Court was asked to examine the correctness of the decision given by the court in Mohini Jain's case. The five judge bench of the Superme Court by 3-2 majority held right to education is a fundamental right under Art 21 and held that right to free education is available only to children until attaining the age of 14 years, but after that the obligation of the sate to provide education is subject to the limit of economic capacity and development. Consequently the Parliament executed the Constitution (86th Amendment) Act, 2002 and added a new Aricle, Art 21-A made education for all childern of the age of 6 to 14 is a fundamental right.

India as an independent nation has always taken pride as being the world's largest democracy and being governed by the Rule of Law. Our leaders lose no time in proclaiming from the rooftops of international arena that, in India, democracy is deep rooted and it pervades all walks of life. But if one were to examine how far various institutions have fulfilled its Constitutional mandate and gained the approval of the public, only the judiciary and more particularly Supreme Court can claim to have made some success. While executive and legislature competed with one another to lose the confidence of the public, it was the judiciary that strive to achieve the constitutional mandate. The Supreme Court of India became a torch bearer and in that process not only turned out to be the savior of the people inside the country but also earned the respect of the counterparts of other countries. It could be said in the area of public interest that the supreme Court of India, by its pro-active role has become a forerunner and courts of other countries quote with approval, many of the decisions of our Supreme Court.

## References


1. *Kesavananda Bharathi v. State of Kerala AIR* (1973), SC 1461
2. *Ibid.* p.1510
3. Seervai, *Constitutional Law of India* Vol.VI, 14th edn. (1997) p.158.
4. *Kesavananda Bharati v. State of Kerala* (1973) 4 SCC 255: AIR (1973) SC 1461.
5. *Minerva Mills v. Union of India* (1980) 3 SCC 625.
6. *Ramachandra Deshpande v. Maruti Balaram Haibatti,* (1995) Supp (2) SCC 539.
7. *Masthan Sahib v. Chief Sommr.* Pondicherry AIR (1962) SC 797, 804, See also *Fertiliser Corpn Kamgar Union v. Union of India* (1981) 1 SCC 568, 574-75.
8. *Ashok Nagar Welfare Assn. v. R.K. Sharma* (2002 1 SCC 749.
9. *Manjula v. Director of Public Instruction*, AIR 1952 Ori 344, See also *Kailash Chander v. State of Haryana*, 1989 Supp (2) SCC 669.
10. *AIR* 1981 SC 298
11. S.P.Guptha v. President of India AIR 1982 SC 149

11(a)*Ibid* pp. 1882 & 189.

12. *AIR* 1984 SC 803
13. People's Union for Democratic Rights v. Union of India AIR 1982, SC 1473.
14. AIR 1982 SC 149.
15. (1982) 3 SCC 235
16. (1984) 3 SCC 161
17. (1987) SCC 265
18. (1980) 3 SCC 488
19. (1980) 4 SCC 162; 1980 SCC (Cri) 933: AIR 1980 SC 1622.
20. (1990) 1 SCC 613.
21. (1997) 6 SCC 241
22. (2007) 6 SCC 506
23. (2005) 1 SCC 590
24. AIR (1978) SC 597

24(a) AIR(1981) SC 746

25. Air (1982) SC 1473
26. AIR (1998) AP 302
27. AIR (1986) SC 180
28. AIR 1989 SC 1988
29. (1994) 6 SCC 632
30. AIR 1991 SC 207
31. AIR 1997 SC 568
32. AIR 1989 SC 2039

32(a) (1996) 4 SCC 37

33. (1996) 4 SCC 37

34. AIR 1974 SC 2092
35. AIR 1978 SC 1976
36. AIR 1980 SC 1579
37. AIR 1979 SC 1360
38. AIR 1979 SC 1369
38(a) AIR 1982 SC 1167
39. AIR 1979 1377
40. AIR 1992 SC 1630
41. AIR 1979 SC 1575
42. AIR 1978 SC 1548
43. (1986) 2 SCC 401
44. AIR 1981 SC 625
45. AIR 1980 SC 1535
46. (1990) 3 SCC 119
47. (1995) 3 SCC 743
48. AIR 1981 SC 625
49. AIR 1983 SC 465
50. (AIR 1989 SC 142)
51. (1994) 4 SCC 260
52. (1993) 2 SCC 746
53. AIR 1997 SC 610
54. (1983) 4 SCC 141
55. (1985) 4 SCC 677
56. (AIR 1990 SC 513)
57. (AIR 1997 SC 3011)
58. (AIR 1999 SC 625)
59. (1995) 1 SCC 14
60. (MC *Mehta v. Union of India* (1986) 2 SCC 176)
61. (1987) 4 SCC 463
62. (AIR 1991 SC 420)
63. (1992) 3 SCC 666
64. (1993) 1SCC 645

# 27

# HUMAN RIGHTS AND POLICING IN A PLURAL DEMOCRACY

*"In safeguarding our freedoms, the police play a vital role. Society for its defence needs a well led, well-trained well disciplined force of police whom it can trust: and enough of them to be able to prevent crime before it happens, or if it does happen, to detect it and bring the accused to justice"*

*Lord Denning-*

**K. Padmakumar**

In an ideal world where everybody respects everyone else's Human Rights, there will be no need for a police force. However, such a situation exists only in the realm of dreams which is why an unwritten social contract got evolved over the years out of which the concept of state and it's various organs including the police were born. Modern police organization and methods in a plural democracy evolved as results of the ascendancy of humanistic democratic ideas over feudalistic and theocratic political philosophies. Professional police as a trained structured body- distinct from military guards and religious police-came into existence only because adherence to rule of law, elimination of arbitrariness and liability for public accountability in criminal justice enforcement became paramount principles consistent with the sovereignty of the people. Human Rights are therefore the very raison d'etre of a modern police service. The fundamental basis of ethics, morality and proper social conduct for police is virtually the same as that for human rights. Human Rights are not the gift of any political sovereign but are rights inherent in human existence. A truly professional and democratic system for the police can evolve only from this realization.

We live in an imperfect world. We need the police to prevent and detect crime, to maintain or preserve social order, to provide assistance to people in time of emergency and above all to protect human rights. Human Rights are an integral part of the law. The police are employed to enforce the law. When they enforce the law while keeping within the limits prescribed by law, they are protecting the human rights of every individual belonging to the community. The police themselves as well as the community must look upon policing from this point of view. At the same time, we must not forget that police officials are thereby human and they also have human rights.

The primary function of a police force in a democracy is the protection of Human Rights. This may sound as an anachronism for large sections of society who view police as prime culprits in human rights violations. The common perception is that, police and Human Rights are poles apart. This is a totally wrong and an extremely dangerous perception which arise out of a total lack of understanding of the concept police and the state in a democracy. This view is dangerous for the well being of society itself and is perilous for democracy.

When a law is enforced on a offender who has committed a transgression, what police is actually doing is to protect the human rights of the victim. Arresting an accused in a murder case and bringing him up before a Court of law amounts to protecting an extremely precious human rights. ie; right to live. Rule of law is a primary requirement for the protection of Human Rights. It is the primary duty of the police service in a democracy to ensure that, every individual is able to live with dignity and is able to enjoy the inalienable human rights to the maximum practical extent possible. While enforcing the law, the procedures prescribed by law has to be followed by police force in both letter and spirit. Law cannot be enforced through a violation of the law. When a law is violated to implement a law the law enforcement agency looses the moral authority to implement laws. In every democracy there are laid down rules and procedures for implementing a law. The entire Criminal Justice System is governing by such laws.

Supreme Court and other various courts in the Country have clearly laid down rules regarding the manner and procedures through which policing is to be conducted in the country. The most above important direction is the decision of the Supreme Court regarding the procedure of arrest in the case of D.K. Basu Vs. State of West Bengal. In the judgment of the Apex Court in. D.K. Basu Vs. State of West Bengal, the Court says, "If the functionaries of the government become lawbreakers, it is bound to breed contempt for law and would encourage lawlessness and every man would have the tendency to become law unto himself". This judgment clearly lays down 10 principles which are to be mandatorily followed by a law enforcement agency while arresting and detaining a person.

The end does not justify the means. Suspected criminals may possess information necessary for the protection of others of the state, but they must not be tortured. Getting information from a criminal after torturing him may give a police officer a false reputation for efficiency. When the criminal is one involved in some sensational crime, even the public may be crying for his blood and the police officer may even be applauded for his strong-arm methods and "no-nonsense approach". But such methods are counter productive in the long run. The torture process dehumanizes the police officer himself and he tends to use the same kind of methods in other situation also. Anybody who applauds and encourages third degree methods has not imbibed the spirit of freedom and concern for human rights. Such people should realize that, this method if encouraged may even be used against them at a later stage. Once torture is tolerated the brutalization involved will motivate officers to complete among themselves to achieve and show 'results' and 'efficiency'. This will results in \massive human rights violations and put democracy itself at peril.

Another major factor which threatens the enjoyment of human rights in a plural democracy is corruption in public life. Police force has a major role in combating the cancer of corruption. Not only Police, should remain above all inducement and corrupt practices, but, it should also effectively and focussedly use the authority given to them by law to combat corruption. A corrupt practice by a public servant prevents citizens from enjoying a right which accrues to him by being a citizen in a plural democracy. Every citizen has a right to expect a public servant to work with dignity, efficiency, integrity and impartiality. Corruption endangers good governance leading to social insecurity which can ultimately end in anarchy and destruction of the democracy itself. Decisions must be made without fear or favor and in accordance with the principle that all are equal before the law. Corruption threatens the rule of law. It assails the very foundations of the edifice of democratic governance and respect for human rights. Ultimately the right to live with dignity, equality and conscience is endangered by the rampant growth of corruption. Checking, preventing, eliminating and publishing acts of corruption thus becomes an abiding human rights concern. A responsible police force in a democracy must aim at eliminating corruption in all its forms while they themselves remain incorruptible.

Although enforcement of law is the primary duty of police, the relationship between the police and the public in a plural democracy is not a master servant relationship. By enforcing the law, police are doing service to the victims of the transgression of law. Relationship between police and public in a democracy is symbiotic in nature. Policing is a service in a democracy. Ordinary people should have free access to police with problems and communicate information to help the police. If one is scared to enter a police station, one is not likely to go there and complain about petty crime, suspicious activity in neighbourhoods, rowdy problems etc. The police man in turn loses the opportunity to known law-abiding public-spirited members of the community to whom he can turn for help in a serious crime situation or whom he can contact informally for information. The natural instinct is to keep away from a feared object, Fear of Police, unless consciously eliminated and discouraged, keeps the common man away from the police.

In this context, the importance of evolving of the Community policing become important. Community Policing contains the essence of policing in a plural democracy. Understanding the need and aspirations of the community and catering to them is the way in which a police force gets converted into a police service.

In Kerala, concept of community policing initiatives has become embedded in the system in the last couple of years. The 'Janamaithri Suraksha Project' which is being implemented in selected police station all over the state in the last few years has been a resounding success and has brought about a sea change in the attitude of the common man towards Police. The success of the scheme is reflected in the crime figures as well as in the prevailing sense of security at the places in which the scheme has been implemented. Community Policing is the outcome of realization of that, Police is not agency functioning from outside the community, but forms an integral part that of the community as a whole and functions from within.

Police service in a plural democracy needs to respect the society it tries to serve. It should not consider themselves as having an exclusive responsibility (to the isolation of everybody else) to fight crime and keep public order totally relying on their own manpower and weapons. They must realize that they are partners in a social progress and that they need to be in constant dialogue with the other partners forming part of government, social organizations, local authorities, leaders of public opinion and the public at large.

A professional working culture based on human rights will mean that police official will be able to function professionally without discrimination or racism, fraud or corruption. When planning specific police operations, respect for human rights should always be included among operational objectives. Law defines crime and criminality and police rely on such definitions to take action against those suspected of committing crime. The professional policeman must simultaneously remember that law defines not only crime and criminality but also how the police should treat a criminal. The sanctity and inviolability of law cannot be arbitrarily confined to crime and criminality alone without extending such values to the manner of treatment of criminals. People have entrusted the police with the authority for law enforcement. Police professionals must discharge that trust by ensuring that police act in conformity with the law, following procedures sanctioned by enacted law and judicial pronouncements. If this is accepted as a working condition, then there can never be any conflict of interest between professionalism in Police and adherence to human rights principles which is the essence of the very concept of plural democracy.

# 28

# POLICE AND HUMAN RIGHTS IN KERALA: NEED FOR REFORM

**K. Alexander**

The concept of 'Human Rights' is associated with 'Liberty, Equality and Dignity' of human life. This concept gained momentum with the United Nation's charter and the 'Universal Declaration of Human Rights' on 10, December, 1948. Democratic governments are committed to safeguard these basic rights of individuals. Good governance implies governance in an effective and citizen - friendly manner. Governments in democratic systems are crafted as instruments to preserve the authority of the state, pursue its goals and provide security of citizens. Thus every state should accept protection of its citizens, promotion of their growth, sustained development and social justice as their prime duty. Maintenance of peace and order is critically vital to the process of development. In fact, development and order go hand in hand (D.H. Bayley, 1969)[1]. Without order the process of development will be hindered and the fruits of development will not reach the clientele. In order to ensure a well-ordered society, there have to be laws having the sanction of force capable of implementation and enforcement. Therefore, the state needs a force like the police for achieving the objectives of security and tranquility.

Police are in fact, the protectors of life, liberty and property of the people. It is the operative agency for ensuring the essentials of civilized life and a touchstone for testing the spirit and quality of civil administration (John Coatman, 1959)[2]. The presence of the police itself will instill a sense of security and confidence in law abiding people. The manner in which the police respond to violations of law and order, place restraints on personal freedom, prevent the occurrence of crime and detect crime; all are vital benchmarks to evaluate civilized and dignified living. When the laws are fairly clear about their intent and purposes, the modalities of enforcement are not hampered by considerations other than requirements of law and when law is enforced without fear or favour, it contributes significantly to 'Rule of Law.' The police maintain law and order by which the normal pace of life is assured in the society. Police is defined as "A body of people whose job is to keep order and enforce regulations" (T.N. Dhar, 2002)[3]. It is also a "Department of government responsible for the promotion of order, protection from crime and enforcement of civil law" (T.N. Dhar, 2002)[4]. Prevention of crime detection of crime, traffic control, maintenance of order, internal security etc., are identified as the normal functions of the police in any society. In brief, the functions of the Police encompasses almost all areas of basic human freedom and people considered the effectiveness of the police as a reliable indicator of the protection of human rights. People use to have high expectations of the police as August Follmer, the Chief of police, Berkely, USA, once observed "A Police man should have the wisdom of Solomon, the patience of Job, the leadership of Moses, the kindness of the Good Samaritan, the strategy of Alexander, the faith of David, the diplomacy of Lincoln, the tolerance of the Carpenter of Nazareth and finally, an intimate knowledge of every branch of the natural , biological and social sciences" (T.N. Dhar, 2002)[5]

The framers of Indian Constitution influenced by the UDHR, were pragmatic enough to see that those rights which are essential and not bargain, able are included in Part–III of the Constitution while those which can be implemented gradually in Part–IV. In respect of the Police from 1861 onwards in the IPC and later in the Cr PC and I. E. Act, there are guarentees against police misuse of basic freedoms. For instance, arrested persons to be produced before the magistrate within twenty four (24) hours, presumption of innocence, double jeopardy, due process concept etc.

Contrary to the expectations, a wide gap is visible between the perceptions of the people and the performance of the police in Kerala. Almost on a daily basis reports are appearing in the media painting police as violators rather than protectors of human rights. As the horizon of human rights is expanding, so is the crime rate rising and the atrocities by the police increasing. As a result, police are more feared than respected. It is not a surprise to say that they are feared not by the law less but by the law abiding citizenry. This has to be viewed from the context of the diverse socio-political challenges gripping the state of Kerala in the short span of about a few decades. Kerala has had the rare opportunity to have every political party guide its destiny. Over the years or from the formation of the State in 1956 the population of the State has increased and stabilized. There has been rapid urbanization. The number of vehicles in all descriptions has registered substantial growth (Govt. of Kerala, 2009)[6] without matching road development which has resulted in almost daily fatal motor accidents. There has been unionization of practically every section of society and there have been almost continuous demonstrations on the streets for ventilating their grievances. Students of both schools and colleges have been getting organized on political lines and often their elections have led to violent clashes, which have prompted the Hon. High Court to ban election on political lines in schools and to have a re-thinking on such elections in the colleges. There have been violent demonstrations and direct action by Tribals and other marginalized sections of the society, leading to offences accompanied by violence and loss of life like Muttanga, Chengara etc.

Extremist movements like Naxlites and assorted militant groups have had their presence in the state for long. Caste and communal tensions leading to clashes and loss of life have not been rare. In crime, the state has seen a phenomenal growth under all heads. The operation of interstate gangs in the state has surfaced quite often. Loss of revenue through economic offences have been an alarming feature of crime in the state. Organized gangs have been freely indulging in white-collar crimes like the various quick – rich schemes in the state. There have been several instances of offence against women, both gender violence and other serious offences like rape and molestation. The state has been in the grip of a spate of suicides mostly as a result of the consumption fever and the craze to 'keep up with the Jones'. The fast aging population of the state has increased the geriatric problems faced by the community and the elderly have been easy target of violence in the state. Migratory labour from neighbouring states and also from faraway states like Bihar and from some neighbouring countries have generated new trends of crime. There have also been a substantial increase in non-traditional crimes, crimes aided by technology, cyber crimes and other sophisticated crimes, in the state (Kerala Police High-Tech Cell, 2009)[7]. In short, the problems the Police have to deal with have become very complex and massive. This background of the steady escalation of the crime graph, the mounting incidents of violent and serious crimes and also the emergence of terror linked crimes warrants appropriate measures to reform the police.

Every organization is a living and dynamic entity. Each activity is born, has its periods of experimental development, of reforms and stable activity and in some cases, of decline. One effort at arresting such decay is to inject into the corpus of the organization, elements of reconstruction and reform. This process has to be dove-tailed into the organization whenever it is faced with challenges. Infact, as and when new convulsions grip the society, new demands are made of it and it is exposed to new threats, the Police organization needs to be reformed. A close look would indicate that there is a pressing need for reforming our Police to make them acceptable to the people and to make the people accept their police.

The first state in Independent India to appoint a police commission was Kerala which appointed the 'Kerala Police Re-organization Committee' on 15 January, 1957 by the Government led by E.M. Sankaran Namboodiripad (K.P.R.C. Report, 1959)[8]. The Committee was given an elaborate Terms of Reference with 18 items covering almost all areas of policing. However, after the removal of the ministry consequent to the 'Liberation Struggle', the Committee was asked to submit the report urgently, suggesting that it may confine itself to study and report only six (6) items comparatively less important, in the Terms of Reference. The Committee, therefore, decided to confine its study to the items mentioned by the government and submitted an excellent report with 51 recommendations. But the political change in the state affected its implementation. The next attempt at Police reform was on 16, August 1982, when the 'Kerala Police Re-organization Commission' was appointed (K.P.R.C. Report.1984)[9]. The Terms of Reference of this commission was in about half of the items identical to the Terms of Reference of the National Police Commission appointed by the Central Government in 1977 which had submitted its 8th and final report in 1981 (Govt. of India, 1981)[10]. The Political leadership in this state did neither accept the National Police Commission report nor structured a Terms of Reference which would have been an improvement on the NPC report taking into account the special circumstances of the state. They rather aimed at reorganizing the police than reforming it. The appointment of this panel can be seen as a diversionary tactic to obviate the need for taking up the recommendations of the NPC for implementation. (K.P.R.C. Report.1984)[11] In brief, no serious attempt has been made to evaluate the performance of the police to identify deficiencies, strength and weakness and introduce necessary and desirable changes so as to enable the Police to march in tune with the expectations of the society.

Instead of reforming the Police we are giving importance to modernization of the force. Modernization is an attempt to replace equipments and facilities which have become useless due to wear and tear and also to make available the gains of science and technology to the police in their quest for keeping pace with the lawless and criminal elements. On the other hand Reform is an approach towards reforming the police by re-writing the basic laws, supplying required legal enactments and statutes, realigning the focus of the police department towards emerging challenges to order and tranquility in society and enabling it to keep pace with the rapid changes taking place all around. In other words, any effort to supply the police force with modern transport and communication facilities, cyber science support, strengthening of the Forensic Science backup, giving the police sophisticated weapons and accoutrements for crowd control and traffic management and generally making the police spit and polish to match with forces elsewhere, would not be police reform since they are only 'aids to performance and not guides to performance'. Any genuine attempt to reform the police must target to liberate them from the control of the political executive.

Though almost all the important political parties in Kerala had the fortune of controlling the police, no earnest effort has been made to free them from political control. It is axiomatic that if the political class has got no complaint against a system, it is obvious that that system is not affecting their political fortunes or it is made to subserve their political interest. The police leadership in a democratic political system should take the views of the political executive into consideration in the management of law and order. But in investigating crime they should go by the book. Police performance in investigation has to be strictly accountable to the provisions of the law and nothing else, which may help in refurbishing the image of the Police and re-establishing its credibility. The civil society has to be alive and should strive to mobilize public opinion demanding police reform, if they would like their police to be the guardians of Human Rights.

**Notes and References**

1. David. H. Bayley, (1969): "*Police and Political Development in India*". New Jersey, Princeton Press, p. 38
2. John Coatman, (1959): '*Police*', Oxford University Press, London,
3. T.N. Dhar, (2002): "Governance, Policing and Human Rights", in *Policing India in the New Millennium*, Allied Publishers, New Delhi, PP:335
4. *Ibid* p. 335
5. *Ibid* p. 336
6. There are 53.27 lakh vehicles registered in the state of Kerala. 505713 vehicles were registered in Kerala in the year 2009, as per the records of the Motor Transport Dept., Govt. of Kerala.
7. The number of cyber crimes has recorded a phenomenal growth in the state. As per the data provided by the High-Tech cell in the Police Headquarters, 504 cases were reported in 2007. In 2008 it has grown to 1329 and in 2009, 2736 were reported.
8. Government of Kerala, (1959): *Report of the Kerala Police Re-organization Committee*, Trivandrum.
9. Government of Kerala, (1984): *Report of the Kerala Police Re-organization Commission.*
10. Refer the 'Note' by the Member-Secretary of the Kerala Police Re-organization Commission, 1984 appended as Appendix I in the Report and the Report of the National Police Commission, 1981.
11. *Ibid.*

# 29

# ROLE OF NGOs IN HUMAN RIGHTS DEFENCE

**B.R.P. Bhaskar**

A vibrant society is one that has a body of civic and social organizations and institutions that are not under the control of the state or of powerful political and commercial interests and take up public causes. Credit is due to the United Nations for recognizing the role non-governmental organizations can play in articulating and solving the problems of people. It was the strenuous efforts of a few NGOs that resulted in the inclusion of human rights standards in the UN Charter in 1945. The term "non-governmental organization" gained currency only after it found mention in the Charter. The reference to NGOs occurs in Article 71 which empowers the Economic and Social Council (ECOSOC), an important limb of the world body, to "make suitable arrangements for consultation with non-governmental organizations which are concerned with matters within its competence." By 1948 there were 41 NGOs which had consultative status with ECOSOC but few among them were engaged in the promotion and protection of human rights.

By 1992 the number of NGOs enjoying consultative status with ECOSOC rose to more that 700. Since then number has galloped to 3,400, and many among these NGOs are involved in activities relating to human rights. ECOSOC accreditation allows NGOs access to and right of participation in all its subsidiary bodies such as the Commission on the Status of Women, the Commission on Sustainable Development, and the Permanent Forum on Indigenous Issues. It also permits them to participate in the meetings of the Human Rights Council and the UN's many human rights treaty bodies.

The UN, which is an organization in which governments represent countries, now brings together NGO representatives too whenever world leaders meet to discuss important issues. Even as heads of states and governments consider sensitive issues, activists belonging to NGOs engaged in grassroots-level activity in the context of such issues gather in the same city and articulate their ideas for resolving them.

In the field of human rights, the role of NGOs is particularly important as governments or their agencies often become violators of the very rights they are committed to protect and promote. In an essay titled "Human Rights NGOs: The Power of Persuasion", published in the journal "Ethics and International Affairs" in December1999, William Korey, former professor of history at Columbia University, points out that at the end of World War II, the phrase "human rights" was virtually unknown, whether in the media, in standard textbooks, or as a guideline for state conduct in the international community. It was non-governmental organizations that made the phrase a core element of the UN Charter. NGOs, through their persuasion, made human rights a major item in international discourse in the media, state chancelleries and international institutions. NGOs played a leading role in the creation of international standards and establishment of legally binding treaties incorporating these standards. "They are central to the process of adopting implementing organs to these treaties and in providing the essential documentation and briefings to make these organs work," he writes.

The activities of NGOs cover a wide range from creating awareness about rights in the people to preparing them and lead them in struggles against violation of rights.

India presents a complex picture with regard to human rights as the people of the country are at various stages of development. Elements of the tribal society, agrarian society and industrial society have coexisted in the land for a considerable period of time, and now elements of post-industrial society can also be seen. Each of these societies faces human rights problems of a different kind. As a result of the complex social situation, the human rights scene also provides an incredible variety.

Vast sections of the people are illiterate and ill-informed, and that makes it easy for rights violators to act with impunity. Against this background, human rights education assumes importance. This task is performed primarily by NGOs.

Most States – sadly, Kerala, which takes pride in its status as a totally literate state, is also among them – have responded coolly to demands to include human rights education in the school curriculum. At the level of higher education, the situation is slightly better, thanks to the initiative of the University Grants Commission which gives financial assistance for conducting human rights seminars. The law under which the National and State Human Rights Commissions are constituted provides for allocation of funds for human rights training. However, few commissions have cared to implement this provision sincerely.

Many victims of rights violations are extremely poor and lack the capacity to stand up for their rights, let alone put up a fight. They must perforce rely on NGOs or individual human rights defenders. It would have been impossible for the Adivasis displaced by the Narmada Project to put up a determined fight for survival but for the dedicated services of Medha Patkar and the Narmada Bachao Andolan which she helped organize. The Bhopal gas tragedy victims, too, would have been unable to mount a big campaign for justice without the intervention of various NGOs. Even with the help extended by NGOs and activists, in both these cases the victims have not been able to get complete justice so far. One can imagine how much more miserable their plight would have been if human rights organizations had not come forward to take up their cause.

The Judiciary is widely perceived in India as the last resort of victims of rights violation. The Narmada and Bhopal experiences show that its record in the administration of sociai and economic justice, which is an important aspect of human rights, is not as illustrious as that in the administration of political justice.

The Universal Declaration of Human Rights, in its 30 articles, defines a wide variety of rights. After the UN adopted the declaration in 1948, the member-states continued deliberations on rights-related issues, and in 1966 the world body adopted two important covenants outlining different kinds of rights – the International Covenant on Civil and Political Rights and the International Covenant on Economic, Social and Cultural Rights. Later separate instruments dealing with the problems of various groups like indigenous peoples, children, torture victims etc also emerged. With unregulated economic activities resulting in destruction of the ecology and threatening climate change, the world today faces problems of a kind it had not encountered before.

As the evolving situation raises new challenges, it becomes necessary to address the problems thrown up by them. A case in point is the emergence of the concept of rights of HIV+ patients in the wake of widespread discrimination against them following the spread of AIDS.

The complex scenario calls for a good deal of expertise in human rights defenders. An individual may opt to work in an area of particular interest to him or her. The immense task of mobilizing and deploying an adequate number of human rights defenders with the requisite knowledge in a particular area can only be undertaken by a non-governmental organization.

Human rights violators are often powerful individuals or institutions. An individual human rights defender has clear limitations, imposed by his or her circumstances, in dealing with such violators. An organization will be able to intervene more effectively than an individual in such circumstances.

Again, ordinarily, an individual human rights defender can play an effective role only in his or her immediate neighbourhood. When rights violations are widespread, it becomes necessary to take up issues at regional, national and international levels. This can be done in a meaningful way only by organizations which can operate independently of the state and powerful private interests.

The work done by organizations like Amnesty International, which is rendering yeoman service in the area of civil and political rights, and Transparency International, a global coalition fighting against corruption, underlines the importance of concerted worldwide action. The People's Union for Civil Liberties is a fine example of a national NGO working in the area of civil and political rights. Besides lawyers, a large number of scientists, engineers, doctors and other professionals are engaged in human rights defence under its banner.

NGOs have made a major contribution to the cause of human rights by extensively documenting cases of violation. As Dorothy Q. Thomas, founder-director of Women's Rights division of Human Rights Watch, points out, human rights practice is a method of reporting facts to promote change. One typical method of reporting human rights violations is to investigate individual cases of violations through interviews with victims and witnesses. Negative media exposure generated by publication of the reports of such investigation "can serve as a 'shame sanction' in working to increase a government's compliance with international human rights norms".

In these circumstances, non-governmental organizations are playing a significant role in the protection and promotion of human rights. This role cannot be entrusted to anyone else.

# 30

# NON-GOVERNMENTAL ORGANISATIONS (NGOs) AND HUMAN RIGHTS: ITS PROTOTYPICAL ROLE

**P. Sukumaran Nair**

### Introduction

Human Rights are those rights that are universal in nature and are based upon the belief that each individual should be treated with dignity and respect to which he is entitled as a human being. The first half of the 20th century witnessed two global wars which resulted in grave violations of right to life and freedom. The United Nations which came into existence after the second world war in its charter made specific provisions for protecting Human Rights of all people of the world and it adopted Universal Declaration of Human Rights (UDHR) on 10th December 1948. Thereafter several Human Rights conventions were held at the national and global levels to undertake the responsibility to preserve, protect and defend human rights and fundamental freedoms to all irrespective of race, colour, sex, languages, religion etc. Besides, steps have also been taken at the appropriate level to ensure the enjoyment of these rights by the people. As it has become the bounden duty on the part of all concerned to strengthen the process of protection of Human Rights, the Government of India sent out clear signals to everyone about its commitment to uphold and implement Human Rights. The Government of India set up Human Rights Commissions at the national and state levels to enquire into complaints of Human Rights violations and see how to protect and save the victims of Human Rights violations.

But the functioning of these mechanisms initiated by Government have shown that due to institutional instability and inherent limitations promotion and enforcement of human rights were lagging behind and convictions have become rare. Existing mechanisms seems in sufficient to have grass-roots contact and fail to maintain rapport with the public to study, analyse and explore specific issues/problems confronting the public. NGOs being representative of Civil Society fill the gap by creating awareness among the people about various issues in Society and pursue development activities for the betterment of weaker sections of the society. This paper seeks to examine the role of Non-Governmental Organisations - both national and international-in furthering the cause of human rights.

**Importance of Non-Governmental Organisations (NGOs)**

The term Non-Governmental Organisations (NGOs) first came into lime light within the UN System in 1945. A Non-Governmental Organisation can be defined as an organisation that is not part of local, state or federal government.[1] Article 71 of the UN Charter empowered the Economic and Social Council (ECOSOC), one of the principal organs of the UN, with the power to make suitable arrangements for consultation with NGO's which are concerned with matters within its competence[2]. The ECOSOC Resolution 1296 and 1991 further outlined the criteria for consultative status of NGO's connected with it. It may be noted that initially (there were) only 41 NGO's which had consultative status with ECOSOC. Gradually their number increased to 500 in 1968 and further the number of NGO's having consultative status with ECOSOC had gone up to 1000 in 1996[3]. World Bank sources indicate that there are between 6000 and 30,000 national NGO's in developing countries[4]. NGO's play a very significant role in creating awareness about various issues in society and undertake development activities for the amelioration and betterment of deprived sections of the people in a civil society. The role of NGO's got a significant boost in the world conference of Human Rights held at Vienna in 1993.

Further, Protection of Human Rights Act 1993 and National Committee on Human Rights Act recognised their vital role in furthering the cause of Human Rights. Section 12(1) of PHR Act has enjoined upon National Human Rights Commission (NHRC) to encourage the efforts of NGO's and institutions working in the field of Human Rights[5].

The NHRC in its first report unambiguously identified three areas in which NGO's could play its role to accomplish its mission. They are:

Firstly, because of their grass roots contacts, NGOs can most effectively identify Human Rights violations, articulate them and seek redress from the commission by bringing violations to its notice. Secondly, the Rapport the NGO's maintain with the public will be a great inducement to the Commission by helping the Commission's investigating staff as well as undertake investigations of violations on behalf of the commission. Thirdly, NGOs can undertake research and serious studies on specific problems and issues in view of their specific knowledge[6]. Besides the NHRC also compiled a National Register of NGOs working in Human Rights area to co-ordinate its efforts and make known their contributions to outside world.

There are a large number of NGO's functioning throughout the length and breadth of the world and it is rather difficult to mention all due to technical reasons. They can be classified into Voluntary Organisations, Professional Organisations, Refugee Organisations, New Social Movements etc.

The following are some of the important NGOs at the International and National levels which have succeeded in creating an impact among the people in furthering the cause of Human Rights.

**Amnesty International**

Amnesty International, an independent worldwide organisation founded in 1961 with Headquarters in UK, is one of the largest and most active human rights organisations in the world with consultative status at the UN[7]. It acts as a powerful pressure group for the respect of Human Rights. It gained global attention due to its voluntary character, moral stance and marshalling of facts and figures[8]. It has local groups in 35 countries, an individual membership in 75 countries and an institutional secretariat of 110 people.

It works for the release of political prisoners and abolition of torture and capital punishment and for the implementation of the UN Standard Minimum Rules on the treatment of prisoners, regardless of whether or not the prisoners are charged with the use of advocacy of violence[9].

Thus it concentrates only on political imprisonment, torture and execution. Its focus has been the individual in the cell and it is through persuation and dialogue with the National Government that the organisation fulfills its mission. Its work can be translated by each national sections into modes of action through campaign, press contacts, lobbying etc.

This self-financing organisation derives its income from individual membership fees, donations, fund-raising campaigns, sale of publications, public events and contribution by the groups. Its publication include Annual Report, Country report and News letter. In 1947 this international autonomous organisation received Nobel prize and in 1978 it received UN award for outstanding achievement in the field of Human Rights.

In India, in the past the interference of Amnesty International was criticised on the ground that its reports are not basaed on facts and hence was subjected to vehement criticism for some anti-India stands in its reports. During the emergency period (1975-77) Indira Gandhi raised her accusation against this organisation when it attempted to check the violations of Human Rights in India. Later with the expertise of international pressure and also with greater interaction the Government of India had with concerned agencies, it was convinced that this organisation's observations have become more objective and factual. At present it has established contact with NHRC, enjoys high reputation in India and Human Rights activists are also depending on its reports and publications and data in their work.

**International Council for Voluntary Agencies**

Established in Geneva (Switzerland), this council aims to provide as a platform where voluntary agencies may exchange their views and informations on matters of common interest and to serve as an instrument for development, growth and improvement of voluntary agencies and their activities. It performs its activities by providing information regarding humanitarian problems to peoples, governments, inter- governmental agencies and NGO's throughout the world and seek remedial measures through voluntary agencies. It encourages voluntary agencies to undertake studies, and to collect, co-ordinate and disseminate information regarding the humanitarian problems. Further, it also promotes the establishment of national council and other groupings of voluntary agencies and to sponsor meetings of voluntary agencies and other bodies dealing with the above objective.

**International Federation for the Rights of Man**

This international voluntary agency, having consultative status with ECOSOC, was set up in France to convey the principles of Justice, Liberty and Equality as laid down in the French Declaration of Rights of Man in 1789 and 1793 as well as the Universal Declaration of Human Rights 1948. It also makes public protest in countries where rights of man are violated and tries to see how such rights are respected.

**International League for Human Rights**

International League for Human Rights is an US based international NGO which works to develop and establish international Human Rights standards. It aims at the establishment of those guarantees for political freedom, racial and religious equality and civil liberties. It focuses the attention of the World Community on "Gross violation of human rights such as slavery, genocide, torture, imprisonment without trial, denial of the right to leave ones country, representation of free speech and the press and racial and religious discrimination". It confronts such violations through the publication of special reports, preparation and submission of documented complaints to Governments and inter-governmental bodies, the organisation of investigative mission to countries whose serious violations are reported and organisation of public campaigns[10]. The League enjoy consultative status with UN, UNESCO, the Council of Europe, the ILO and the OAS.

**Women's International League for Peace and Freedom**

This league, located in Geneva, was established to bring together women of different political and philosophical situations to unite in their determination to study, make known and help "to abolish social, economic and psychological concern of war and work for a constructive peace". It campaigns for disarmament; work for the protection of minorities, for the prevention of discrimination and to solve the problem of refugees and displaced persons. It strives to implement human rights and liberties and works for the pacific settlement of disputes.

**Human Rights Net Work**

Established in 1974 in London Human Rights Network comprises Human Rights organisations and numerous pacifist and church-related groups and civil right organisations. The Network aims to promote a cross-fertilisation of ideas. Its function include exchange notes on campaigns, techniques and new developments in their field. Besides, they make appeals for support in initiatives like circulating petitions etc. A task force for co-operative action on South Africa has been constituted by this network to pool information, ideas and support among interested network members on external pressure groups[11].

**Parliamentary Human Rights Group**

This organisation was established in 1976, as a brain child of UNA, to focus attention within Parliament on particular issues of concern. It is an all party group founded with the support of a number of NGO's concerned with Human Rights. It aims at mustering a core of around 100 MPs who can be called upon to provide support when human rights issues arise in the course of debate in Parliament. It maintains contact with various human right organisations and raises parliamentary questions. Further, it seeks to stimulate interest and debate on these matters with the houses and promote action on them.

**Human Rights Watch**

Human Rights Watch was initially founded as Helsinki Watch in 1978 to monitor the erstwhile Soviet Union's compliance with Helsinki accord. It adopted a methodology of publicly 'naming and shaming'[12] abusive governments through media coverage and through direct exchange with policy makers. In 1981 American Watch was formed to focus its attention on the Human Rights abuses in South America, Central America and Carribbeans. Similar international NGO's like Asia Watch (1985) Africa Watch (1988) and Middle East Watch were formed and added to what was known as 'The Watch Committee'. In 1988 all these committees were united under on roof 'Human Rights Watch'.

It opposes violations of human rights like capital punishment and discrimination on the basis of sexual orientation. Human Rights watch advocates freedom in connection with fundamental human rights like freedom of religion and the press.

Human Rights Watch provide research reports on violations of Human Rights norms as set out by UDHR. Research reports include issues like social and gender discrimination, torture, political corruption, abuses in criminal justice laws and the legislation of abortion etc.

## NGOs at the National Level

Non- Governmental Organisation is relatively a new concept in India. In India the role of NGOs have been performed in the past by local organisations or voluntary organisations registered under Societies Registration Act 1860[13]. It was as a result of a strong reaction against the atrocities committed during emergency (1975-77) that led to the emergence of a large number of Human Rights Organisation in India. During the emergency period, mass scale arrest including the leaders of opposition, Censorship of the Press, misuse of MISA & NSA, etc. were seen as gross violations of Human Rights and freedom. This reaction developed into a movement of human rights activists and voluntary organisations and this (movement) gradually followed positive measures for bringing these excess into light and towards securing punishment to the guilty. Accordingly, protectionof human rights has become the chief concern of these organisations. In India, there have been many social action groups-women groups, environment groups, groups which extend support to the struggle for democracy and justice, legal fora etc. which form the broadbase of Human Rights groups.

The role played by following NGO's are noteworthy.

## People's Union for Civil Liberty (PUCL)

This voluntary organisation was founded by veteran leader Jayaprakash Narayan, as Peoples Union for Civil Liberty and Democratic Rights (PUCLDR) in 1976. His intention was to make PUCLDR an organisation irrespective of political ideologies and to act as a platform for all people belonging to various political parties for the defence of Civil liberties and Human Rights. In 1980 this organisation was renamed as PUCL. It has branches all over the country. It publishes an English journal entitled PUCL Bullettin and the same is widely read all over the world among human rights groups. Every year on March 23 it organises J.P. Memorial lecture and presents its Human Rights Journlism Award to inculcate interest in Civil liberties and Human Rights among journalists and those who are making substantial contribution in this field.

The members of the organisation undertake their activities by visiting the places where human right violations take place, conduct enquiries with the victims, police officers, public and those who are concerned, before it draws up a conclusion regarding violation of Human Rights.

Peoples Union for Civil Liberty does not accept money from any funding agency and all expenses are met by its members and activists.

## Peoples Union for Democratic Rights (PUDR)

Civil Rights movement in India has been functioning as an autonomous forum for the protection of Civil Liberties and Democratic Rights of the people for the last three decades. Peoples Union for Democratic Rights

(PUDR) came in to existence in 1976-77 as the Delhi Unit of a larger national forum and has become PUDR in December 1981[14].

PUDR was established to fight for the cause of Democratic Rights, to conduct investigations, issue statements, distribute leaflet etc, organises public meetings, demostrations and dharnas and fight legel cases to highlight the violations of peoples right and help towards their redressal. It also takes up issues of general importance that affects the rights of people through general campaigns, publications and legal interventions. These include: gender equality; rights of forest dwellers and forest policy; working class rights; agrarian conflict, caste oppression, rape, atrocities in police custody and undemocratic legislation and various incarnations of terrorists Act (TADA & POTA).

It has taken up a number of cases of democratic rights covering most parts of the country since its existence. As a genuine voluntary organisation, it is actively engaged in defence of Civil Liberties and democratic rights.

### Citizen for Democracy (CFD)

Another Delhi based organisation that works for the defence of human rights is Citizen For Democracy which was founded in 1977.

In addition to the above, there are large number of voluntary organisations functioning in the country with the sole objective of safeguarding human rights. Such organisation include: Andhra Pradesh Civil Liberties Committee (APCLC), Association for the Protection of Democratic Rights (APDR) (Mumbai), Citizen's Committee for Civil Liberties and Democratic Rights (Goa), Lok Adhikar Sangh (Gujarat), Karnataka Civil Liberty's Committee (KCLC) (Bangalore), Organising Committee for Democratic Right (OCDR), Indian Peoples Human Rights Committee etc. Moreover, the movements like Narmada Bachao Andolan, the Chipko Movement, the Voluntary De-addiction Centres, Organisation for preventing the use of drugs, etc. can be included in this category. These organisations and institutions have succeeded in furthering the cause of human rights of people.

### NGO's Role in Protecting Human Rights

It is true that NGO's have been successful in attracting peoples committed to work for the cause of defending rights both at national and global level. These NGOs have strived hard to generate awareness among the people identifying their problems in the protection and enjoyment of human rights. Accordingly people are getting more and more conscious of their rights, the need to protect them and the means to protect them.

A study of the various NGOs functioning at National and International level have shown that they pursue measures like fact finding mission and investigation, public interest litigation, citizens awareness programmes, campaign and production of supportive literature for independent movement and organisations[15], etc. to accomplish their mission. It's significant role in furthering to the cause of human rights was aptly stated by William Korey thus "NGO's played a decisive role in transforming human rights from a charter provision/Declaration into a critical element of Foreign policy discussions in and out of Governmental or inter-Governmental circles[16].

NGO's prototypical role in furthering human rights may be stated in three ways viz, by setting standards, documenting violations and lobbying for effective enforcement.

'Standard Setting' implies the establishment of international norms by which the conduct of states can be measured or judged. The NGOs exert influence upon their government at the national level to sign and ratify treaties that embody human rights norms and have tried to increase use of complaint mechanism of these treaties. In the 1993 world conference on human rights at Vienna over 800 NGOs (2/3 of which were grass roots organisation) participated and they were instrumental for the creation of U.N. High Commissioner for Human Rights. Further, Women NGO's were a prominent force at this world conference and were instrumental in pushing for the inclusionof ground breaking language in the conference document[17].

To document violations of human right standards is another modus operandi used by NGOs in promoting the cause of human rights. Investigation and documentation by NGO's have become an effective device in bringing the human right abuses to the attention of international institutions and agencies and the general public. Reporting facts to promote change is an important trait in the process of practice of human rights. To report human rights violation in specific countries, the NGOs investigate individual cases of human rights violations through interviews with victims and witnesses on the basis of supporting informations regarding the abuses from other authentic sources.

Finally, inorder to transform the phrase human rights from charter provisions or declarations into actual practice so as to get the benefits to the victims, enforcement mechanism are also important. NGOs strives hard to create enforcement mechanism for the same. The NGOs were also the impetus behind the creation of special UN mechanisms to enforce human rights especially when international human rights standards gained prominence. Some of the UN mechanisms that have been created through their lobbying include the thematic and country made mandates under the office of the High Commissioner for Human Rights[18]. These include Working Groups on issues such as disappearance and detention; Special Rapporteurs on topics such as torture, arbitrary and extra judicial killing, violence against women etc. Thus on all the three fronts the NGOs prototypical role has been significant.

## Conclusion

The concept of human rights postulates the existence and respect for a particular value system which seeks to realize human existence between freedom and justice. The first article of Universal Declaration of Human Rights provides that all human beings are born free and equal in dignity and rights. The Indian constitution which came into existence on January 26, 1950 also bears the impact of Universal Declaration of Human Rights. Accordingly protection and promotion of human rights has become the chief concern of all at the national and international level. Considering the importance of upholding the eternal and inalienable rights of the people, the Government of India established human rights institutions at the national and state level to work for securing and protecting human rights of all people of the country. Despite these institutional arrangements, it has observed that violation of human rights in India is endemic. Amnesty International Report (1993) states "..........torture is pervasive and a daily routine in everyone of Indias 25 states, irrespective of whether arrest are made by the police, the paramilitary forces or the army"[19] Large number of people of our country lacks adequate accesses to basic amenities and are unaware of their rights and the need to protect them and the means by which to defend it. Human Rights institution formed by Government, though they are autonomous in nature and function, also suffers from setbacks in discharging their functions effectively. It is against this background that NGO's role assumes importance in a civil society. Their sole objective is to bring about a change and defend the Human rights by propagating, advocating, campaigning and by creating consciousness among people.

It is obvious that NGOs have been playing their due role both at national and international level by adopting devices like fact-finding missions and investigations, public interest litigation, by organizing citizen awareness programmes, production of supportive literature for independent movement and by critically evaluate governmental actions / policies relating human rights. They are also very particular is establishing international norms to sign and ratify treaties that embody human rights norms, document violation of human rights and seek enforcement measures to implement human rights declarations into actions.

In India human rights issues have been brought to light mainly by organizations owing allegiance to left political parties. It was during the emergency period (1975-77) that a considerable number of human rights organizations emerged in India. These organizations attracted several committed people towards them. Since 1980, these organizations and movements diversified their field of activities from pursuing civil and political rights to economic, social, cultural, environmental and women's rights.

In this connection, it may not be out of place to state that in India NGOs and Governmental mechanisms are not functioning in the same direction towards fulfilling the objectives of defending human rights. There are differences in their approaches and policies. While NGOs critically evaluate the Governmental policies and actions relating to human rights, Government also puts restrictions on the activities of NGOs through strict application of FCRA (Foreign Currency Regulation Act) to curtail the flow of foreign funds and assistance. Critics points out that NGOs are largely western in origin and concept. There are Government organized NGOs through which the Government defend human rights violations by the state. Critics are of the view that these Government sponsored NGOs are aggressive and create confusion, politicize the sphere of human rights, and has diminished the credibility and independence of Non-Government Organizations[20].

Emphasizing the undeniable role of NGOs in the UN system, the former UN Secretary General in his 2002 report to the United Nations pointed out that "formal deliberations and decisions of many such meetings are now often enriched by the debates carried out in non-governmental forum and events held in parallel with the official conferences".

No doubt, NGOs have been playing a crucial role in upholding human rights. It is time that Governments all over the world should realize the important role played by the NGOs in protecting Human Rights and fundamental freedoms. Governments should desist from imposing unnecessary restrictions on the legitimate functioning of NGOs with regard to the protection of Human Rights. NGOs are representative of civil society and it is imperative that human rights be meaningfully linked to public participation. For accomplishing this great task both NGOs and Government mechanisms should work hand in glove, in other words the two agencies have to put their heads together in furthering the cause of human rights.

## References


1. *Introducing Human Rights*, South Asia Human Rights Documentation Centre, Oxford University Press, p. 92.
2. For details see the UN Charter.
3. William Korey, (1998) *NGOs and United Nations Human Rights*.
4. *Ibid*
5. S.Subramoniam, (1997) Human Rights, International Challenges (Vol.II) New Delhi, p. 577
6. *Ibid*, p. 576
7. *Ibid*, p. 576
8. *Ibid*, p. 583
9. *The Human Rights Handbook*, (1979), *A Guide to British and American International human rights organisations* compiled by Marguerite Garbing, Macmillan Pvt Ltd, London.
10. *Ibid*, p. 249
11. *Ibid*, p.16
12. http://www.pucl.org
13. *Opcit*, No.1. p. 92
14. *Opcit*.
15. *Introducing Human Rights, Op. cit*, p. 92

16. William Korey, *Opcit*. p. 3
17. James A Paul, *NGO's and Global Policy making* (2000).
18. William Korey, *op cit* N. 3.
19. K.S.Srivasthava, (2007), *Women in Indian Constitution and Human Rights*, APH Publishing Corporation, New Delhi, p.105.
20. For details see G.Haragopal, (1993), *The Study of Human Rights in the last decade of 20th Century. Reflections on Vienna Conference*, Institute for the Study of Society and Culture, Sambalpur, p. 20.

# APPENDIX – I

# UNIVERSAL DECLARATION OF HUMAN RIGHTS

Adopted and proclaimed by General Assembly resolution 217 A (III) of 10 December 1948

## Preamble

Whereas recognition of the inherent dignity and of the equal and inalienable rights of all members of the human family is the foundation of freedom, justice and peace in the world, Whereas disregard and contempt for human rights have resulted in barbarous acts which have outraged the conscience of mankind, and the advent of a world in which human beings shall enjoy freedom of speech and belief and freedom from fear and want has been proclaimed as the highest aspiration of the common people,

Whereas it is essential, if man is not to be compelled to have recourse, as a last resort, to rebellion against tyranny and oppression, that human rights should be protected by the rule of law, Whereas it is essential to promote the development of friendly relations between nations,

Whereas the peoples of the United Nations have in the Charter reaffirmed their faith in fundamental human rights, in the dignity and worth of the human person and in the equal rights of men and women and have determined to promote social progress and better standards of life in larger freedom.

Whereas Member States have pledged themselves to achieve, in cooperation with the United Nations, the promotion of universal respect for and observance of human rights and fundamental freedoms.

Whereas a common understanding of these rights and freedoms is of the greatest importance for the full realization of this pledge, Now, therefore, the General Assembly proclaims this Universal Declaration of Human Rights as a common standard of achievement for all peoples and all nations, to the end that every individual and every organ of society, keeping this Declaration constantly in mind, shall strive by teaching and education to promote respect for these rights and freedoms and by progressive measures, national and international, to secure their universal and effective recognition and observance, both among the peoples of Member States themselves and among the peoples for territories under their jurisdiction.

**Article I**

All human beings are born free and equal in dignity and rights. They are endowed with reasons and conscience and should act towards one another in a spirit of brotherhood.

**Article 2**

Everyone is entitled to all the rights and freedoms set forth in this Declaration, without distinction of any kind, such as race, colour, sex, language, religion, political or other opinion, national or social origin, property, birth or other status. Furthermore, no distinction shall be made on the basis of the political, jurisdictional or international status of the country or territory to which a person belongs, whether it be independent, trust, non-self-governing or under any other limitation of sovereignty.

**Article 3**

Everyone has the right to life, liberty and security of person.

**Article 4**

No one shall be held in slavery or servitude; slavery and the slave trade shall be prohibited in all their forms.

**Article 5**

No one shall be subjected to torture or to cruel, inhuman or degrading treatment or punishment.

**Article 6**

Everyone has the right to recognition everywhere as a person before the law.

**Article 7**

All are equal before the law and are entitled without any discrimination to equal protection of the law. All are entitled to equal protection against any discrimination in violation of this Declaration and against any incitement to such discrimination.

**Article 8**

Everyone has the right to an effective remedy by the competent national tribunals for acts violating the fundamental rights granted him by the constitution or by law.

**Article 9**

No one shall be subjected to arbitrary arrest, detention or exile.

**Article 10**

Everyone is entitled in full equality to a fair and public hearing by an independent and impartial tribunal, in the determination of his rights and obligations and of any criminal charge against him.

**Article 11**

Everyone charged with a penal offence has the right to be presumed innocent until proved guilty according to law in a public trail at which he has had all the guarantees necessary for his defence.

No one shall be held guilty of any penal offence on account of any act or omission which did not constitute a penal offence, under national or international law, at the time when it was committed. Nor shall a heavier penalty be imposed than the one that was applicable at the time the penal offence was committed.

**Article 12**

No one shall be subjected to arbitrary interference with his privacy, family, home or correspondence, nor to attacks upon his honour and reputation. Everyone has the right to the protection of the law against such interference or attacks.

**Article 13**

Everyone has the right to freedom of movement and residence within the borders of each State. Everyone has the right to leave any country, including his own, and to return to his country.

**Article 14**

Everyone has the right to seek and to enjoy in other countries asylum from persecution.

The right may not be invoked in the case of prosecutions genuinely arising from non-political crimes or from acts contrary to the purposes and principles of the United Nations.

**Article 15**

Everyone has the right to a nationality. No one shall be arbitrarily deprived of his nationality nor denied the right to change his nationality.

**Article 16**

Men and women of full age, without any limitation due to race, nationality or religion, have the right to marry – and to found a family. They are entitled to equal rights as to marriage, during marriage and at its dissolution.

Marriage shall be entered into only with the free and full consent of the intending spouses. The family is the natural and fundamental group unit of society and is entitled to protection by society and the State.

**Article 17**

Everyone has the right to own property alone as well as in association with others. No one shall be arbitrarily deprived of his property.

**Article 18**

Everyone has the right to freedom of thought, conscience and religion; this right includes freedom to change his religion or belief, and freedom, either alone or in community with others and in public or private, to manifest his religion or belief in teaching, practice, worship and observance.

**Article 19**

Everyone has the right to freedom of opinion and expression; this right includes freedom to hold opinions without interference and to seek, receive and impart information and ideas through any media and regardless of frontiers.

**Article 20**

Everyone has the right to freedom of peaceful assembly and association. No one may be compelled to belong to an association.

**Article 21**

Everyone has the right to take part in the government of his country, directly or through freely chosen representatives. Everyone has the right to equal access to public service in his country. The will of the people shall be the basis of the authority of government; this will shall be expressed in periodic and genuine elections which shall be by universal and equal suffrage and shall be held by secret vote or by equivalent free voting procedures.

**Article 22**

Everyone, as a member of society, has the right to social security and is entitled to realization, through national effort and international co-operation and in accordance with the organization and resources of each State, of the economic, social and cultural rights indispensable for his dignity and the free development of his personality.

**Article 23**

Everyone has the right to work, to free choice of employment, to just and favourable conditions of work and to protection against unemployment. Everyone, without any discrimination, has the right to equal pay for equal work. Everyone who works has the right to just and favourable remuneration ensuring for himself and his family an existence worthy of human dignity, and supplemented, if necessary, by other means of social protection. Everyone has the right to form and to join trade unions for the protection of his interests.

**Article 24**

Everyone has the right to rest and leisure, including reasonable limitation of working hours and periodic holidays with pay.

**Article 25**

Everyone has the right to a standard of living adequate for the health and well-being of himself and of his family, including food, clothing, housing and medical care and necessary social services, and the right to security in the event of unemployment, sickness, disability, widowhood, old age or other lack of livelihood in circumstances beyond his control. Motherhoods and childhood are entitled to special care and assistance. All children, whether born in our out of wedlock, shall enjoy the same social protection.

**Article 26**

Everyone has the right to education. Education shall be free, at least in the elementary and fundamental stages. Elementary education shall be compulsory. Technical and professional education shall be made generally available and higher education shall be equally accessible to all on the basis of merit.

Education shall be directed to the full development of the human personality and to the strengthening of respect for human rights and fundamental freedoms. It shall promote understanding, tolerance and friendship among all nations, racial or religious groups, and shall further the activities of the United Nations for the maintenance of peace. Parents have a prior right to choose the kind of education that shall be given to their children.

**Article 27**

Everyone has the right freely to participate in the cultural life of the community, to enjoy the arts and to share in scientific advancement and its benefits. Everyone has the right to the protection of the moral and material interests resulting from any scientific, literary or artistic production of which he is the author.

**Article 28**

Everyone is entitled to a social and international order in which the rights and freedoms set forth in this Declaration can be fully realized.

**Article 29**

Everyone has duties to the community in which alone the free and full development of his personality is possible. In the exercise of his rights and freedoms, everyone shall be subject only on such limitations as are determined by law solely for the purpose of securing due recognition and respect for the rights and freedoms of others and of meeting the just requirements of morality, public order and the general welfare in a democratic society.

These rights and freedoms may in no case be exercised contrary to the purposes and principles of the United Nations.

**Article 30**

Nothing in this Declaration may be interpreted as implying for any State, group or person any right to engage in any activity or to perform any act aimed at the destruction of any of the rights and freedoms set forth herein.

# INDEX

**F**

## G

J



K

## U

## V



## W